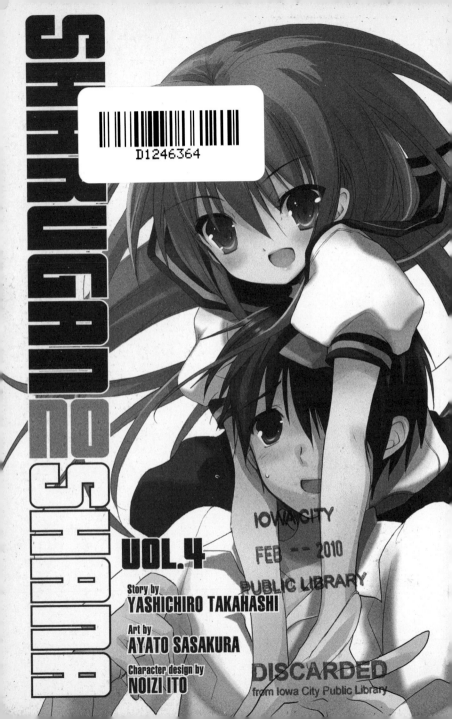

SHAKUGAN NO SHANA

VOL.4

Story by
YASHICHIRO TAKAHASHI

Art by
AYATO SASAKURA

Character design by
NOIZI ITO

SHAKUGAN NO SHANA

VOL.4

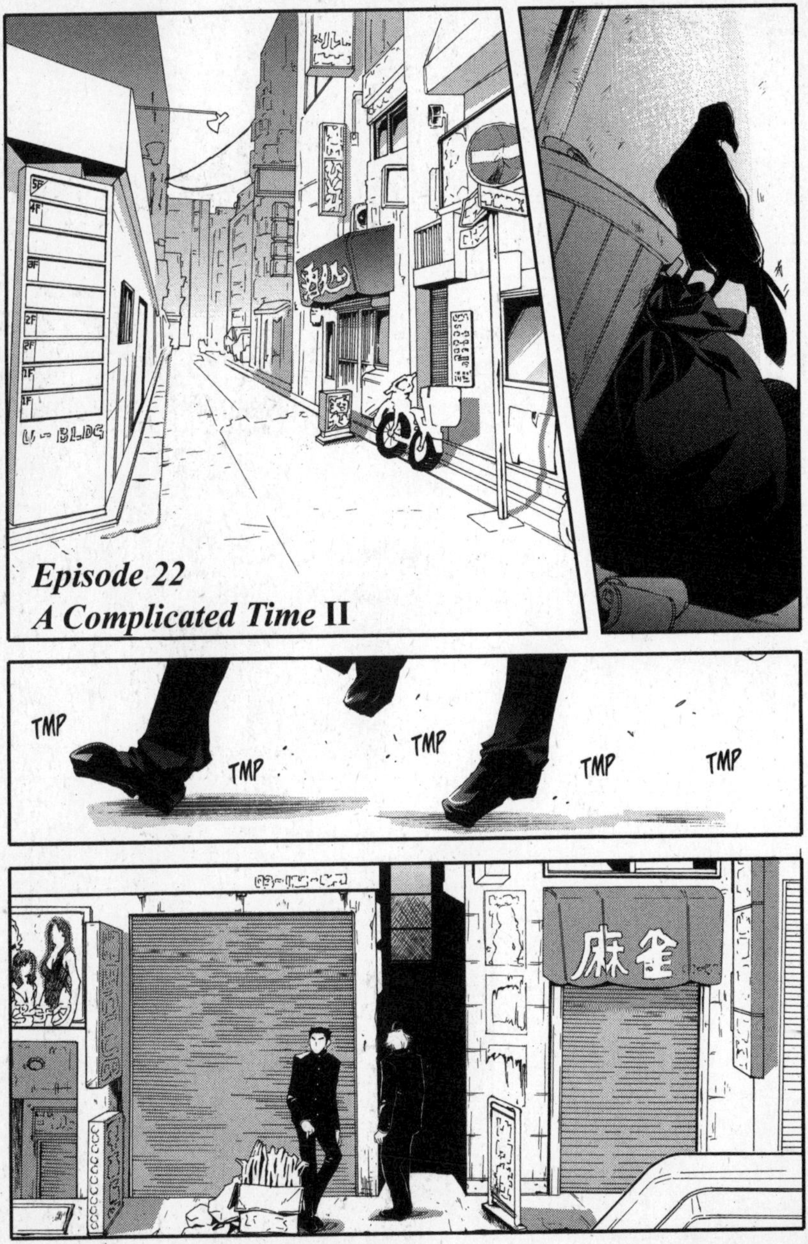
5F
4F
3F
2F
2F
1F
1F
U-BLDG
Episode 22
A Complicated Time II
TMP
TMP
TMP
TMP
TMP
麻雀

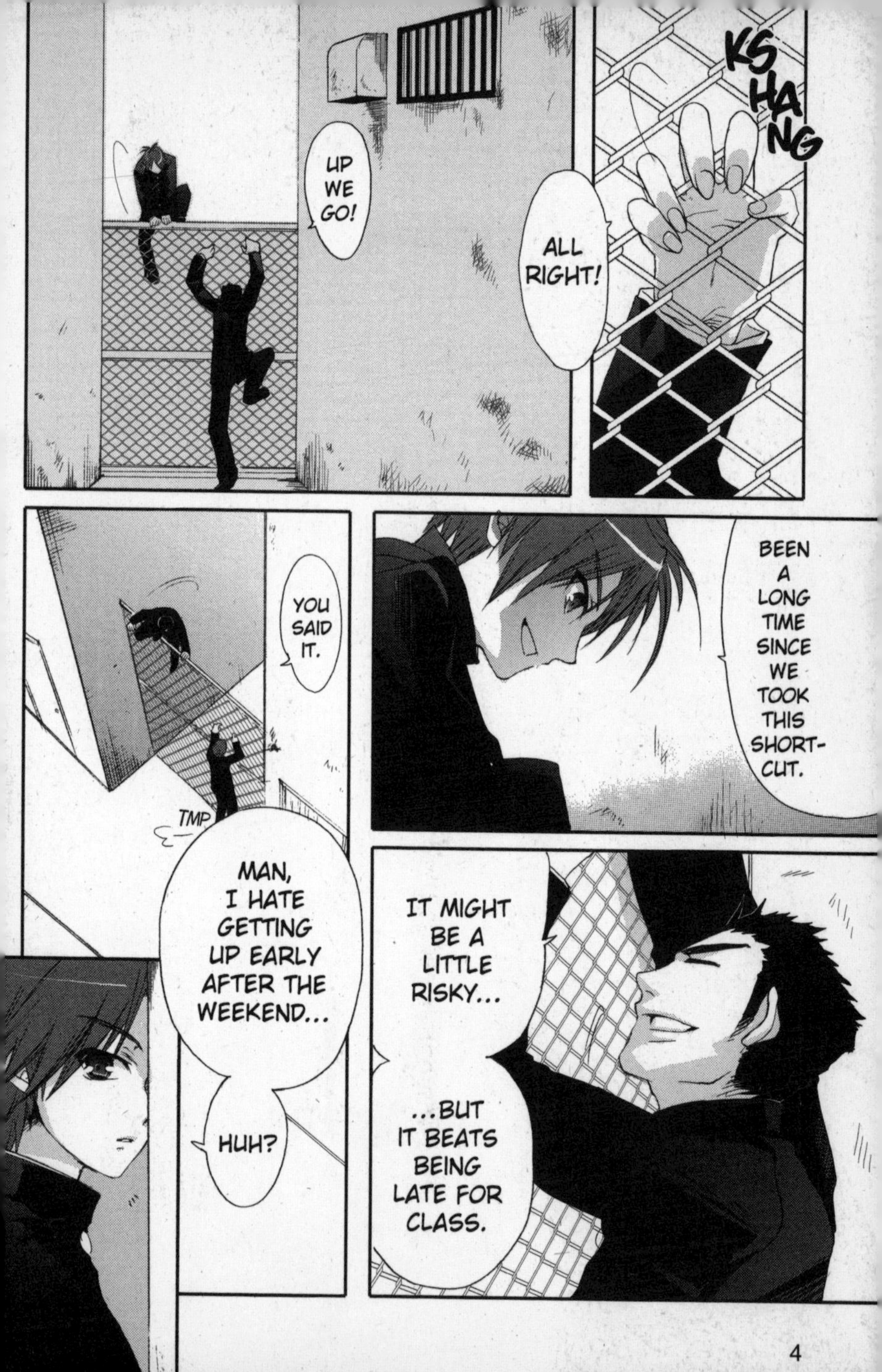
KSHANG
ALL RIGHT!
UP WE GO!
BEEN A LONG TIME SINCE WE TOOK THIS SHORTCUT.
YOU SAID IT.
TMP
IT MIGHT BE A LITTLE RISKY...
...BUT IT BEATS BEING LATE FOR CLASS.
MAN, I HATE GETTING UP EARLY AFTER THE WEEKEND...
HUH?

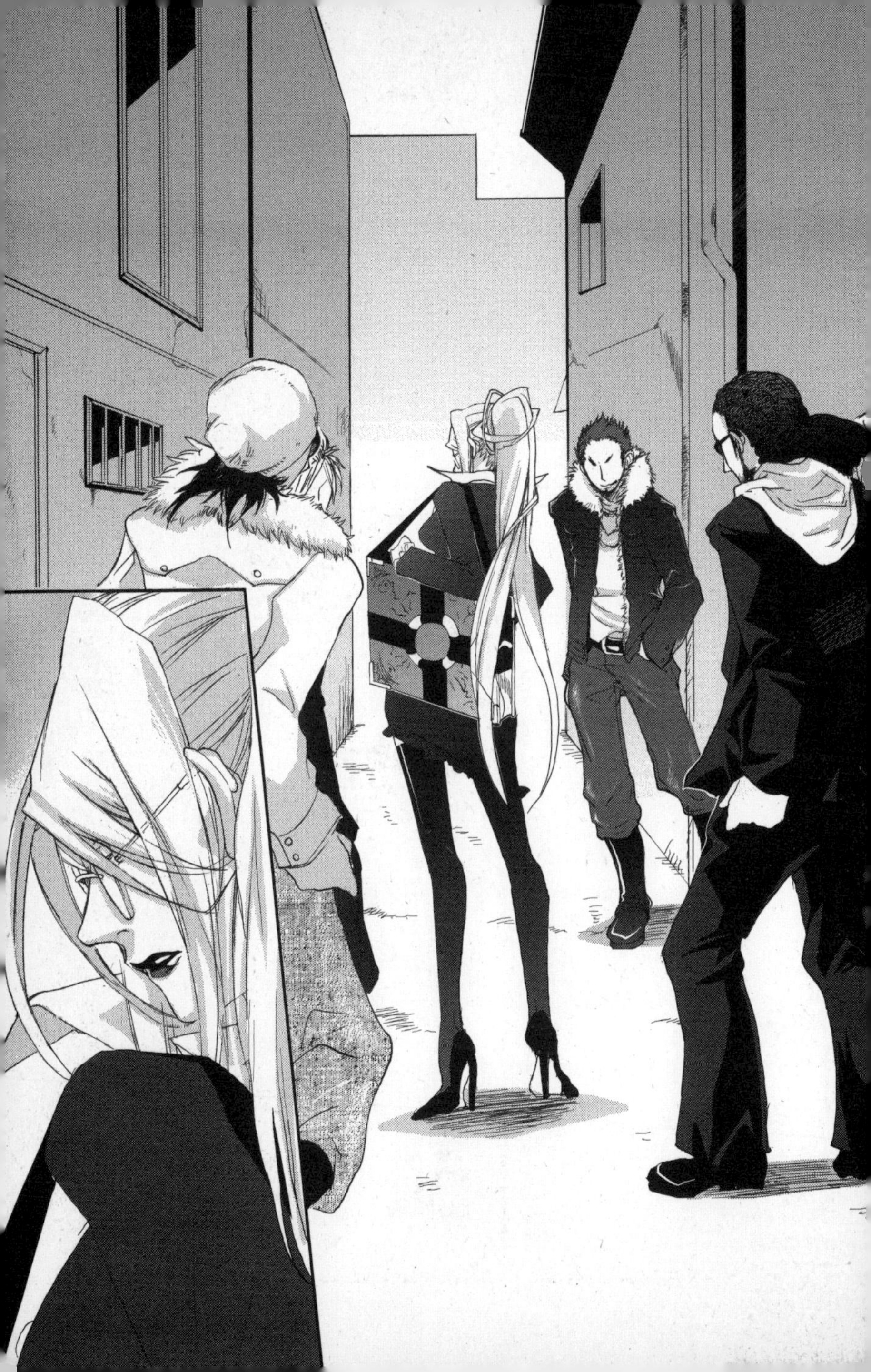

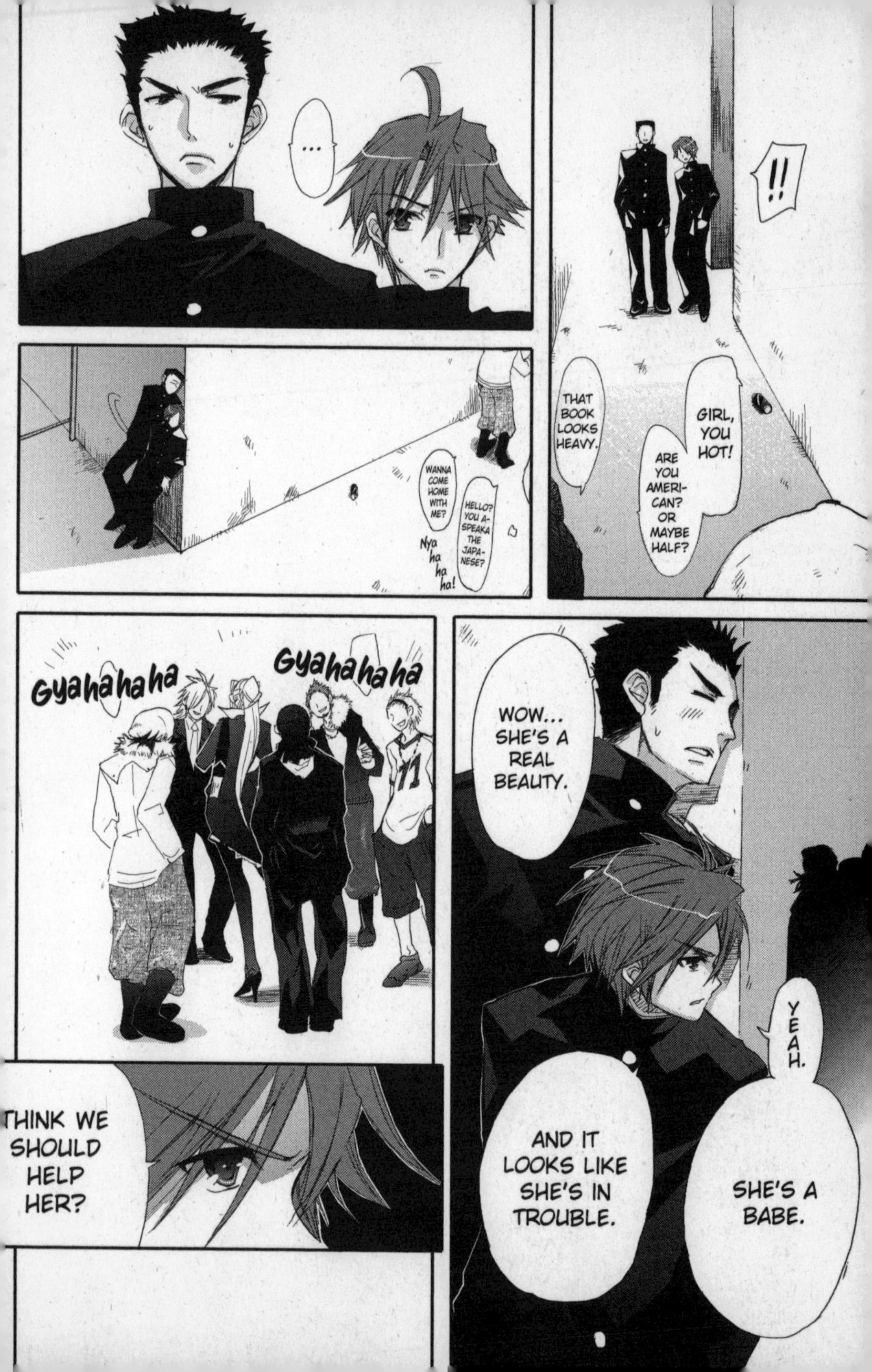
!!
GIRL, YOU HOT!
ARE YOU AMERI-CAN? OR MAYBE HALF?
THAT BOOK LOOKS HEAVY.
...
HELLO? YOU A-SPEAKA THE JAPA-NESE?
WANNA COME HOME WITH ME?
Nya ha ha ha!
WOW... SHE'S A REAL BEAUTY.
YEAH.
SHE'S A BABE.
AND IT LOOKS LIKE SHE'S IN TROUBLE.
Gyahahaha
Gyahahaha
THINK WE SHOULD HELP HER?

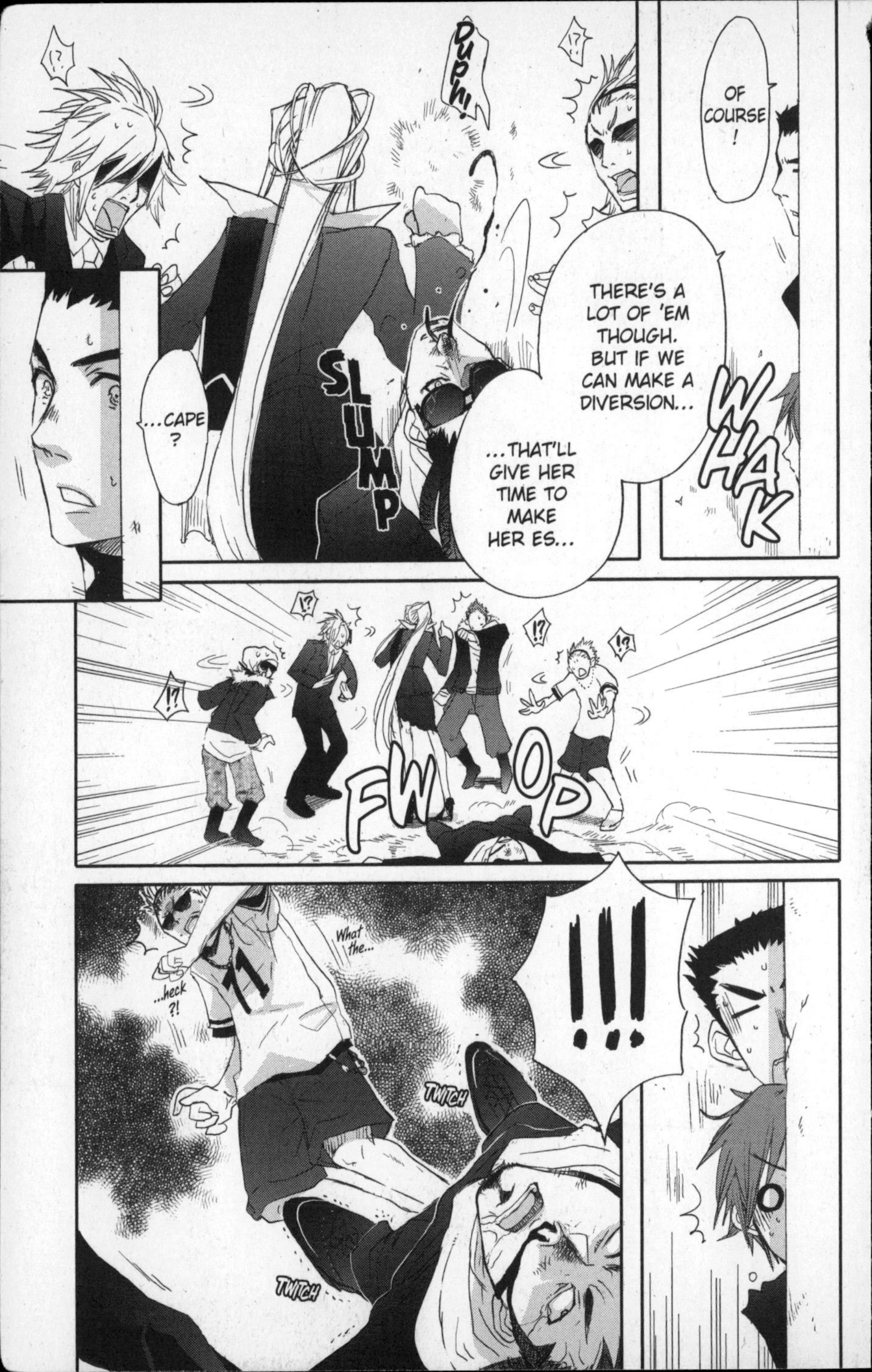
OF COURSE !
THERE'S A LOT OF 'EM THOUGH. BUT IF WE CAN MAKE A DIVERSION...
...THAT'LL GIVE HER TIME TO MAKE HER ES...
WHAK
!?
Duph!
SLUMP
!?
...CAPE ?
!?
!?
!?
!?
FWOOP
!!!
TWITCH
What the...
...heck ?!
TWITCH

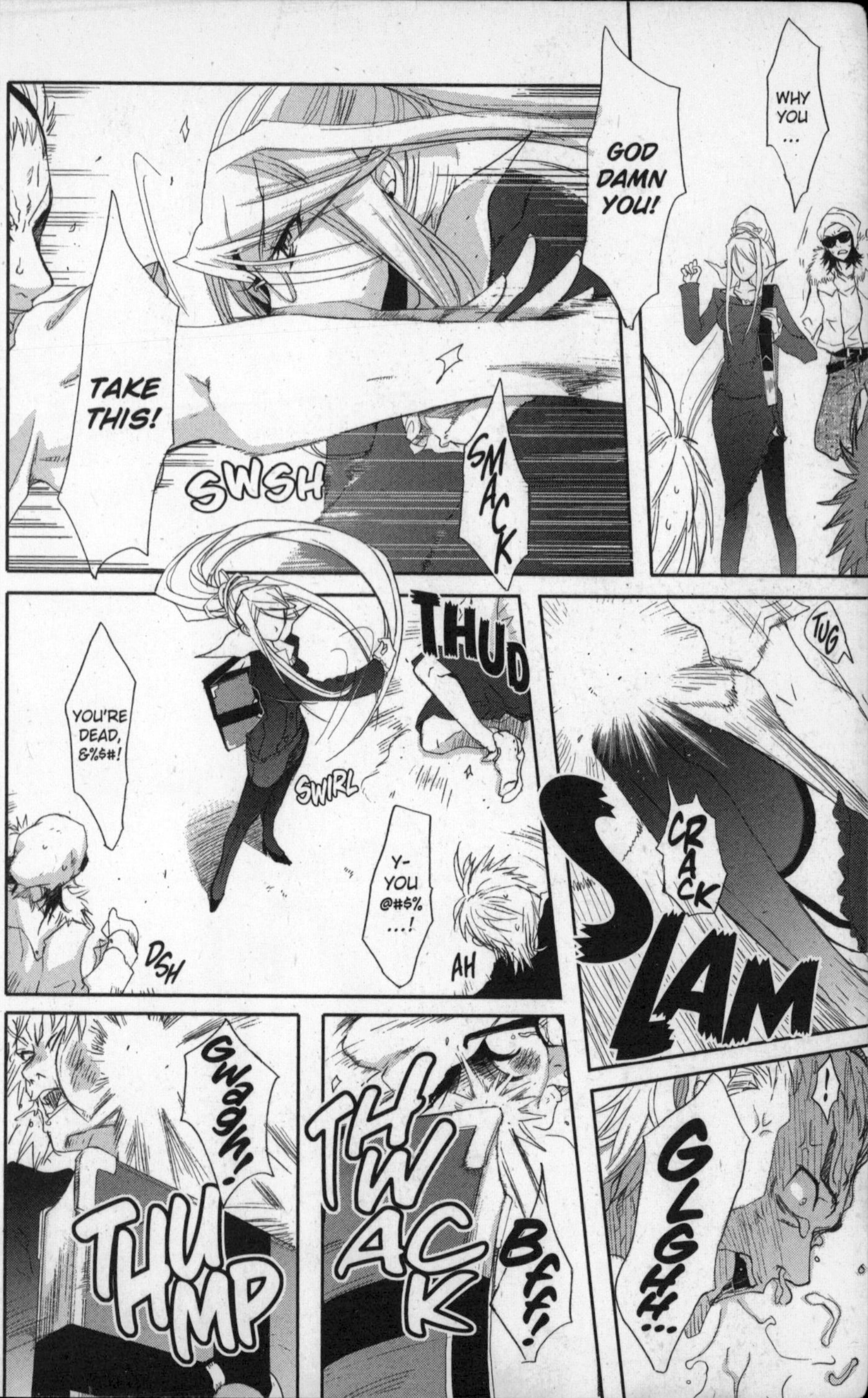
WHY YOU ...
GOD DAMN YOU!
TAKE THIS!
SMACK
SWSH
TUG
CRACK
SLAM
THUD
YOU'RE DEAD, &%$#!
SWIRL
Y-YOU @#$%...!
AH
DSH
!
GLGHH...
BFF!
THWACK
Gwagh!
THUMP

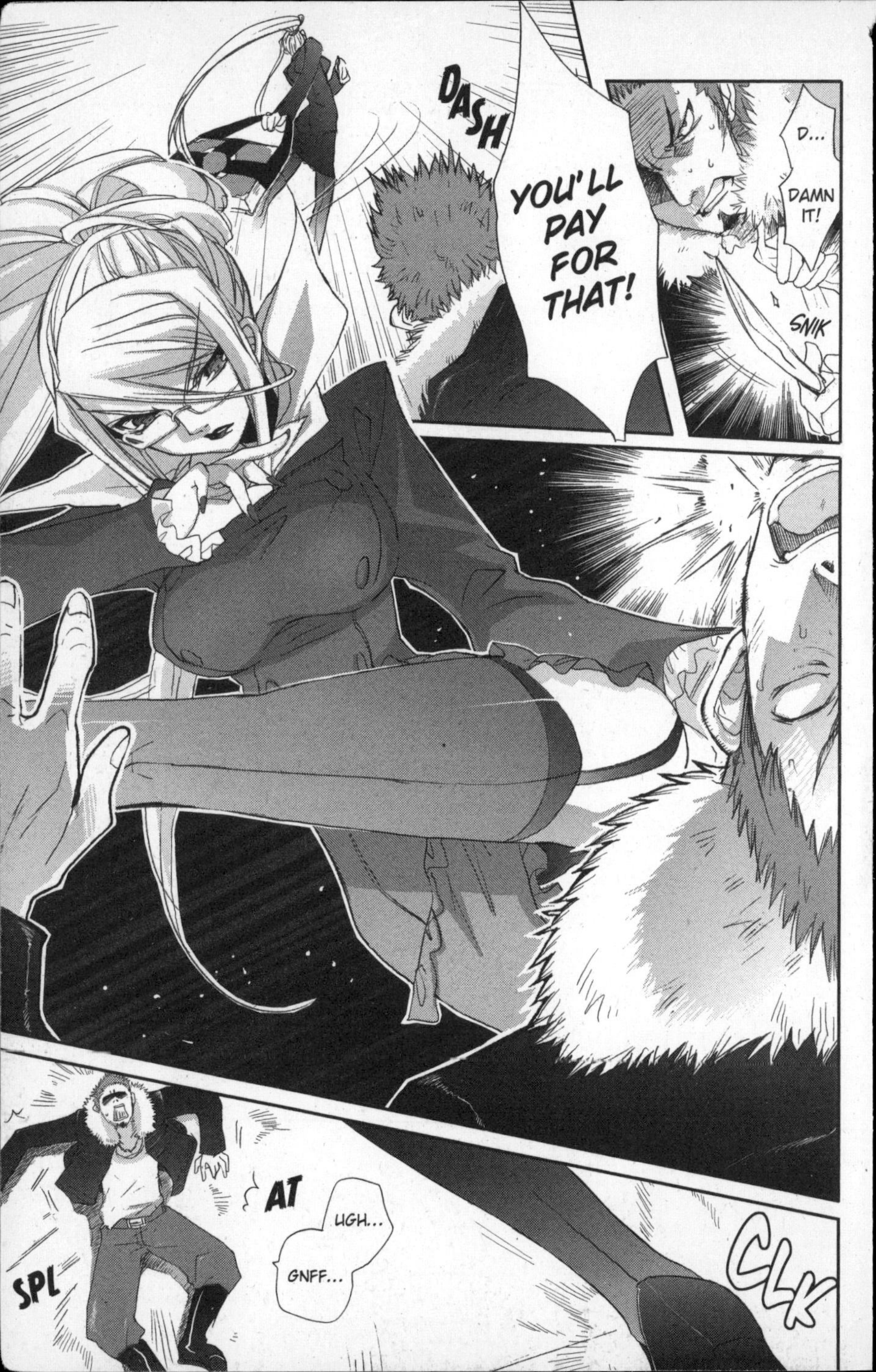
D...
DAMN IT!
SNIK
YOU'LL PAY FOR THAT!
DASH
CLK
UGH...
GNFF...
AT
SPL

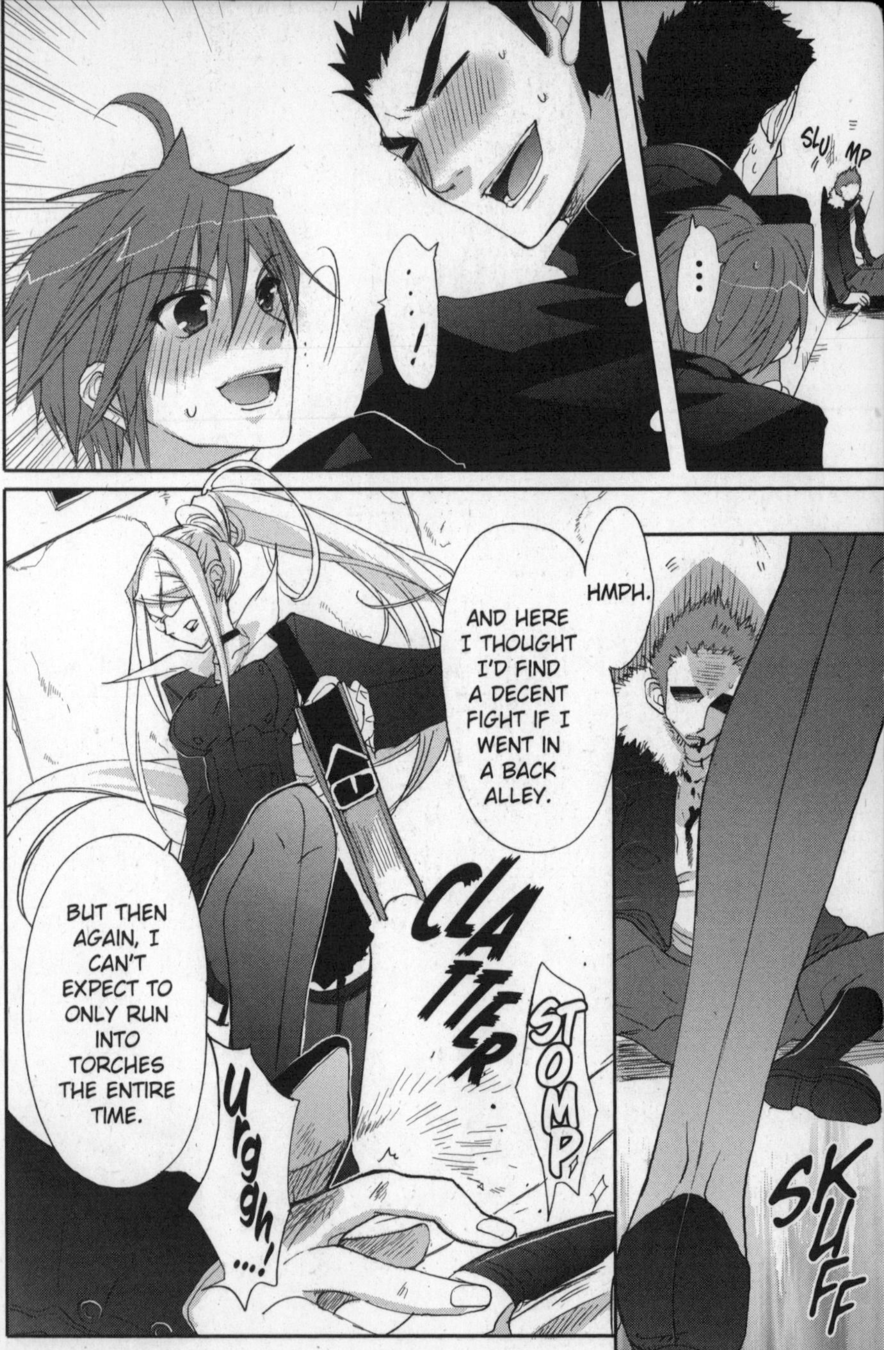
SLUMP
...
...!
SKUFF
HMPH.
AND HERE I THOUGHT I'D FIND A DECENT FIGHT IF I WENT IN A BACK ALLEY.
CLATTER
STOMP
BUT THEN AGAIN, I CAN'T EXPECT TO ONLY RUN INTO TORCHES THE ENTIRE TIME.
Urggh...!

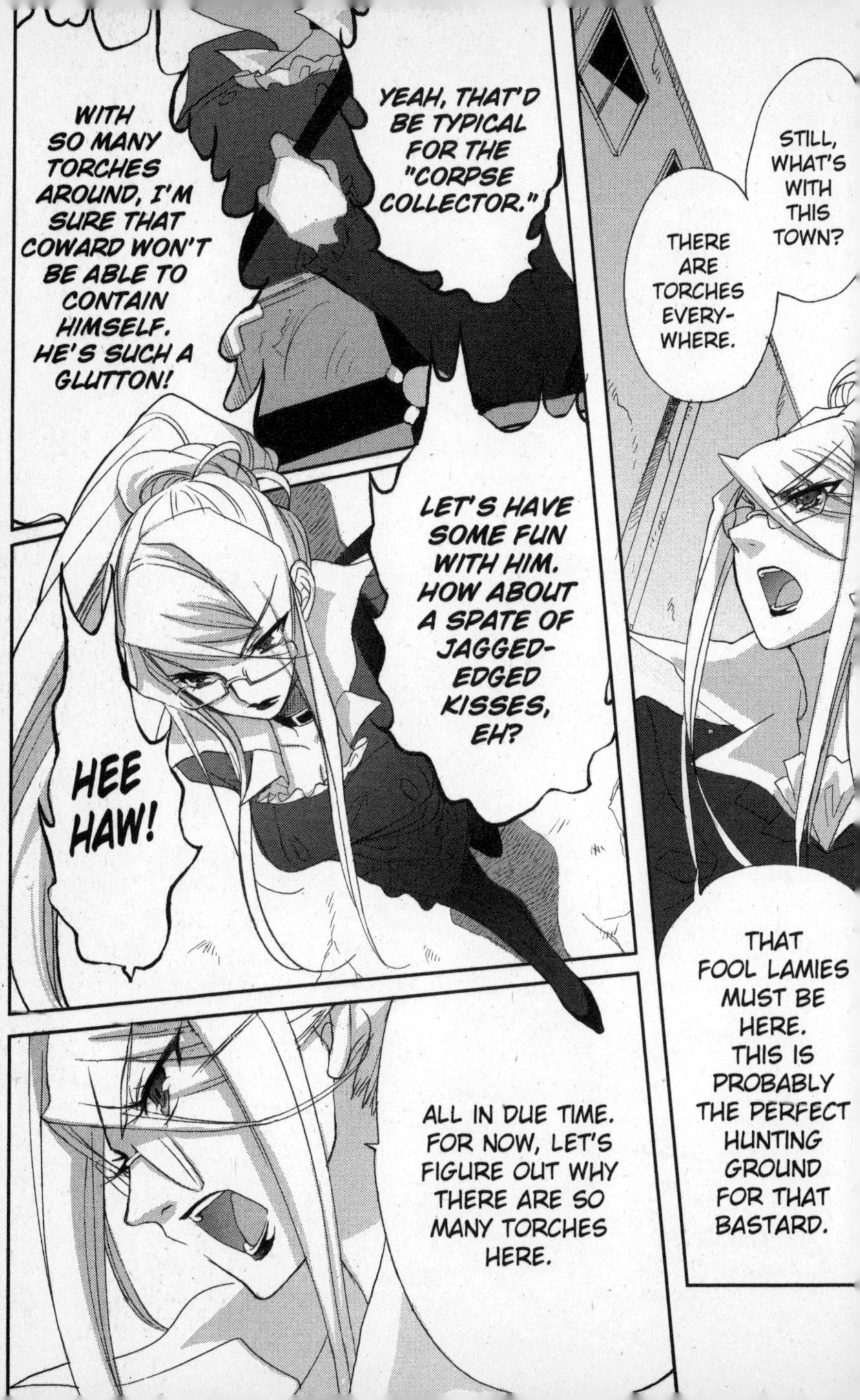
STILL, WHAT'S WITH THIS TOWN?
THERE ARE TORCHES EVERY-WHERE.
THAT FOOL LAMIES MUST BE HERE. THIS IS PROBABLY THE PERFECT HUNTING GROUND FOR THAT BASTARD.
YEAH, THAT'D BE TYPICAL FOR THE "CORPSE COLLECTOR."
WITH SO MANY TORCHES AROUND, I'M SURE THAT COWARD WON'T BE ABLE TO CONTAIN HIMSELF. HE'S SUCH A GLUTTON!
LET'S HAVE SOME FUN WITH HIM. HOW ABOUT A SPATE OF JAGGED-EDGED KISSES, EH?
HEE HAW!
ALL IN DUE TIME. FOR NOW, LET'S FIGURE OUT WHY THERE ARE SO MANY TORCHES HERE.

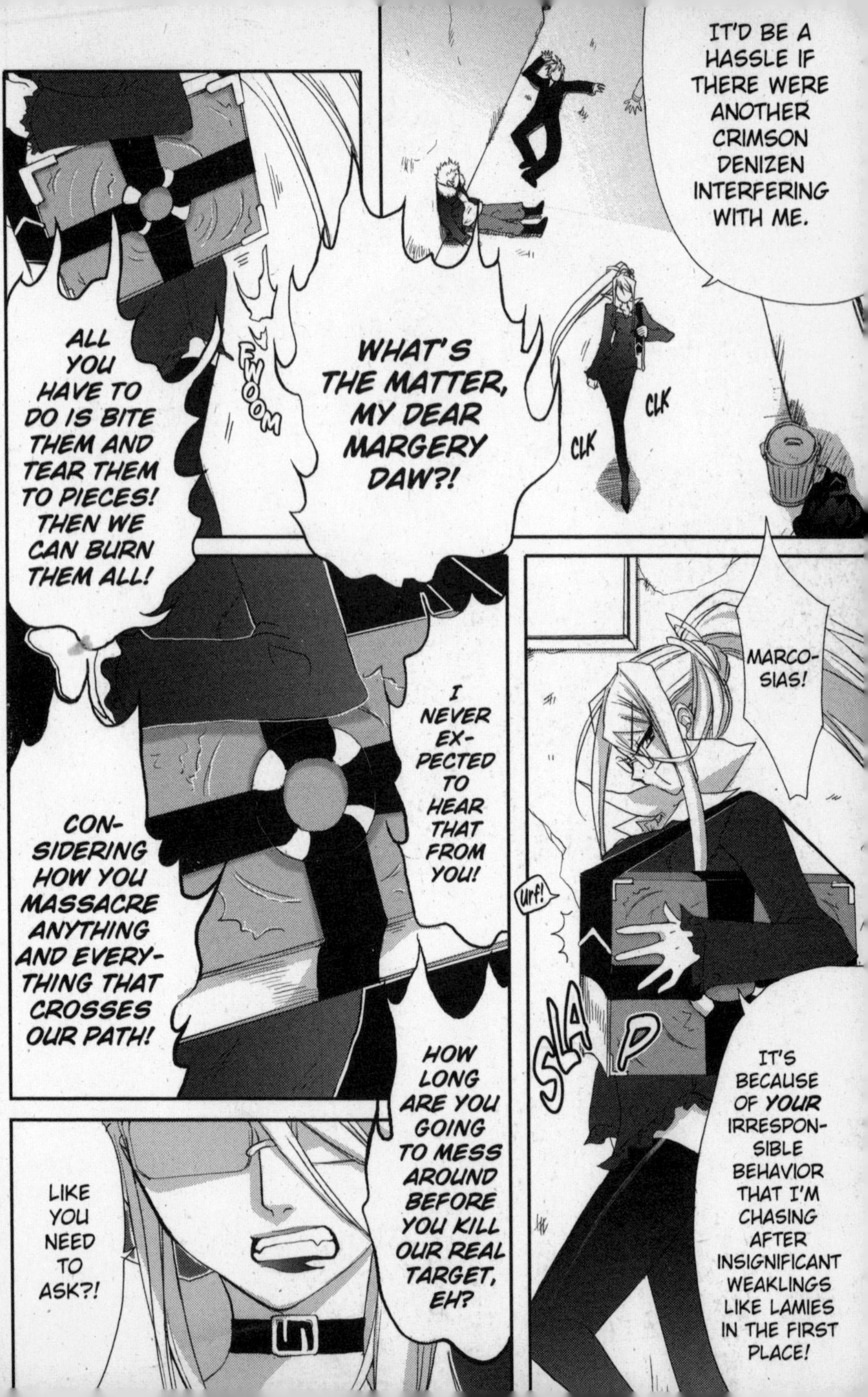
IT'D BE A HASSLE IF THERE WERE ANOTHER CRIMSON DENIZEN INTERFERING WITH ME.
CLK
CLK
FWOOM
WHAT'S THE MATTER, MY DEAR MARGERY DAW?!
ALL YOU HAVE TO DO IS BITE THEM AND TEAR THEM TO PIECES! THEN WE CAN BURN THEM ALL!
MARCO-SIAS!
Urf!
SLAP
IT'S BECAUSE OF YOUR IRRESPON-SIBLE BEHAVIOR THAT I'M CHASING AFTER INSIGNIFICANT WEAKLINGS LIKE LAMIES IN THE FIRST PLACE!
I NEVER EX-PECTED TO HEAR THAT FROM YOU!
CON-SIDERING HOW YOU MASSACRE ANYTHING AND EVERY-THING THAT CROSSES OUR PATH!
HOW LONG ARE YOU GOING TO MESS AROUND BEFORE YOU KILL OUR REAL TARGET, EH?
LIKE YOU NEED TO ASK?!

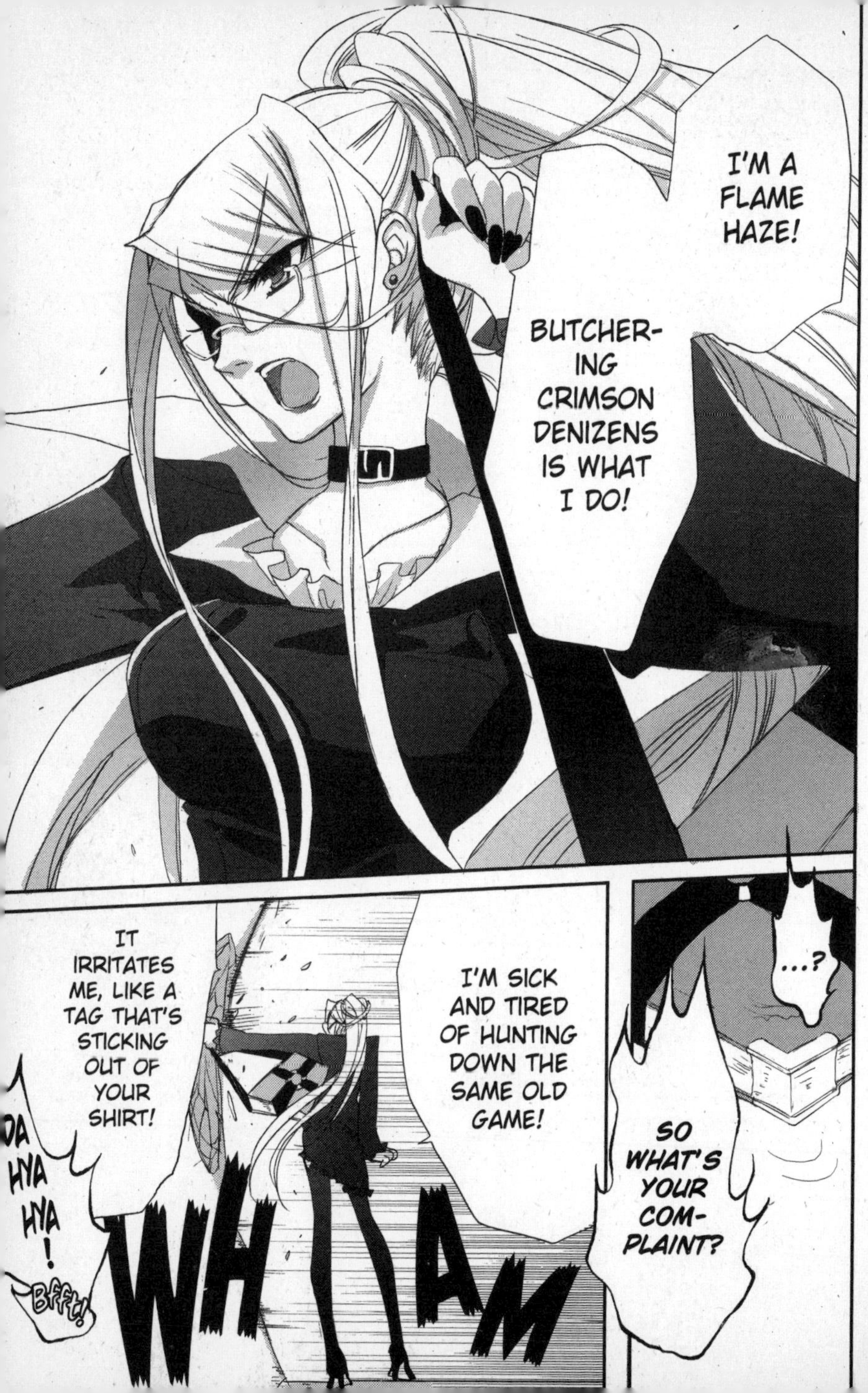
I'M A FLAME HAZE!
BUTCHERING CRIMSON DENIZENS IS WHAT I DO!
...?
SO WHAT'S YOUR COMPLAINT?
I'M SICK AND TIRED OF HUNTING DOWN THE SAME OLD GAME!
IT IRRITATES ME, LIKE A TAG THAT'S STICKING OUT OF YOUR SHIRT!
WHAM
DA HYA HYA!
Bffft!

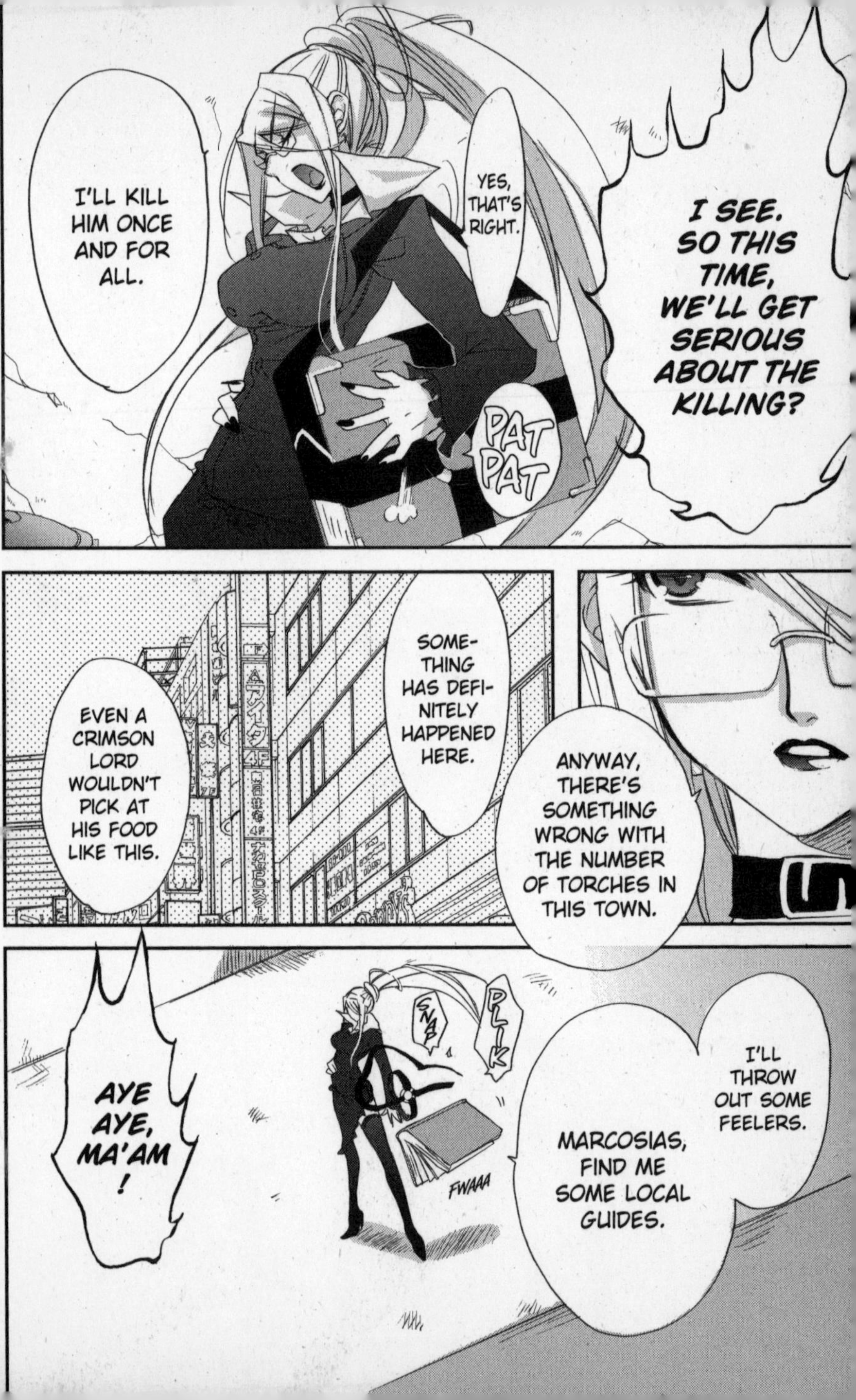
I SEE. SO THIS TIME, WE'LL GET SERIOUS ABOUT THE KILLING?
YES, THAT'S RIGHT.
PAT PAT
I'LL KILL HIM ONCE AND FOR ALL.
SOME-THING HAS DEFI-NITELY HAPPENED HERE.
EVEN A CRIMSON LORD WOULDN'T PICK AT HIS FOOD LIKE THIS.
ANYWAY, THERE'S SOMETHING WRONG WITH THE NUMBER OF TORCHES IN THIS TOWN.
I'LL THROW OUT SOME FEELERS.
MARCOSIAS, FIND ME SOME LOCAL GUIDES.
PLIK
SNAP
FWAAA
AYE AYE, MA'AM!

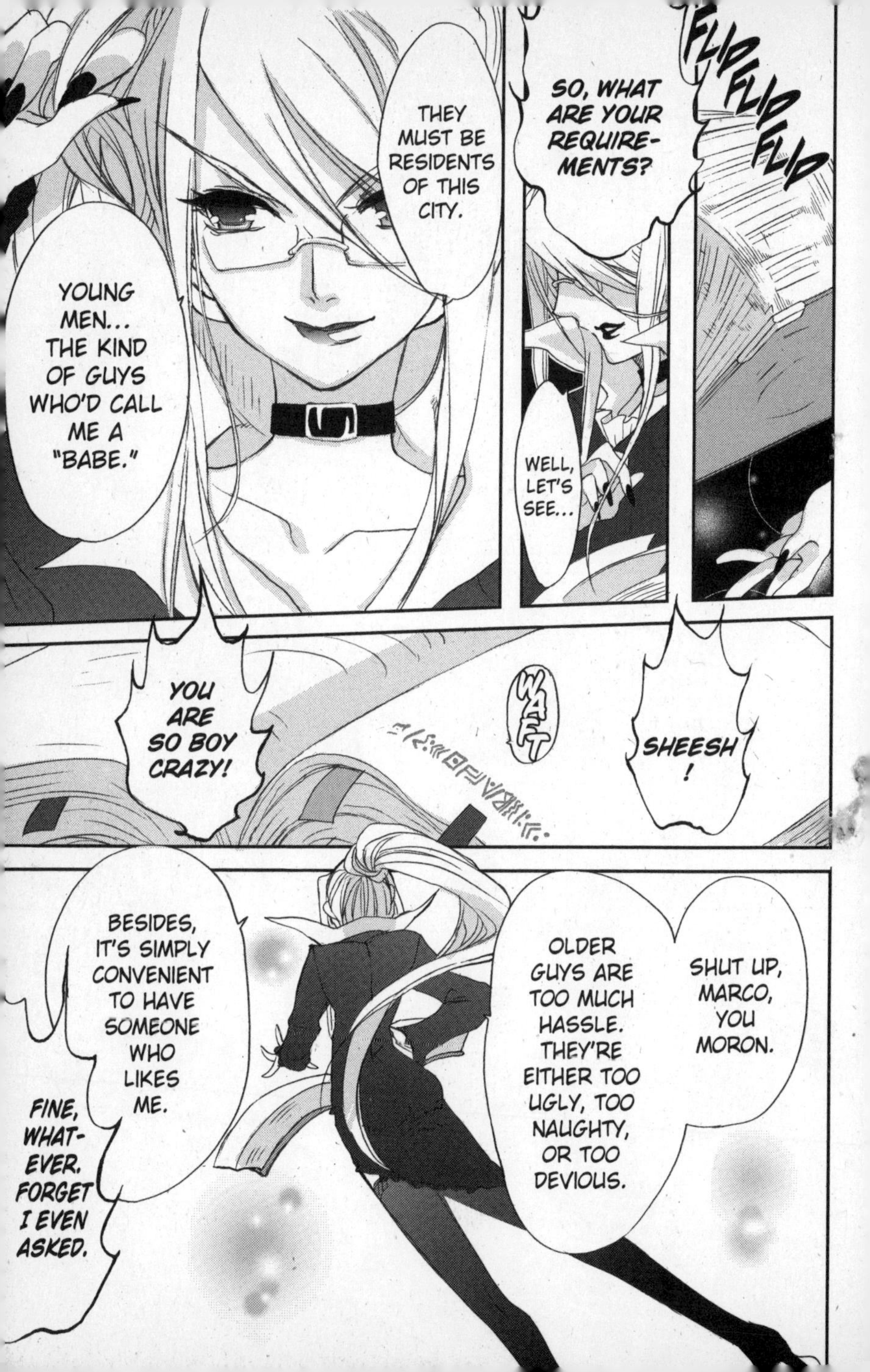
FLIP FLIP FLIP
SO, WHAT ARE YOUR REQUIRE-MENTS?
WELL, LET'S SEE...
THEY MUST BE RESIDENTS OF THIS CITY.
YOUNG MEN... THE KIND OF GUYS WHO'D CALL ME A "BABE."
SHEESH!
WAFT
YOU ARE SO BOY CRAZY!
SHUT UP, MARCO, YOU MORON.
OLDER GUYS ARE TOO MUCH HASSLE. THEY'RE EITHER TOO UGLY, TOO NAUGHTY, OR TOO DEVIOUS.
BESIDES, IT'S SIMPLY CONVENIENT TO HAVE SOMEONE WHO LIKES ME.
FINE, WHAT-EVER. FORGET I EVEN ASKED.

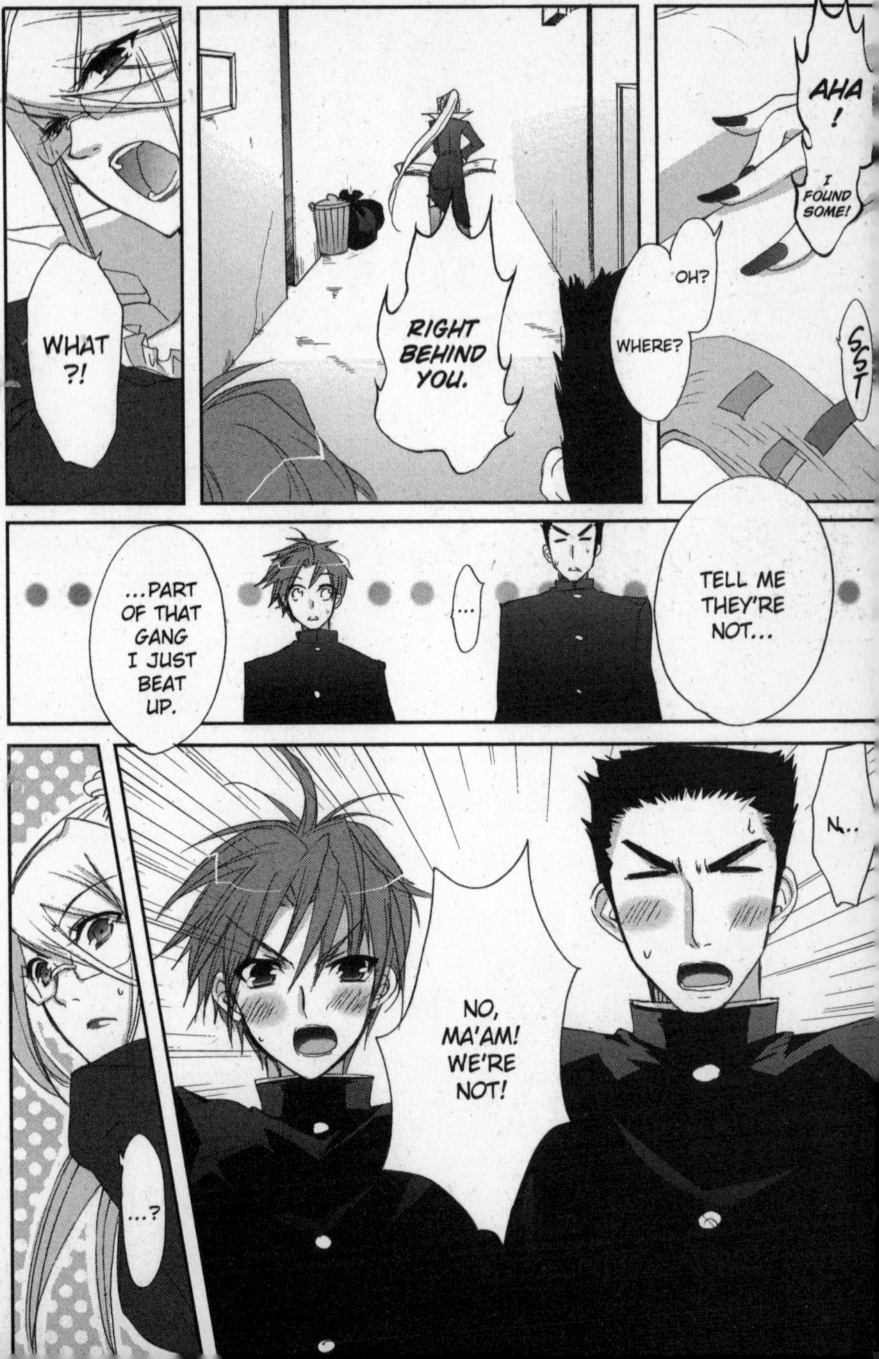
AHA!
I FOUND SOME!
OH? WHERE?
SST
RIGHT BEHIND YOU.
WHAT?!
TELL ME THEY'RE NOT...
...
...PART OF THAT GANG I JUST BEAT UP.
N..
NO, MA'AM! WE'RE NOT!
...?

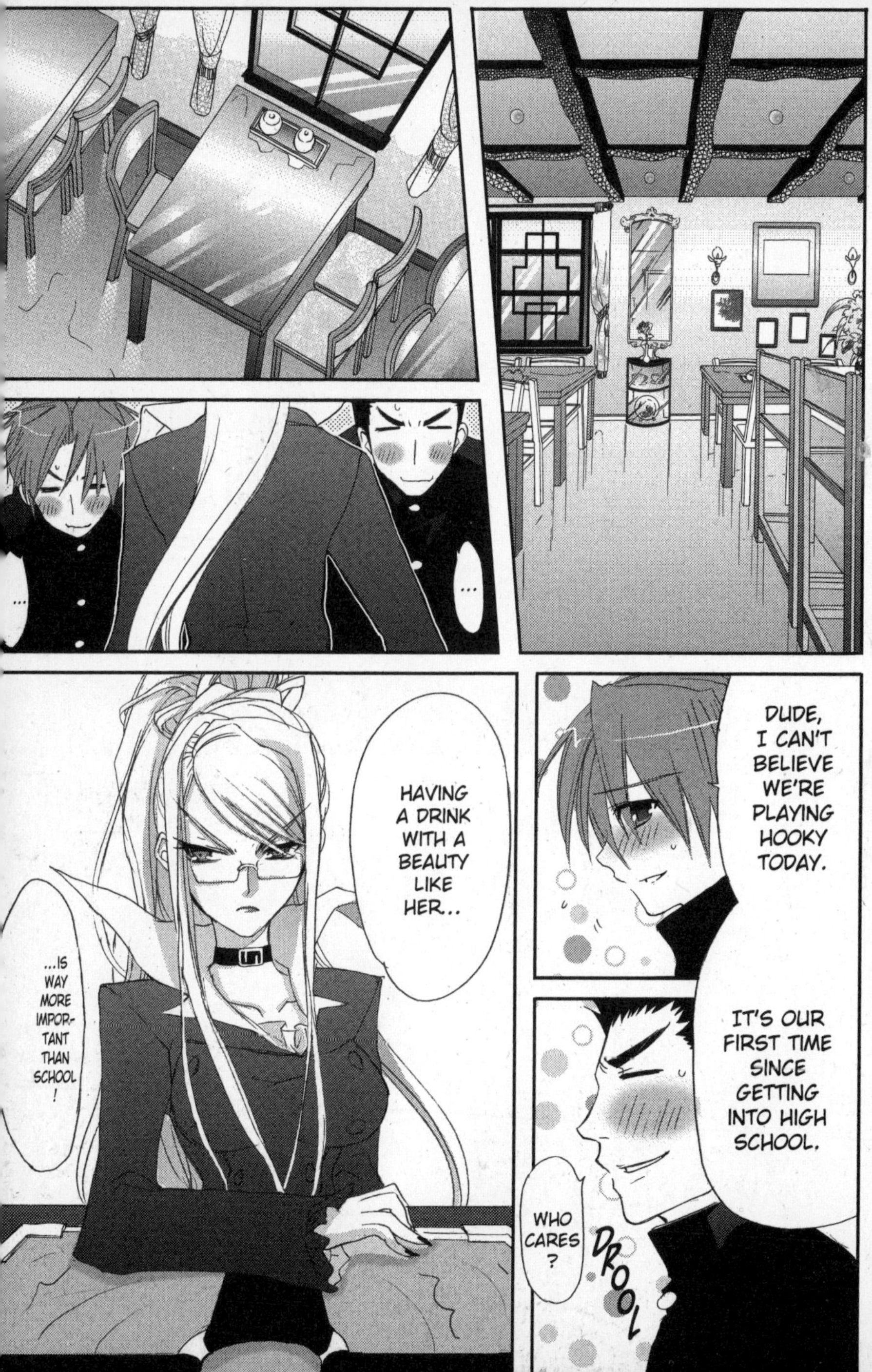
...
...
DUDE, I CAN'T BELIEVE WE'RE PLAYING HOOKY TODAY.
IT'S OUR FIRST TIME SINCE GETTING INTO HIGH SCHOOL.
WHO CARES?
DROOL
HAVING A DRINK WITH A BEAUTY LIKE HER...
...IS WAY MORE IMPOR-TANT THAN SCHOOL!

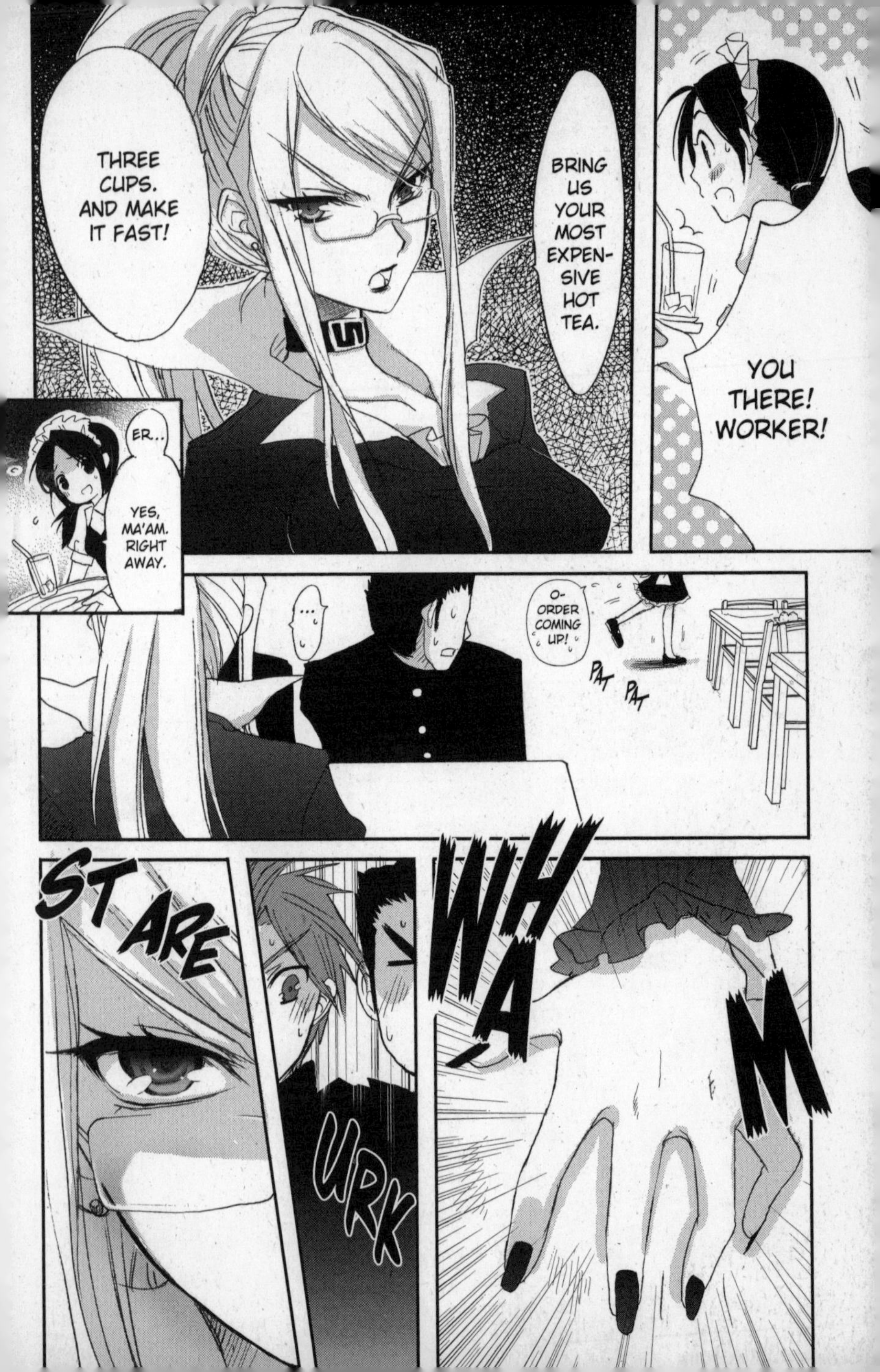
YOU THERE! WORKER!
BRING US YOUR MOST EXPENSIVE HOT TEA.
THREE CUPS. AND MAKE IT FAST!
ER...
YES, MA'AM. RIGHT AWAY.
O-ORDER COMING UP!
PAT PAT
...
WHAM
URK
STARE

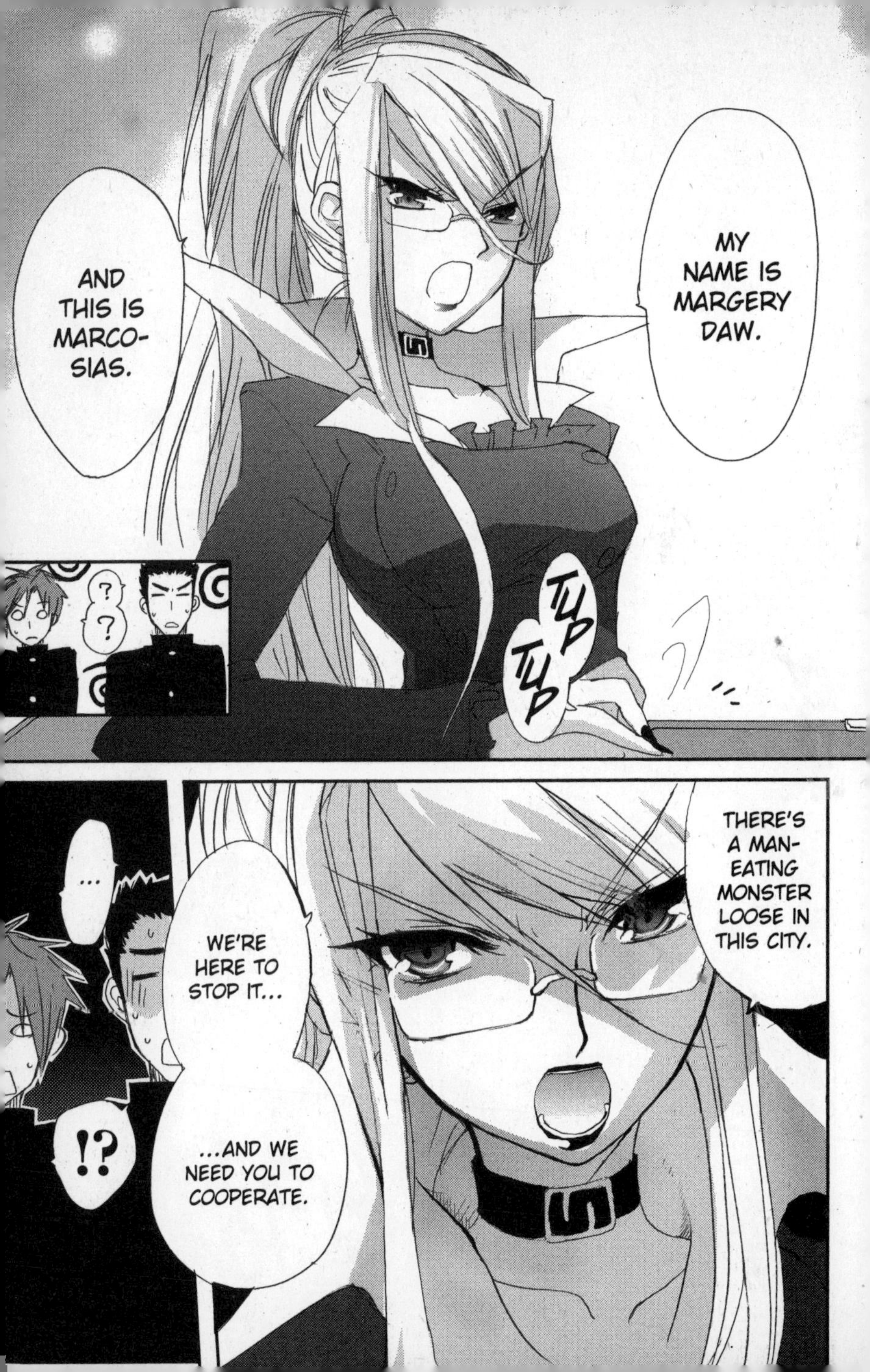
MY NAME IS MARGERY DAW.
AND THIS IS MARCO-SIAS.
TUP TUP TUP
? ?
THERE'S A MAN-EATING MONSTER LOOSE IN THIS CITY.
WE'RE HERE TO STOP IT...
...AND WE NEED YOU TO COOPERATE.
...
!?

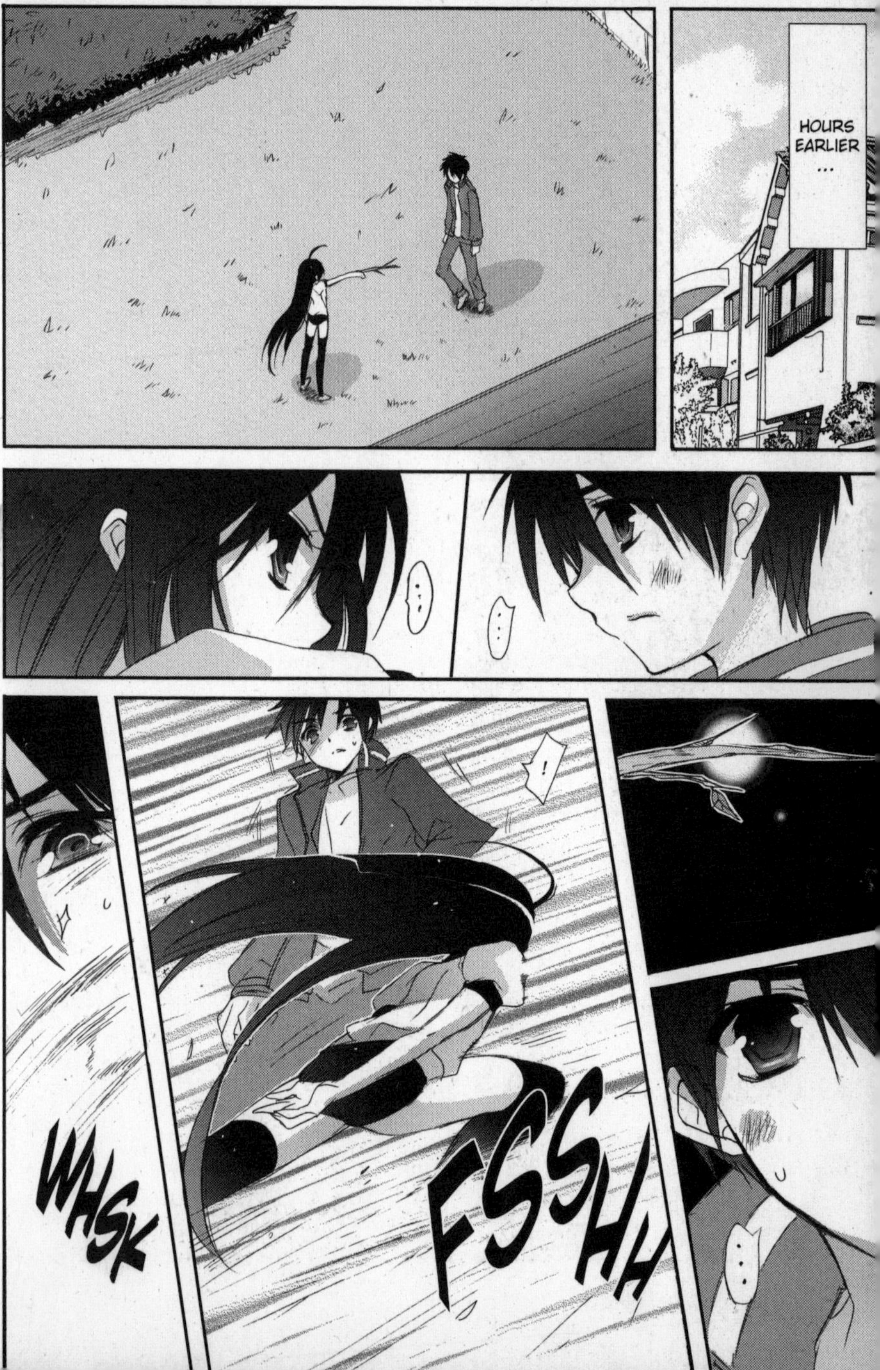
HOURS EARLIER ...
...
...
!
...
FSSHH
WHSK

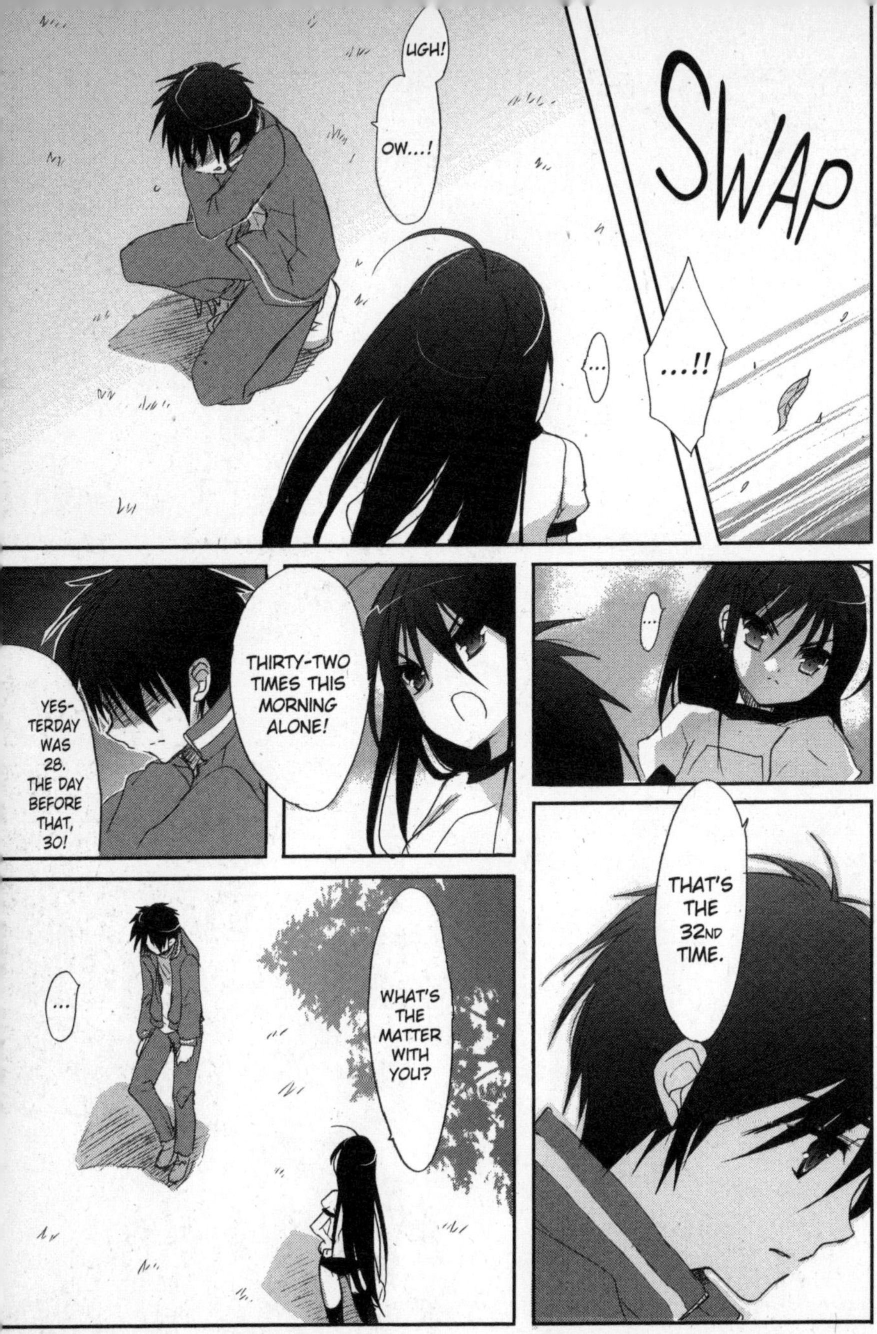
SWAP
...!!
...
UGH!
OW...!
...
THAT'S THE 32ND TIME.
THIRTY-TWO TIMES THIS MORNING ALONE!
YESTERDAY WAS 28. THE DAY BEFORE THAT, 30!
WHAT'S THE MATTER WITH YOU?
...

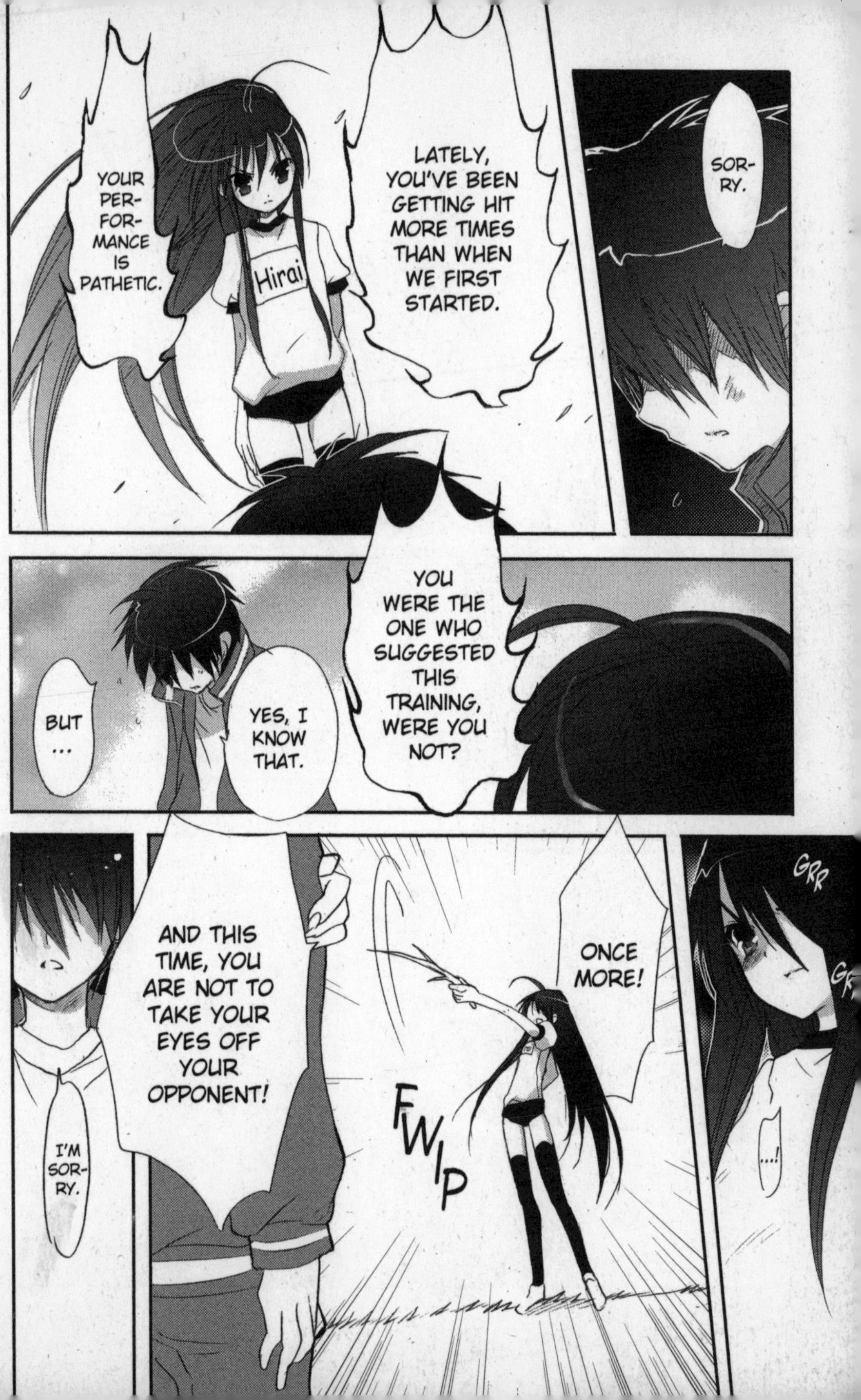
SOR-RY.
LATELY, YOU'VE BEEN GETTING HIT MORE TIMES THAN WHEN WE FIRST STARTED.
Hirai
YOUR PER-FOR-MANCE IS PATHETIC.
YOU WERE THE ONE WHO SUGGESTED THIS TRAINING, WERE YOU NOT?
YES, I KNOW THAT.
BUT ...
GRR
GRR
...!
ONCE MORE!
FWIP
AND THIS TIME, YOU ARE NOT TO TAKE YOUR EYES OFF YOUR OPPONENT!
I'M SOR-RY.

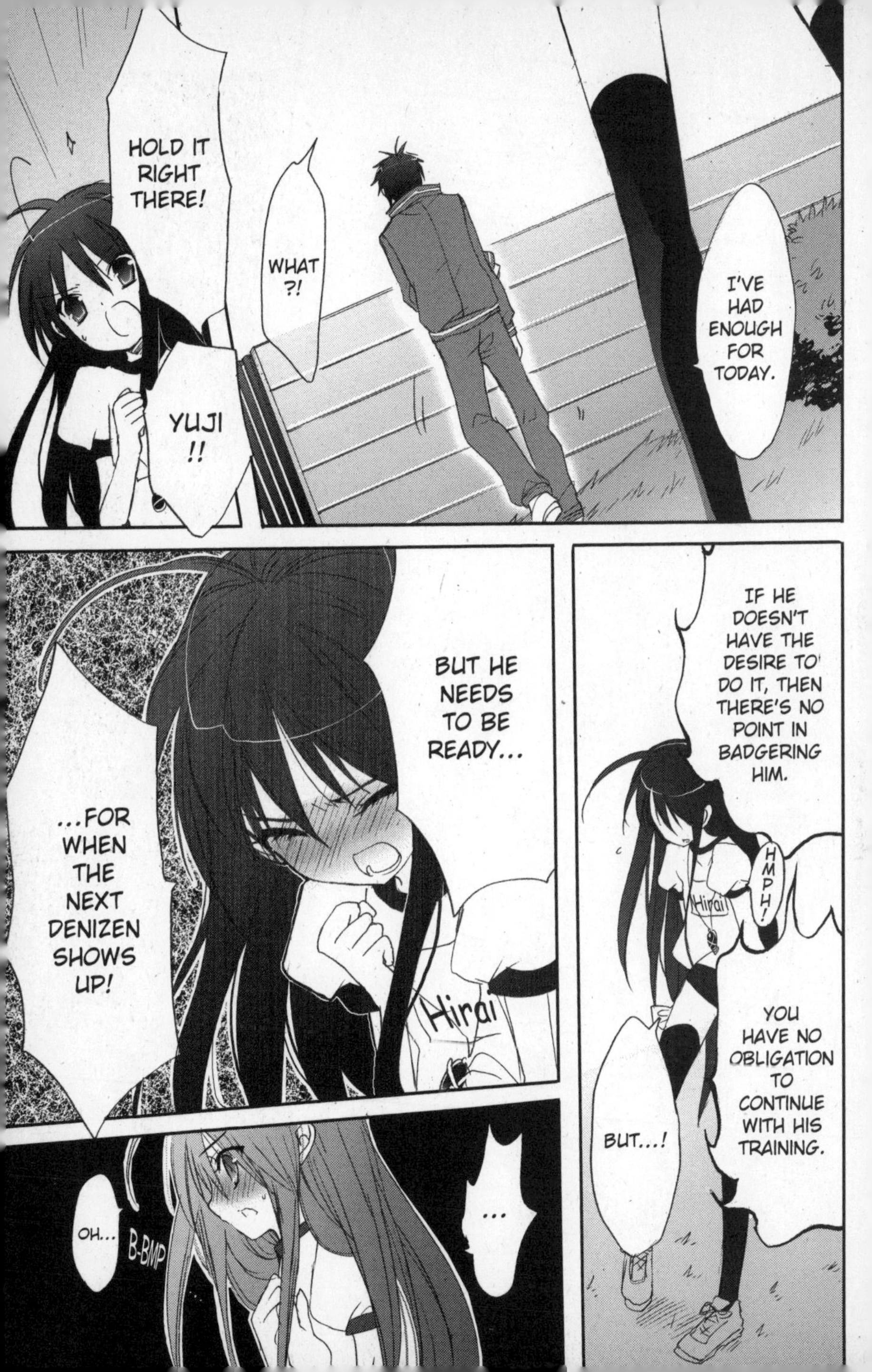
I'VE HAD ENOUGH FOR TODAY.
WHAT ?!
HOLD IT RIGHT THERE!
YUJI !!
IF HE DOESN'T HAVE THE DESIRE TO DO IT, THEN THERE'S NO POINT IN BADGERING HIM.
HMPH!
Hirai
YOU HAVE NO OBLIGATION TO CONTINUE WITH HIS TRAINING.
BUT...!
BUT HE NEEDS TO BE READY...
...FOR WHEN THE NEXT DENIZEN SHOWS UP!
Hirai
...
B-BMP
OH...

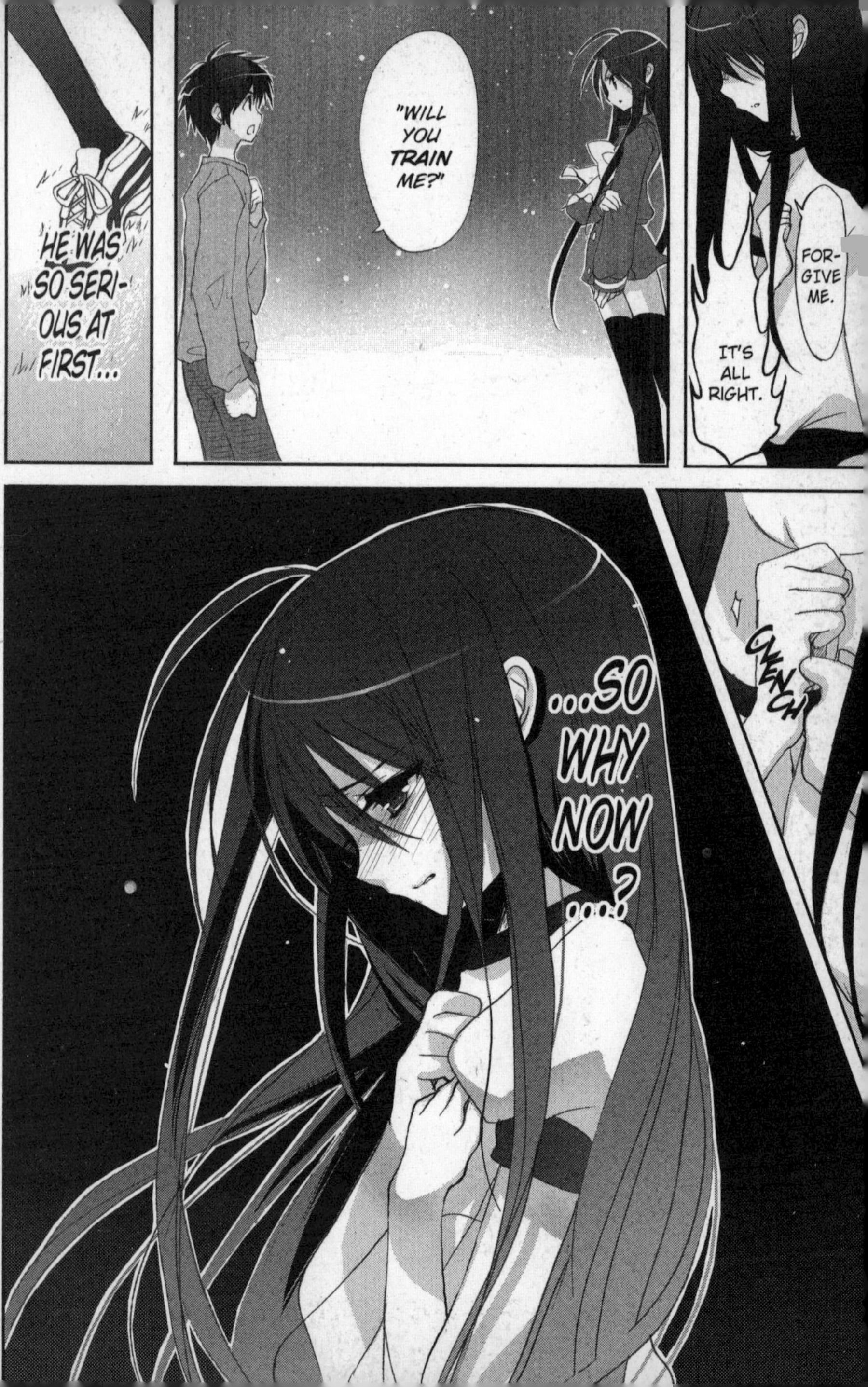
FOR-GIVE ME.
IT'S ALL RIGHT.
"WILL YOU TRAIN ME?"
HE WAS SO SERI-OUS AT FIRST...
GWENCH
...SO WHY NOW ...?

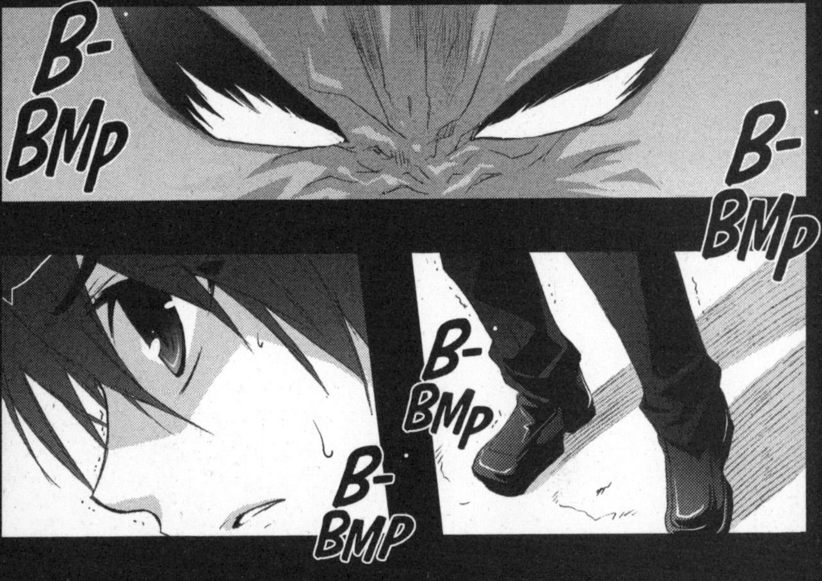
B-BMP
B-BMP
B-BMP
B-BMP

SHAKUGAN NO SHANA™

Episode 23: A Complicated Time III

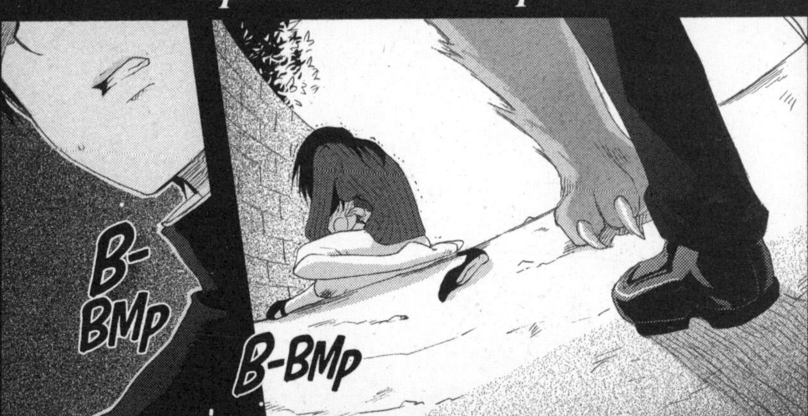
B-BMP
B-BMP

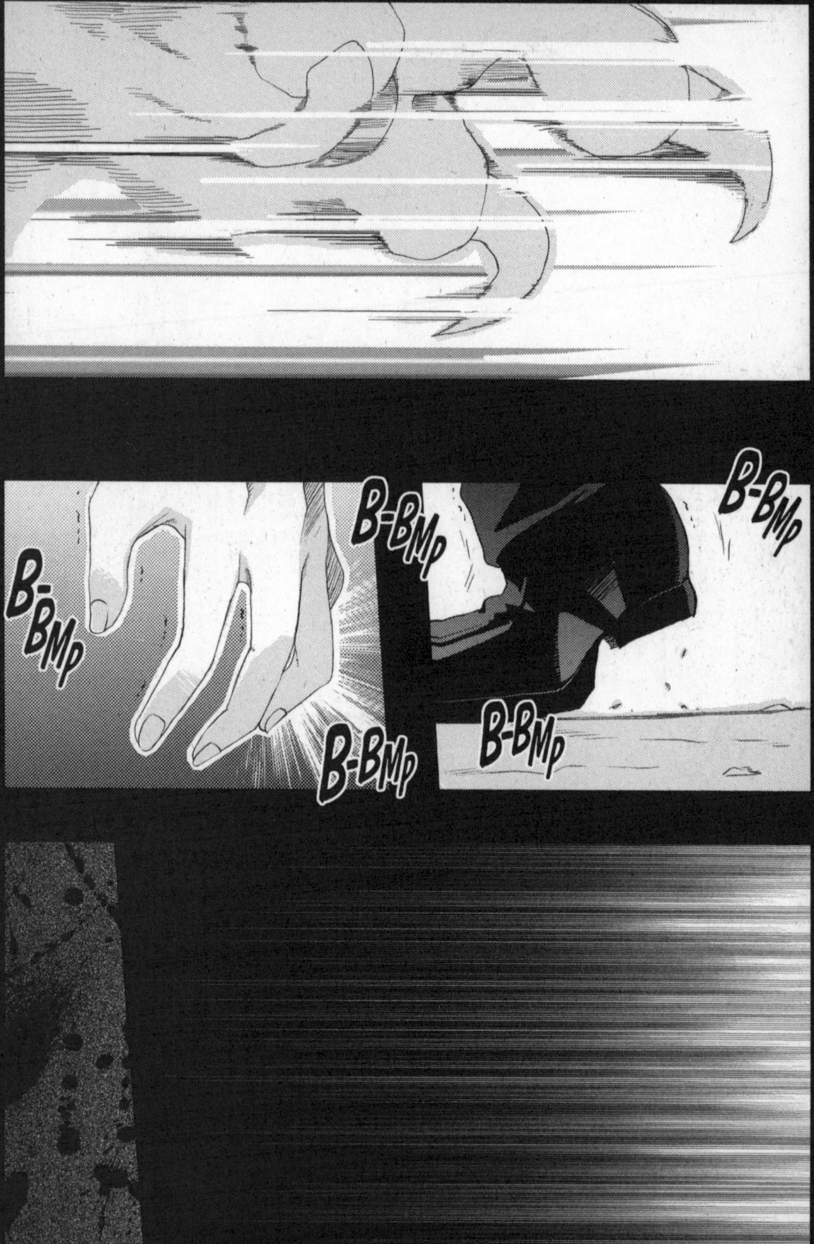
B-BMP
B-BMP
B-BMP
B-BMP
B-BMP

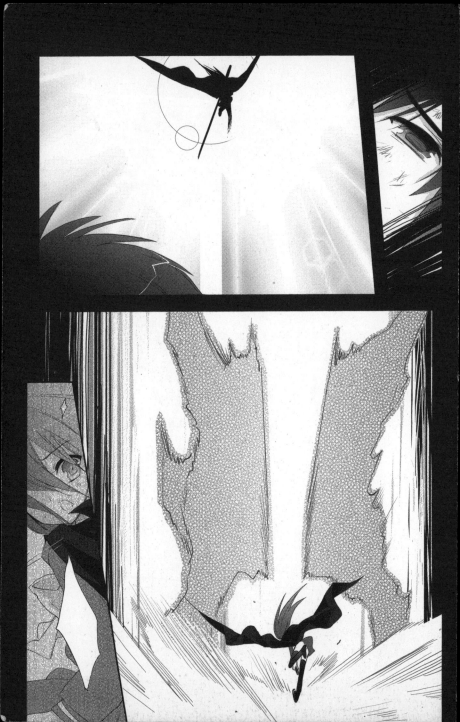

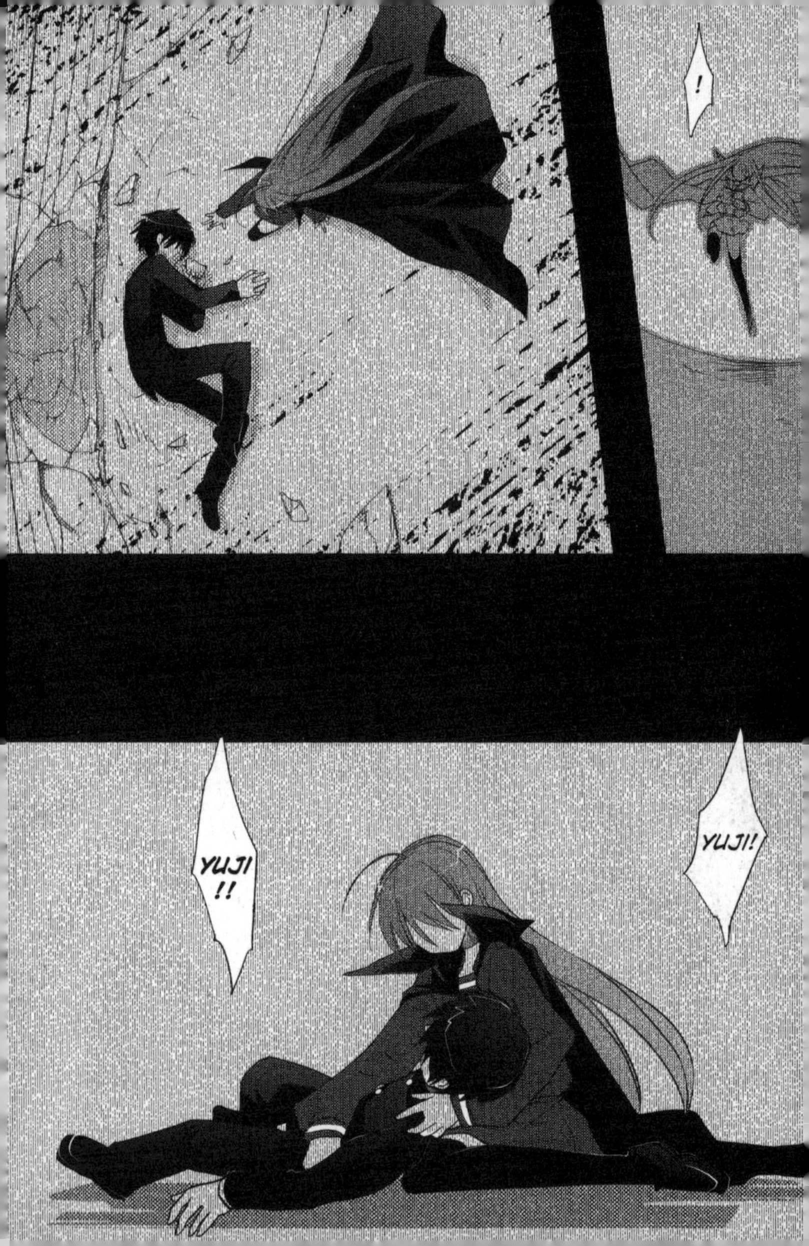
!
YUJI!
YUJI !!

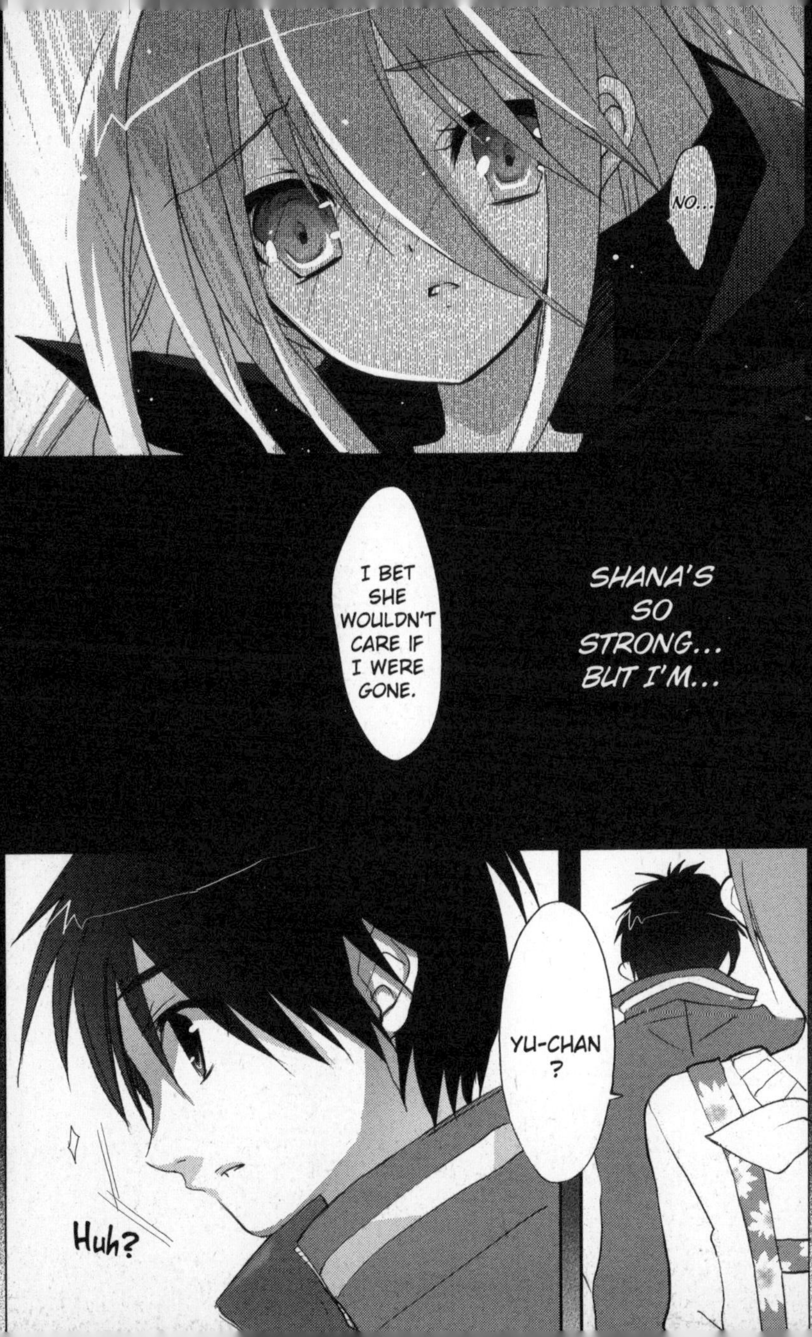
NO...
SHANA'S SO STRONG... BUT I'M...
I BET SHE WOULDN'T CARE IF I WERE GONE.
YU-CHAN?
Huh?

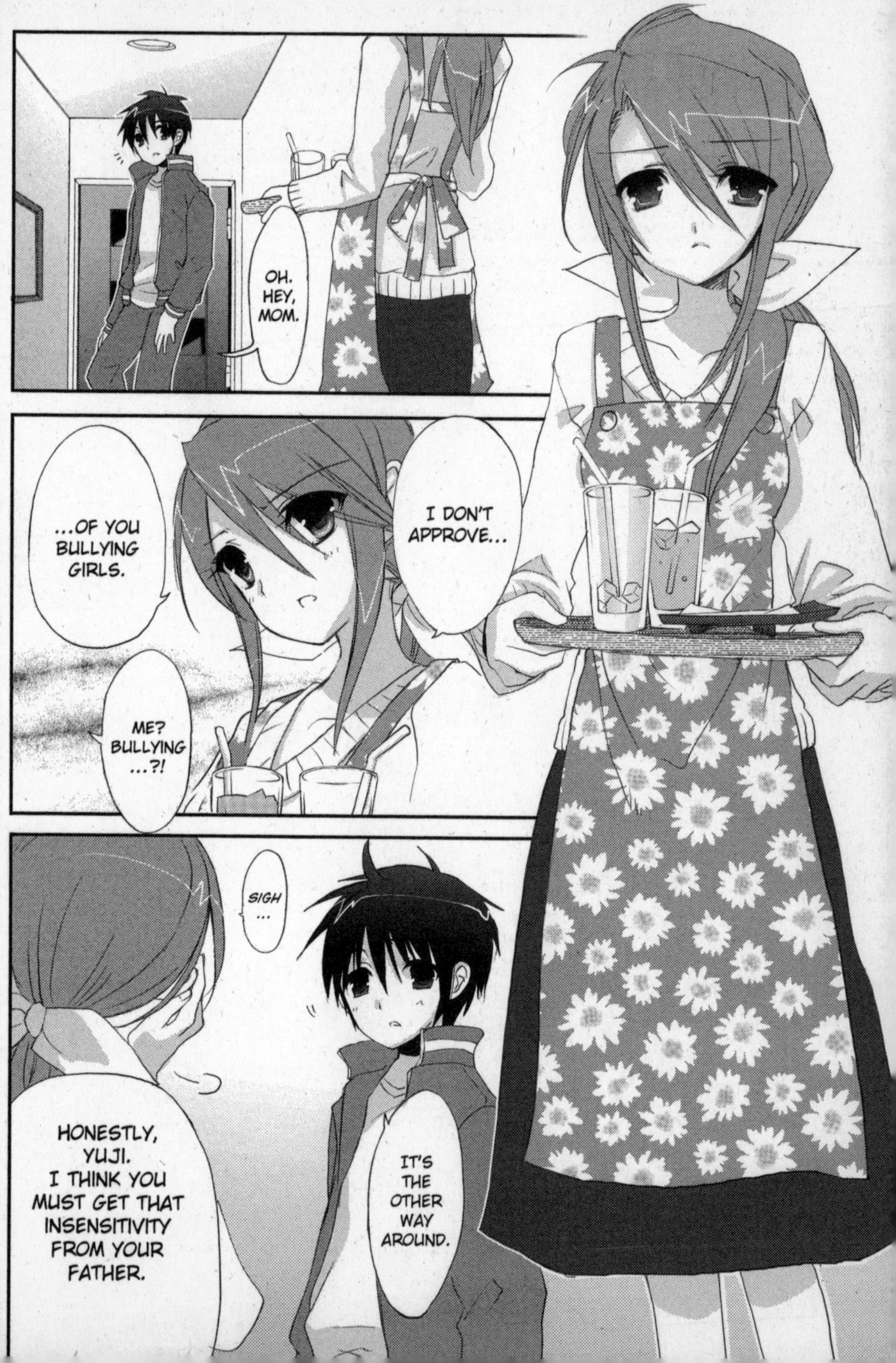
OH. HEY, MOM.
I DON'T APPROVE...
...OF YOU BULLYING GIRLS.
ME? BULLYING...?!
SIGH...
IT'S THE OTHER WAY AROUND.
HONESTLY, YUJI. I THINK YOU MUST GET THAT INSENSITIVITY FROM YOUR FATHER.

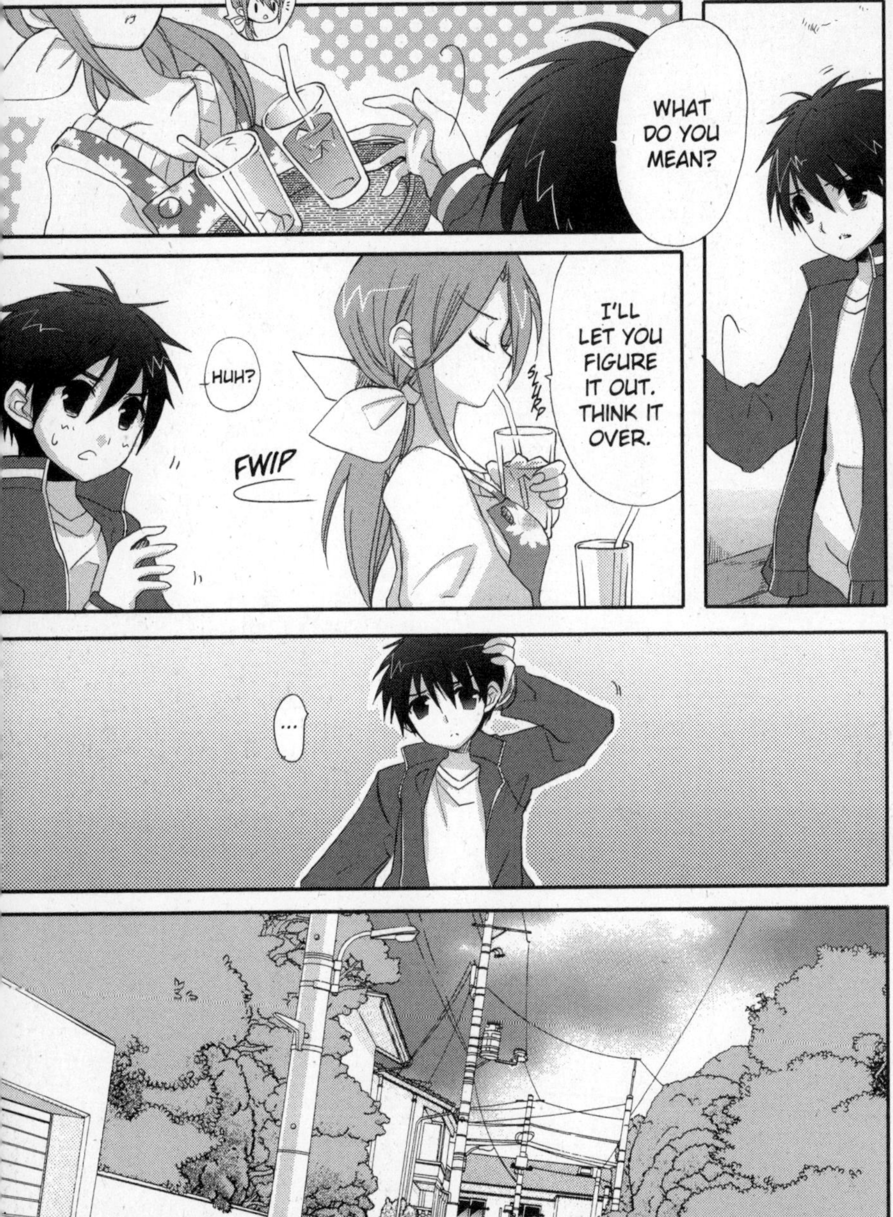
WHAT DO YOU MEAN?
I'LL LET YOU FIGURE IT OUT. THINK IT OVER.
SLURRP
FWIP
HUH?
...

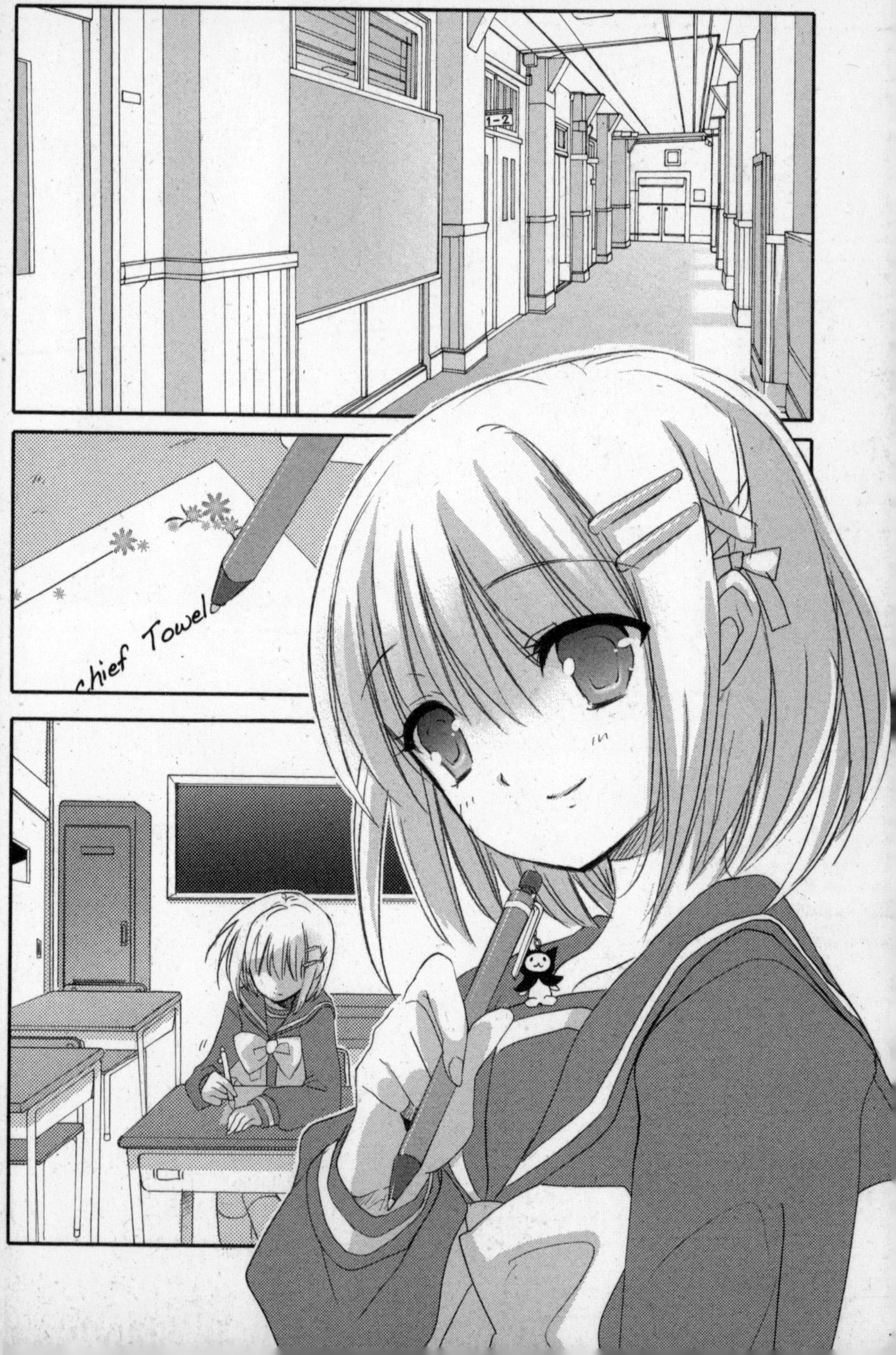
1-2
chief Towel

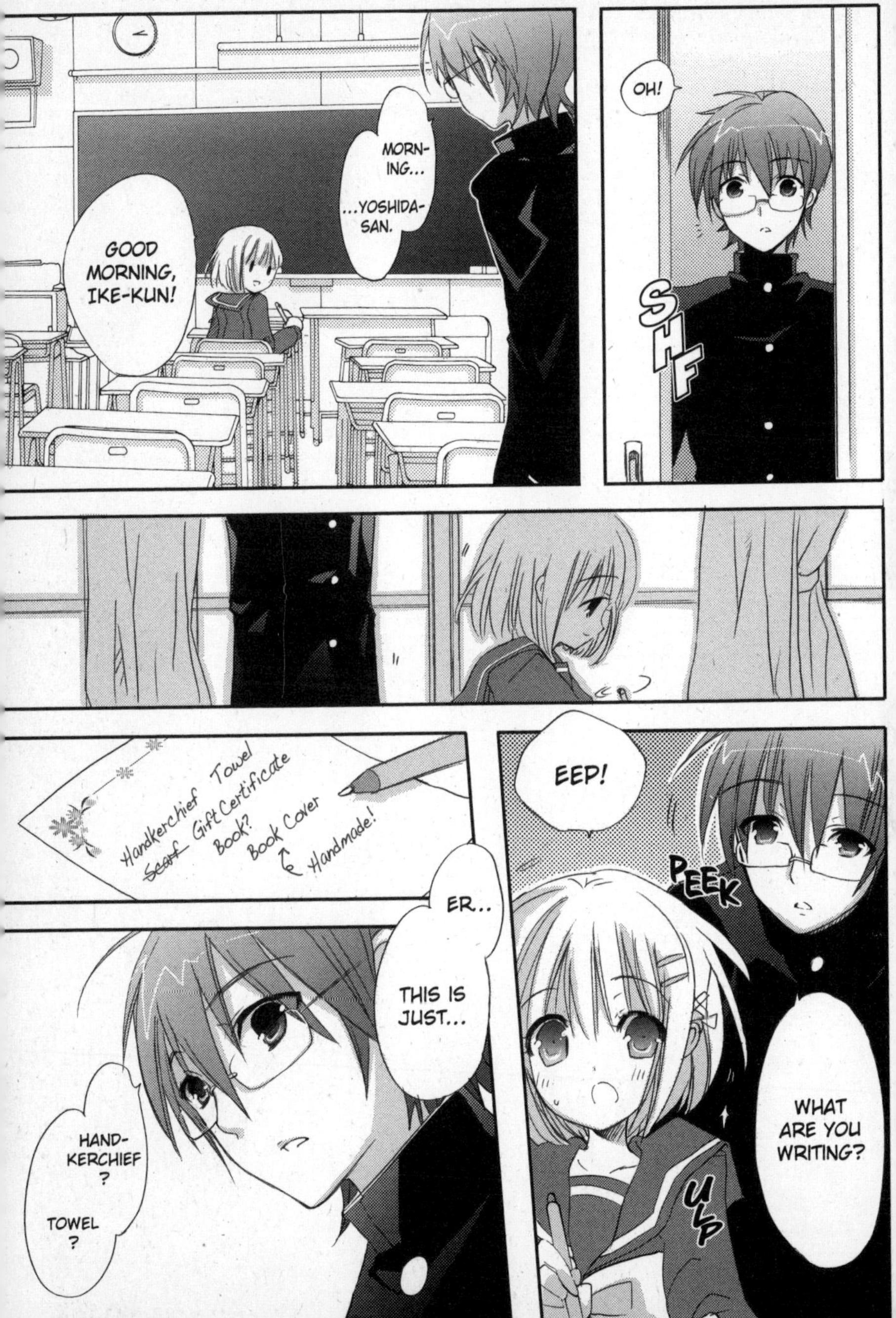
OH!
SHF
MORNING... ...YOSHIDA-SAN.
GOOD MORNING, IKE-KUN!
EEP!
PEEK
WHAT ARE YOU WRITING?
ULP
Handkerchief Towel
~~Scarf~~ Gift Certificate
Book?
Book Cover
Handmade!
ER...
THIS IS JUST...
HANDKERCHIEF?
TOWEL?

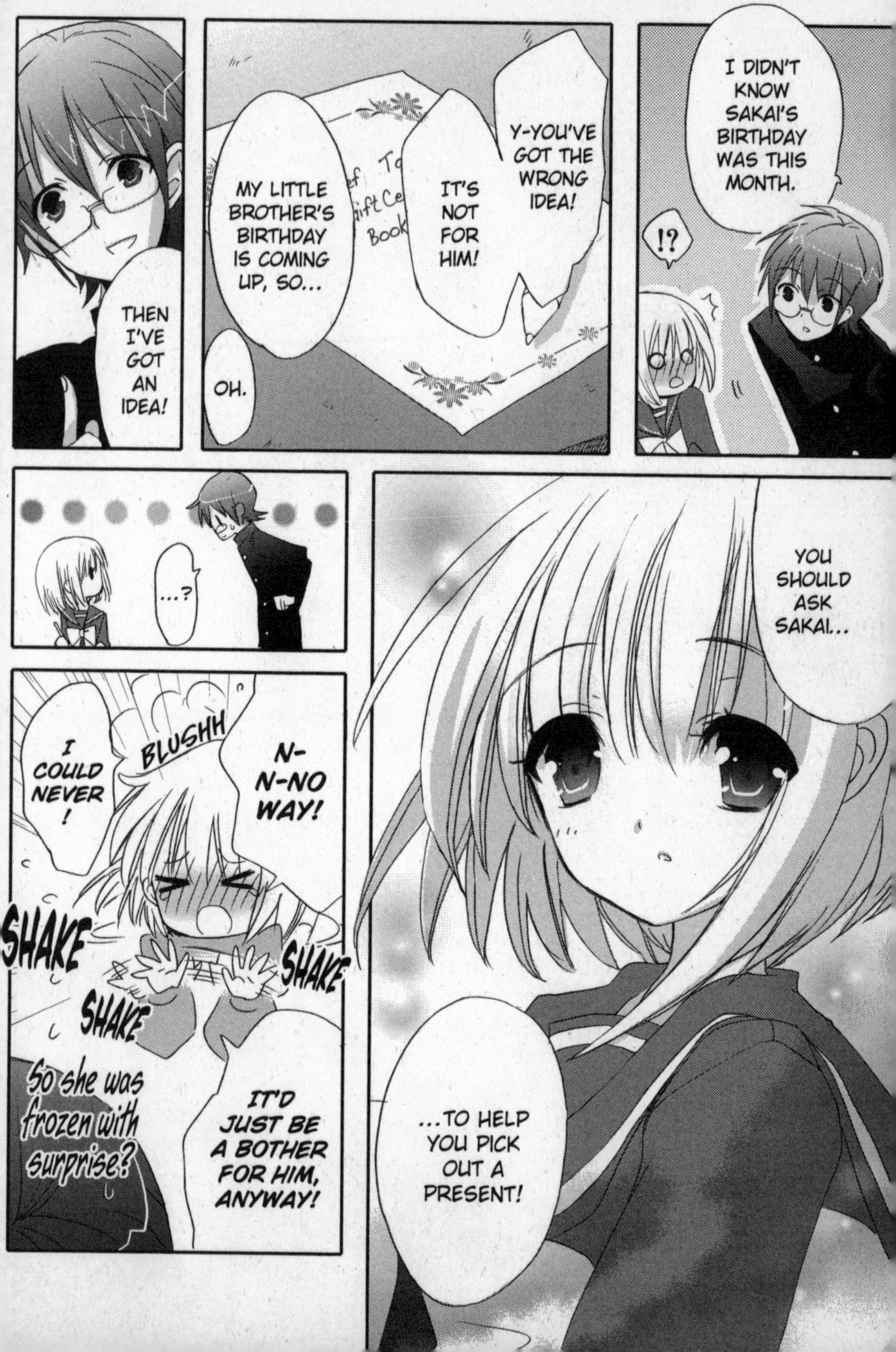
I DIDN'T KNOW SAKAI'S BIRTHDAY WAS THIS MONTH.
!?
Y-YOU'VE GOT THE WRONG IDEA!
IT'S NOT FOR HIM!
MY LITTLE BROTHER'S BIRTHDAY IS COMING UP, SO...
OH.
THEN I'VE GOT AN IDEA!
YOU SHOULD ASK SAKAI...
...TO HELP YOU PICK OUT A PRESENT!
...?
N-N-NO WAY!
BLUSHH
I COULD NEVER!
SHAKE
SHAKE
SHAKE
IT'D JUST BE A BOTHER FOR HIM, ANYWAY!
So she was frozen with surprise?

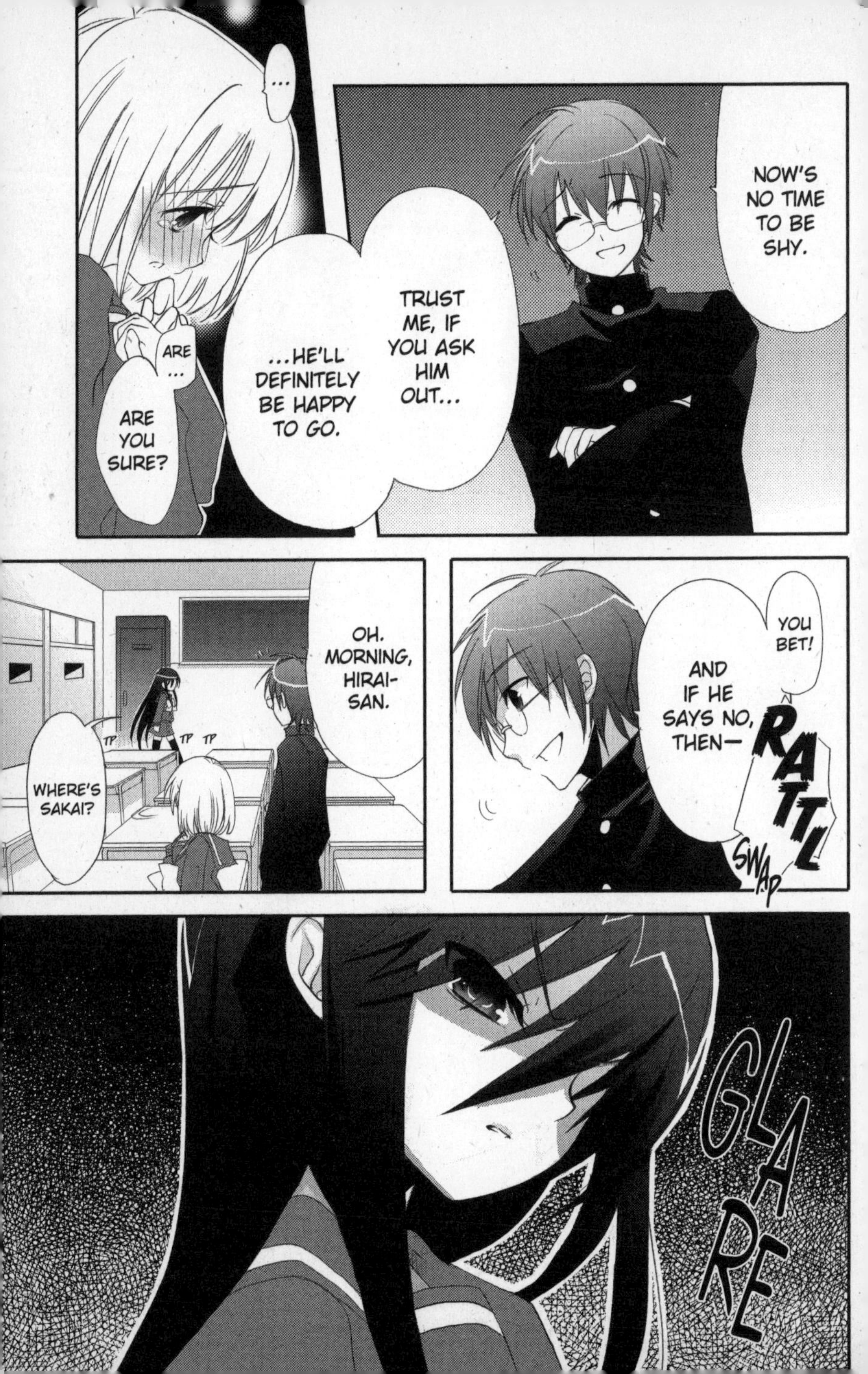
NOW'S NO TIME TO BE SHY.
TRUST ME, IF YOU ASK HIM OUT...
...HE'LL DEFINITELY BE HAPPY TO GO.
...
ARE...
ARE YOU SURE?
YOU BET!
AND IF HE SAYS NO, THEN—
RATTL
SWAP
OH. MORNING, HIRAI-SAN.
TP TP TP
WHERE'S SAKAI?
GLARE

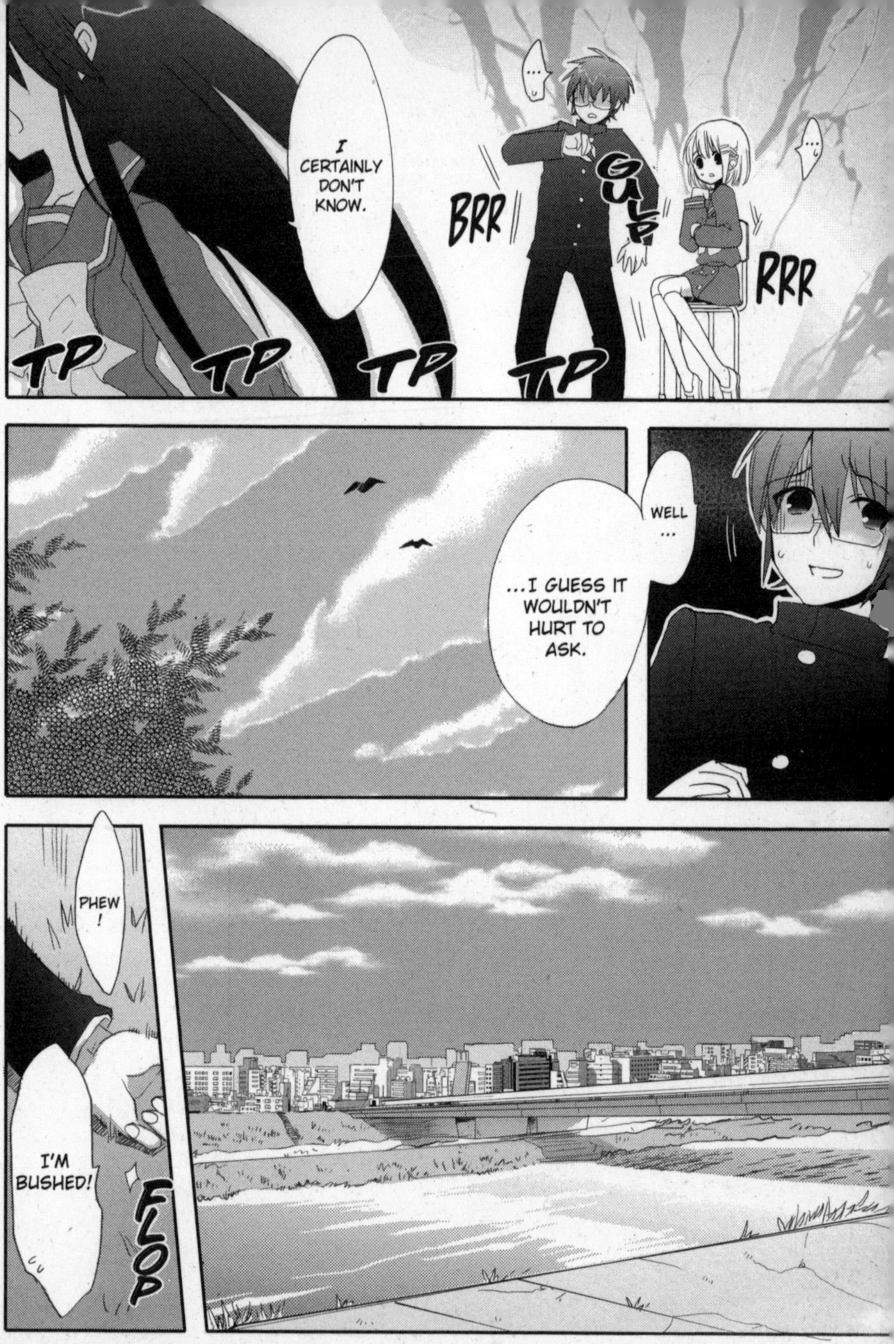
...
...
RRR
GULP
BRR
I CERTAINLY DON'T KNOW.
TP TP TP TP
WELL...
...I GUESS IT WOULDN'T HURT TO ASK.
PHEW!
FLOP
I'M BUSHED!

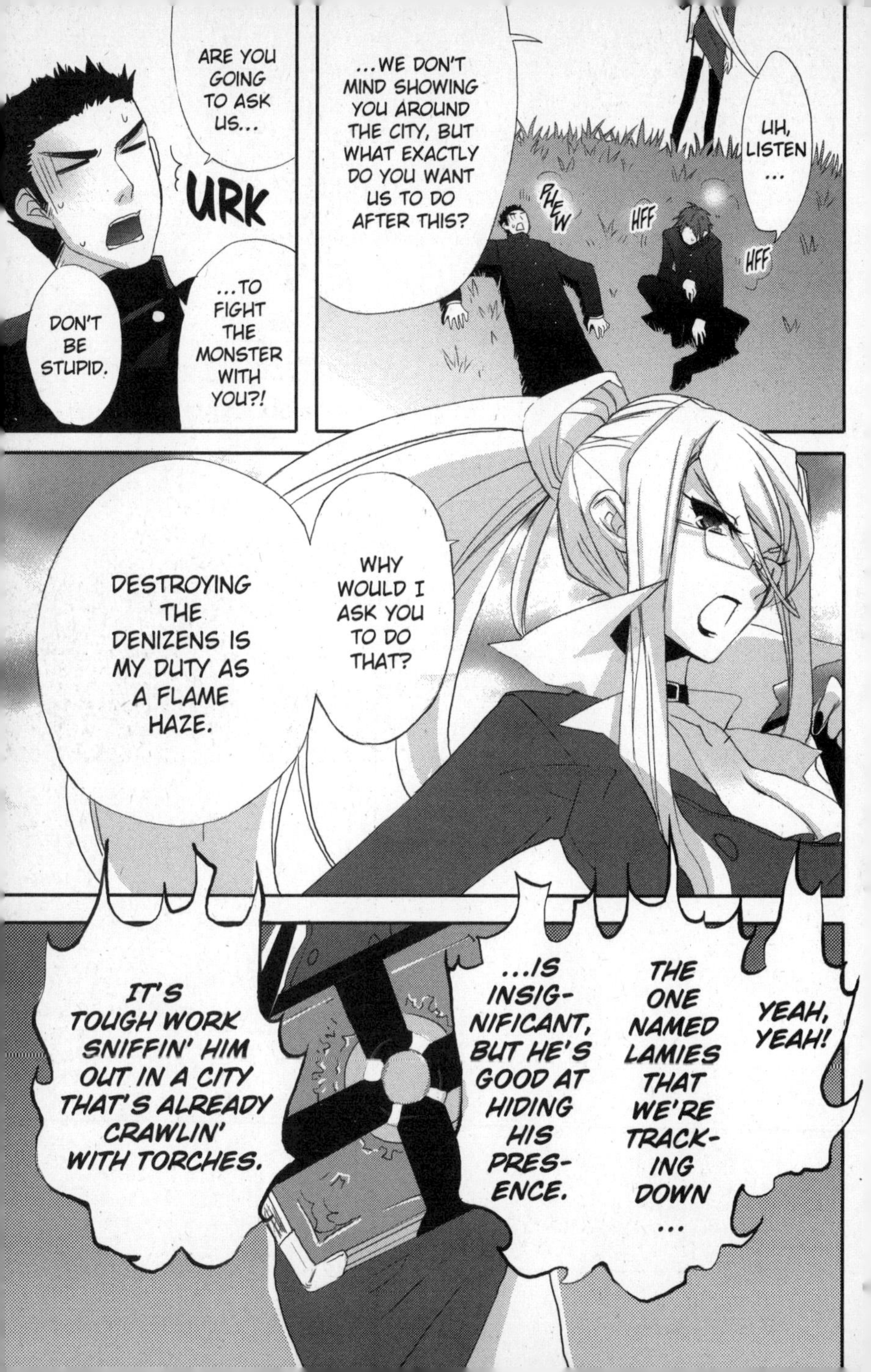
UH, LISTEN ...
...WE DON'T MIND SHOWING YOU AROUND THE CITY, BUT WHAT EXACTLY DO YOU WANT US TO DO AFTER THIS?
PHEW
HFF
HFF
ARE YOU GOING TO ASK US...
URK
...TO FIGHT THE MONSTER WITH YOU?!
DON'T BE STUPID.
WHY WOULD I ASK YOU TO DO THAT?
DESTROYING THE DENIZENS IS MY DUTY AS A FLAME HAZE.
YEAH, YEAH!
THE ONE NAMED LAMIES THAT WE'RE TRACK-ING DOWN ...
...IS INSIG-NIFICANT, BUT HE'S GOOD AT HIDING HIS PRES-ENCE.
IT'S TOUGH WORK SNIFFIN' HIM OUT IN A CITY THAT'S ALREADY CRAWLIN' WITH TORCHES.

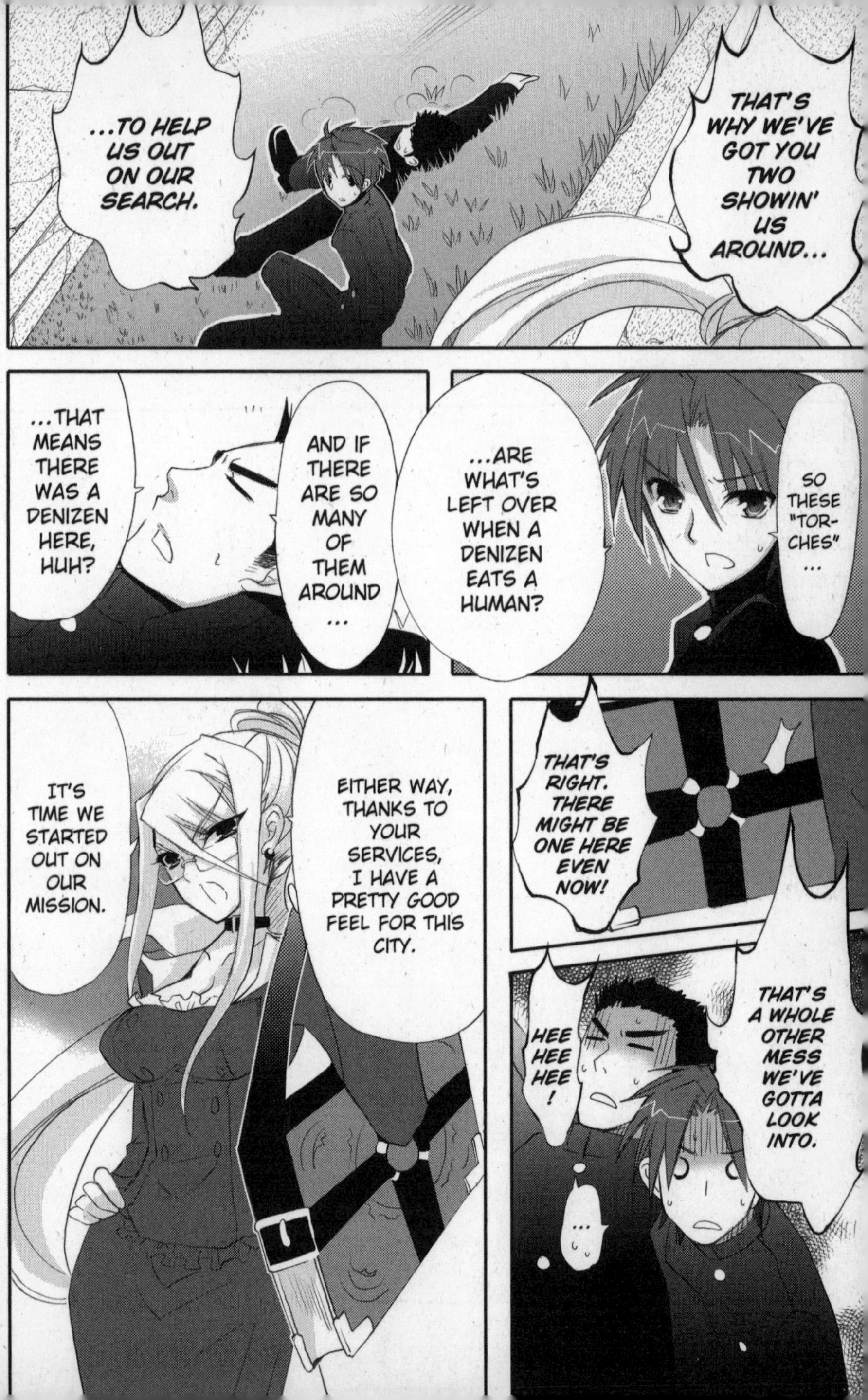
THAT'S WHY WE'VE GOT YOU TWO SHOWIN' US AROUND...
...TO HELP US OUT ON OUR SEARCH.
SO THESE "TORCHES"...
...ARE WHAT'S LEFT OVER WHEN A DENIZEN EATS A HUMAN?
AND IF THERE ARE SO MANY OF THEM AROUND...
...THAT MEANS THERE WAS A DENIZEN HERE, HUH?
THAT'S RIGHT. THERE MIGHT BE ONE HERE EVEN NOW!
THAT'S A WHOLE OTHER MESS WE'VE GOTTA LOOK INTO.
HEE HEE HEE!
...
EITHER WAY, THANKS TO YOUR SERVICES, I HAVE A PRETTY GOOD FEEL FOR THIS CITY.
IT'S TIME WE STARTED OUT ON OUR MISSION.

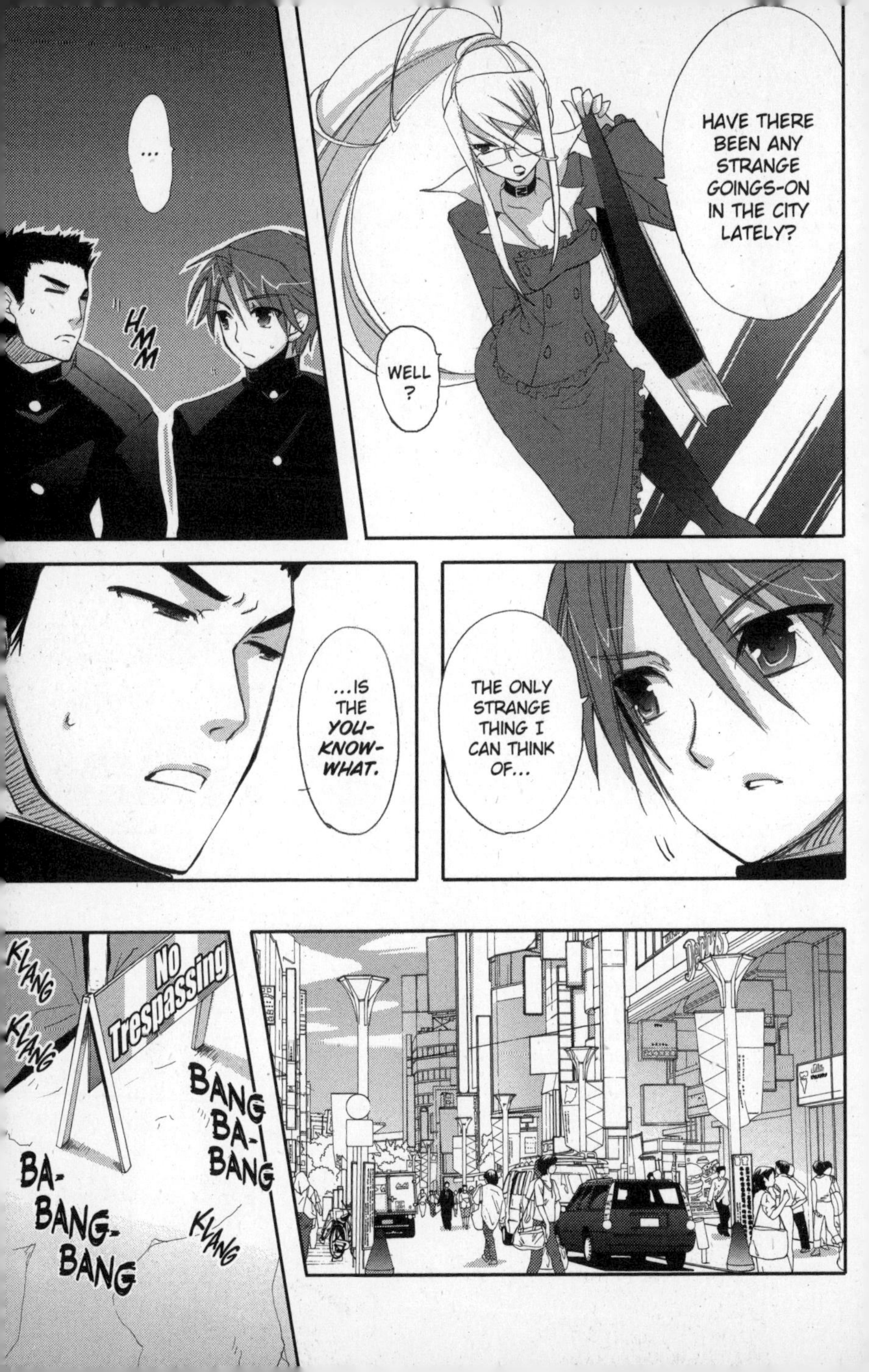
HAVE THERE BEEN ANY STRANGE GOINGS-ON IN THE CITY LATELY?
WELL?
...
HMM
THE ONLY STRANGE THING I CAN THINK OF...
...IS THE *YOU-KNOW-WHAT.*
No Trespassing
KLANG
KLANG
BANG BA-BANG
BA-BANG-BANG
KLANG

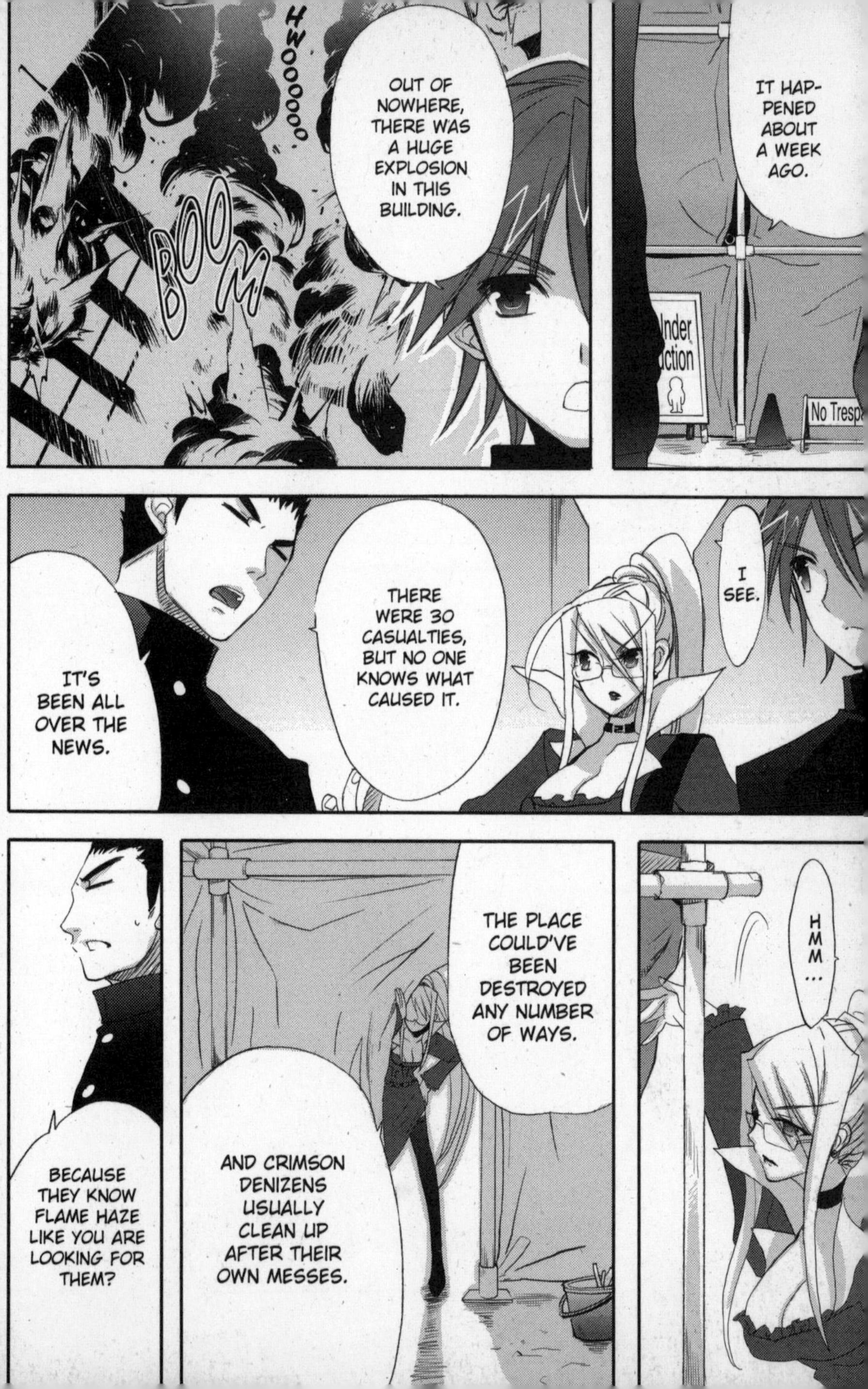
IT HAPPENED ABOUT A WEEK AGO.
OUT OF NOWHERE, THERE WAS A HUGE EXPLOSION IN THIS BUILDING.
HWOOOOOO
BOOM
I SEE.
THERE WERE 30 CASUALTIES, BUT NO ONE KNOWS WHAT CAUSED IT.
IT'S BEEN ALL OVER THE NEWS.
HMM...
THE PLACE COULD'VE BEEN DESTROYED ANY NUMBER OF WAYS.
AND CRIMSON DENIZENS USUALLY CLEAN UP AFTER THEIR OWN MESSES.
BECAUSE THEY KNOW FLAME HAZE LIKE YOU ARE LOOKING FOR THEM?

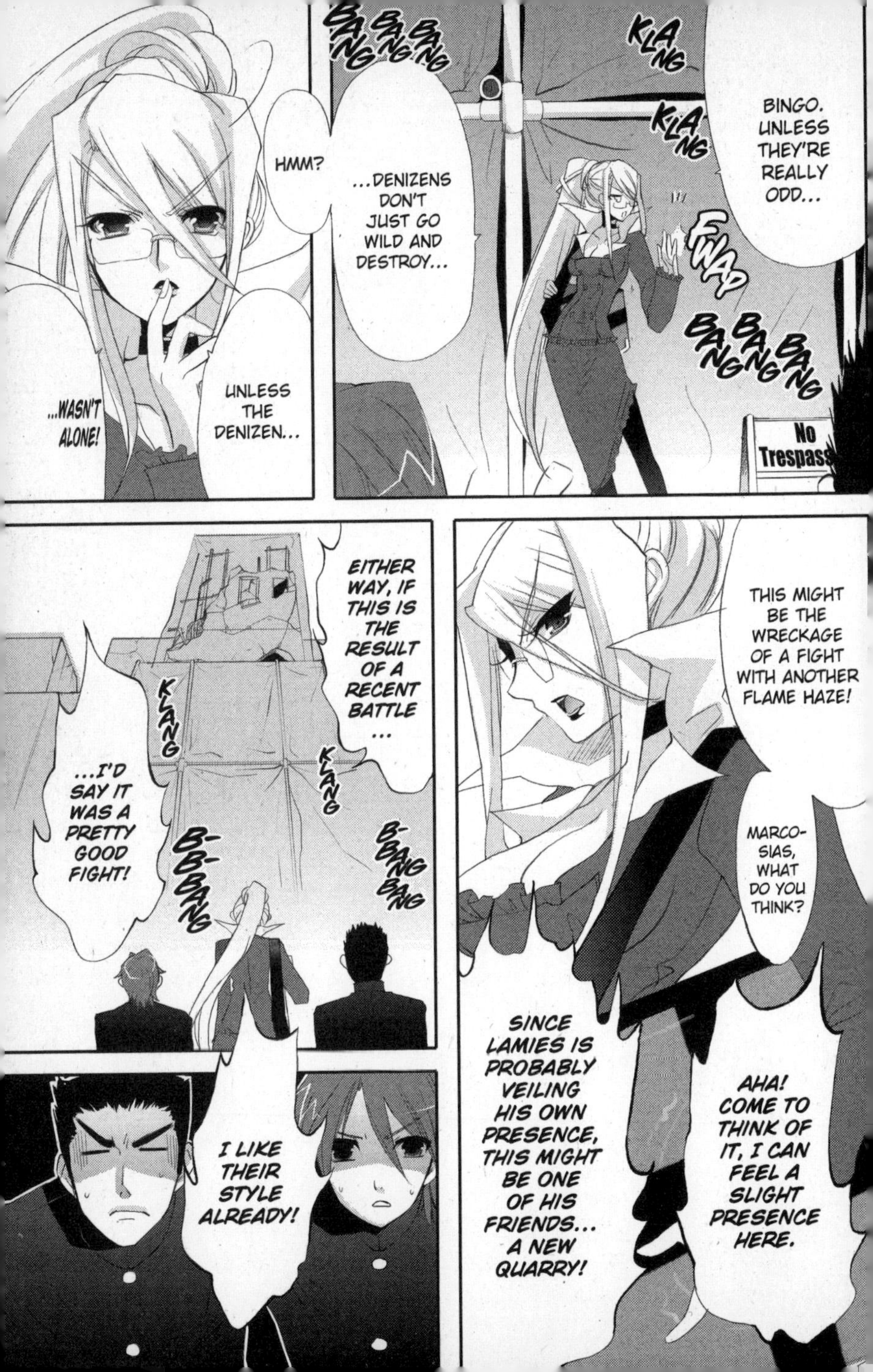
KLANG
KLANG
BINGO. UNLESS THEY'RE REALLY ODD...
FWAP
BANG BANG BANG
No Trespass
BANG BANG BANG
...DENIZENS DON'T JUST GO WILD AND DESTROY...
HMM?
UNLESS THE DENIZEN...
...WASN'T ALONE!
THIS MIGHT BE THE WRECKAGE OF A FIGHT WITH ANOTHER FLAME HAZE!
MARCO-SIAS, WHAT DO YOU THINK?
EITHER WAY, IF THIS IS THE RESULT OF A RECENT BATTLE...
KLANG
B-BANG BANG
...I'D SAY IT WAS A PRETTY GOOD FIGHT!
KLANG
B-B-BANG
AHA! COME TO THINK OF IT, I CAN FEEL A SLIGHT PRESENCE HERE.
SINCE LAMIES IS PROBABLY VEILING HIS OWN PRESENCE, THIS MIGHT BE ONE OF HIS FRIENDS... A NEW QUARRY!
I LIKE THEIR STYLE ALREADY!

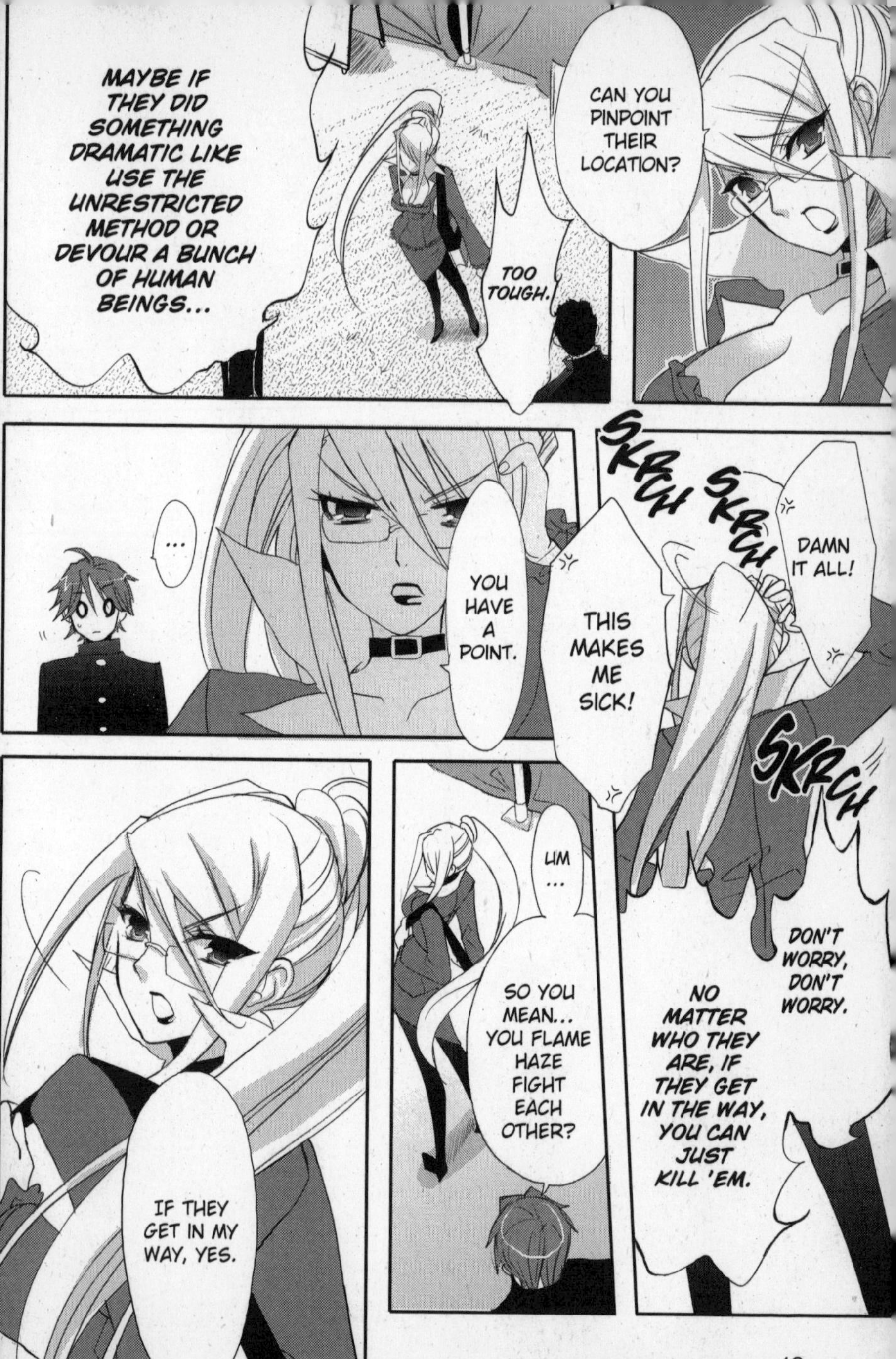
CAN YOU PINPOINT THEIR LOCATION?
MAYBE IF THEY DID SOMETHING DRAMATIC LIKE USE THE UNRESTRICTED METHOD OR DEVOUR A BUNCH OF HUMAN BEINGS...
TOO TOUGH.
SKRCH
SKRCH
DAMN IT ALL!
THIS MAKES ME SICK!
SKRCH
DON'T WORRY, DON'T WORRY.
NO MATTER WHO THEY ARE, IF THEY GET IN THE WAY, YOU CAN JUST KILL 'EM.
YOU HAVE A POINT.
...
UM ...
SO YOU MEAN... YOU FLAME HAZE FIGHT EACH OTHER?
IF THEY GET IN MY WAY, YES.

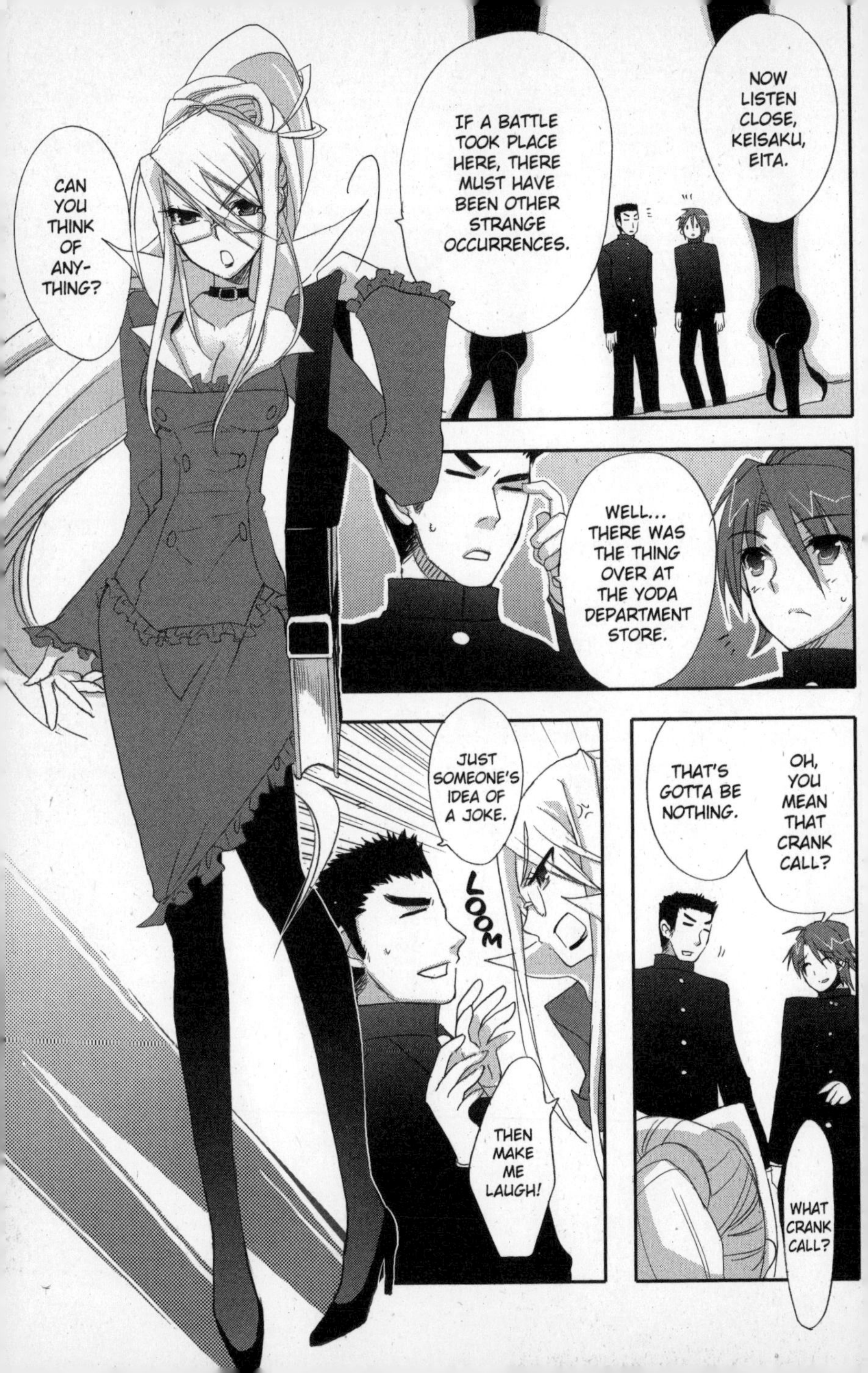
NOW LISTEN CLOSE, KEISAKU, EITA.
IF A BATTLE TOOK PLACE HERE, THERE MUST HAVE BEEN OTHER STRANGE OCCURRENCES.
CAN YOU THINK OF ANY-THING?
WELL... THERE WAS THE THING OVER AT THE YODA DEPARTMENT STORE.
OH, YOU MEAN THAT CRANK CALL?
THAT'S GOTTA BE NOTHING.
WHAT CRANK CALL?
JUST SOMEONE'S IDEA OF A JOKE.
LOOOM
THEN MAKE ME LAUGH!

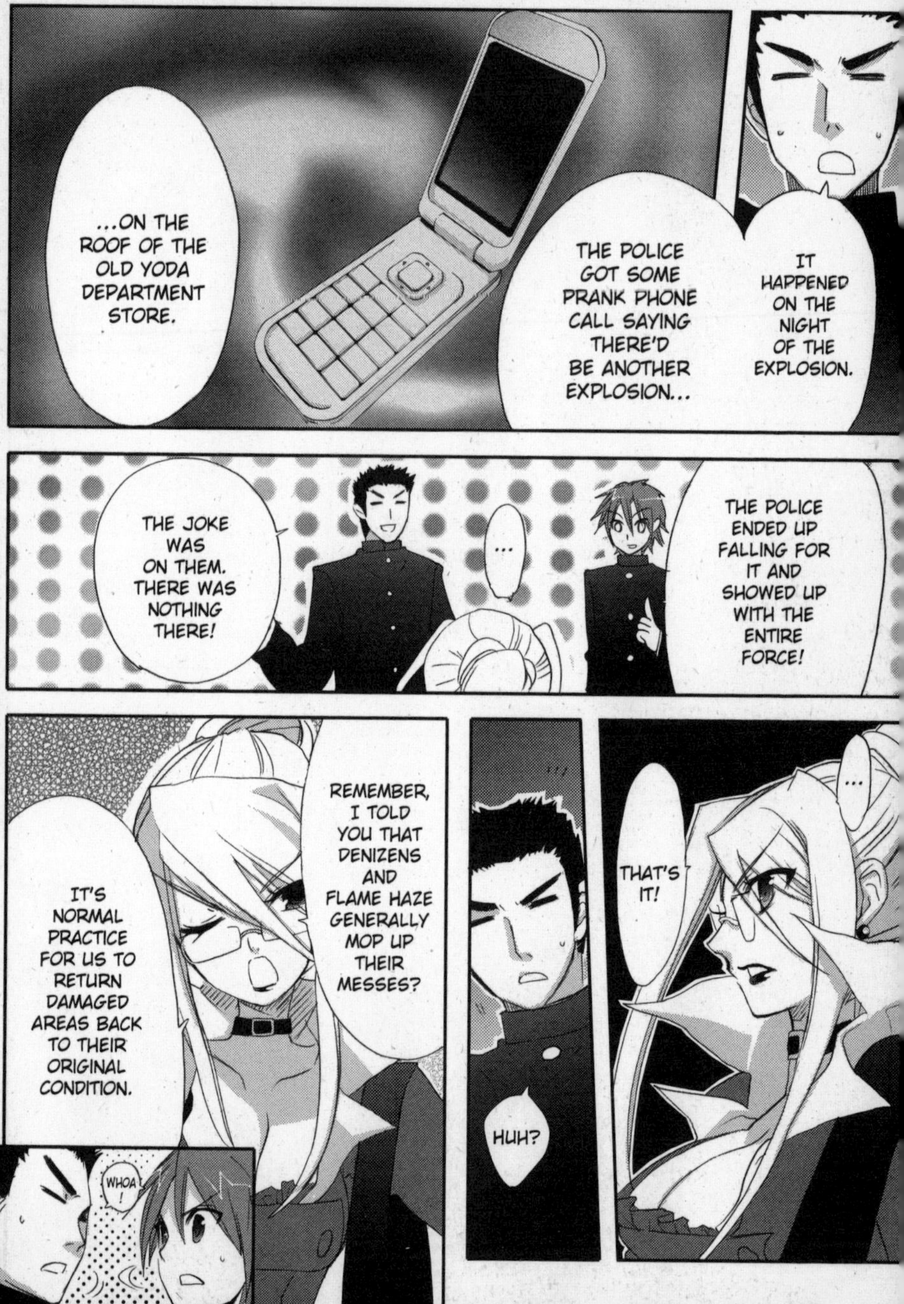
IT HAPPENED ON THE NIGHT OF THE EXPLOSION.
THE POLICE GOT SOME PRANK PHONE CALL SAYING THERE'D BE ANOTHER EXPLOSION...
...ON THE ROOF OF THE OLD YODA DEPARTMENT STORE.
THE POLICE ENDED UP FALLING FOR IT AND SHOWED UP WITH THE ENTIRE FORCE!
...
THE JOKE WAS ON THEM. THERE WAS NOTHING THERE!
...
THAT'S IT!
HUH?
REMEMBER, I TOLD YOU THAT DENIZENS AND FLAME HAZE GENERALLY MOP UP THEIR MESSES?
IT'S NORMAL PRACTICE FOR US TO RETURN DAMAGED AREAS BACK TO THEIR ORIGINAL CONDITION.
WHOA!

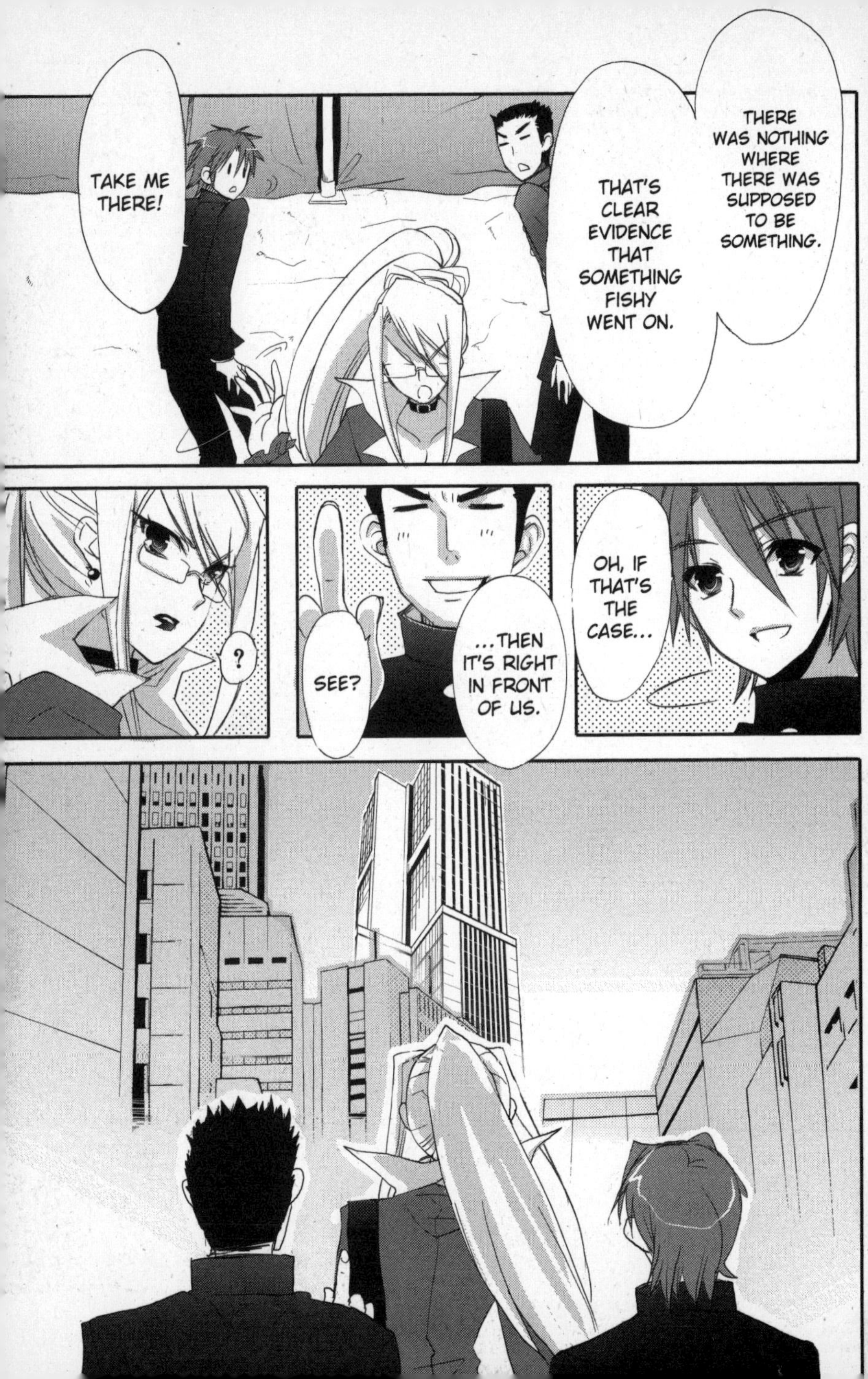
THERE WAS NOTHING WHERE THERE WAS SUPPOSED TO BE SOMETHING.
THAT'S CLEAR EVIDENCE THAT SOMETHING FISHY WENT ON.
TAKE ME THERE!
OH, IF THAT'S THE CASE...
...THEN IT'S RIGHT IN FRONT OF US.
SEE?
?

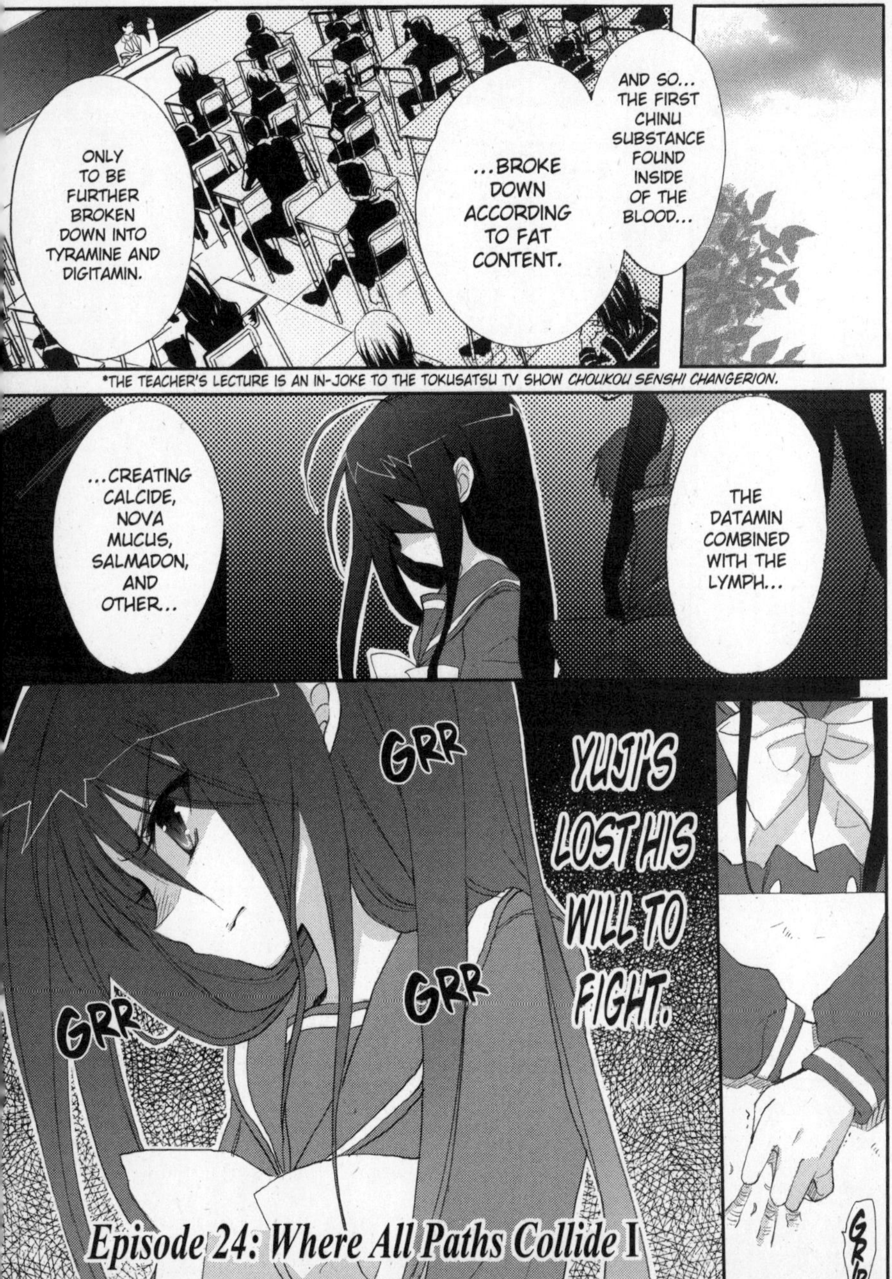
AND SO... THE FIRST CHINU SUBSTANCE FOUND INSIDE OF THE BLOOD...
...BROKE DOWN ACCORDING TO FAT CONTENT.
ONLY TO BE FURTHER BROKEN DOWN INTO TYRAMINE AND DIGITAMIN.
THE DATAMIN COMBINED WITH THE LYMPH...
...CREATING CALCIDE, NOVA MUCUS, SALMADON, AND OTHER...
GRIP
YUJI'S LOST HIS WILL TO FIGHT.
GRR
GRR
GRR
Episode 24: Where All Paths Collide I

*THE TEACHER'S LECTURE IS AN IN-JOKE TO THE TOKUSATSU TV SHOW *CHOUKOU SENSHI CHANGERION.*

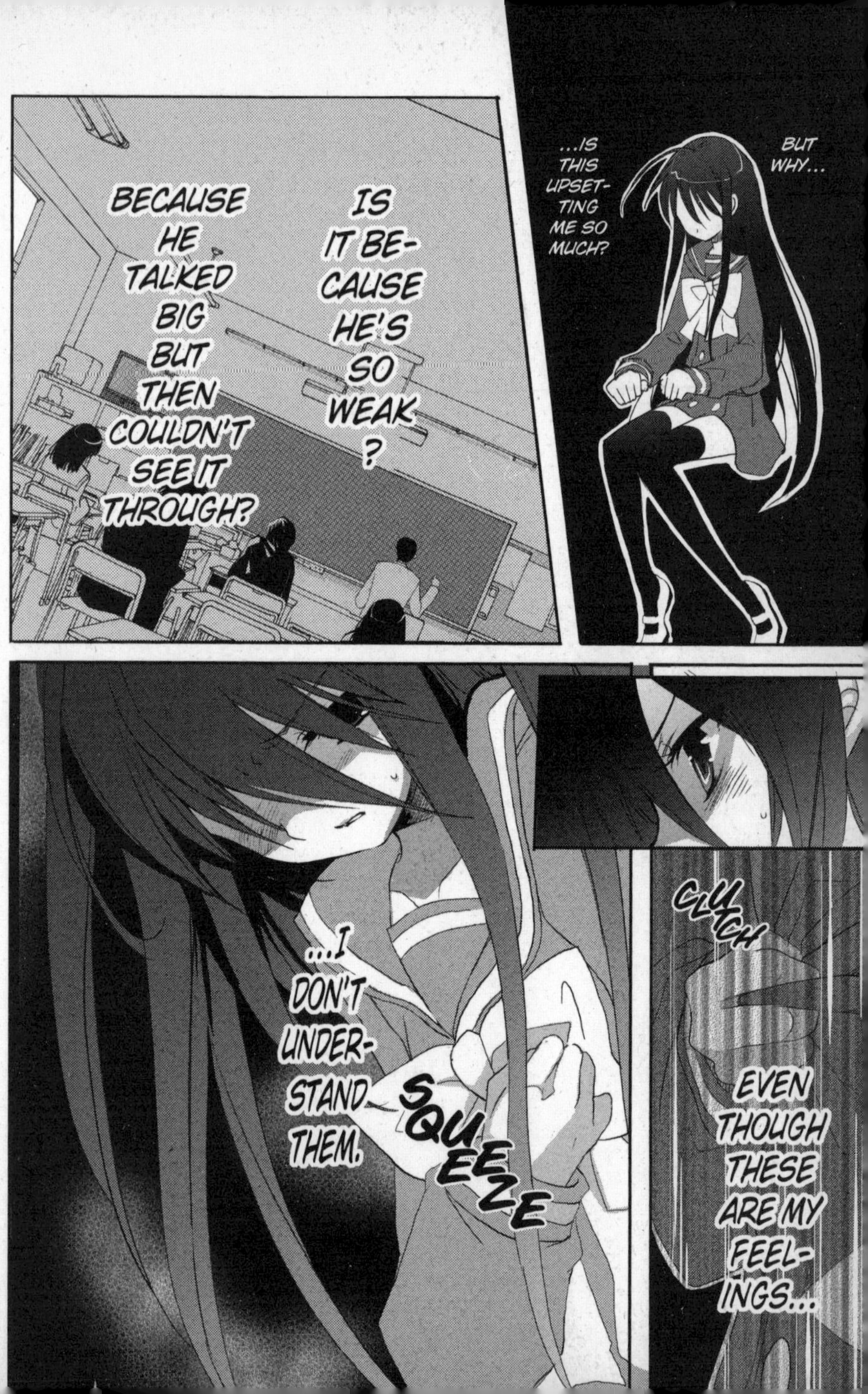
BUT WHY...
...IS THIS UPSETTING ME SO MUCH?
IS IT BECAUSE HE'S SO WEAK?
BECAUSE HE TALKED BIG BUT THEN COULDN'T SEE IT THROUGH?
CLUTCH
EVEN THOUGH THESE ARE MY FEELINGS...
...I DON'T UNDERSTAND THEM.
SQUEEZE

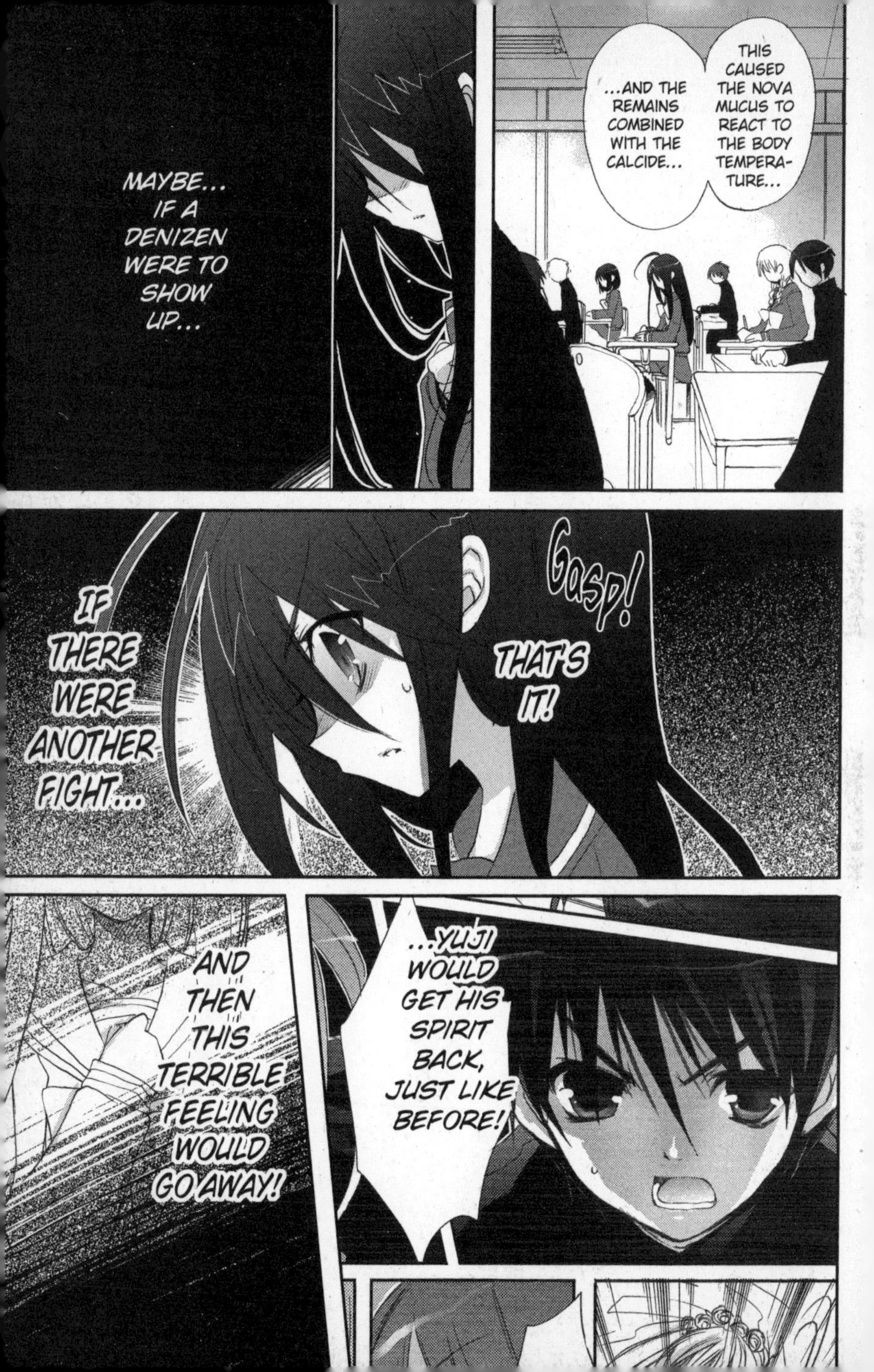
THIS CAUSED THE NOVA MUCUS TO REACT TO THE BODY TEMPERA-TURE...
...AND THE REMAINS COMBINED WITH THE CALCIDE...
MAYBE... IF A DENIZEN WERE TO SHOW UP...
Gasp!
THAT'S IT!
IF THERE WERE ANOTHER FIGHT...
...YUJI WOULD GET HIS SPIRIT BACK, JUST LIKE BEFORE!
AND THEN THIS TERRIBLE FEELING WOULD GO AWAY!

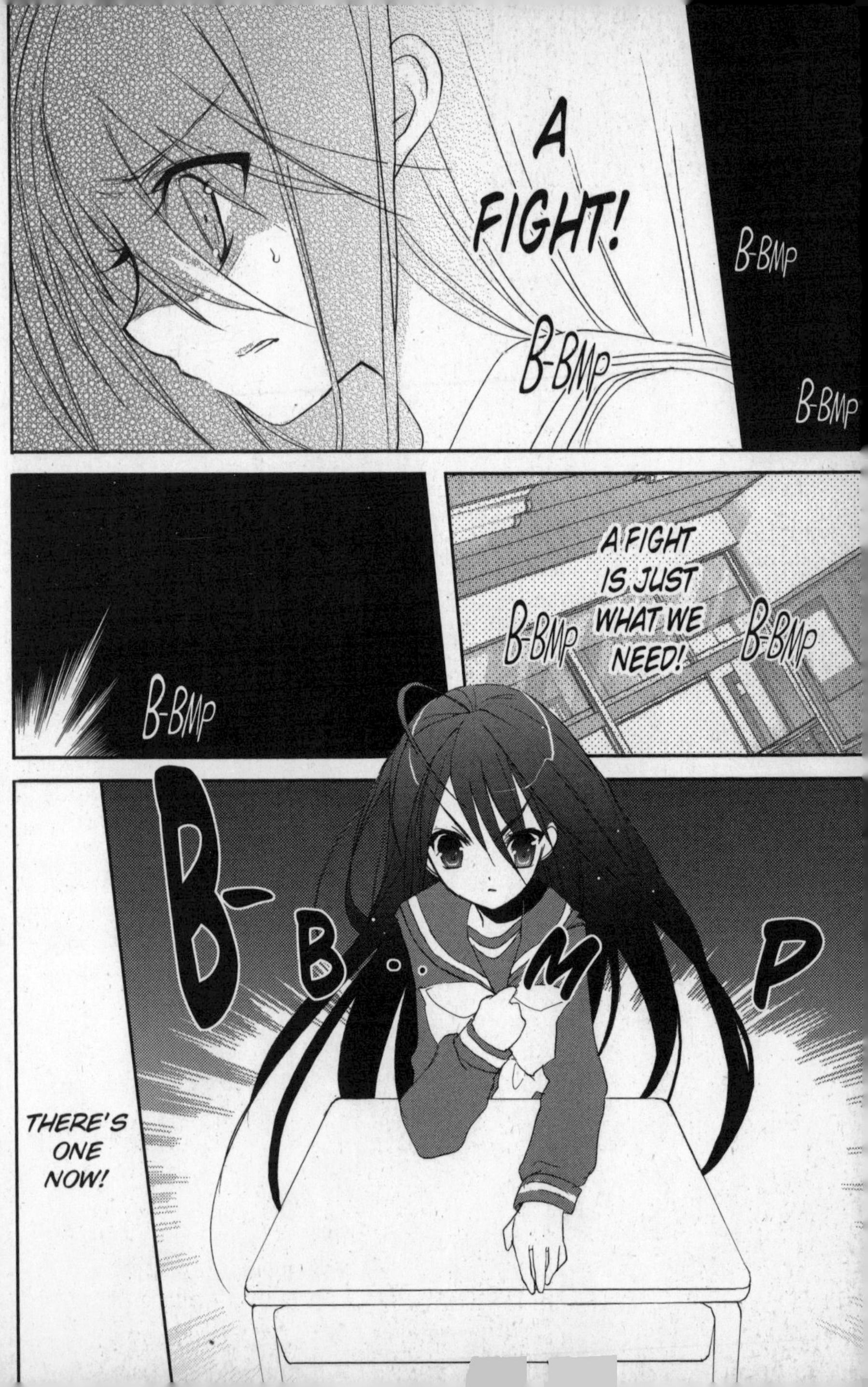
A FIGHT!
B-BMP
B-BMP
B-BMP
B-BMP
A FIGHT IS JUST WHAT WE NEED!
B-BMP
B-BMP
B-BMP
THERE'S ONE NOW!

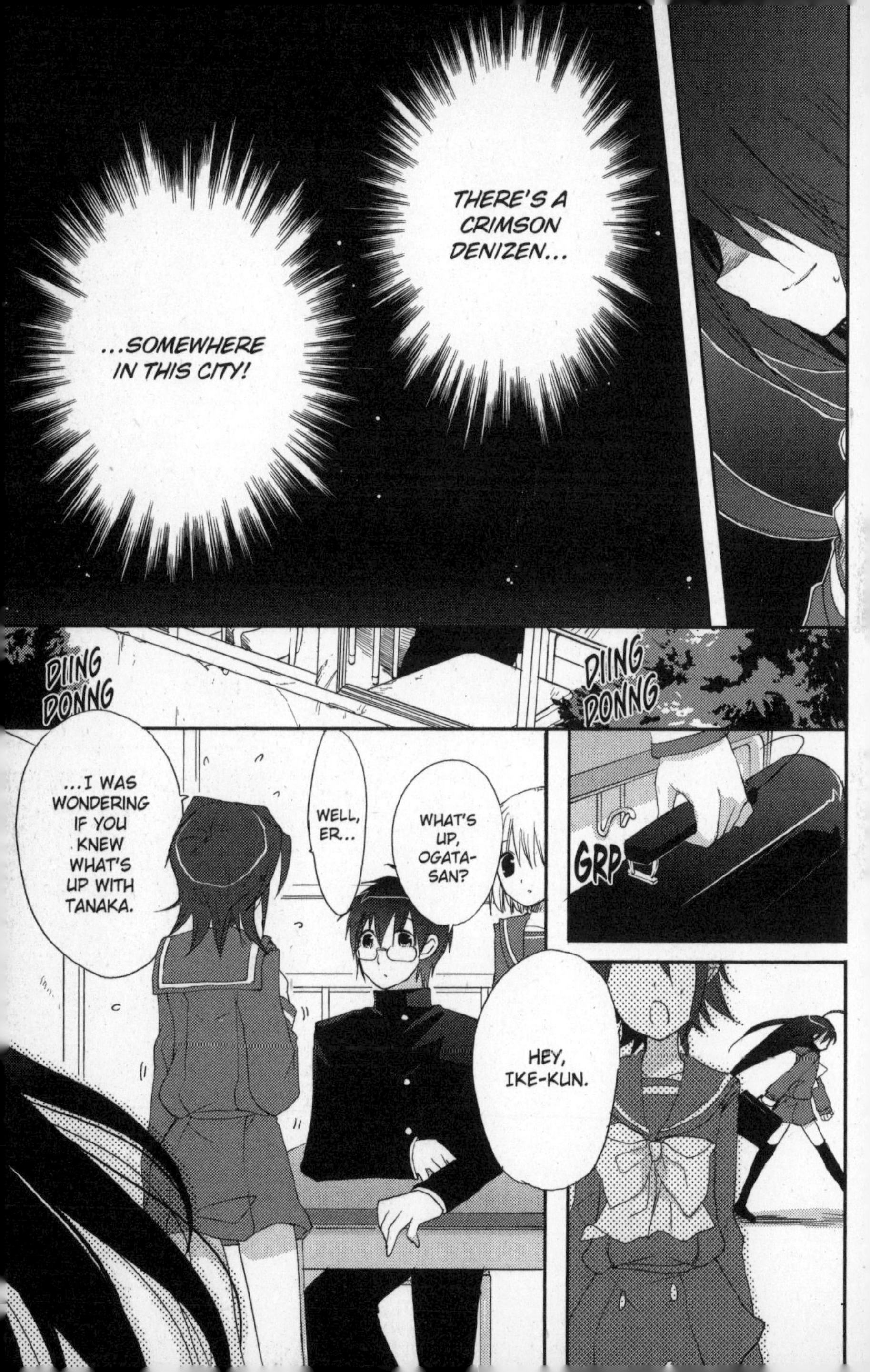
THERE'S A CRIMSON DENIZEN...
...SOMEWHERE IN THIS CITY!
DIING DONNG
DIING DONNG
GRP
HEY, IKE-KUN.
WHAT'S UP, OGATA-SAN?
WELL, ER...
...I WAS WONDERING IF YOU KNEW WHAT'S UP WITH TANAKA.

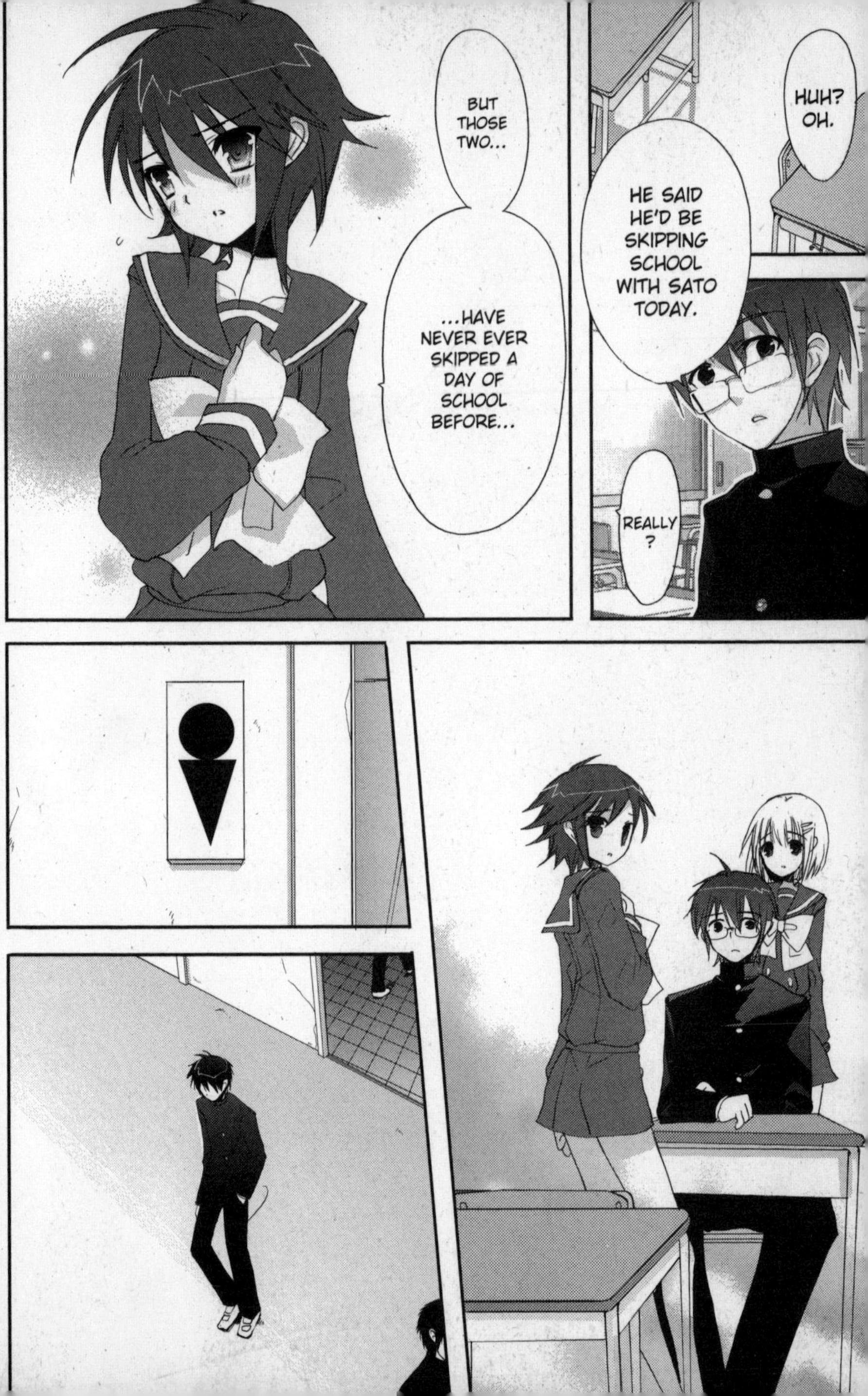
HUH? OH.
HE SAID HE'D BE SKIPPING SCHOOL WITH SATO TODAY.
REALLY?
BUT THOSE TWO...
...HAVE NEVER EVER SKIPPED A DAY OF SCHOOL BEFORE...

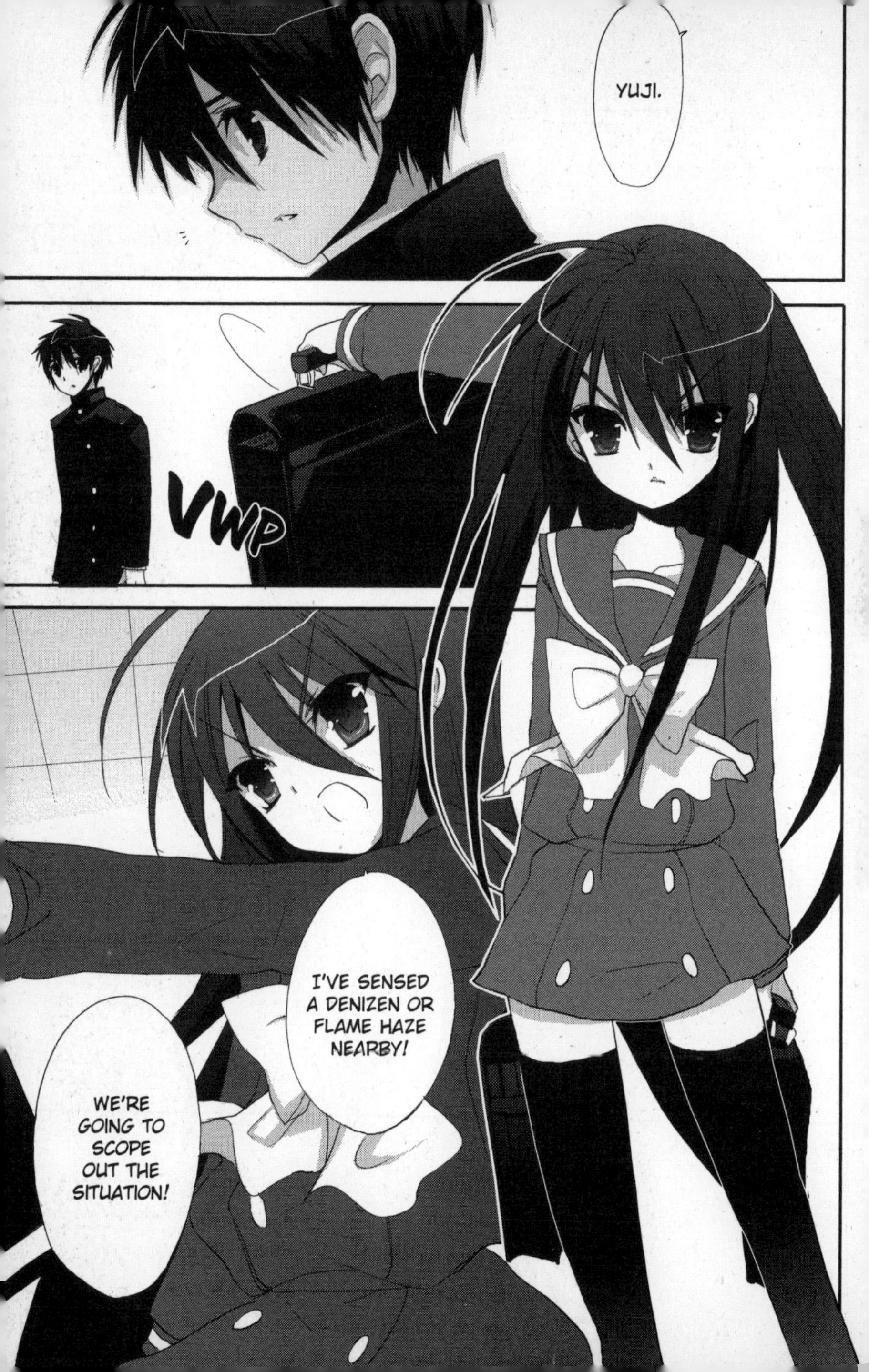
YUJI.
VWP
I'VE SENSED A DENIZEN OR FLAME HAZE NEARBY!
WE'RE GOING TO SCOPE OUT THE SITUATION!

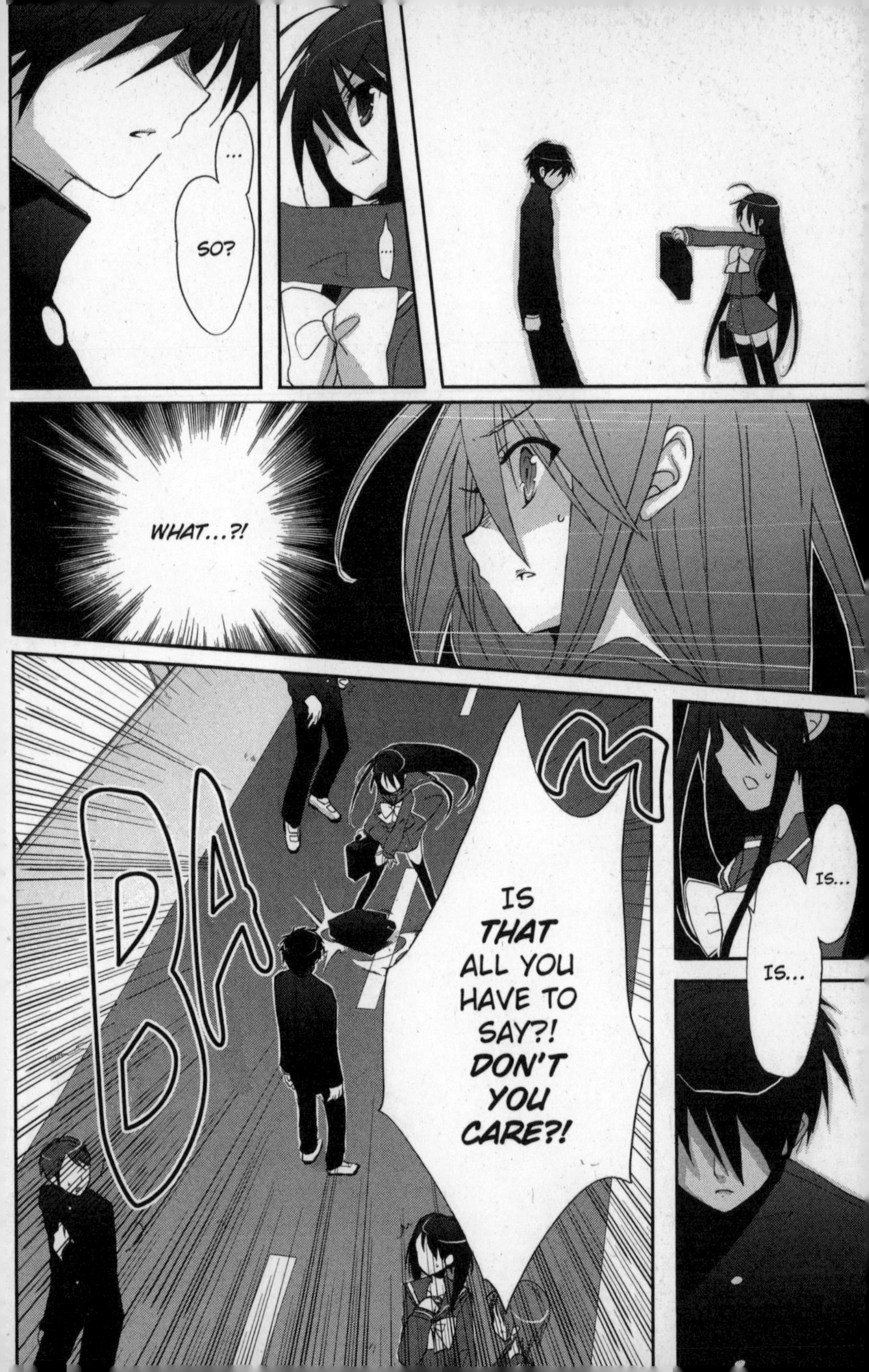
...
...
SO?
WHAT...?!
IS...
IS...
DAM
IS THAT ALL YOU HAVE TO SAY?! DON'T YOU CARE?!

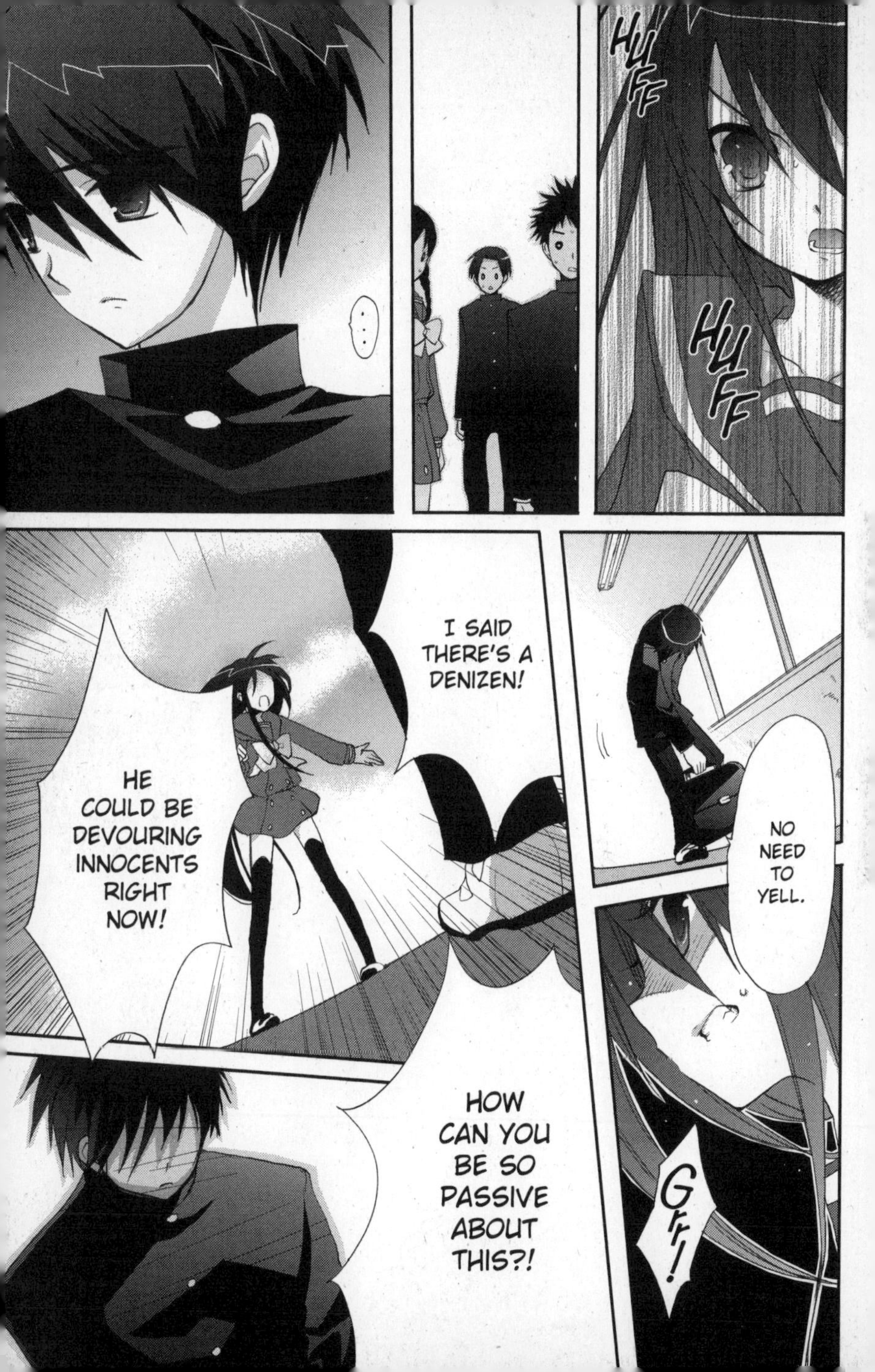
HUFF
HUFF
. . .
I SAID THERE'S A DENIZEN!
HE COULD BE DEVOURING INNOCENTS RIGHT NOW!
NO NEED TO YELL.
Grr!
HOW CAN YOU BE SO PASSIVE ABOUT THIS?!

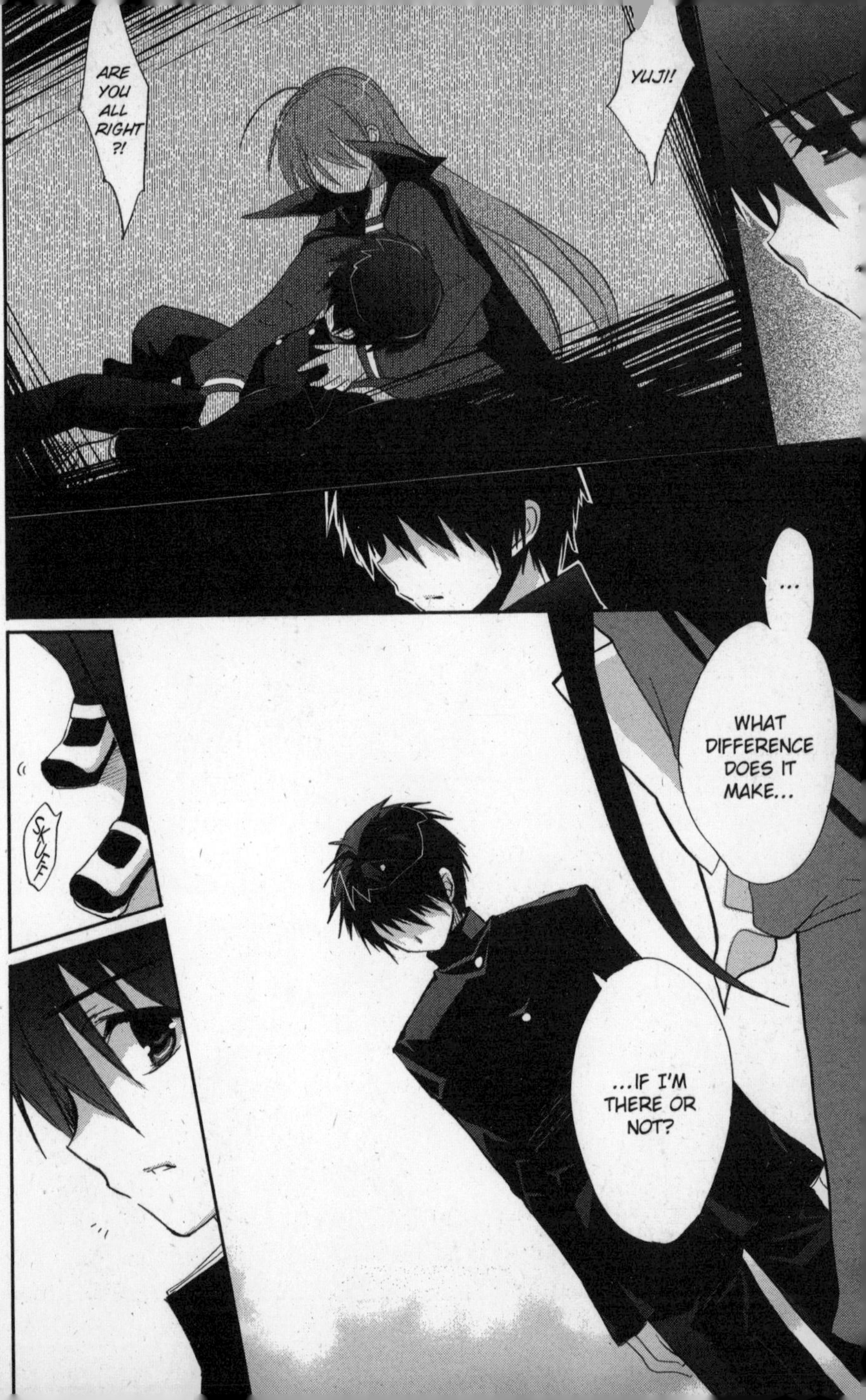
YUJI!
ARE YOU ALL RIGHT?!
...
WHAT DIFFERENCE DOES IT MAKE...
...IF I'M THERE OR NOT?
SKUFF

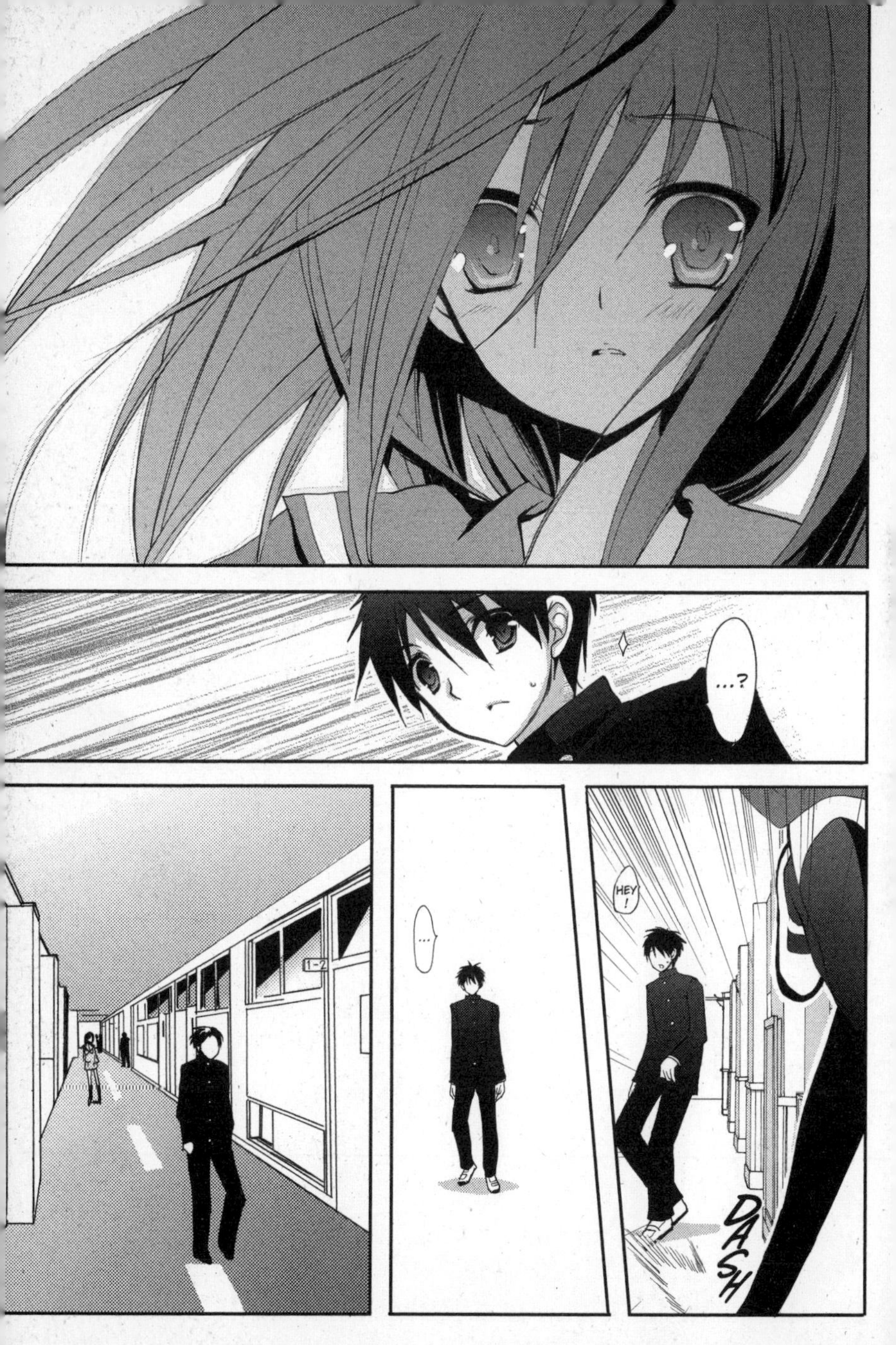
...?
HEY!
DASH
...

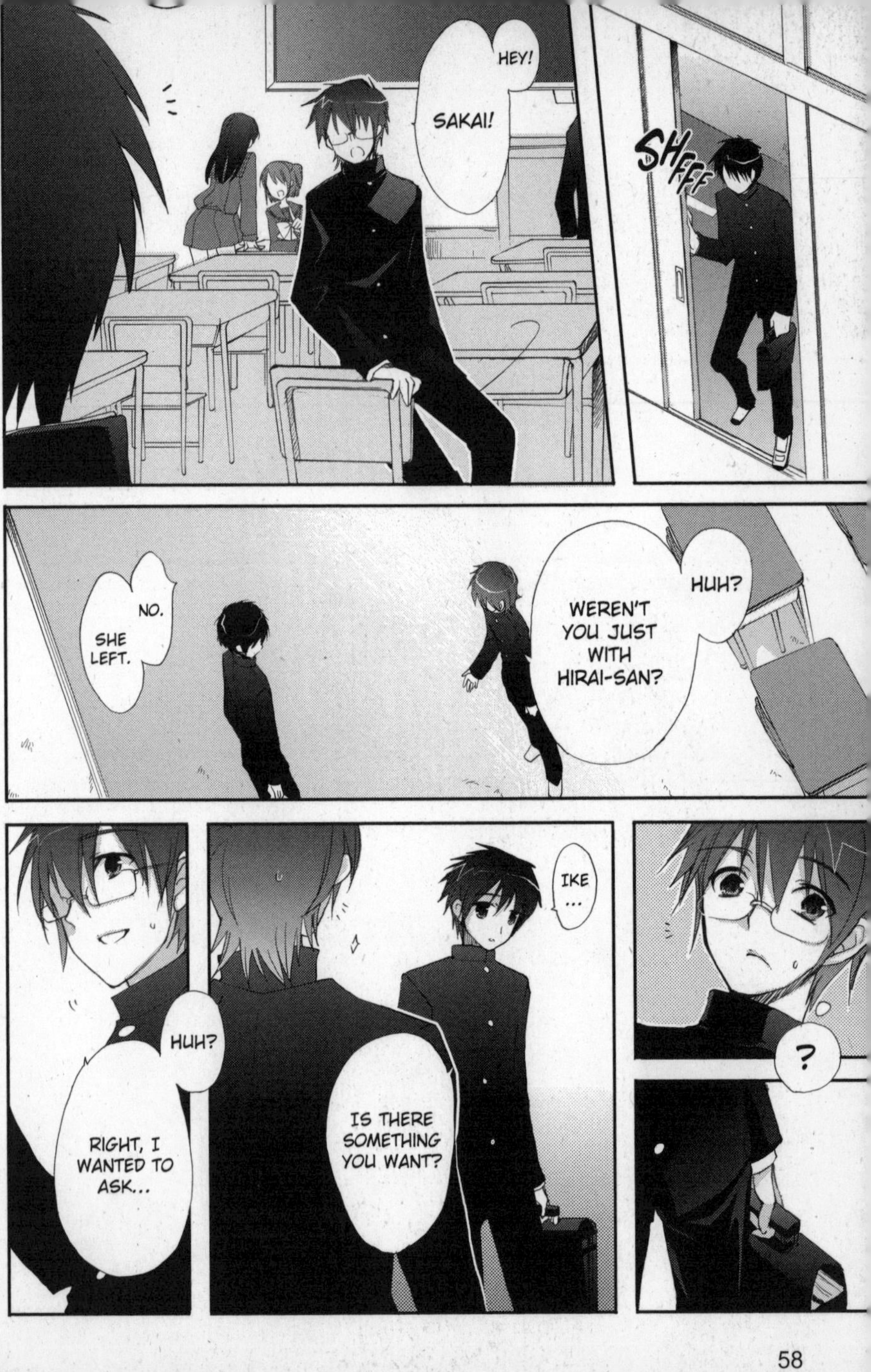
SHFFF
HEY! SAKAI!
HUH? WEREN'T YOU JUST WITH HIRAI-SAN?
NO. SHE LEFT.
?
IKE ...
IS THERE SOMETHING YOU WANT?
HUH?
RIGHT, I WANTED TO ASK...

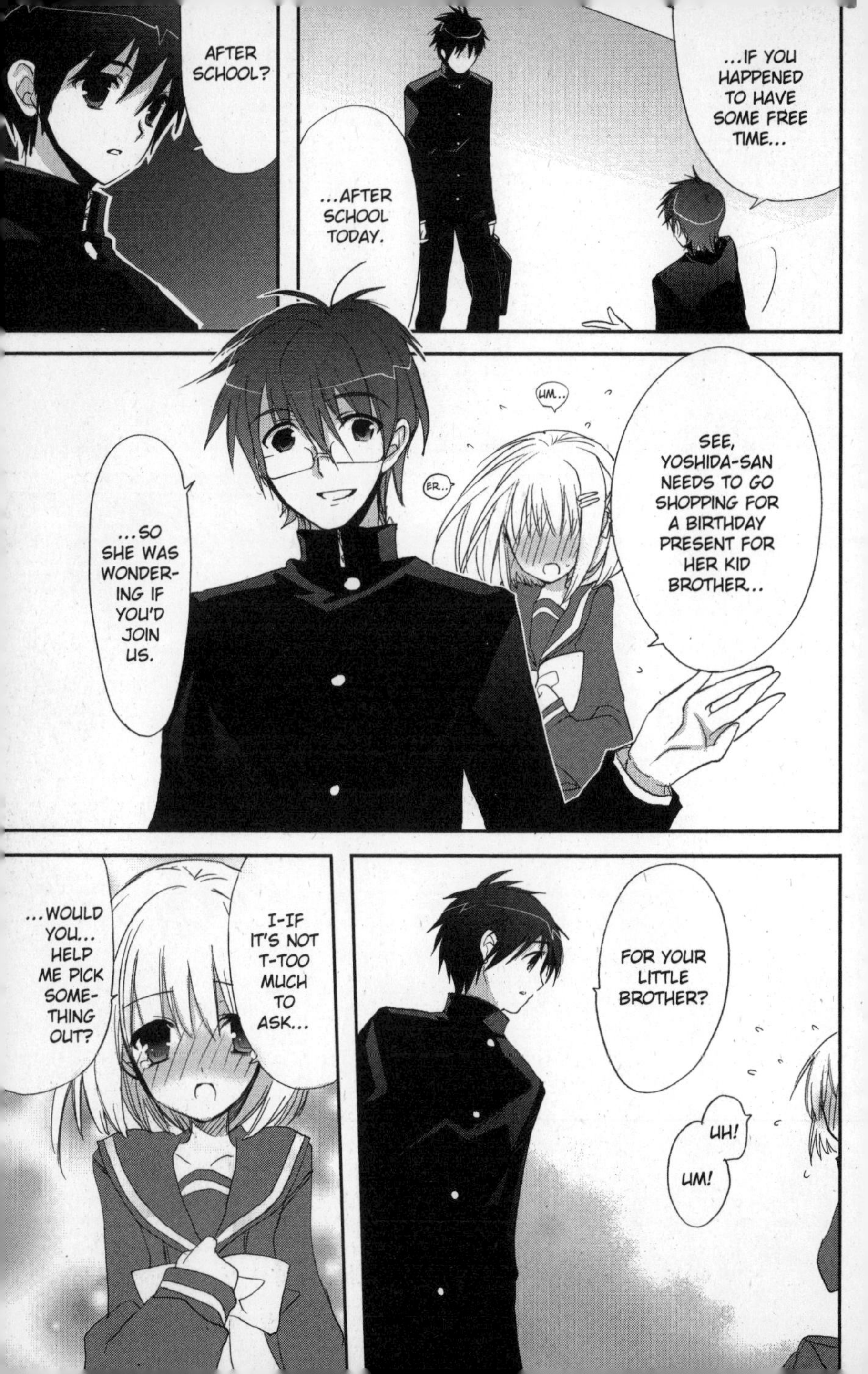
...IF YOU HAPPENED TO HAVE SOME FREE TIME...
...AFTER SCHOOL TODAY.
AFTER SCHOOL?
SEE, YOSHIDA-SAN NEEDS TO GO SHOPPING FOR A BIRTHDAY PRESENT FOR HER KID BROTHER...
UM...
ER...
...SO SHE WAS WONDERING IF YOU'D JOIN US.
FOR YOUR LITTLE BROTHER?
UH!
UM!
I-IF IT'S NOT T-TOO MUCH TO ASK...
...WOULD YOU... HELP ME PICK SOMETHING OUT?

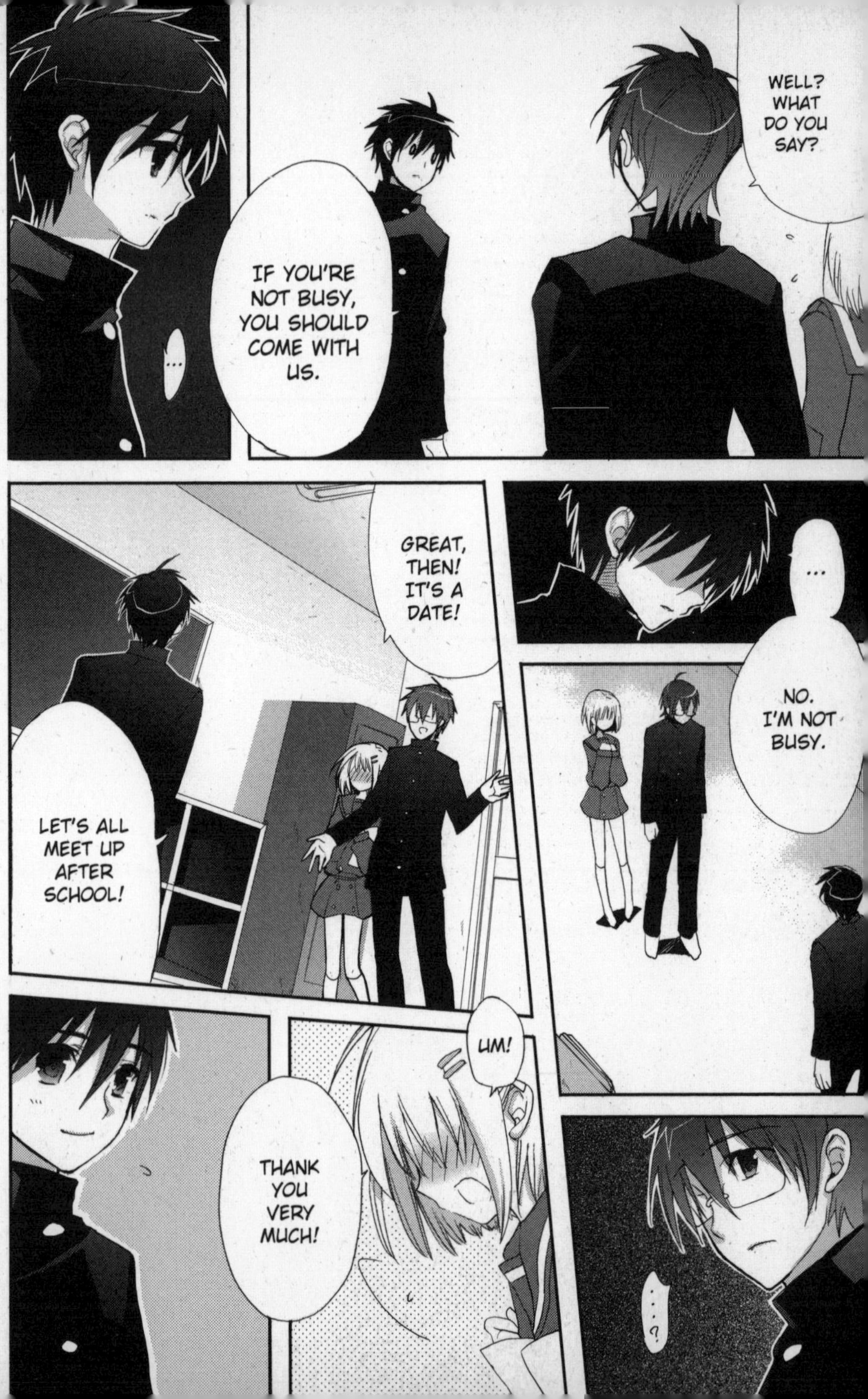
WELL? WHAT DO YOU SAY?
IF YOU'RE NOT BUSY, YOU SHOULD COME WITH US.
...
...
NO. I'M NOT BUSY.
GREAT, THEN! IT'S A DATE!
LET'S ALL MEET UP AFTER SCHOOL!
...?
UM!
THANK YOU VERY MUCH!

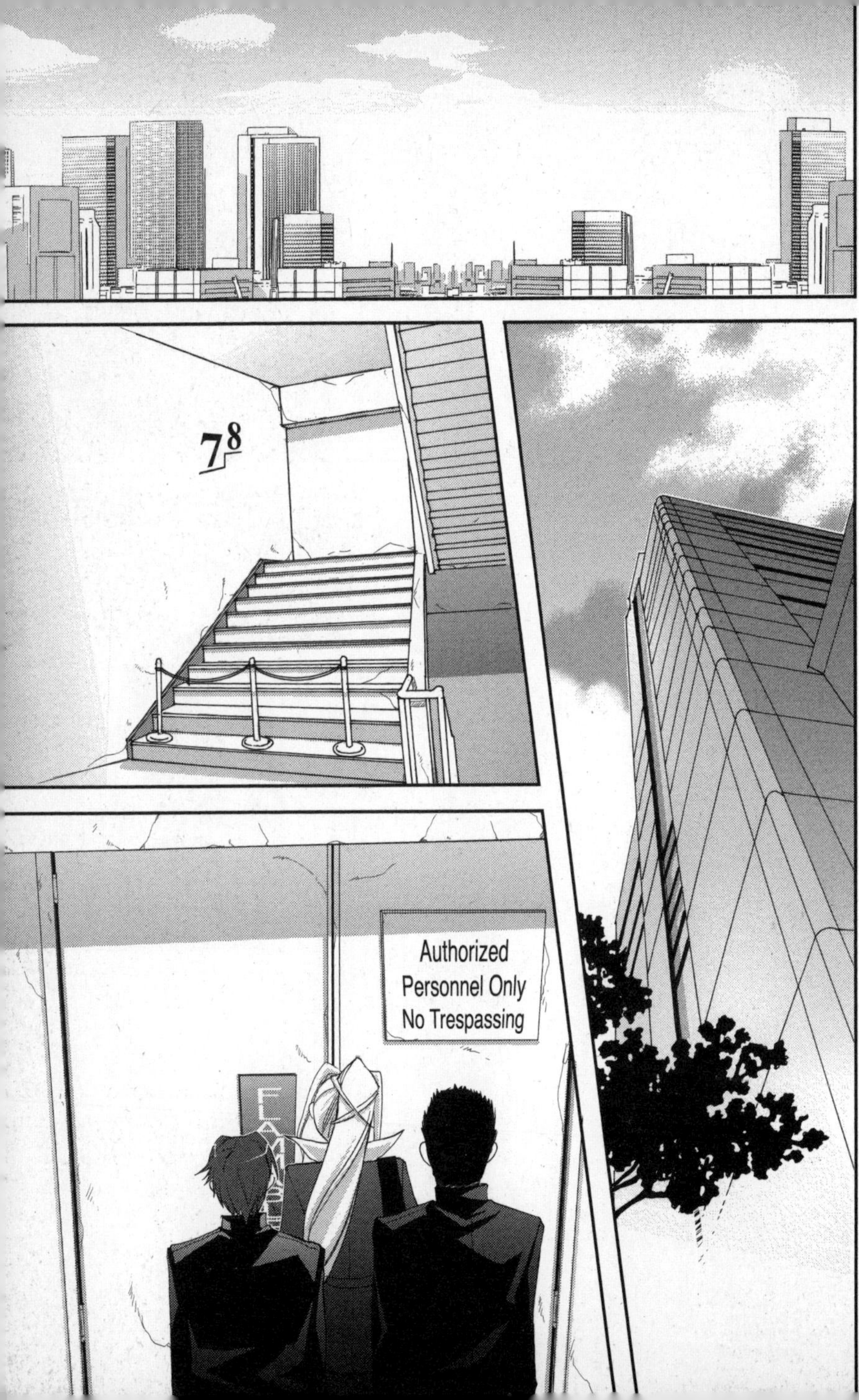
7 8
Authorized
Personnel Only
No Trespassing

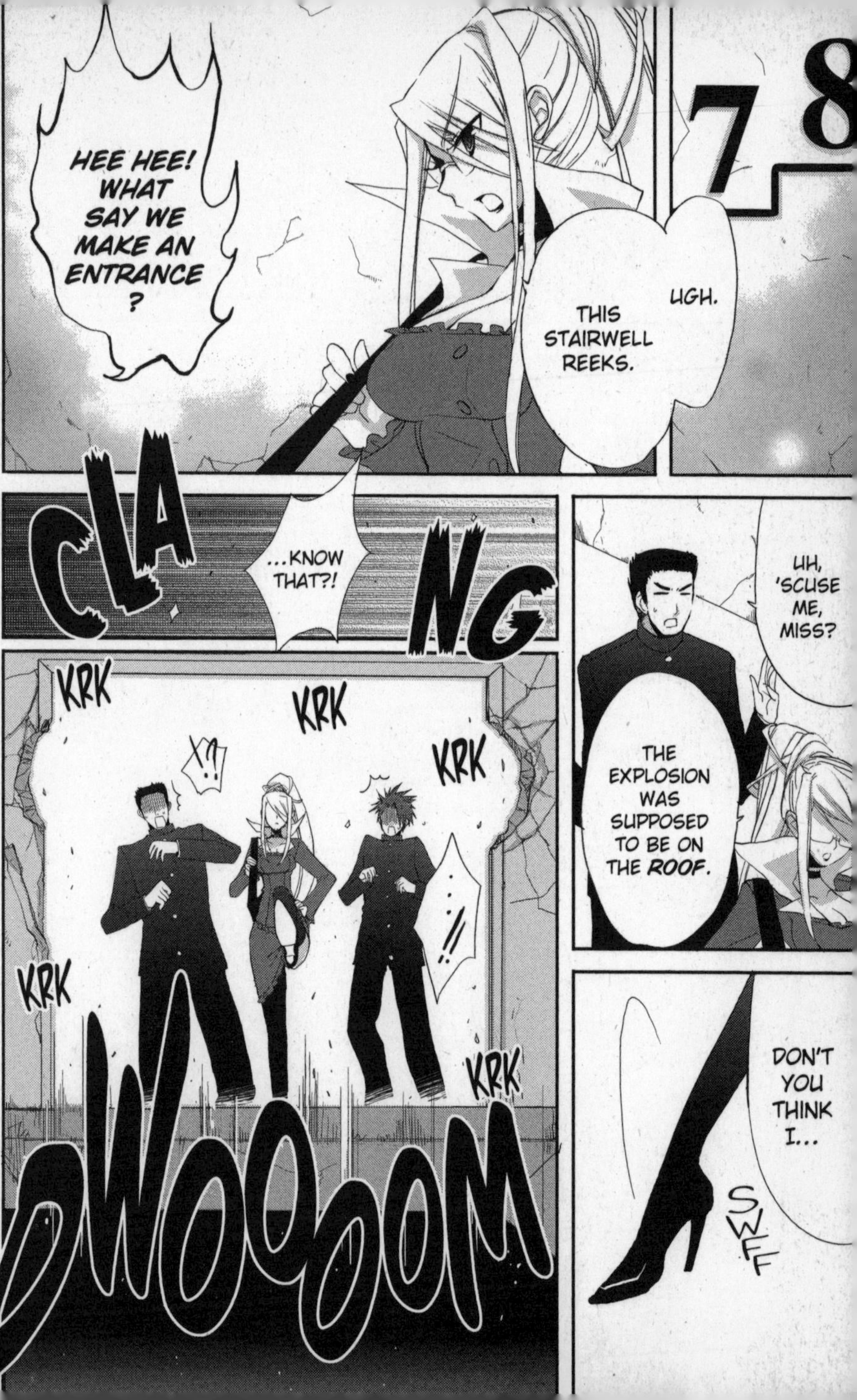

7 8
UGH. THIS STAIRWELL REEKS.
HEE HEE! WHAT SAY WE MAKE AN ENTRANCE?
UH, 'SCUSE ME, MISS?
THE EXPLOSION WAS SUPPOSED TO BE ON THE *ROOF*.
DON'T YOU THINK I...
SWFF
CLANG
...KNOW THAT?!
KRK
KRK
KRK
!?
...!!
KRK
KRK
DWOOOOOM

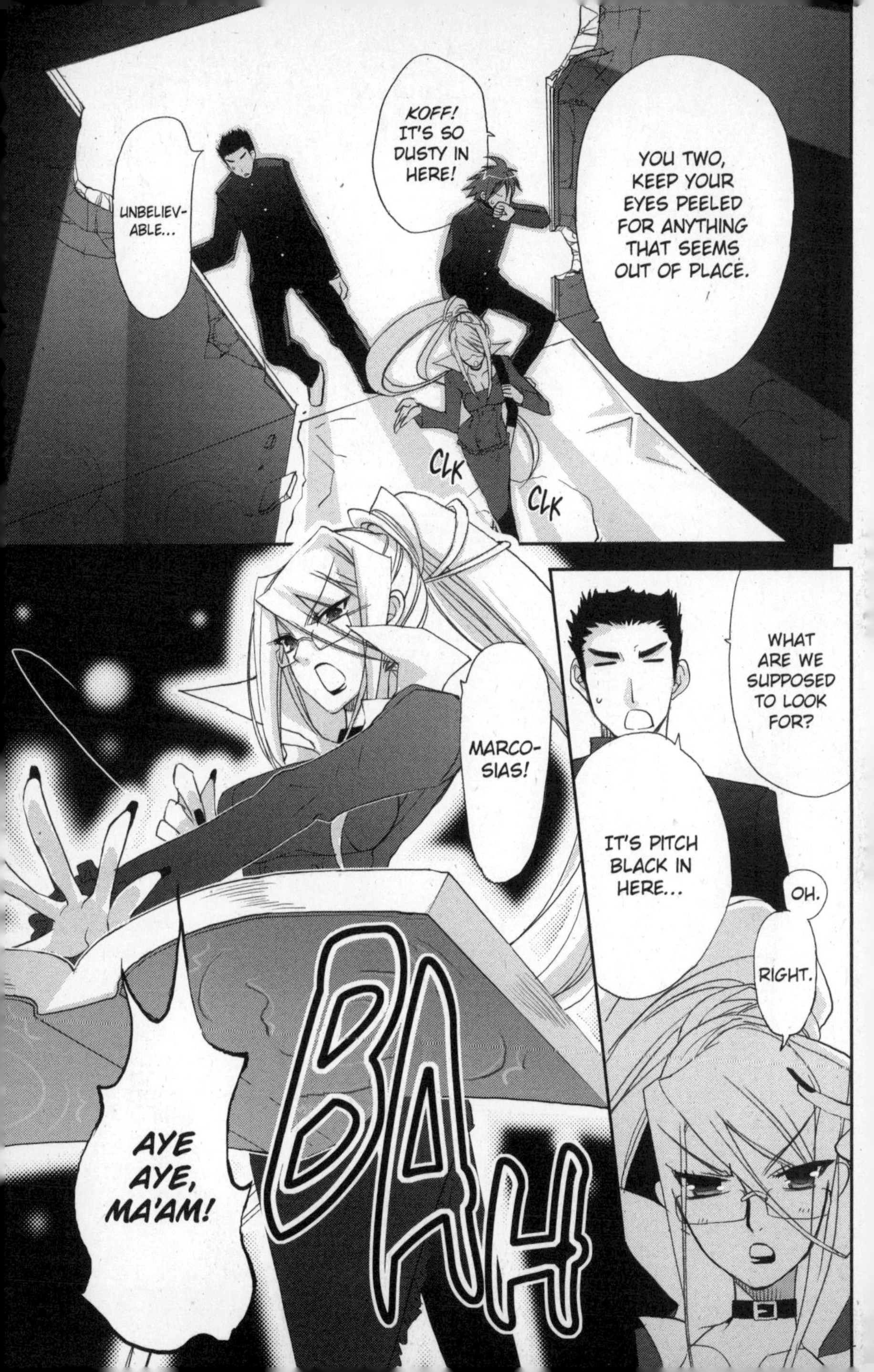
YOU TWO, KEEP YOUR EYES PEELED FOR ANYTHING THAT SEEMS OUT OF PLACE.
KOFF! IT'S SO DUSTY IN HERE!
UNBELIEV-ABLE...
CLK
CLK
WHAT ARE WE SUPPOSED TO LOOK FOR?
IT'S PITCH BLACK IN HERE...
OH.
RIGHT.
MARCO-SIAS!
BAH
AYE AYE, MA'AM!

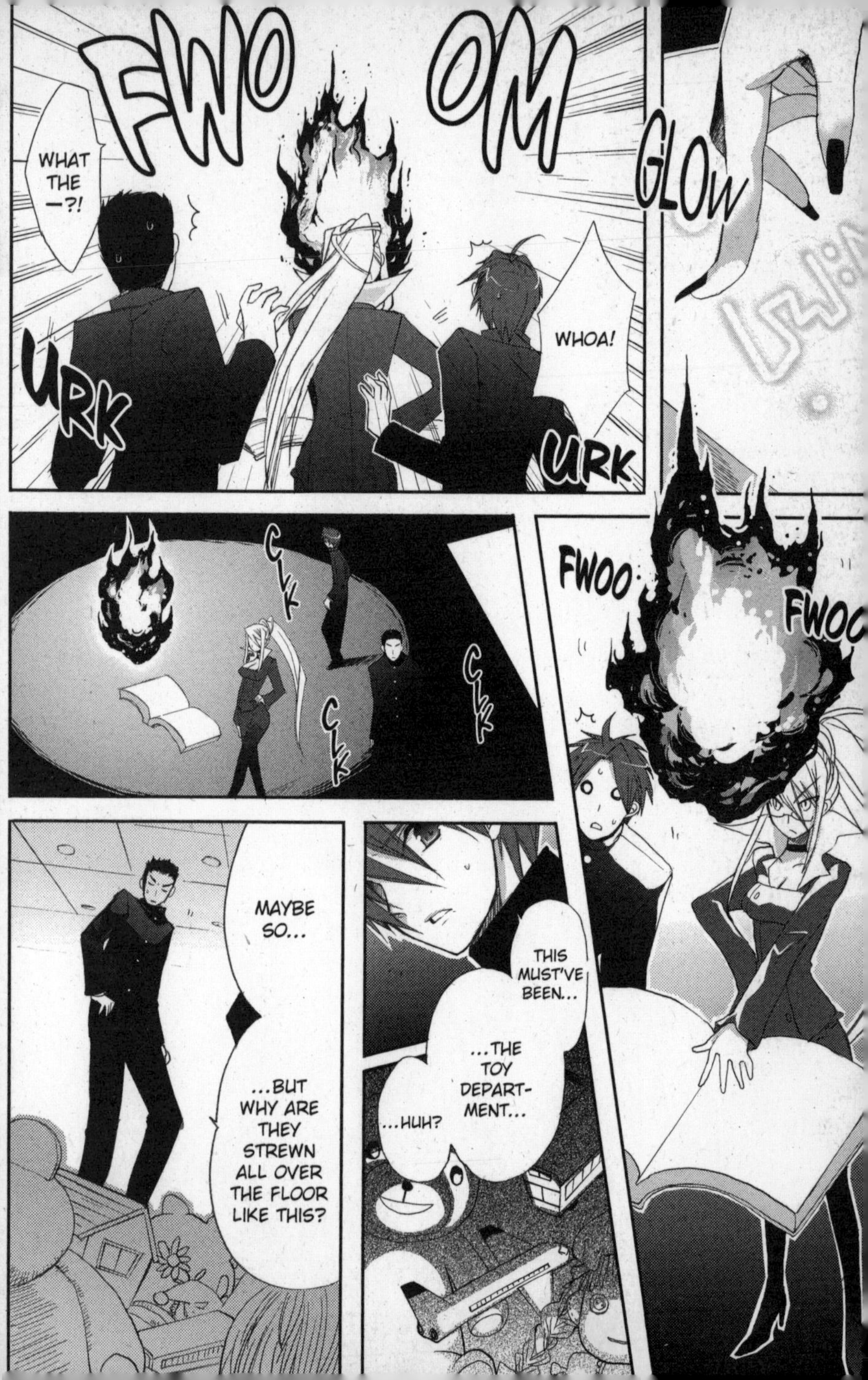
GLOW
FWO OM
WHOA!
WHAT THE —?!
URK
URK
FWOO
FWOO
CLK
CLK
CLK
THIS MUST'VE BEEN...
...THE TOY DEPARTMENT...
...HUH?
MAYBE SO...
...BUT WHY ARE THEY STREWN ALL OVER THE FLOOR LIKE THIS?

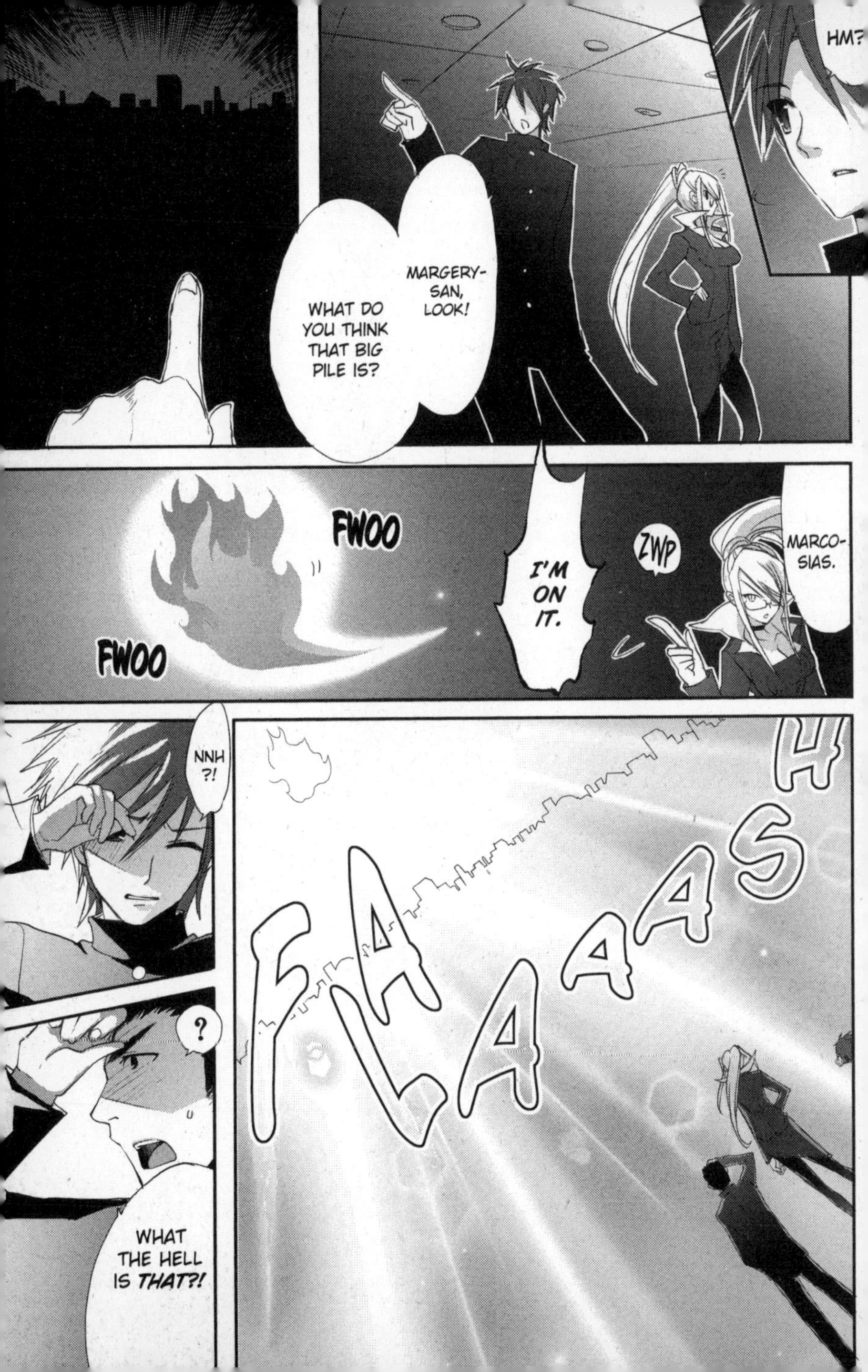
HM?
MARGERY-SAN, LOOK!
WHAT DO YOU THINK THAT BIG PILE IS?
MARCOSIAS.
ZWP
I'M ON IT.
FWOO
FWOO
FLAAAASH
NNH?!
?
WHAT THE HELL IS *THAT?!*

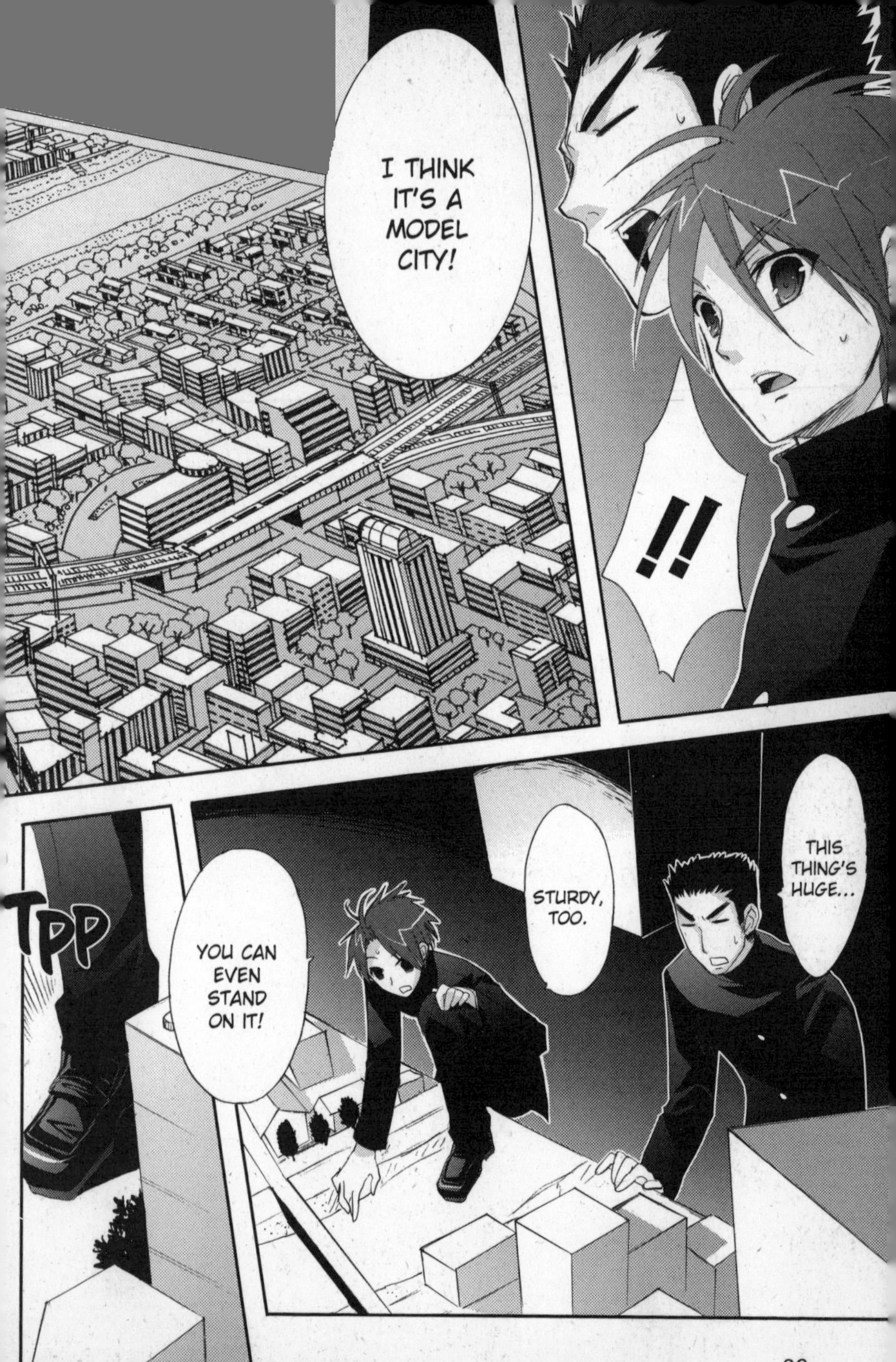
!!
I THINK IT'S A MODEL CITY!
THIS THING'S HUGE...
STURDY, TOO.
YOU CAN EVEN STAND ON IT!
TPP

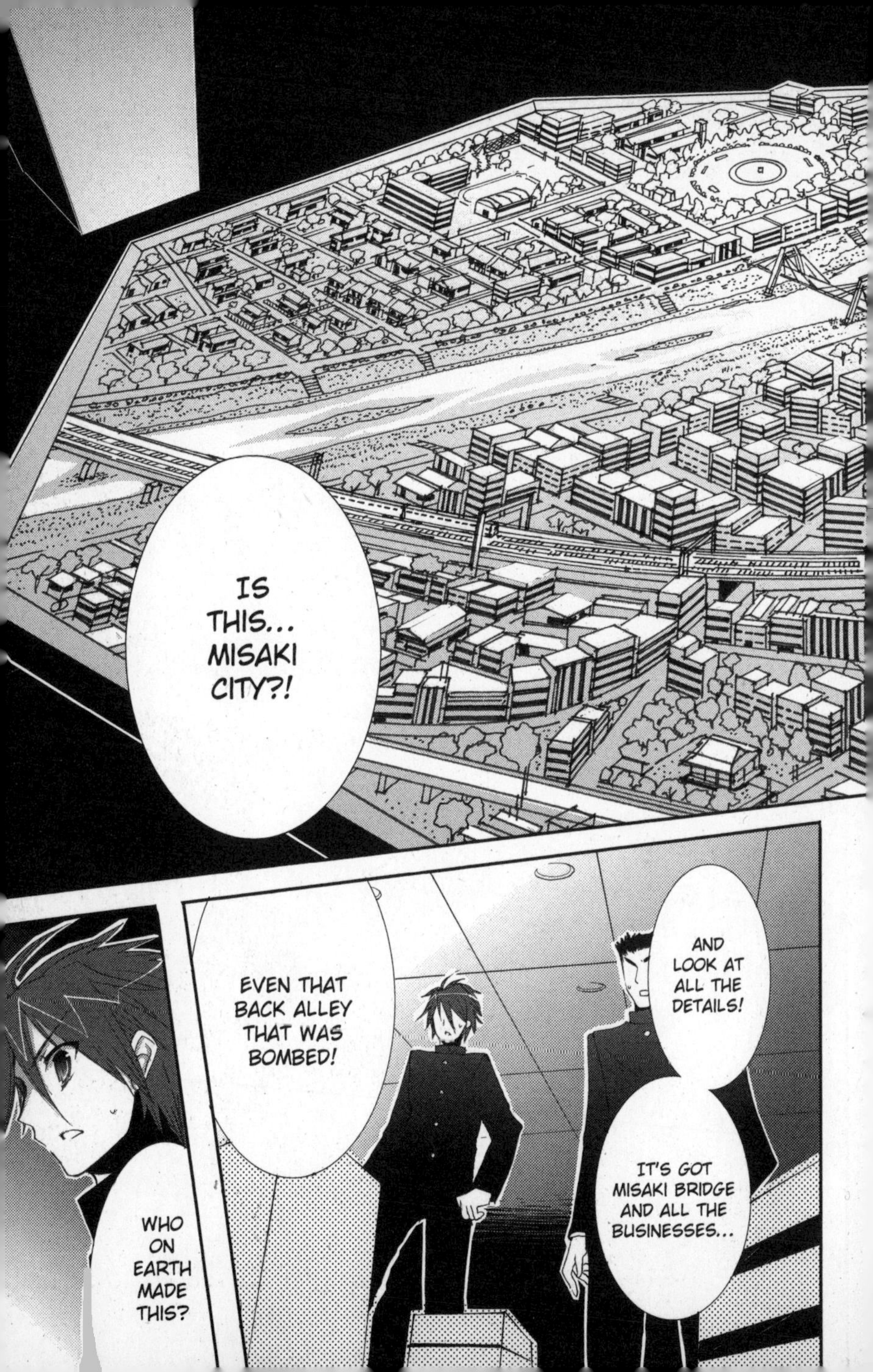
IS THIS... MISAKI CITY?!
AND LOOK AT ALL THE DETAILS!
EVEN THAT BACK ALLEY THAT WAS BOMBED!
IT'S GOT MISAKI BRIDGE AND ALL THE BUSINESSES...
WHO ON EARTH MADE THIS?

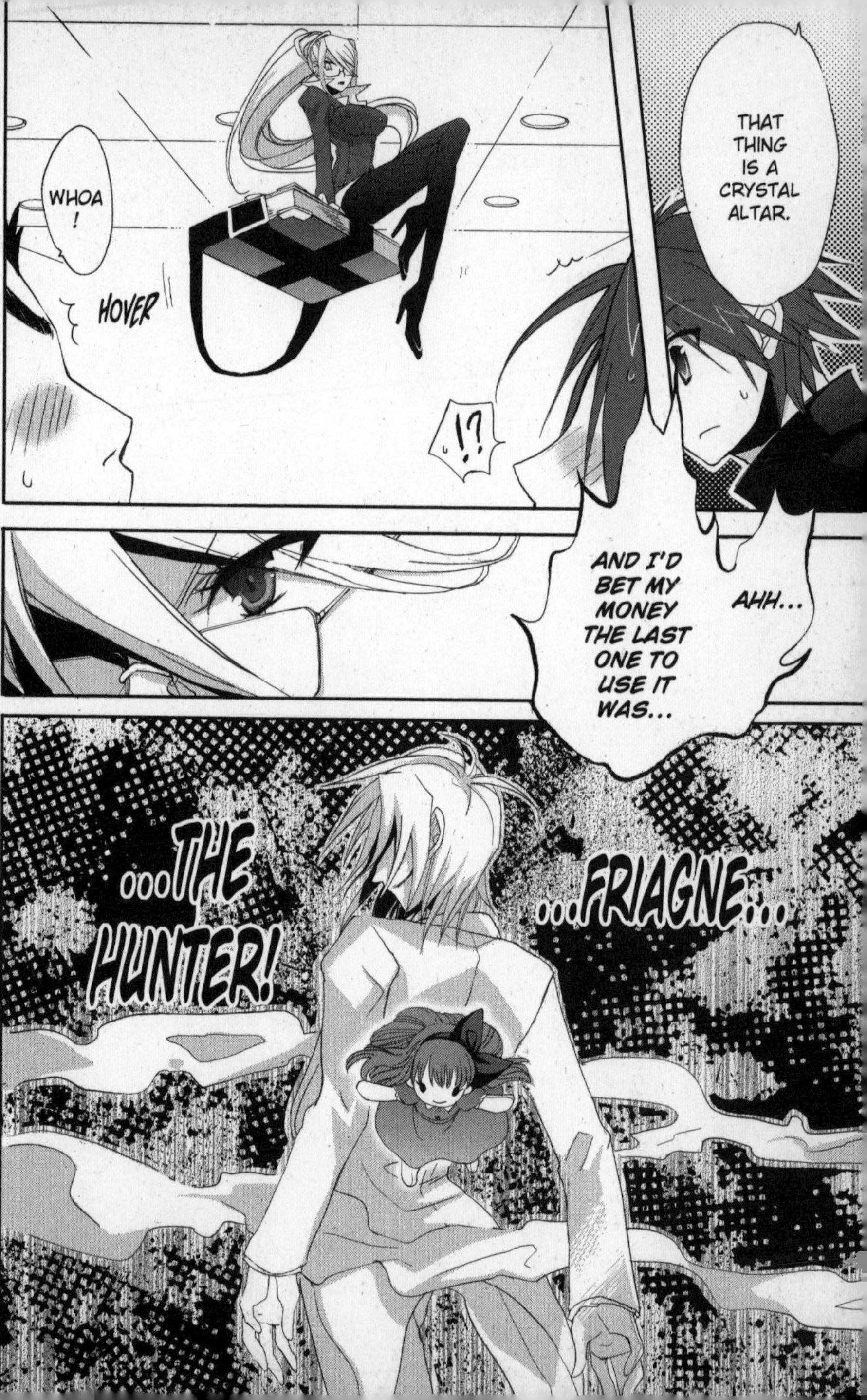
THAT THING IS A CRYSTAL ALTAR.
WHOA!
HOVER
!?
AHH...
AND I'D BET MY MONEY THE LAST ONE TO USE IT WAS...
...FRIAGNE...
...THE HUNTER!

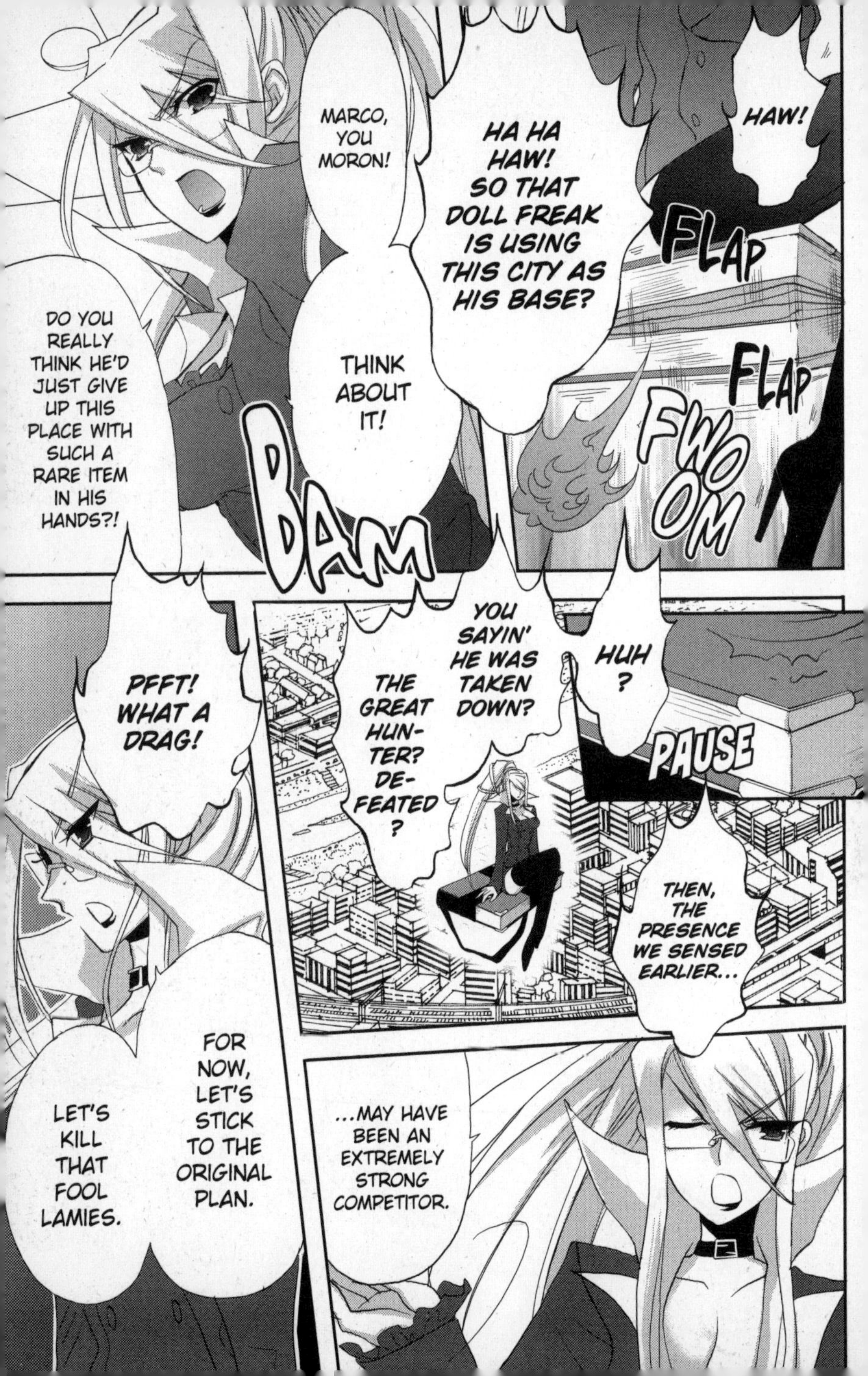
HAW!
FLAP
FLAP
FWOOOM
HA HA HAW! SO THAT DOLL FREAK IS USING THIS CITY AS HIS BASE?
MARCO, YOU MORON!
THINK ABOUT IT!
BAM
DO YOU REALLY THINK HE'D JUST GIVE UP THIS PLACE WITH SUCH A RARE ITEM IN HIS HANDS?!
HUH?
PAUSE
YOU SAYIN' HE WAS TAKEN DOWN?
THE GREAT HUN-TER? DE-FEATED?
THEN, THE PRESENCE WE SENSED EARLIER...
...MAY HAVE BEEN AN EXTREMELY STRONG COMPETITOR.
PFFT! WHAT A DRAG!
FOR NOW, LET'S STICK TO THE ORIGINAL PLAN.
LET'S KILL THAT FOOL LAMIES.

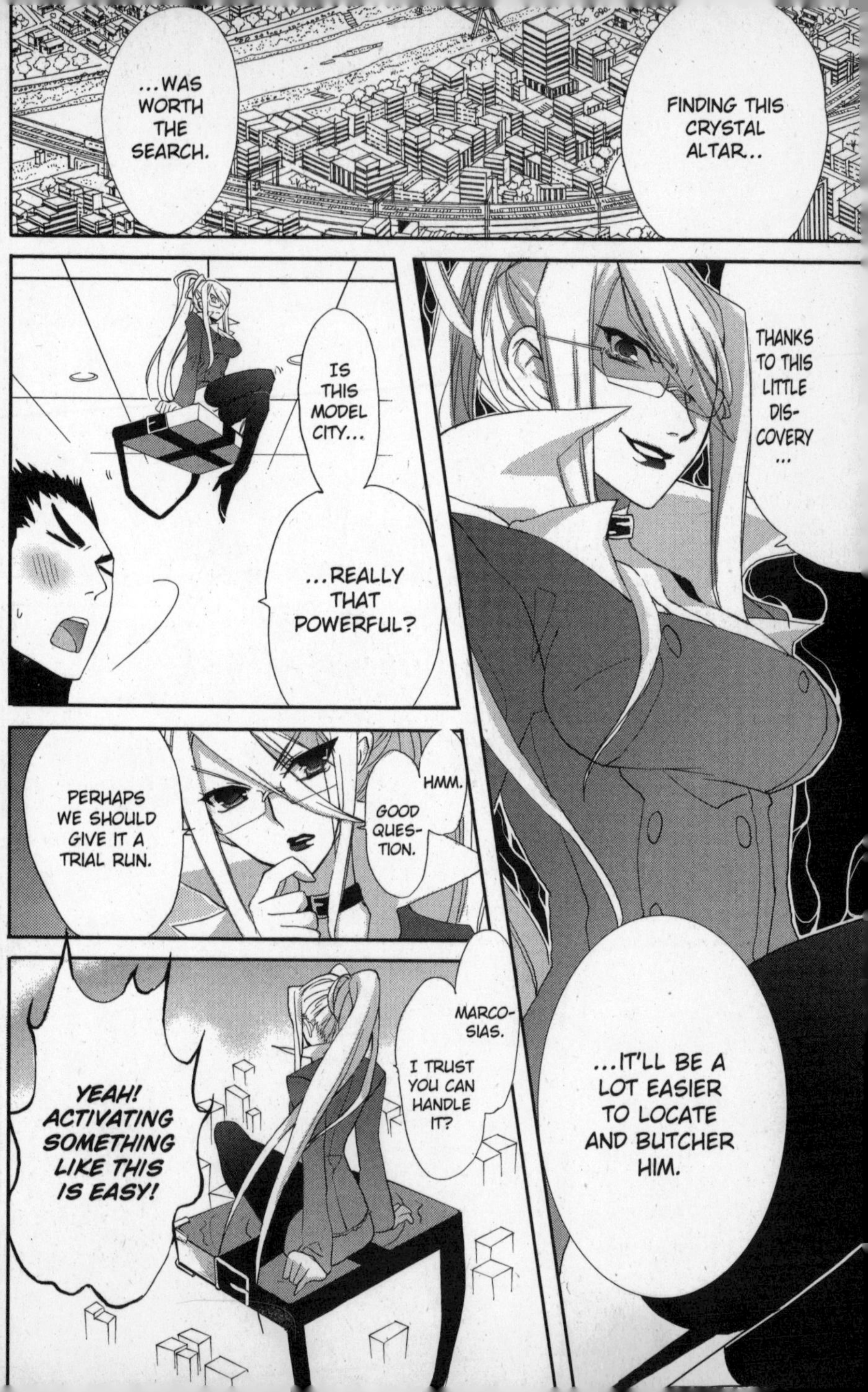
FINDING THIS CRYSTAL ALTAR...
...WAS WORTH THE SEARCH.
THANKS TO THIS LITTLE DIS-COVERY...
...IT'LL BE A LOT EASIER TO LOCATE AND BUTCHER HIM.
IS THIS MODEL CITY...
...REALLY THAT POWERFUL?
HMM.
GOOD QUES-TION.
PERHAPS WE SHOULD GIVE IT A TRIAL RUN.
MARCO-SIAS.
I TRUST YOU CAN HANDLE IT?
YEAH! ACTIVATING SOMETHING LIKE THIS IS EASY!

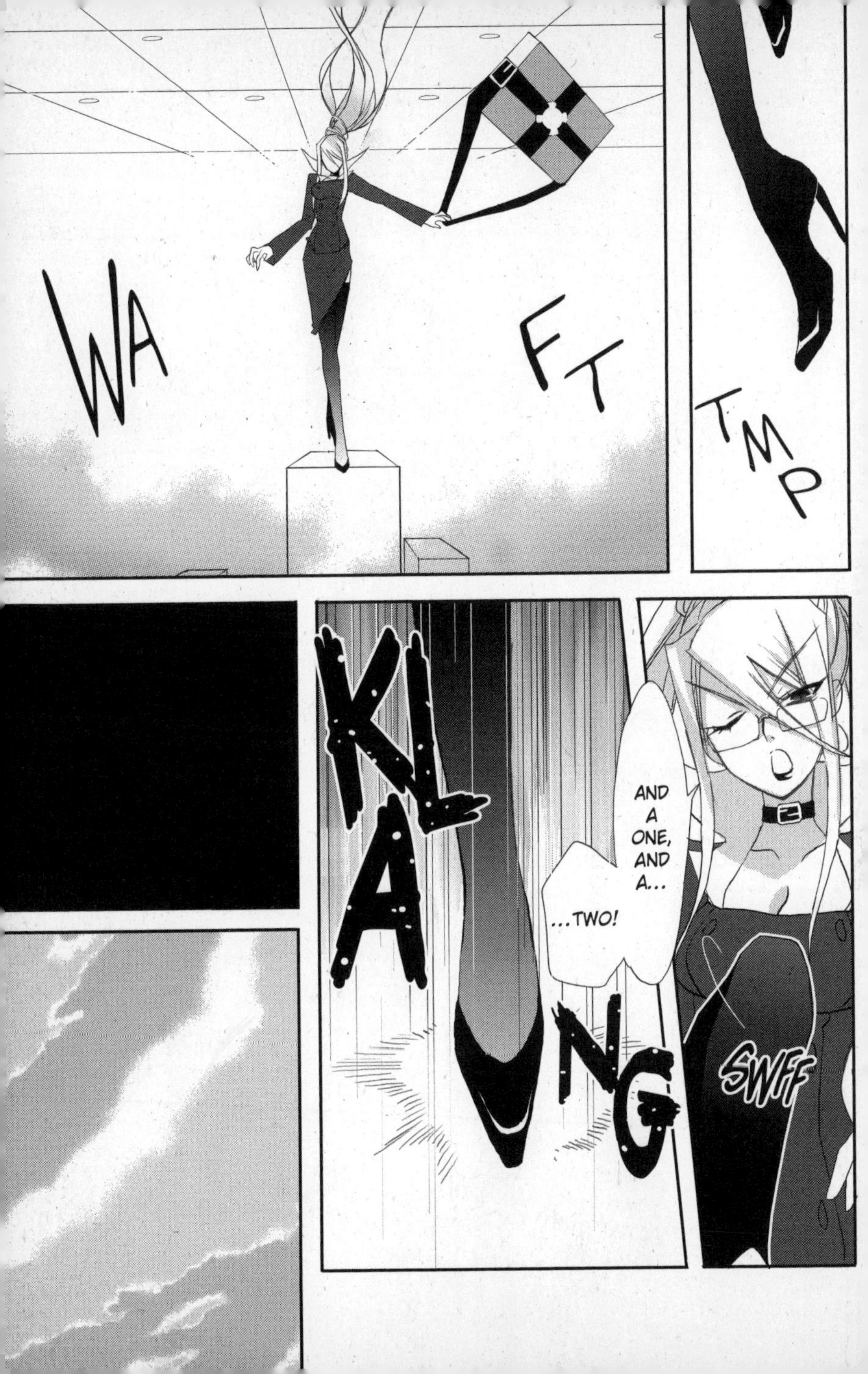
TMP
WAFT
AND A ONE, AND A...
...TWO!
SWFF
KLANG

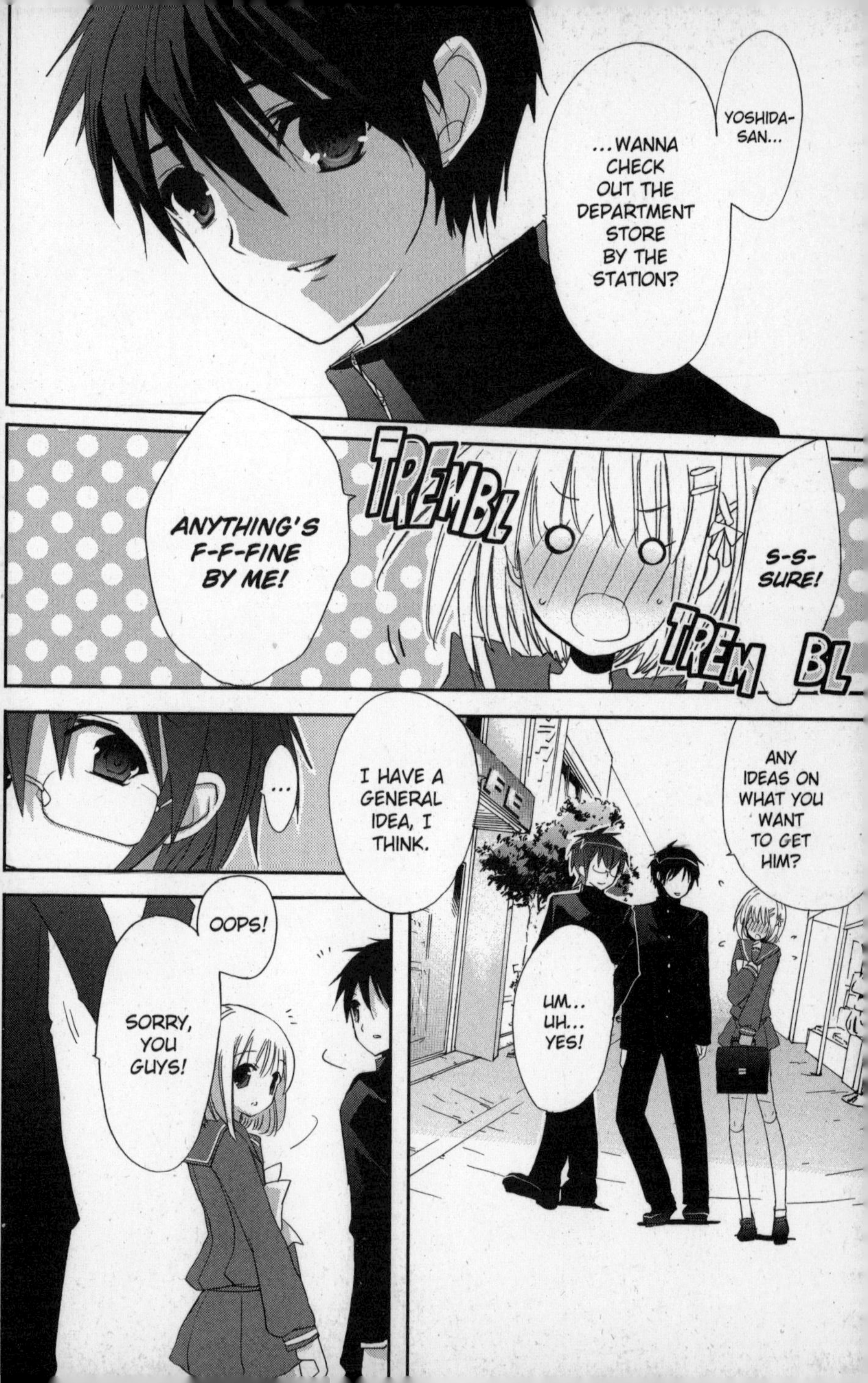
YOSHIDA-SAN...
...WANNA CHECK OUT THE DEPARTMENT STORE BY THE STATION?
S-S-SURE!
TREMBL
TREM BL
ANYTHING'S F-F-FINE BY ME!
ANY IDEAS ON WHAT YOU WANT TO GET HIM?
I HAVE A GENERAL IDEA, I THINK.
UM... UH... YES!
...
OOPS!
SORRY, YOU GUYS!

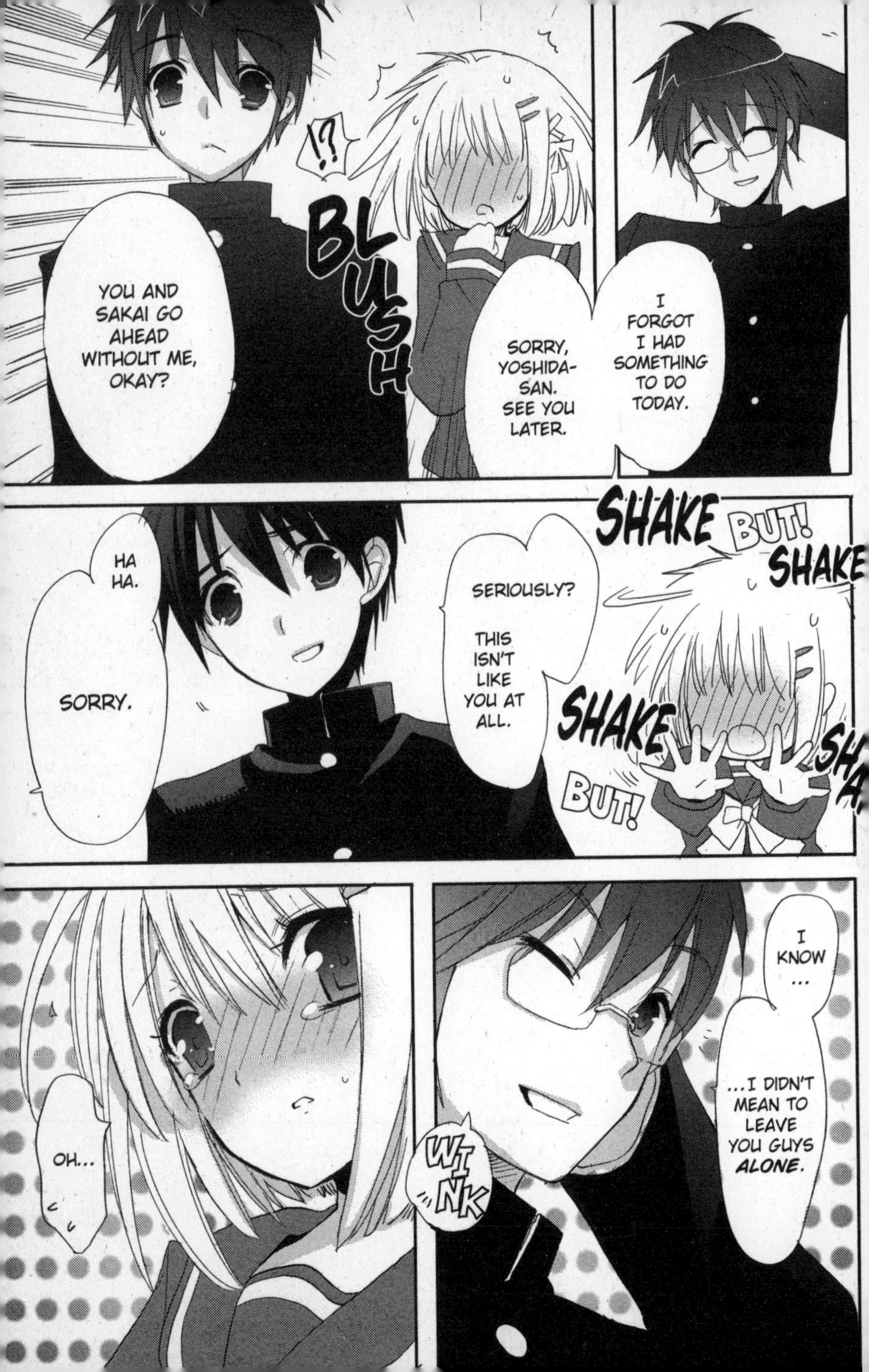
I FORGOT I HAD SOMETHING TO DO TODAY.
SORRY, YOSHIDA-SAN. SEE YOU LATER.
!?
BLUSH
YOU AND SAKAI GO AHEAD WITHOUT ME, OKAY?
SHAKE
BUT!
SHAKE
SERIOUSLY?
THIS ISN'T LIKE YOU AT ALL.
HA HA.
SORRY.
SHAKE
BUT!
I KNOW...
...I DIDN'T MEAN TO LEAVE YOU GUYS *ALONE*.
WINK
OH...

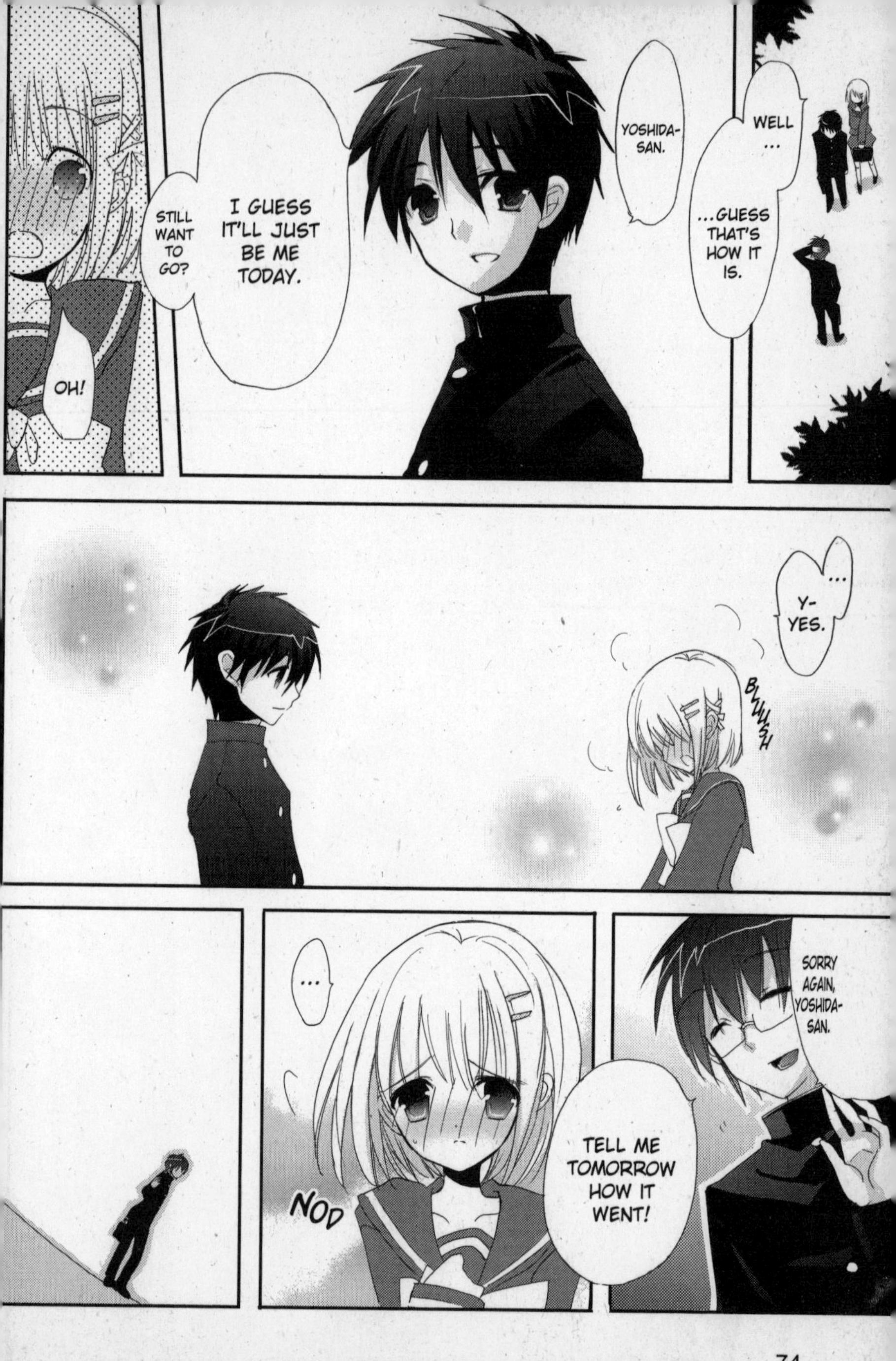
WELL ...
...GUESS THAT'S HOW IT IS.
YOSHIDA-SAN.
I GUESS IT'LL JUST BE ME TODAY.
STILL WANT TO GO?
OH!
...
Y- YES.
BLUUSH
SORRY AGAIN, YOSHIDA-SAN.
TELL ME TOMORROW HOW IT WENT!
...
NOD

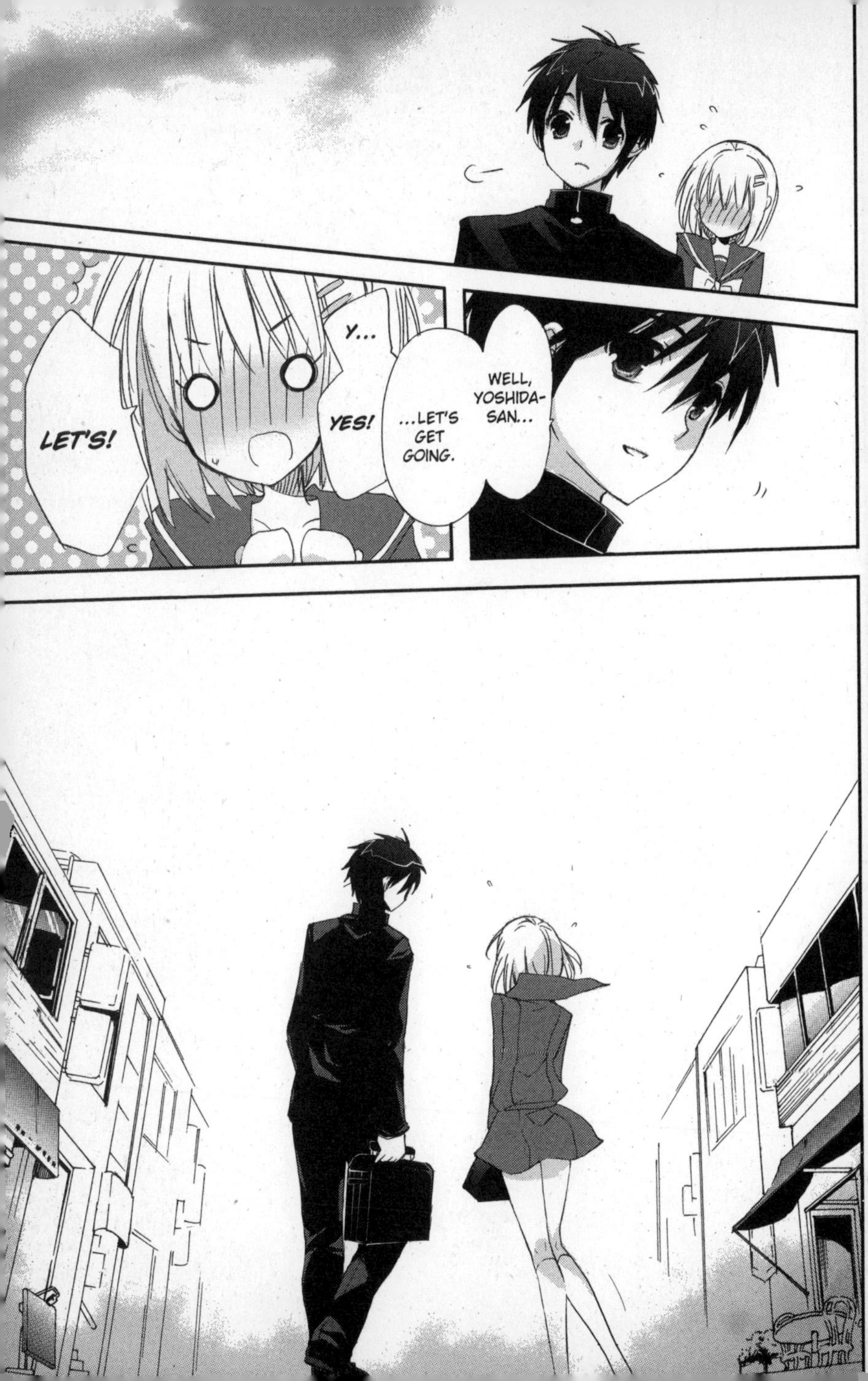
WELL, YOSHIDA-SAN...
...LET'S GET GOING.
Y...
YES!
LET'S!

BAT
BAT

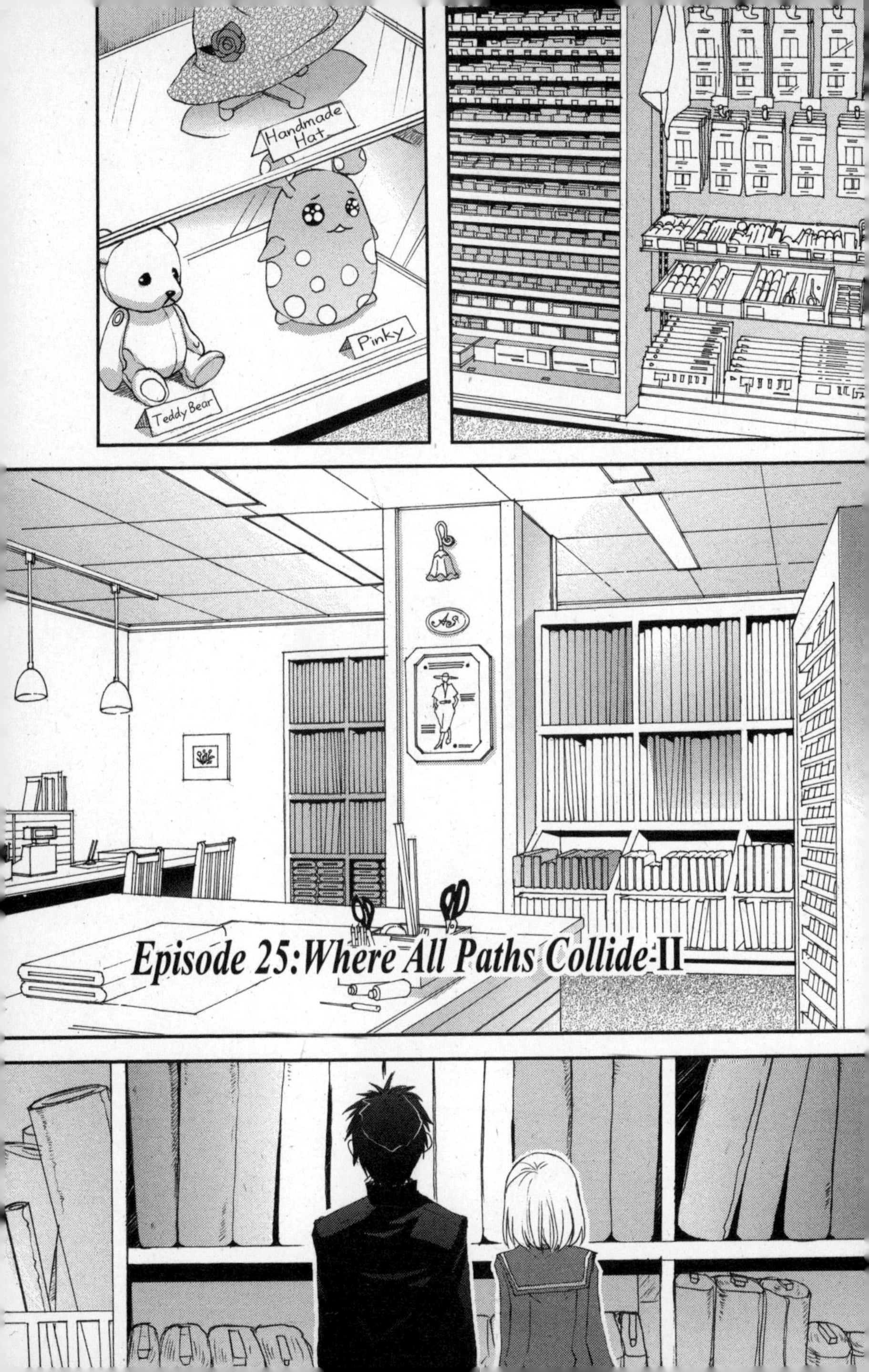
Handmade Hat
Pinky
Teddy Bear
Episode 25: Where All Paths Collide II

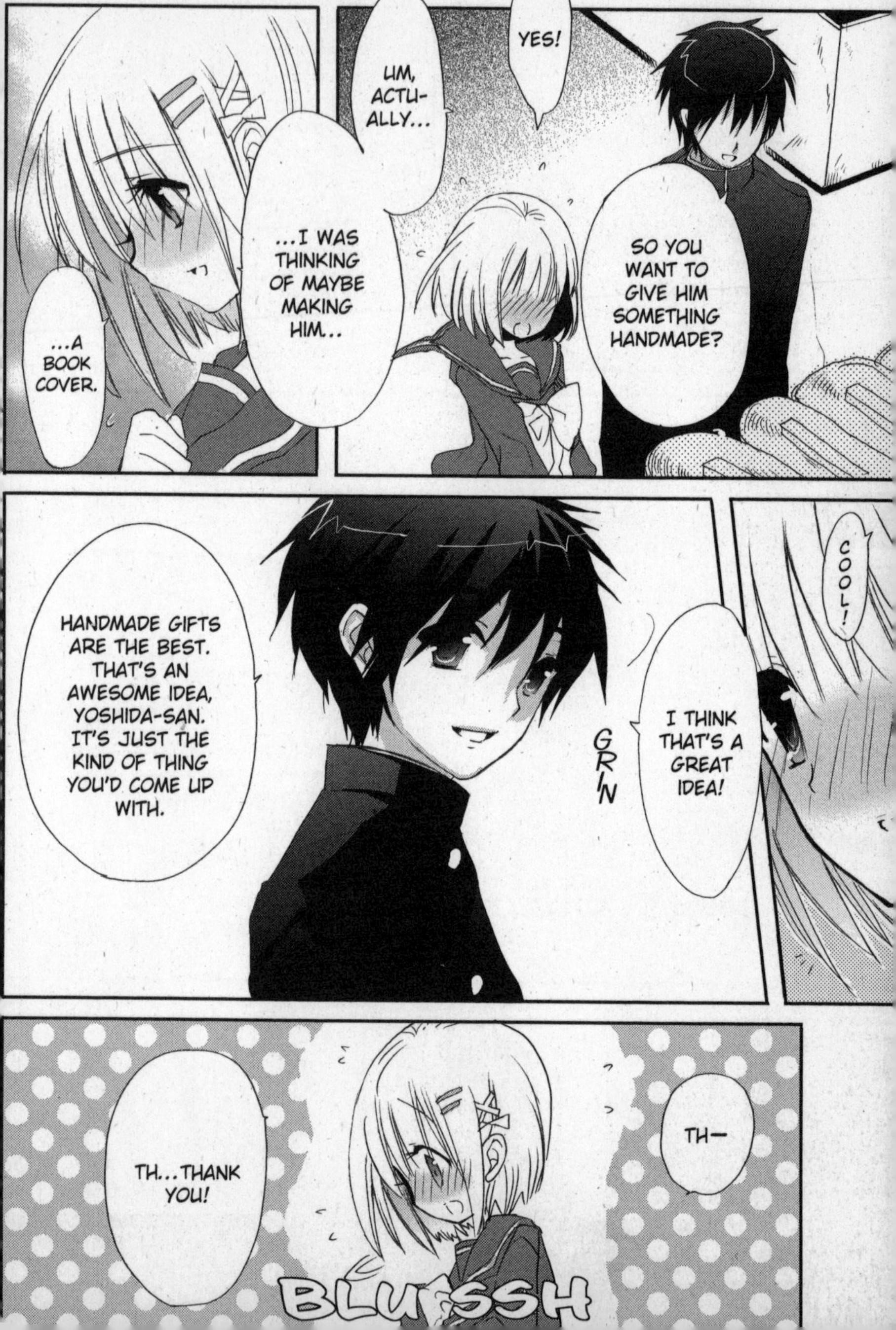
SO YOU WANT TO GIVE HIM SOMETHING HANDMADE?
YES!
UM, ACTU-ALLY...
...I WAS THINKING OF MAYBE MAKING HIM...
...A BOOK COVER.
COOL!
I THINK THAT'S A GREAT IDEA!
GRIN
HANDMADE GIFTS ARE THE BEST. THAT'S AN AWESOME IDEA, YOSHIDA-SAN. IT'S JUST THE KIND OF THING YOU'D COME UP WITH.
TH—
TH...THANK YOU!
BLUSSH

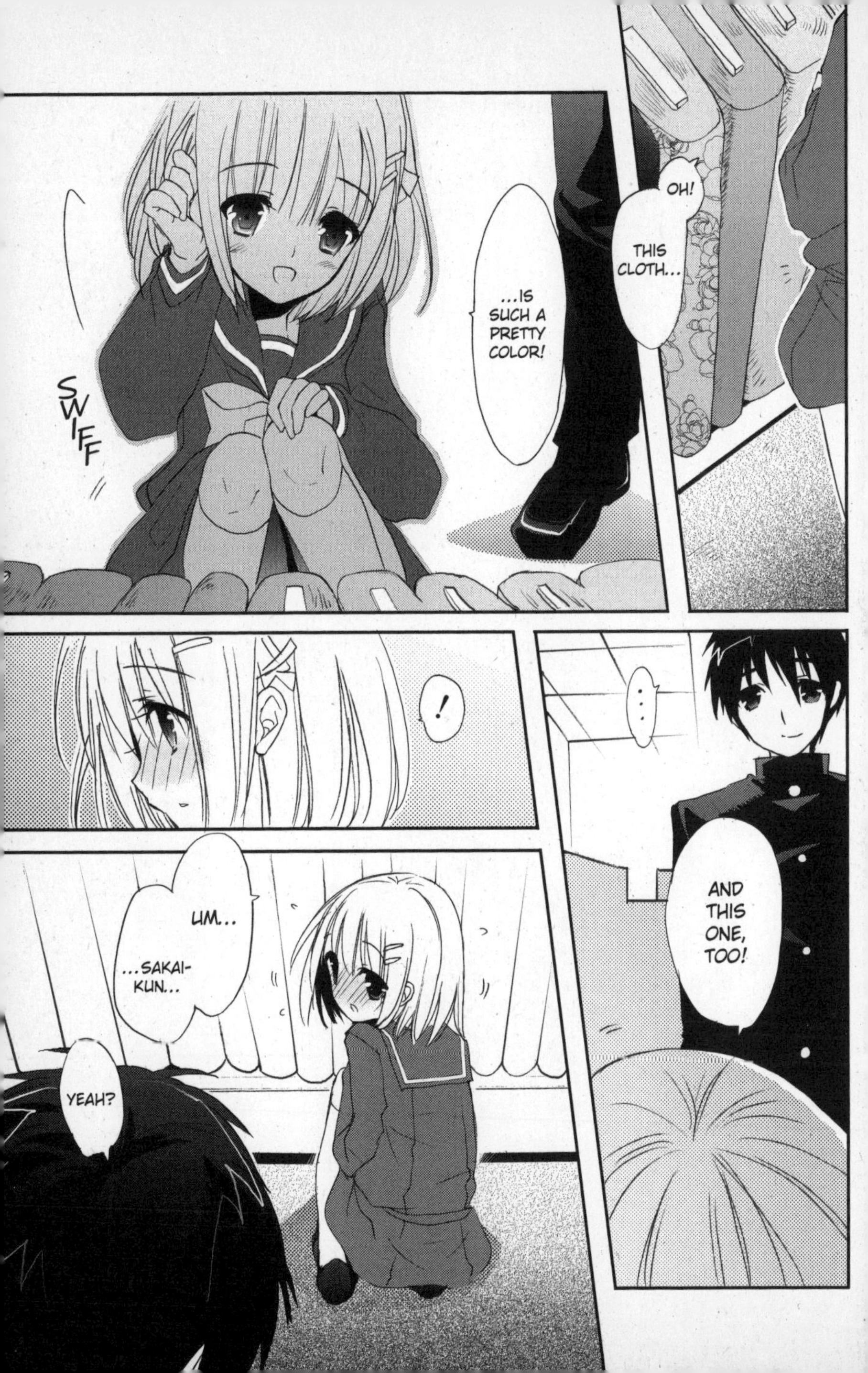
OH!
THIS CLOTH...
...IS SUCH A PRETTY COLOR!
SWIFF
...
AND THIS ONE, TOO!
!
UM...
...SAKAI-KUN...
YEAH?

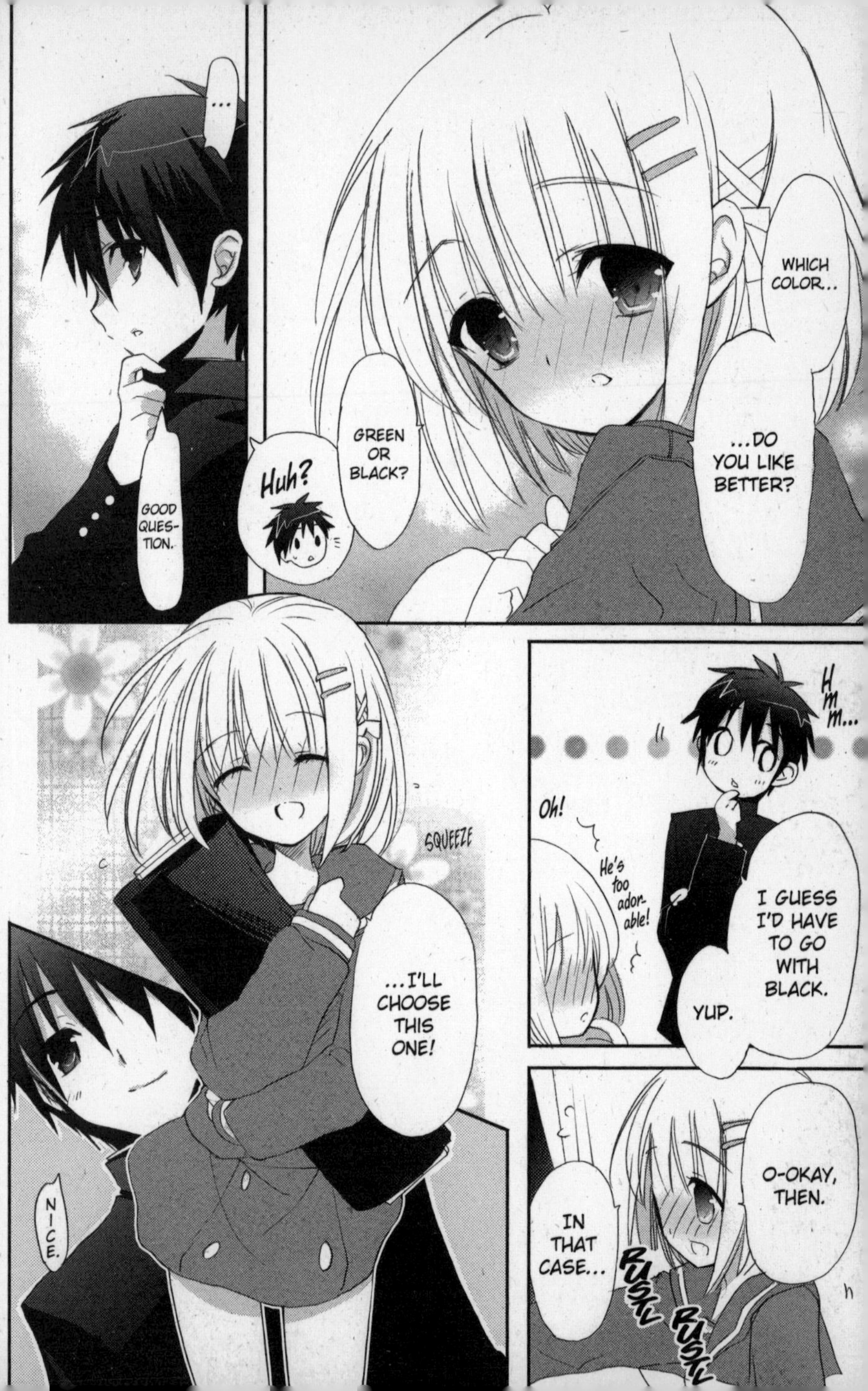
WHICH COLOR...
...DO YOU LIKE BETTER?
GREEN OR BLACK?
Huh?
...
GOOD QUESTION.
Hmm...
Oh!
He's too adorable!
I GUESS I'D HAVE TO GO WITH BLACK.
YUP.
O-OKAY, THEN.
IN THAT CASE...
SQUEEZE
...I'LL CHOOSE THIS ONE!
NICE.

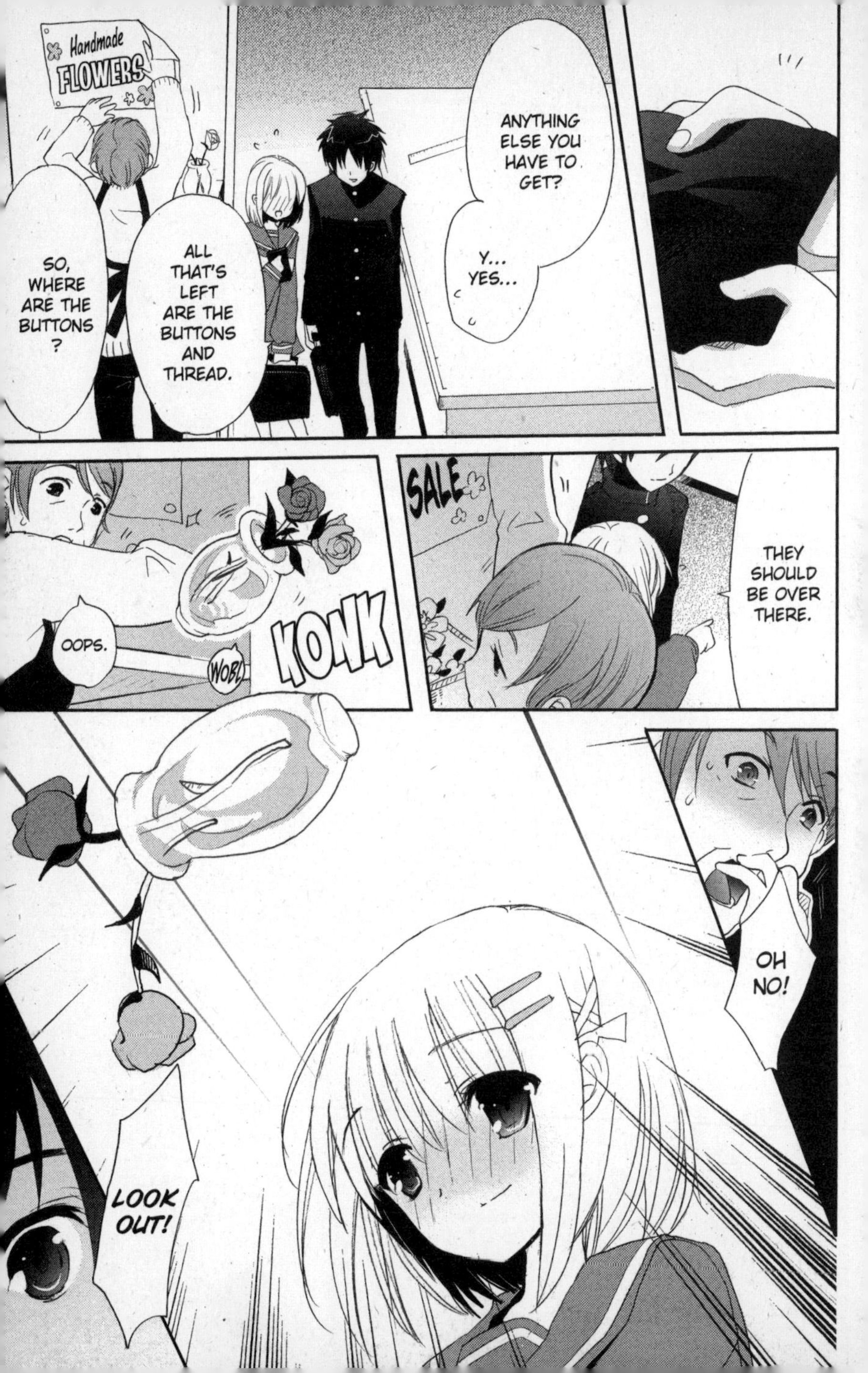
ANYTHING ELSE YOU HAVE TO GET?
Y... YES...
Handmade
FLOWERS
ALL THAT'S LEFT ARE THE BUTTONS AND THREAD.
SO, WHERE ARE THE BUTTONS ?
SALE
THEY SHOULD BE OVER THERE.
KONK
OOPS.
WOBL
OH NO!
LOOK OUT!

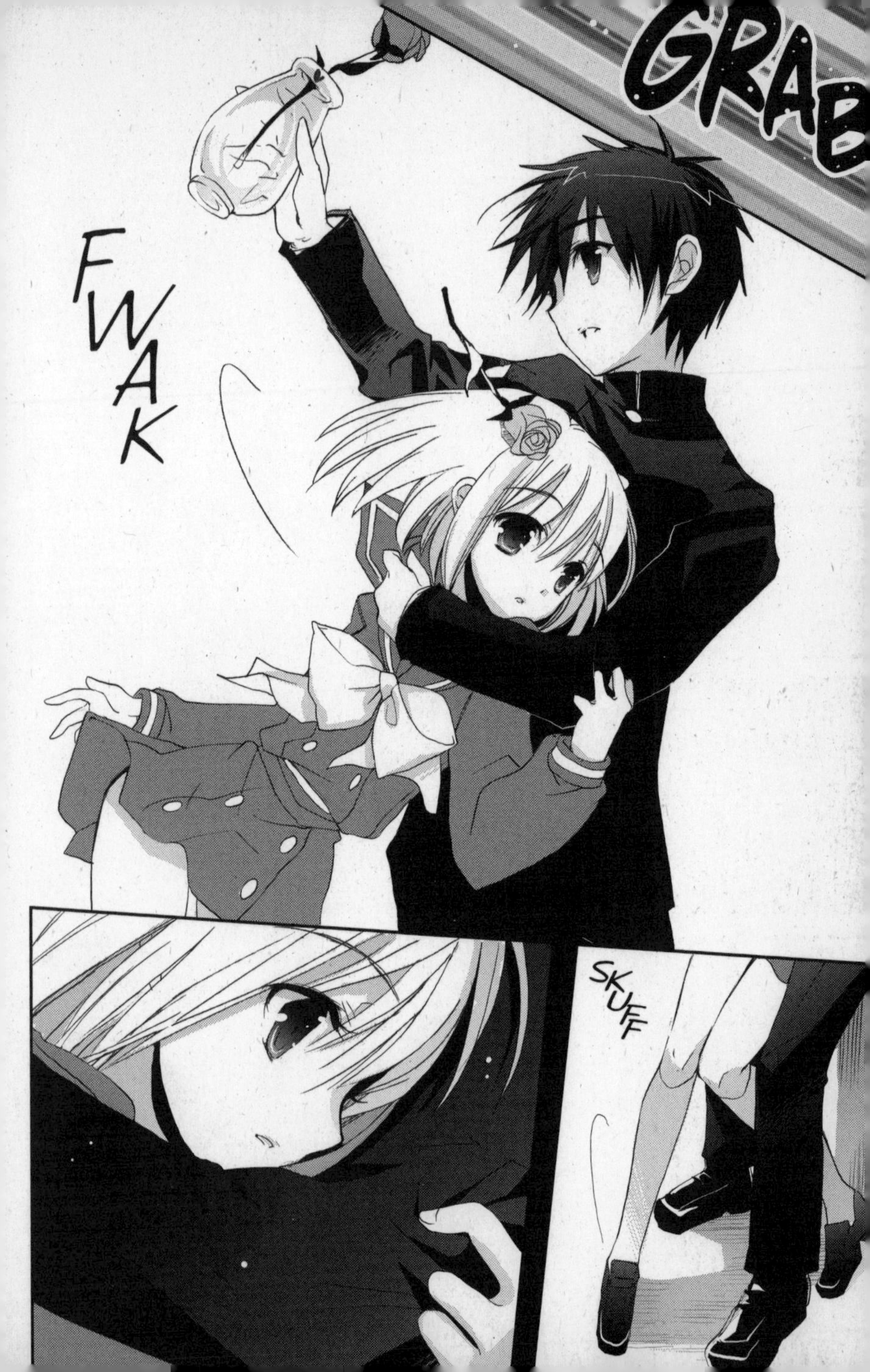
GRAB
FWAK
SKUFF

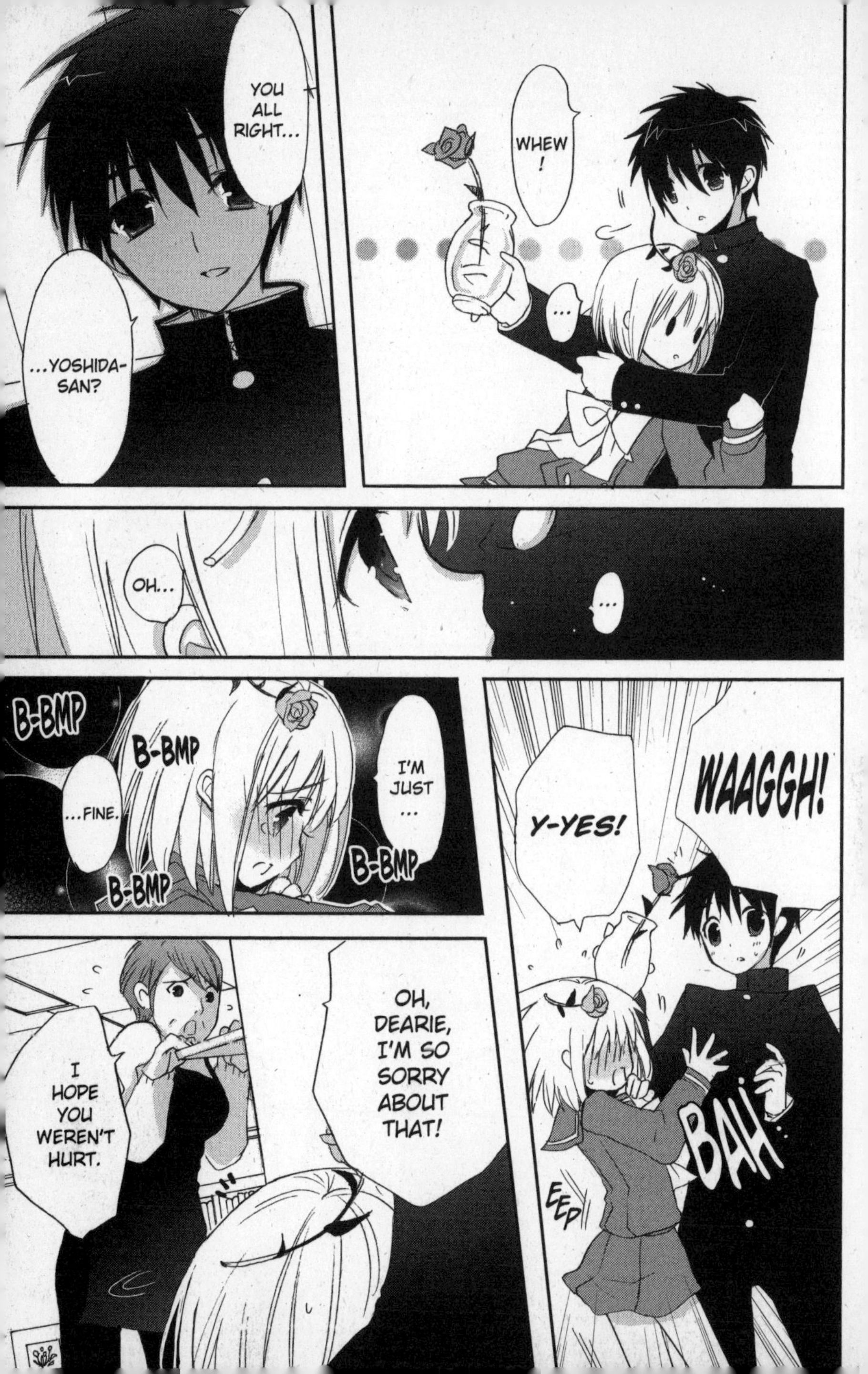
WHEW!
...
YOU ALL RIGHT...
...YOSHIDA-SAN?
...
OH...
WAAGGH!
Y-YES!
BAH
EEP
I'M JUST ...
B-BMP
B-BMP
...FINE.
B-BMP
B-BMP
OH, DEARIE, I'M SO SORRY ABOUT THAT!
I HOPE YOU WEREN'T HURT.

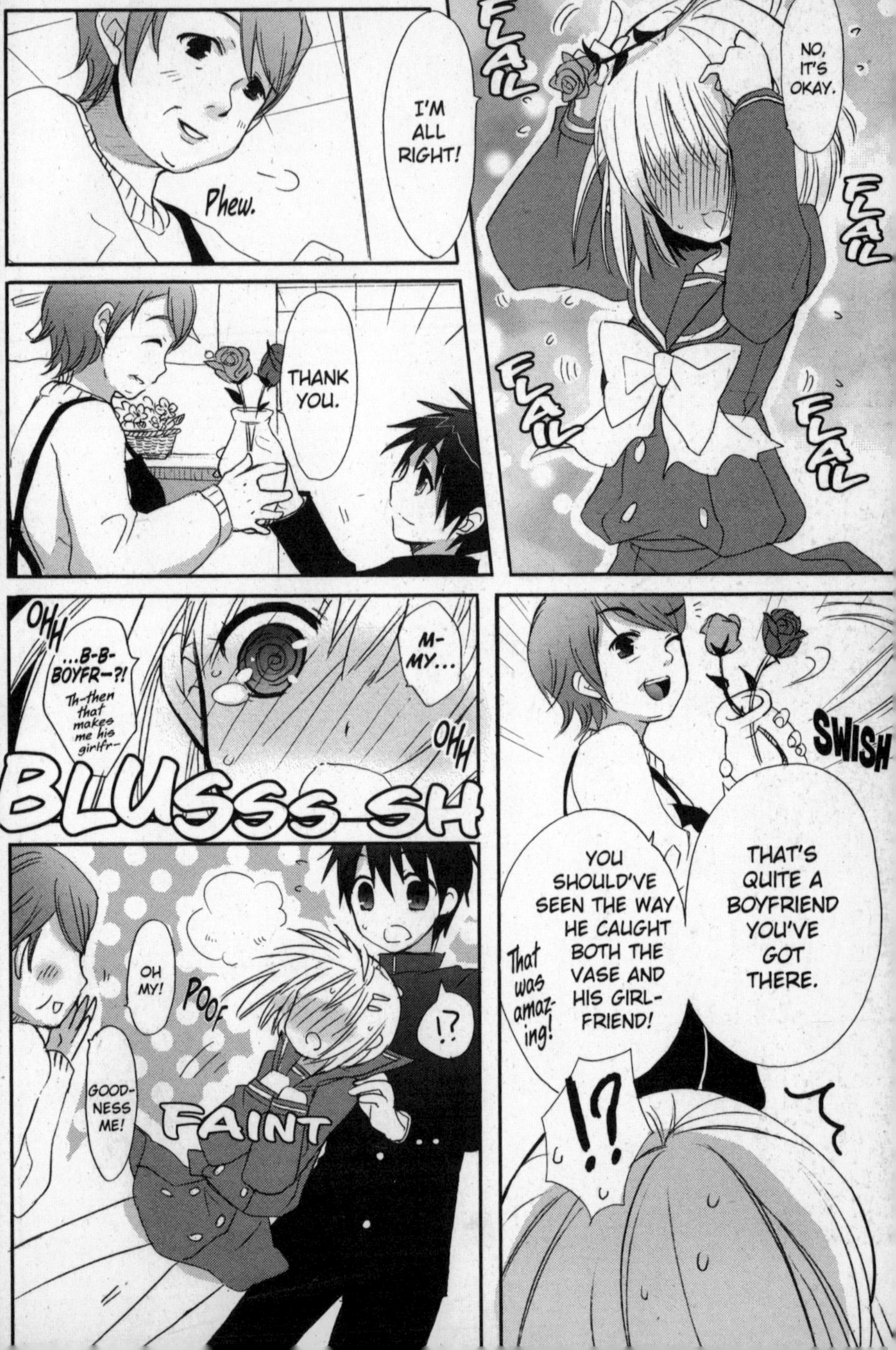
NO, IT'S OKAY.
FLAIL
FLAIL
FLAIL
FLAIL
I'M ALL RIGHT!
Phew.
THANK YOU.
SWISH
THAT'S QUITE A BOYFRIEND YOU'VE GOT THERE.
YOU SHOULD'VE SEEN THE WAY HE CAUGHT BOTH THE VASE AND HIS GIRL-FRIEND!
That was amaz-ing!
!?
M-MY...
OHH
OHH
...B-B-BOYFR--?!
Th-then that makes me his girlfr--
BLUSSS SH
!?
POOF
OH MY!
GOOD-NESS ME!
FAINT

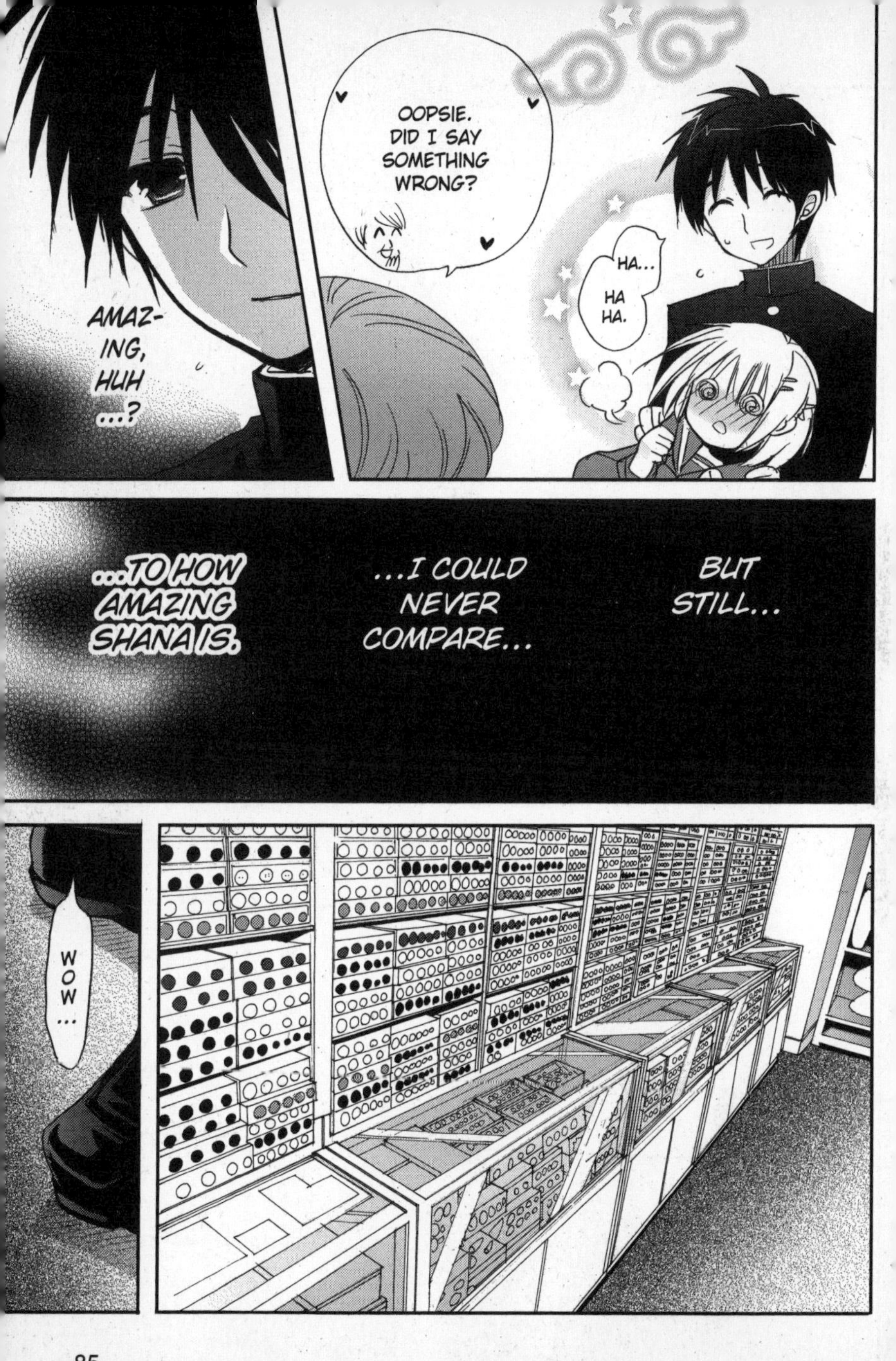
OOPSIE. DID I SAY SOMETHING WRONG?
HA... HA HA.
AMAZ-ING, HUH ...?
BUT STILL...
...I COULD NEVER COMPARE...
...TO HOW AMAZING SHANA IS.
WOW...

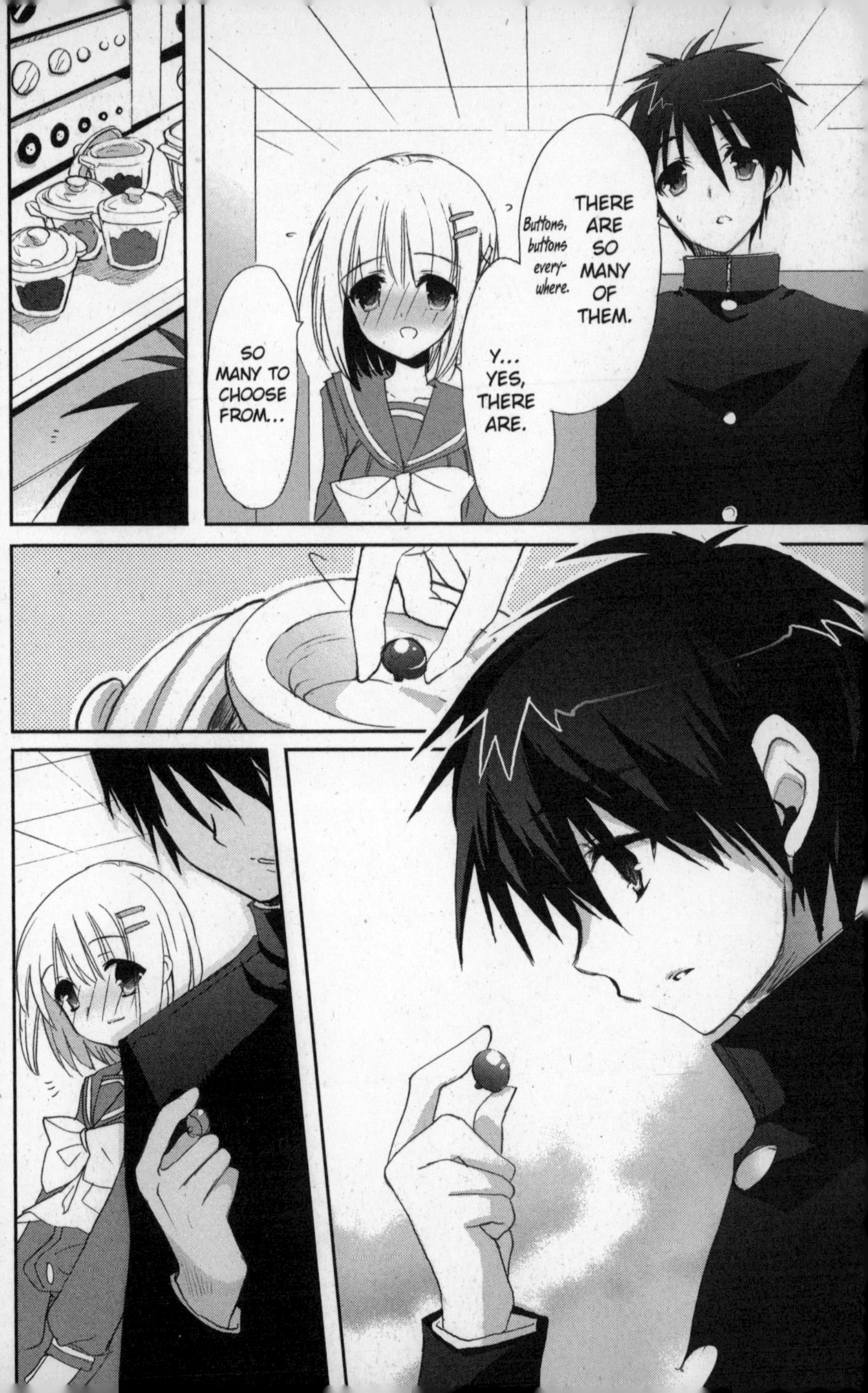
THERE ARE SO MANY OF THEM.
Buttons, buttons every-where.
Y... YES, THERE ARE.
SO MANY TO CHOOSE FROM...

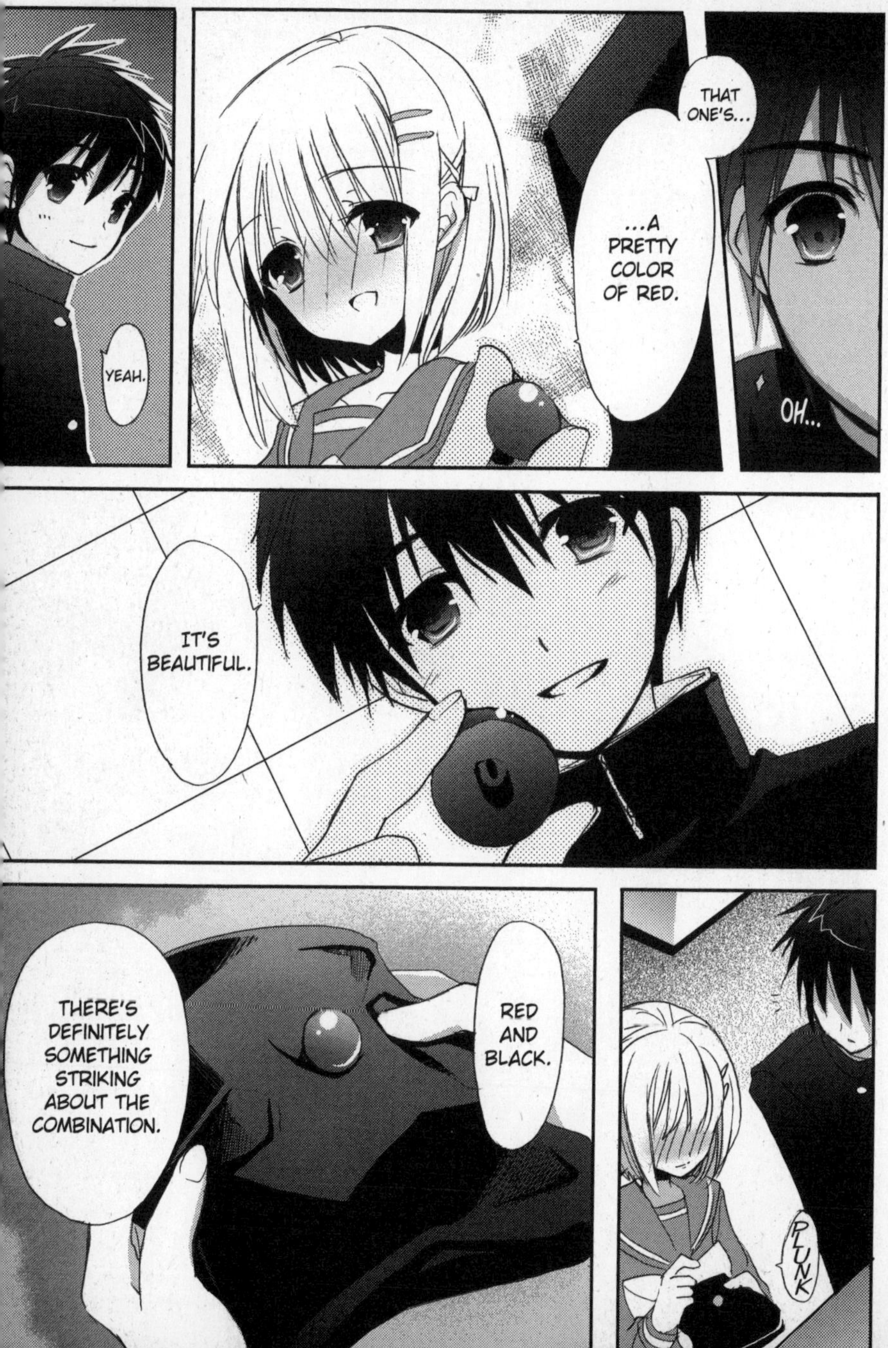
THAT ONE'S...
...A PRETTY COLOR OF RED.
OH...
YEAH.
IT'S BEAUTIFUL.
PLUNK
RED AND BLACK.
THERE'S DEFINITELY SOMETHING STRIKING ABOUT THE COMBINATION.

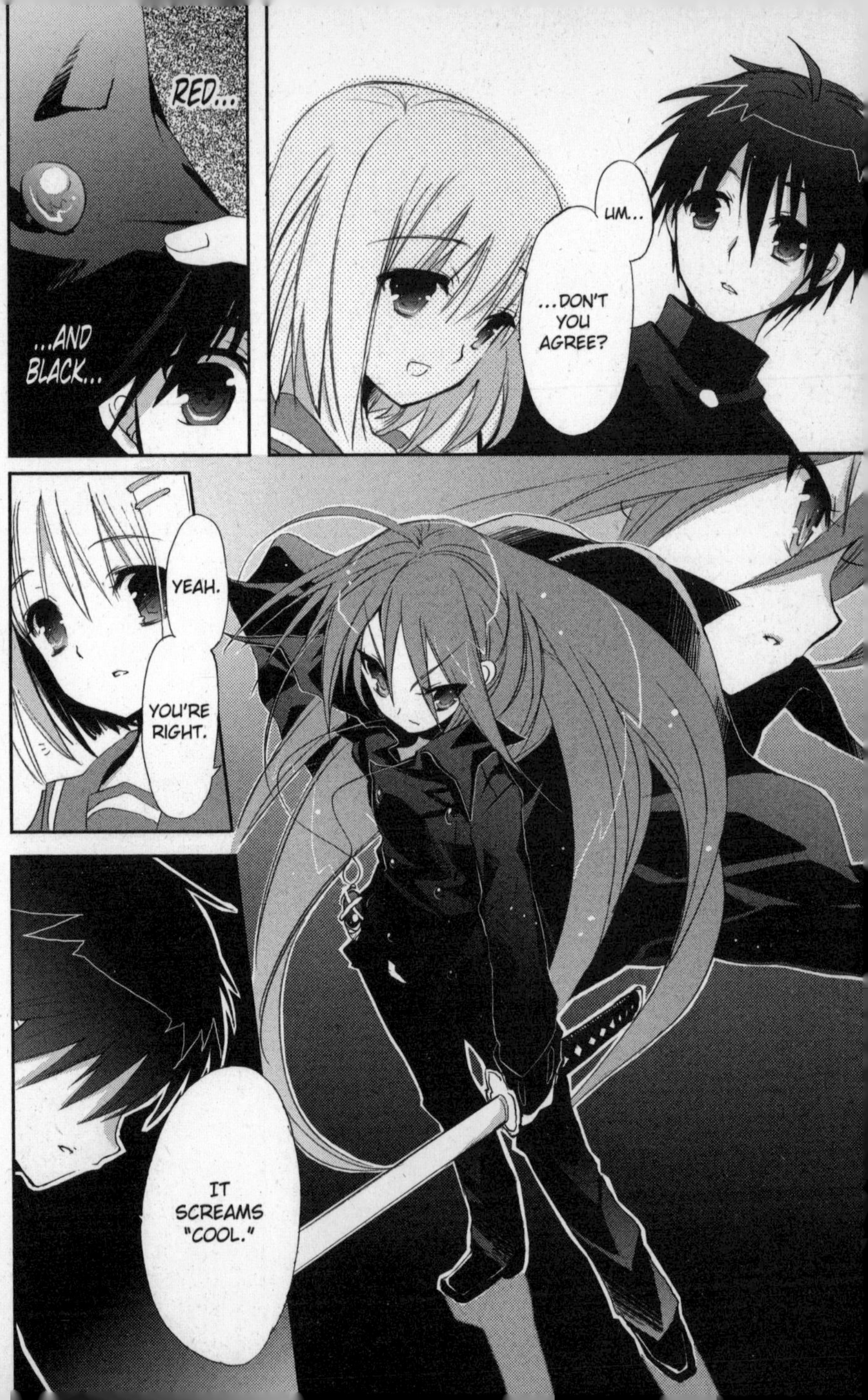
UM...
...DON'T YOU AGREE?
RED...
...AND BLACK...
YEAH.
YOU'RE RIGHT.
IT SCREAMS "COOL."

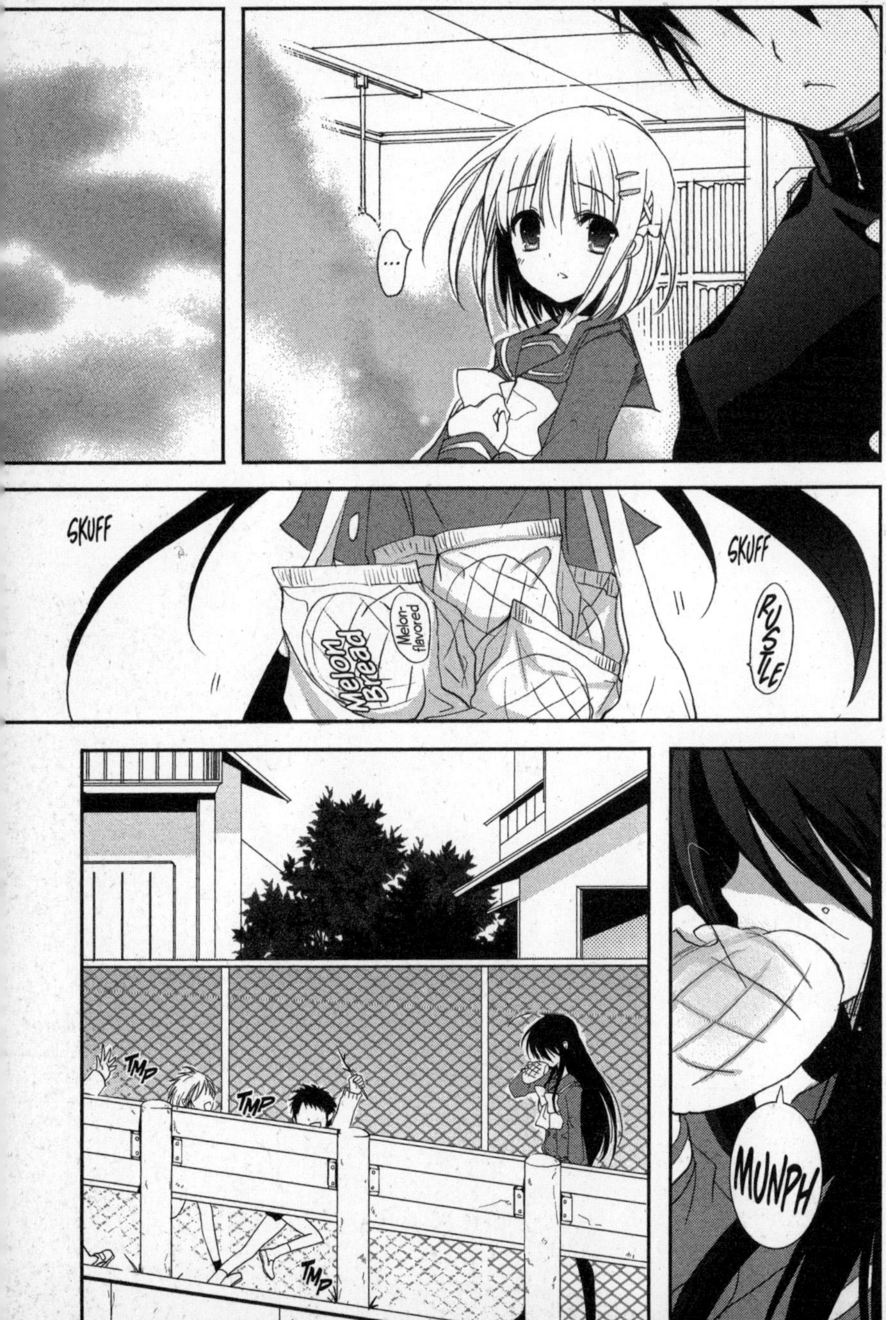
...
SKUFF
RUSTLE
Melon-flavored
Melon Bread
SKUFF
MUNPH
TMP
TMP
TMP

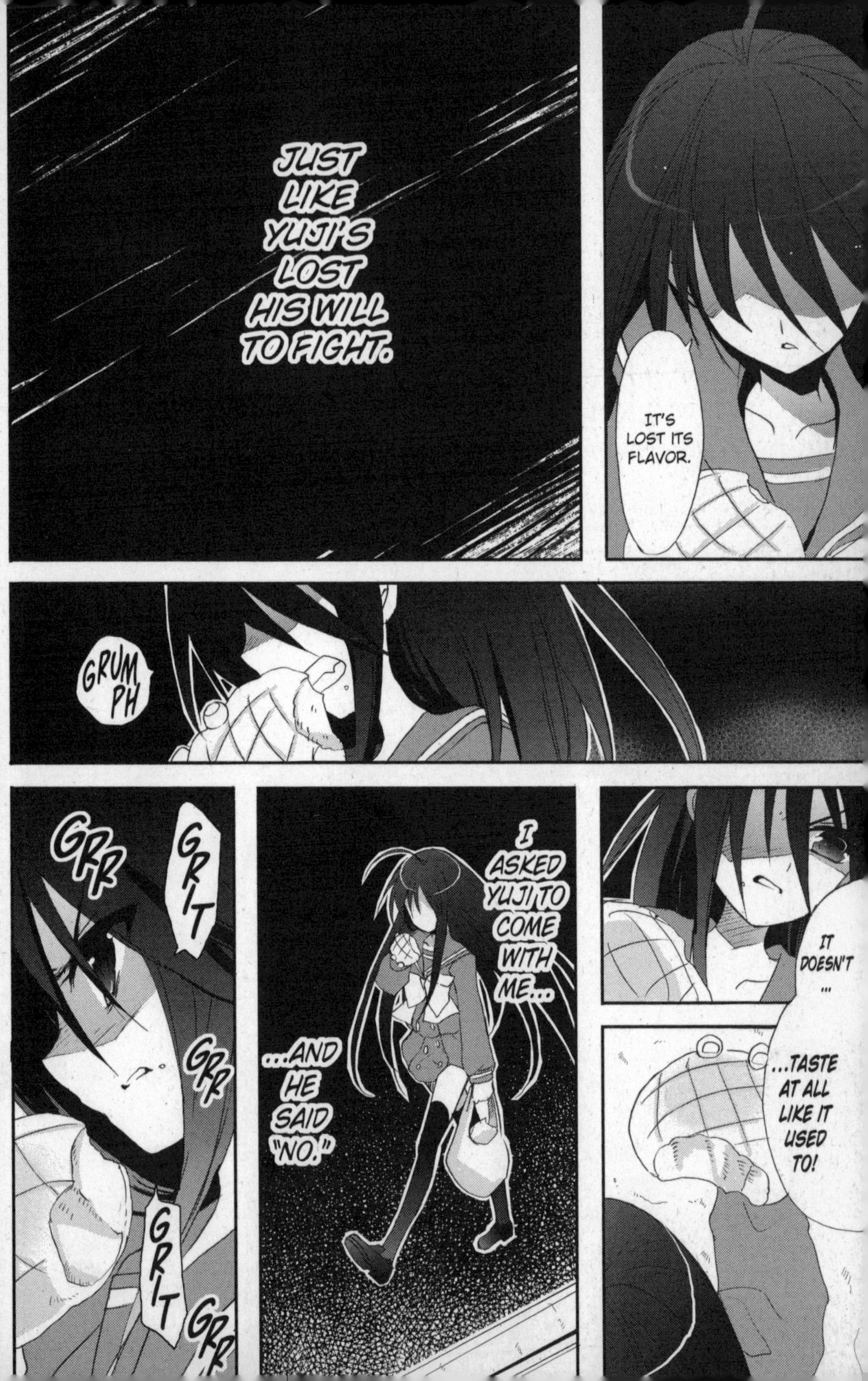
IT'S LOST ITS FLAVOR.
JUST LIKE YUJI'S LOST HIS WILL TO FIGHT.
GRUMPH
IT DOESN'T ...
...TASTE AT ALL LIKE IT USED TO!
I ASKED YUJI TO COME WITH ME...
...AND HE SAID "NO."
GRIT
GRR
GRR
GRIT
GRR

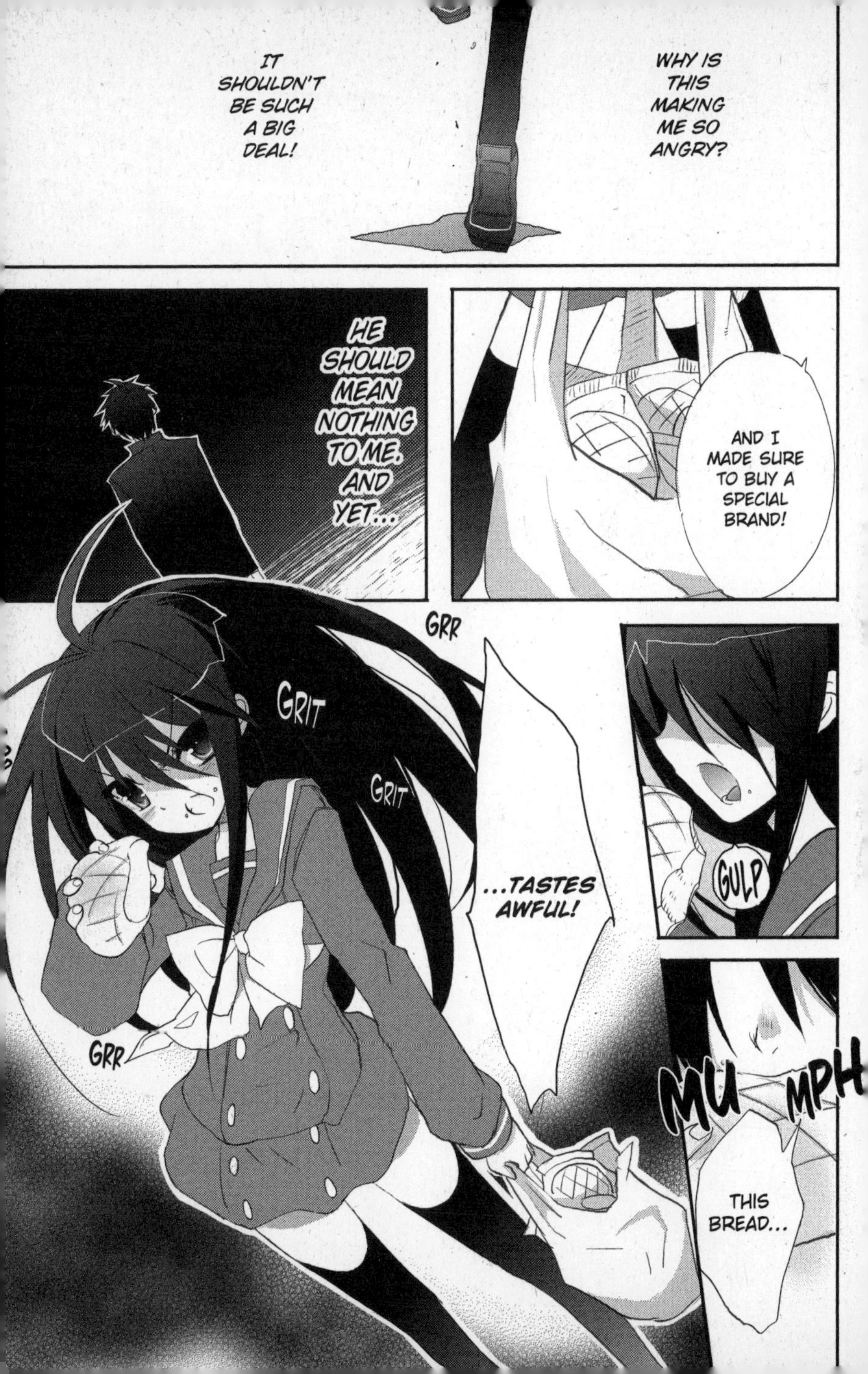
WHY IS THIS MAKING ME SO ANGRY?
IT SHOULDN'T BE SUCH A BIG DEAL!
AND I MADE SURE TO BUY A SPECIAL BRAND!
HE SHOULD MEAN NOTHING TO ME. AND YET...
GULP
MU MPH
THIS BREAD...
...TASTES AWFUL!
GRR
GRIT
GRIT
GRR

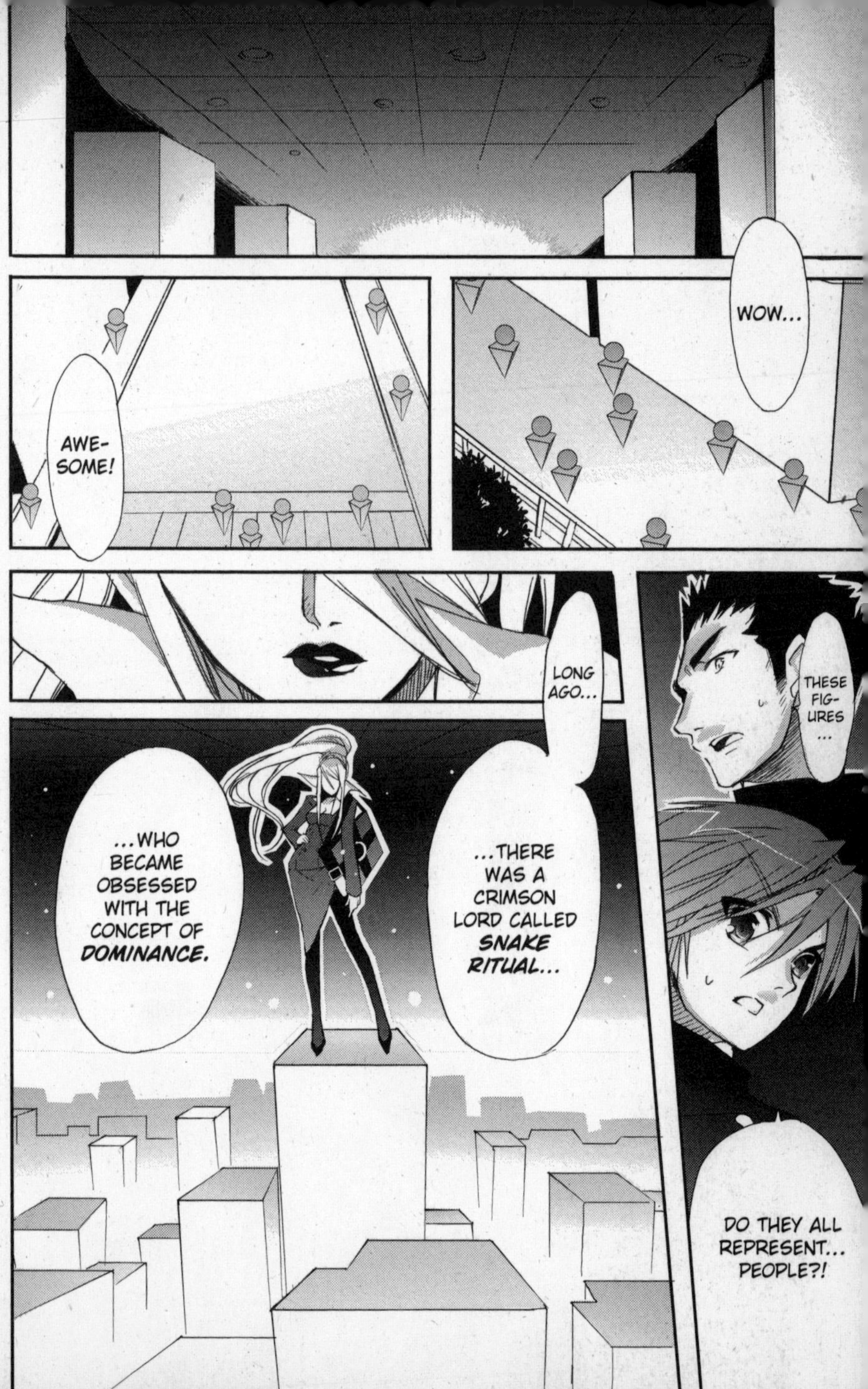
WOW...
AWE-SOME!
THESE FIGURES...
DO THEY ALL REPRESENT... PEOPLE?!
LONG AGO...
...THERE WAS A CRIMSON LORD CALLED SNAKE RITUAL...
...WHO BECAME OBSESSED WITH THE CONCEPT OF DOMINANCE.

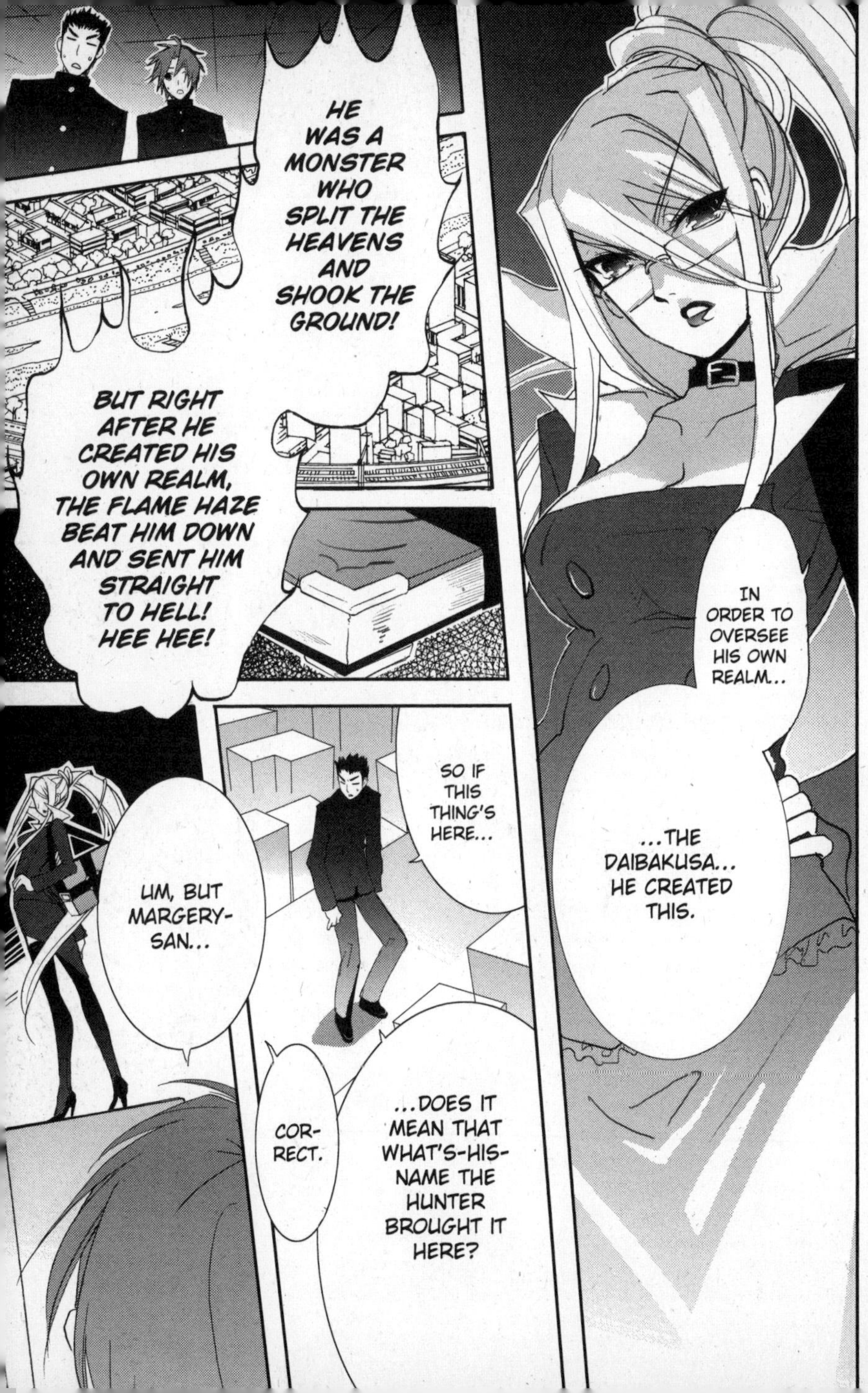
IN ORDER TO OVERSEE HIS OWN REALM...
...THE DAIBAKUSA... HE CREATED THIS.
HE WAS A MONSTER WHO SPLIT THE HEAVENS AND SHOOK THE GROUND!
BUT RIGHT AFTER HE CREATED HIS OWN REALM, THE FLAME HAZE BEAT HIM DOWN AND SENT HIM STRAIGHT TO HELL! HEE HEE!
SO IF THIS THING'S HERE...
UM, BUT MARGERY-SAN...
...DOES IT MEAN THAT WHAT'S-HIS-NAME THE HUNTER BROUGHT IT HERE?
COR-RECT.

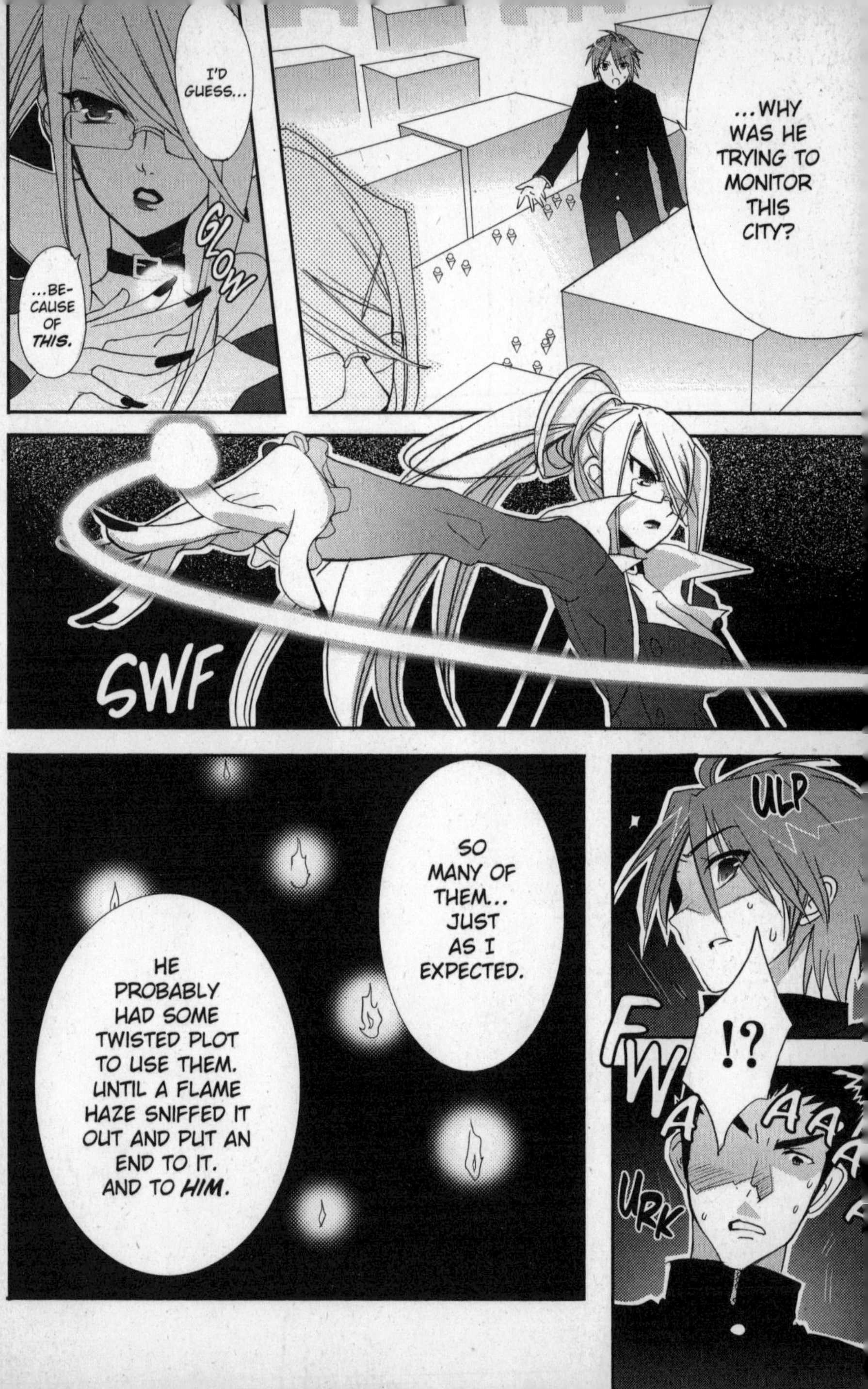
...WHY WAS HE TRYING TO MONITOR THIS CITY?
I'D GUESS...
GLOW
...BE-CAUSE OF THIS.
SWF
ULP
!?
FWAAAA
URK
SO MANY OF THEM... JUST AS I EXPECTED.
HE PROBABLY HAD SOME TWISTED PLOT TO USE THEM. UNTIL A FLAME HAZE SNIFFED IT OUT AND PUT AN END TO IT. AND TO HIM.

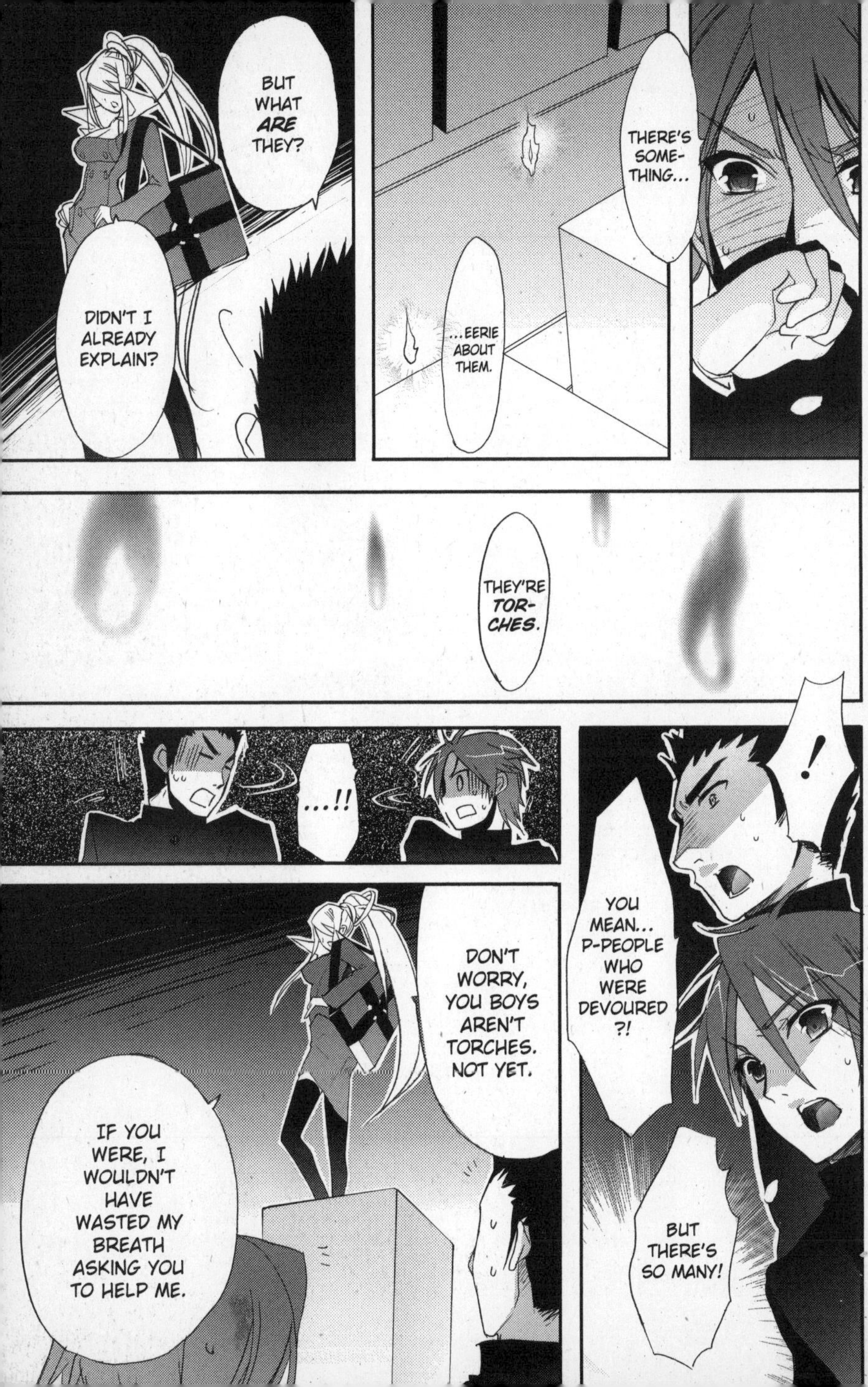
THERE'S SOMETHING...
...EERIE ABOUT THEM.
BUT WHAT *ARE* THEY?
DIDN'T I ALREADY EXPLAIN?
THEY'RE *TORCHES*.
!
YOU MEAN... P-PEOPLE WHO WERE DEVOURED?!
BUT THERE'S SO MANY!
...!!
DON'T WORRY, YOU BOYS AREN'T TORCHES. NOT YET.
IF YOU WERE, I WOULDN'T HAVE WASTED MY BREATH ASKING YOU TO HELP ME.

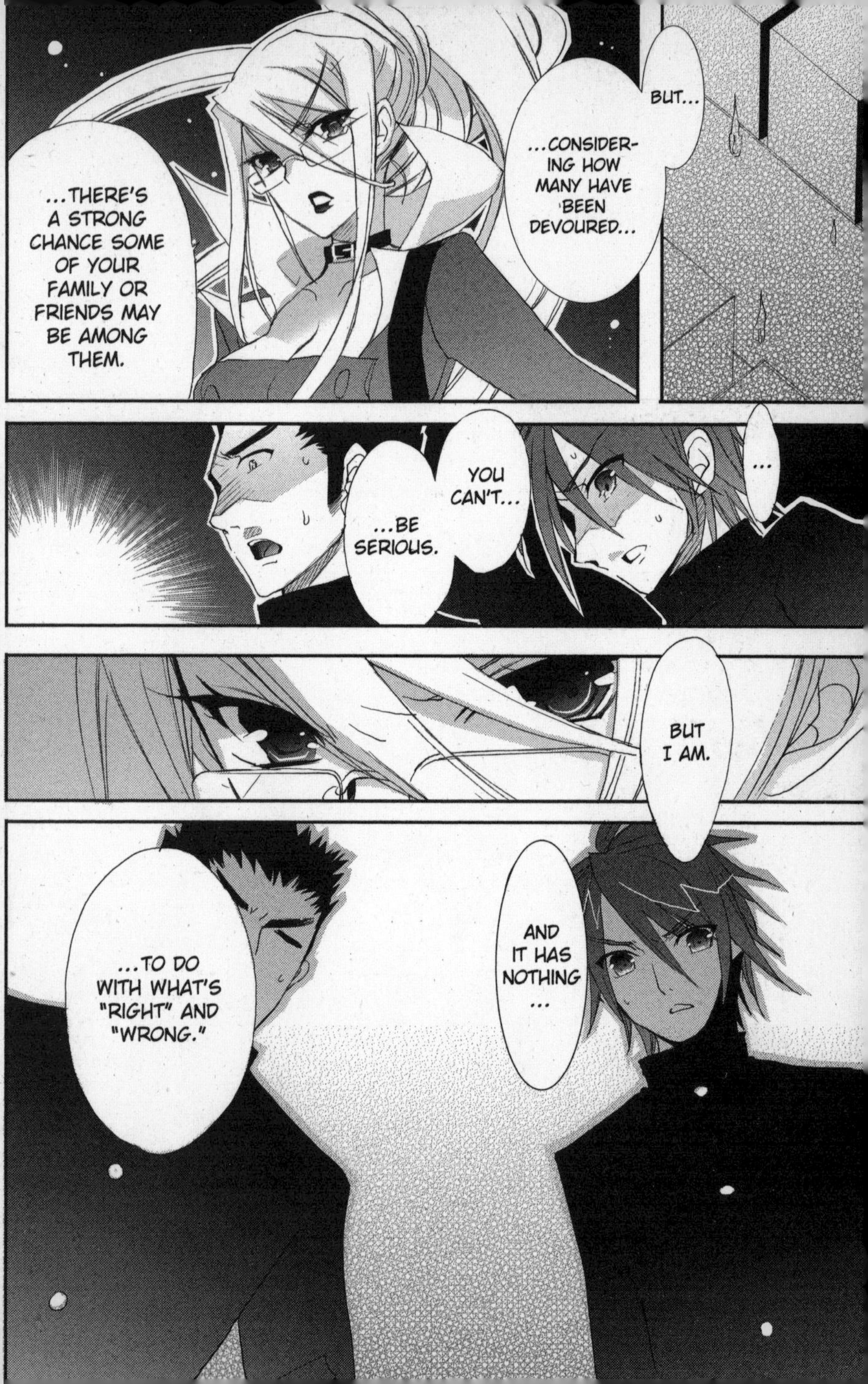
BUT...
...CONSIDERING HOW MANY HAVE BEEN DEVOURED...
...THERE'S A STRONG CHANCE SOME OF YOUR FAMILY OR FRIENDS MAY BE AMONG THEM.
...
YOU CAN'T...
...BE SERIOUS.
BUT I AM.
AND IT HAS NOTHING ...
...TO DO WITH WHAT'S "RIGHT" AND "WRONG."

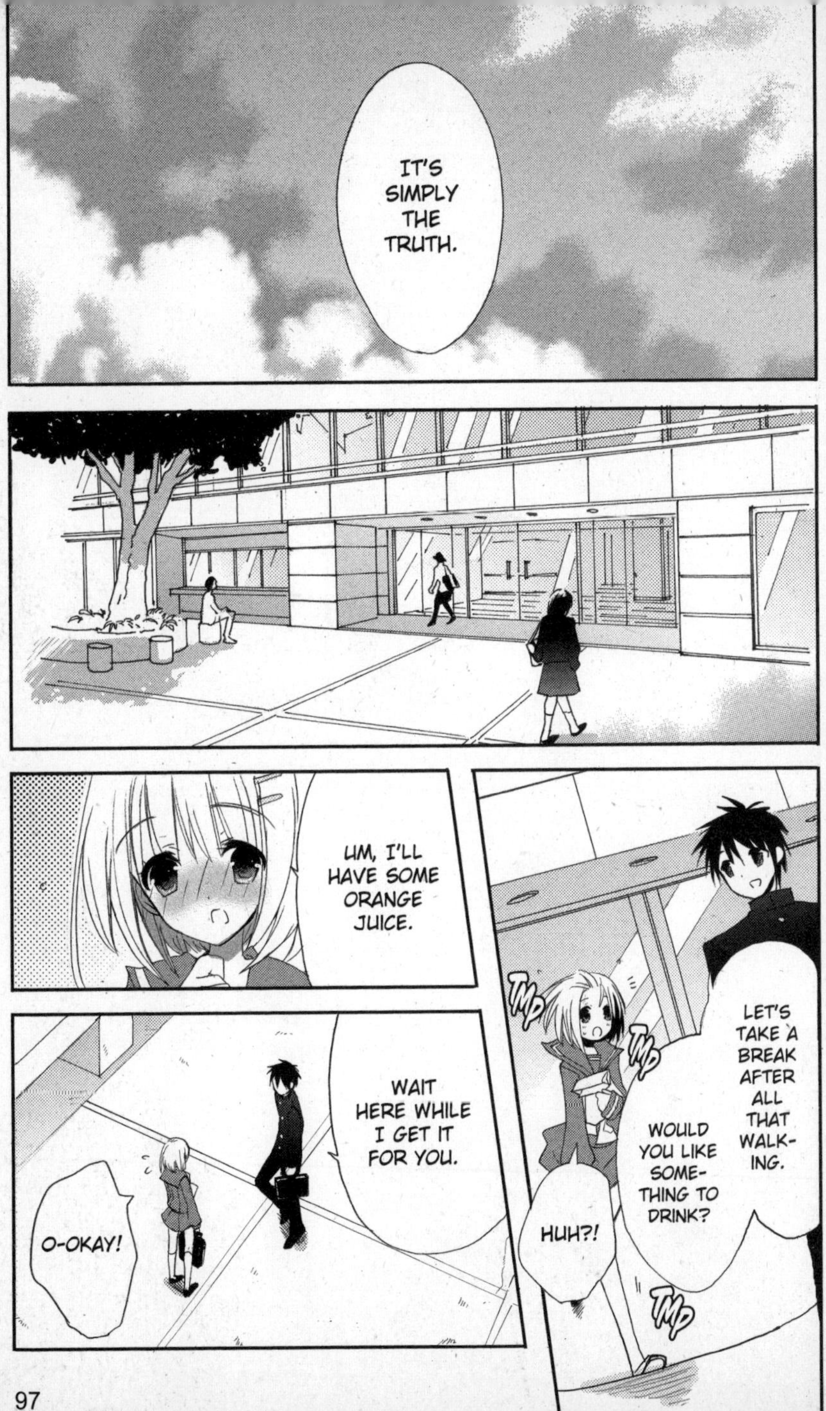
IT'S SIMPLY THE TRUTH.
TMP
TMP
TMP
LET'S TAKE A BREAK AFTER ALL THAT WALKING.
WOULD YOU LIKE SOMETHING TO DRINK?
HUH?!
UM, I'LL HAVE SOME ORANGE JUICE.
WAIT HERE WHILE I GET IT FOR YOU.
O-OKAY!

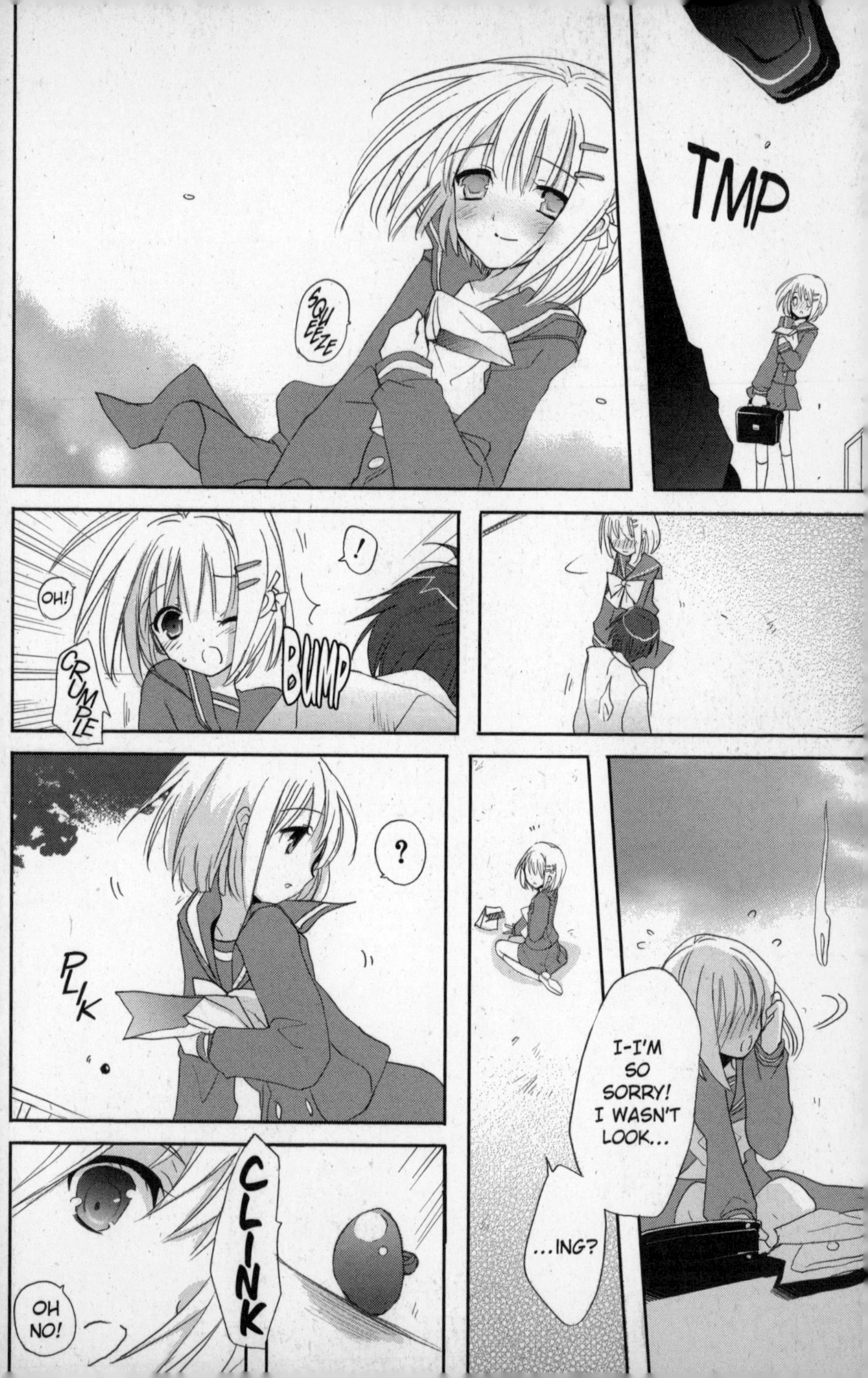
TMP
SQUEEZE
!
OH!
BUMP
CRUMPLE
I-I'M SO SORRY! I WASN'T LOOK...
...ING?
?
PLIK
CLINK
OH NO!

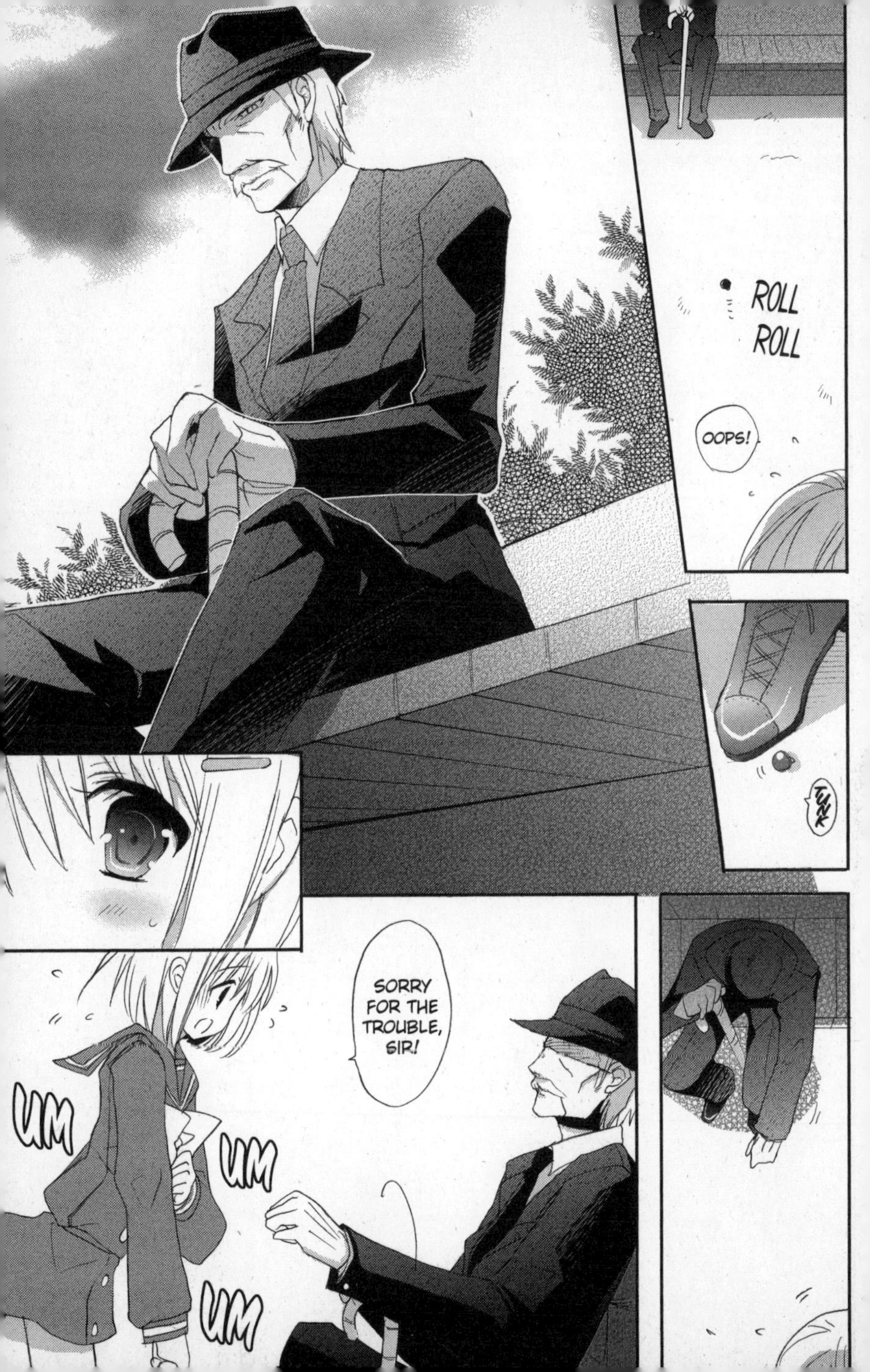
ROLL ROLL
OOPS!
TUNK
SORRY FOR THE TROUBLE, SIR!
UM
UM
UM

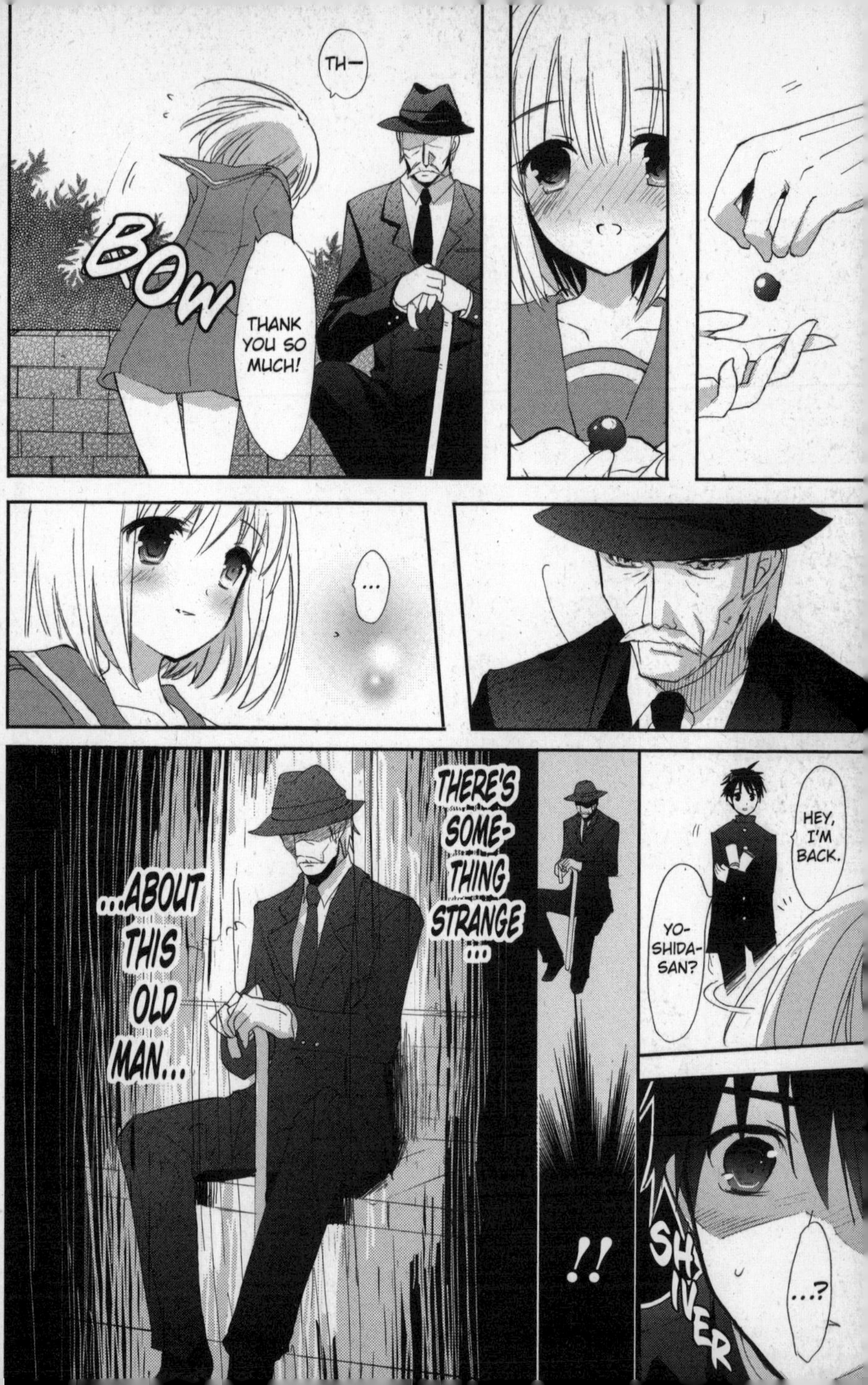
TH—
BOW
THANK YOU SO MUCH!
...
HEY, I'M BACK.
YO-SHIDA-SAN?
SHIVER
...?
!!
THERE'S SOME-THING STRANGE...
...ABOUT THIS OLD MAN...

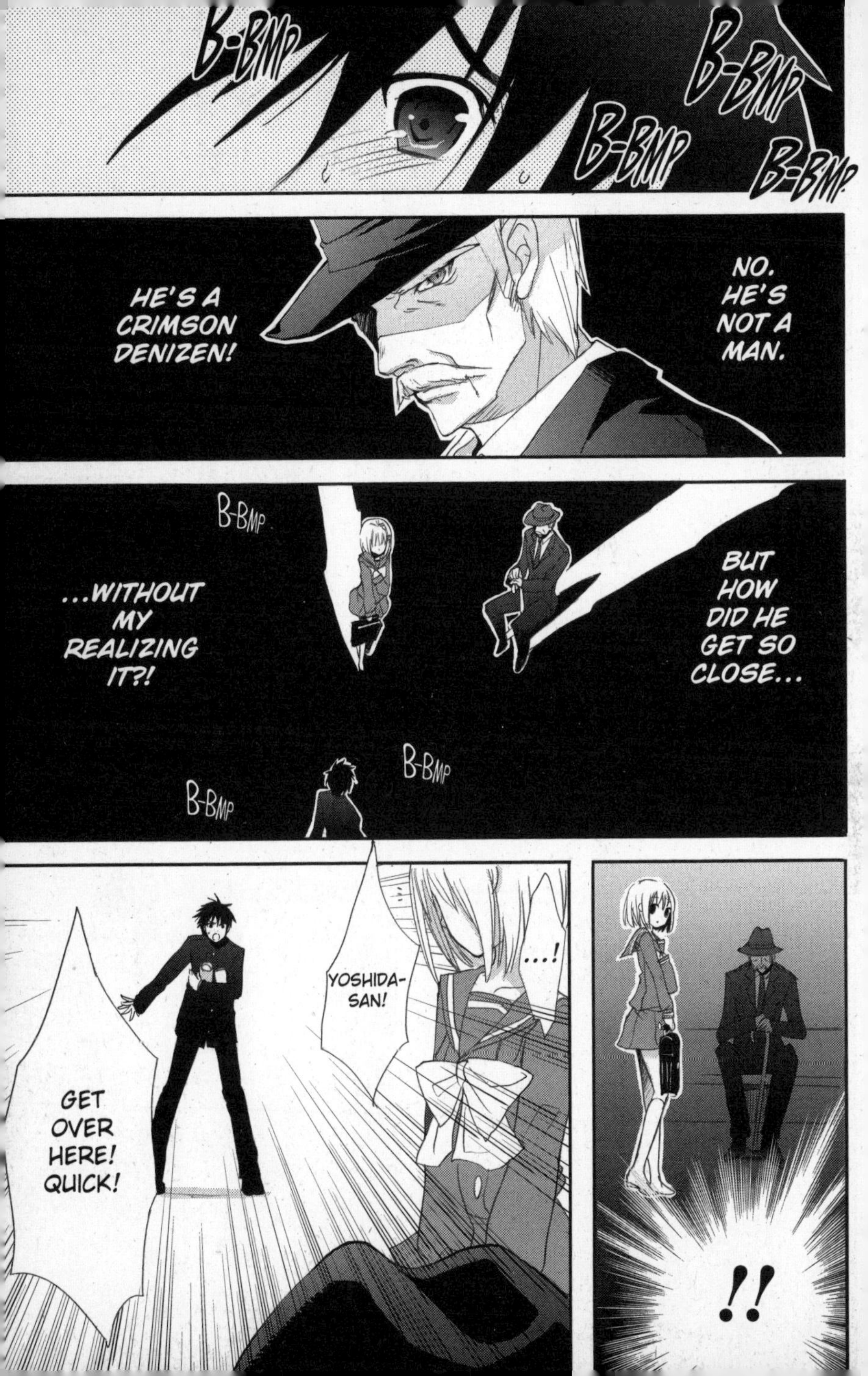
B-BMP
B-BMP
B-BMP
B-BMP
NO. HE'S NOT A MAN.
HE'S A CRIMSON DENIZEN!
B-BMP
BUT HOW DID HE GET SO CLOSE...
...WITHOUT MY REALIZING IT?!
B-BMP
B-BMP
!!
...!
YOSHIDA-SAN!
GET OVER HERE! QUICK!

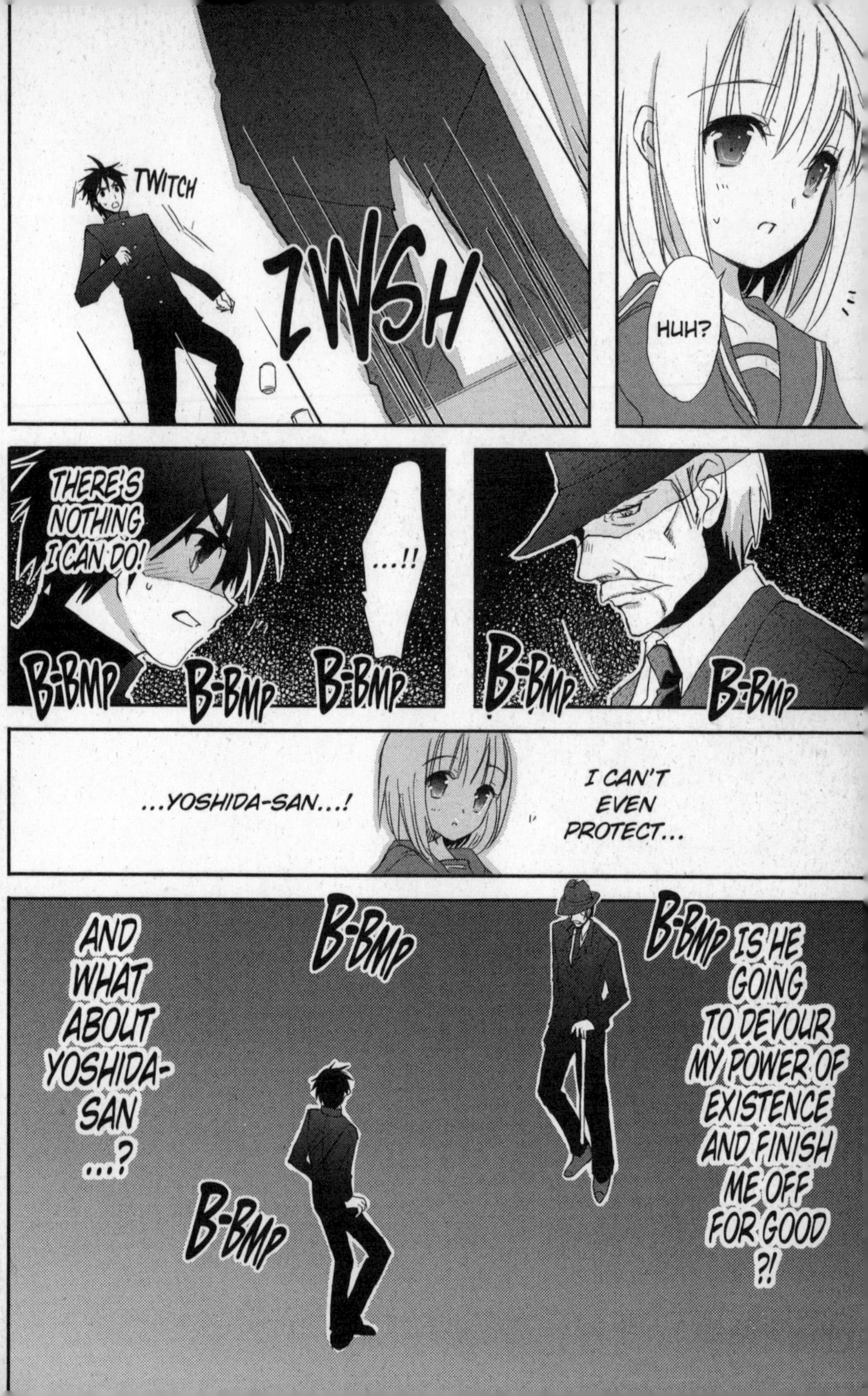
HUH?
TWITCH
ZWSH
B-BMP
B-BMP
...!!
THERE'S NOTHING I CAN DO!
B-BMP
B-BMP
B-BMP
I CAN'T EVEN PROTECT...
...YOSHIDA-SAN...!
IS HE GOING TO DEVOUR MY POWER OF EXISTENCE AND FINISH ME OFF FOR GOOD?!
B-BMP
B-BMP
AND WHAT ABOUT YOSHIDA-SAN...?
B-BMP

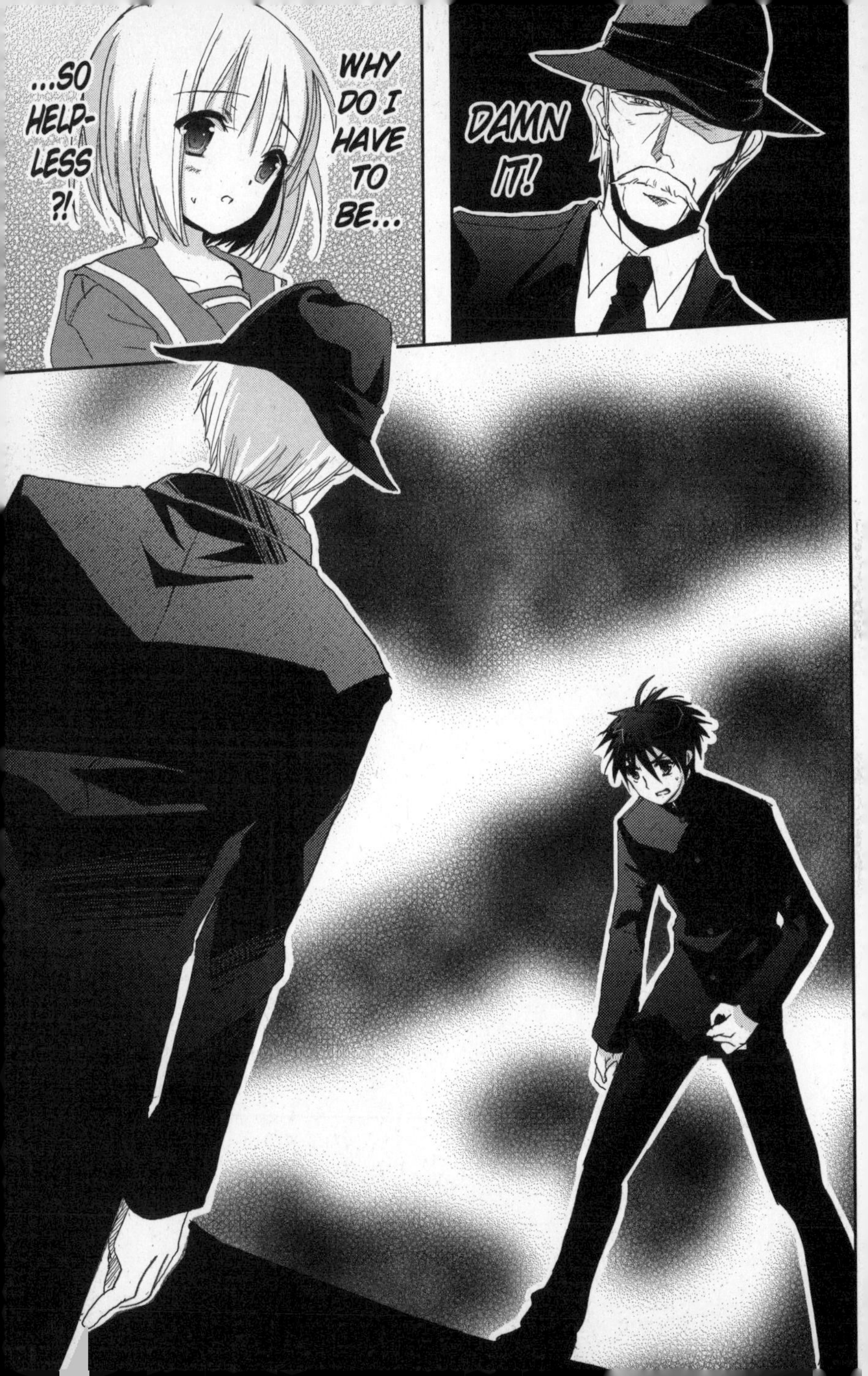
DAMN IT!
WHY DO I HAVE TO BE...
...SO HELP-LESS ?!

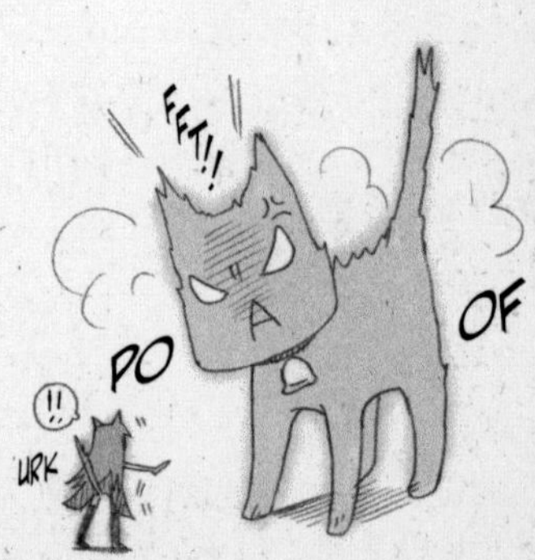
FFFT!!
PO
OF
!!
URK

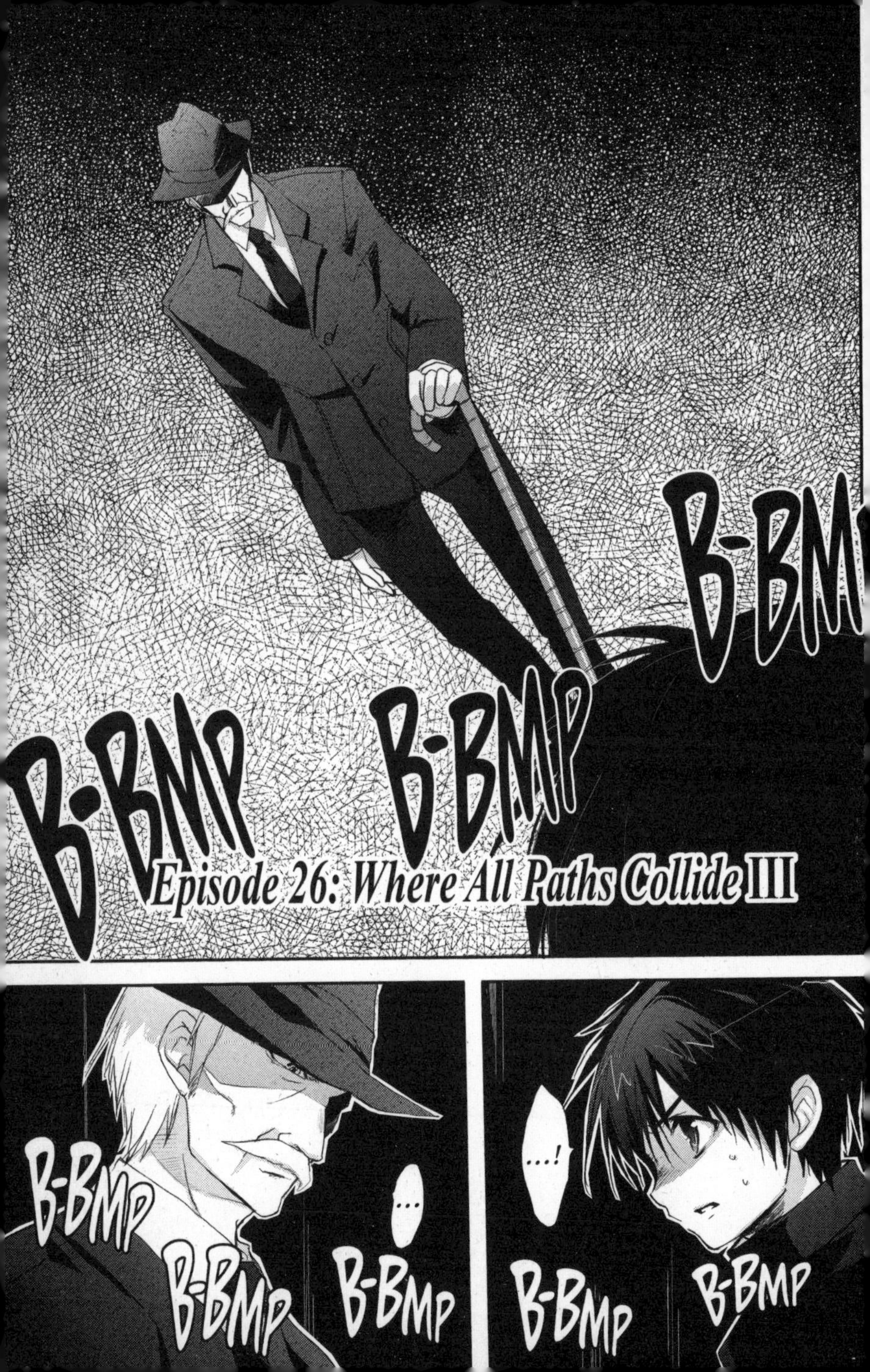
B-BM
B-BMP
B-BMP
Episode 26: Where All Paths Collide III
...!
B-BMP
B-BMP
...
B-BMP
B-BMP
B-BMP

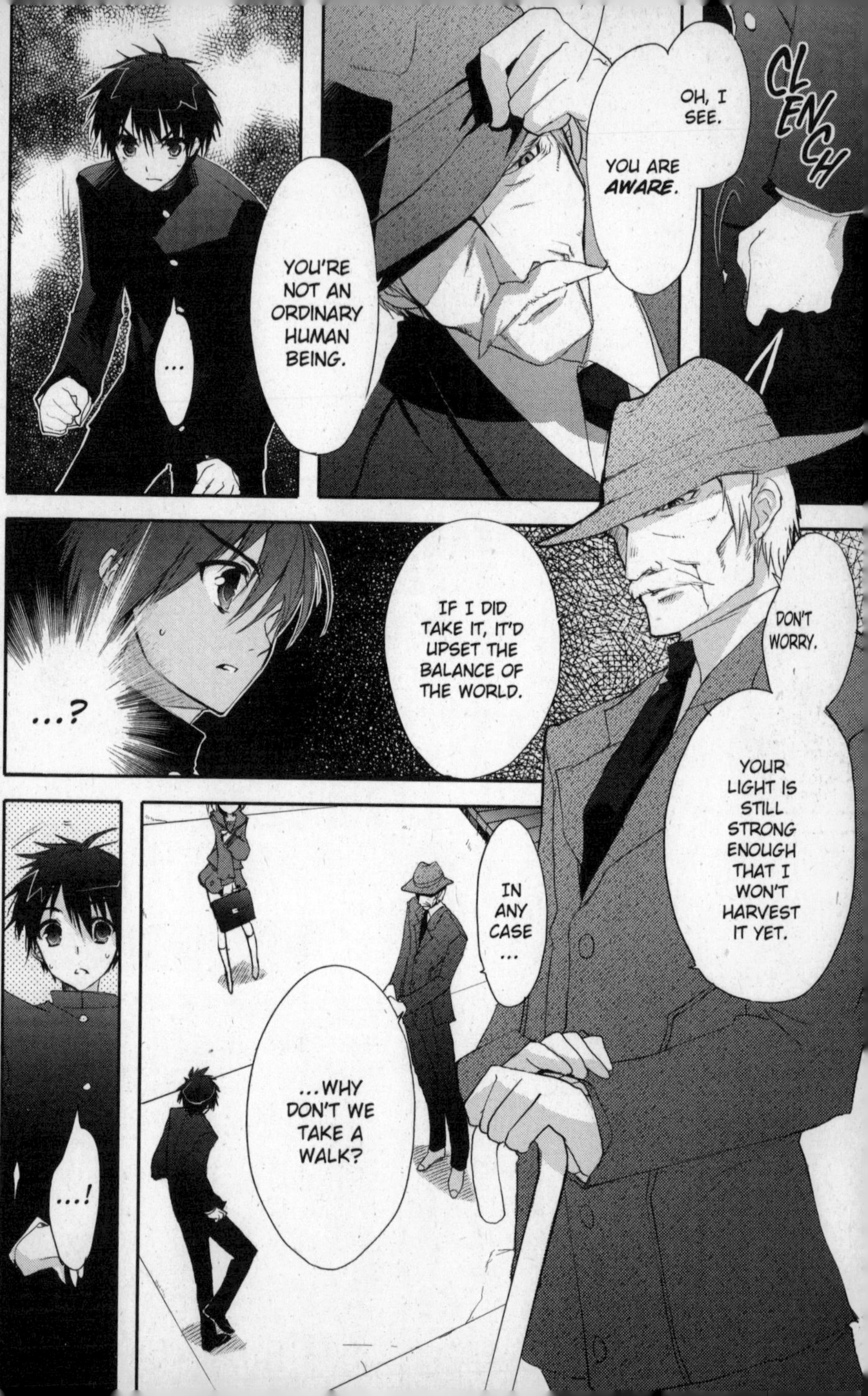
CLENCH
OH, I SEE.
YOU ARE **AWARE**.
YOU'RE NOT AN ORDINARY HUMAN BEING.
...
DON'T WORRY.
YOUR LIGHT IS STILL STRONG ENOUGH THAT I WON'T HARVEST IT YET.
IF I DID TAKE IT, IT'D UPSET THE BALANCE OF THE WORLD.
...?
IN ANY CASE ...
...WHY DON'T WE TAKE A WALK?
...!

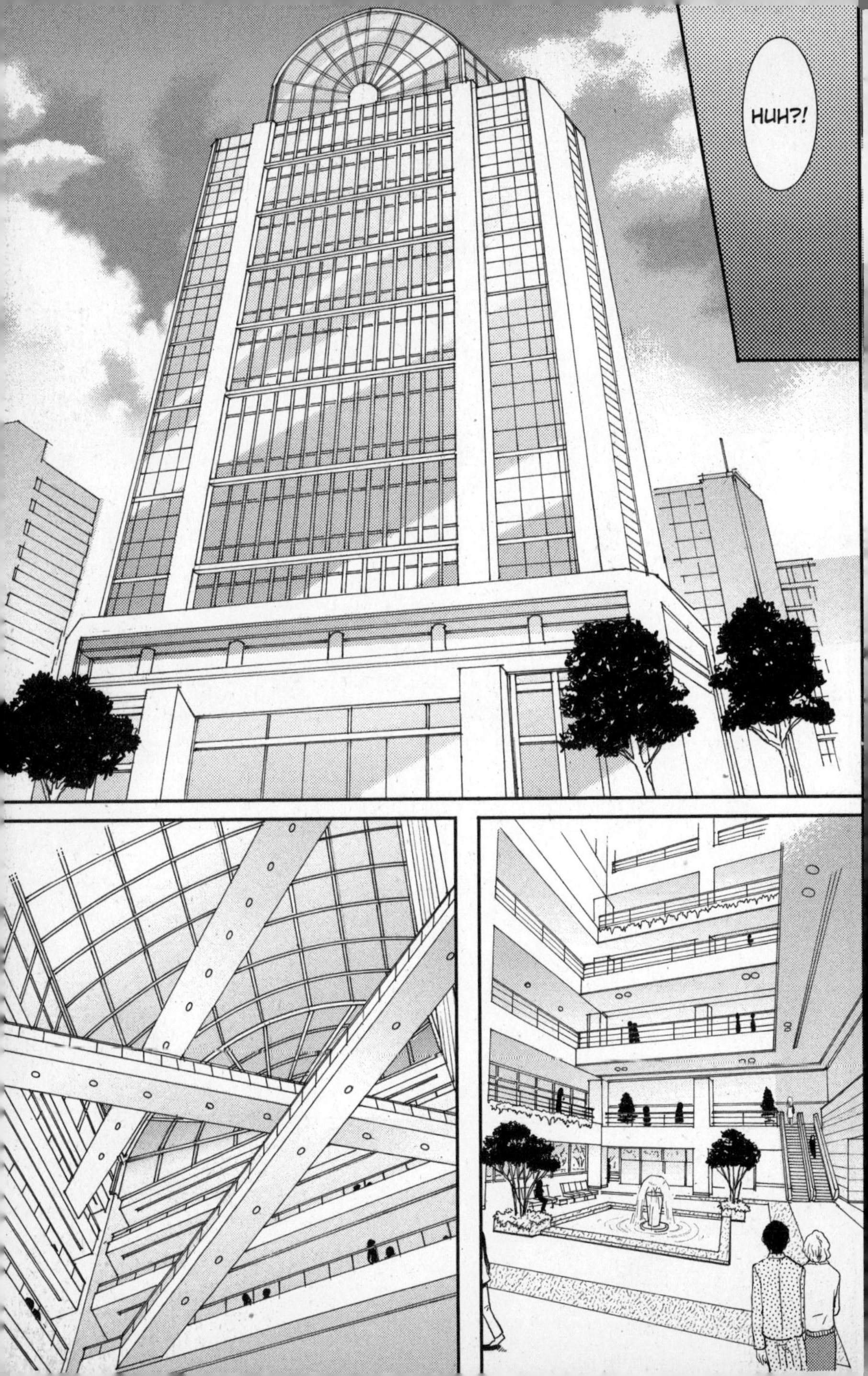
HUH?!

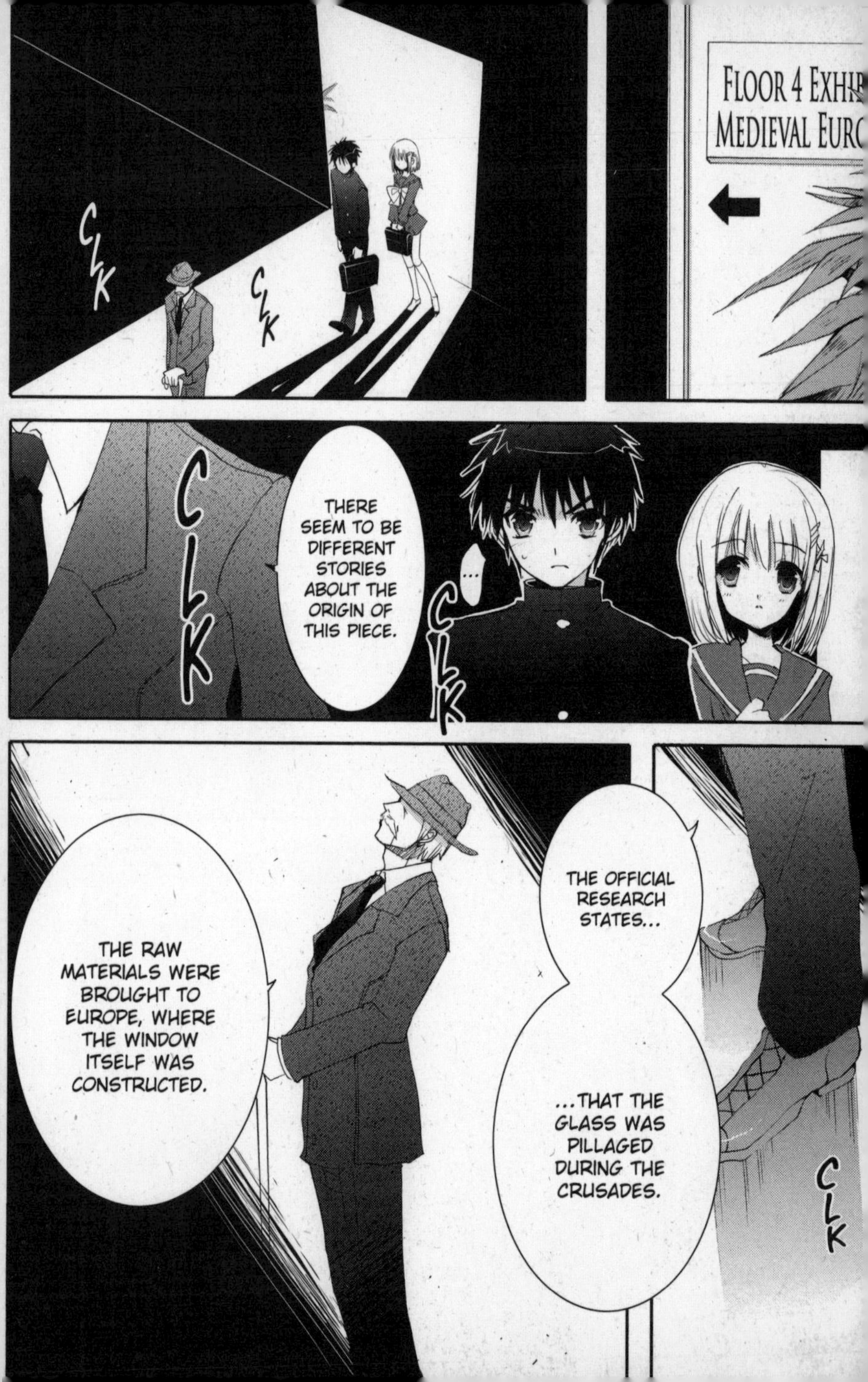
FLOOR 4 EXHI
MEDIEVAL EUR
CLK
CLK
...
THERE SEEM TO BE DIFFERENT STORIES ABOUT THE ORIGIN OF THIS PIECE.
CLK
CLK
CLK
THE OFFICIAL RESEARCH STATES...
...THAT THE GLASS WAS PILLAGED DURING THE CRUSADES.
THE RAW MATERIALS WERE BROUGHT TO EUROPE, WHERE THE WINDOW ITSELF WAS CONSTRUCTED.

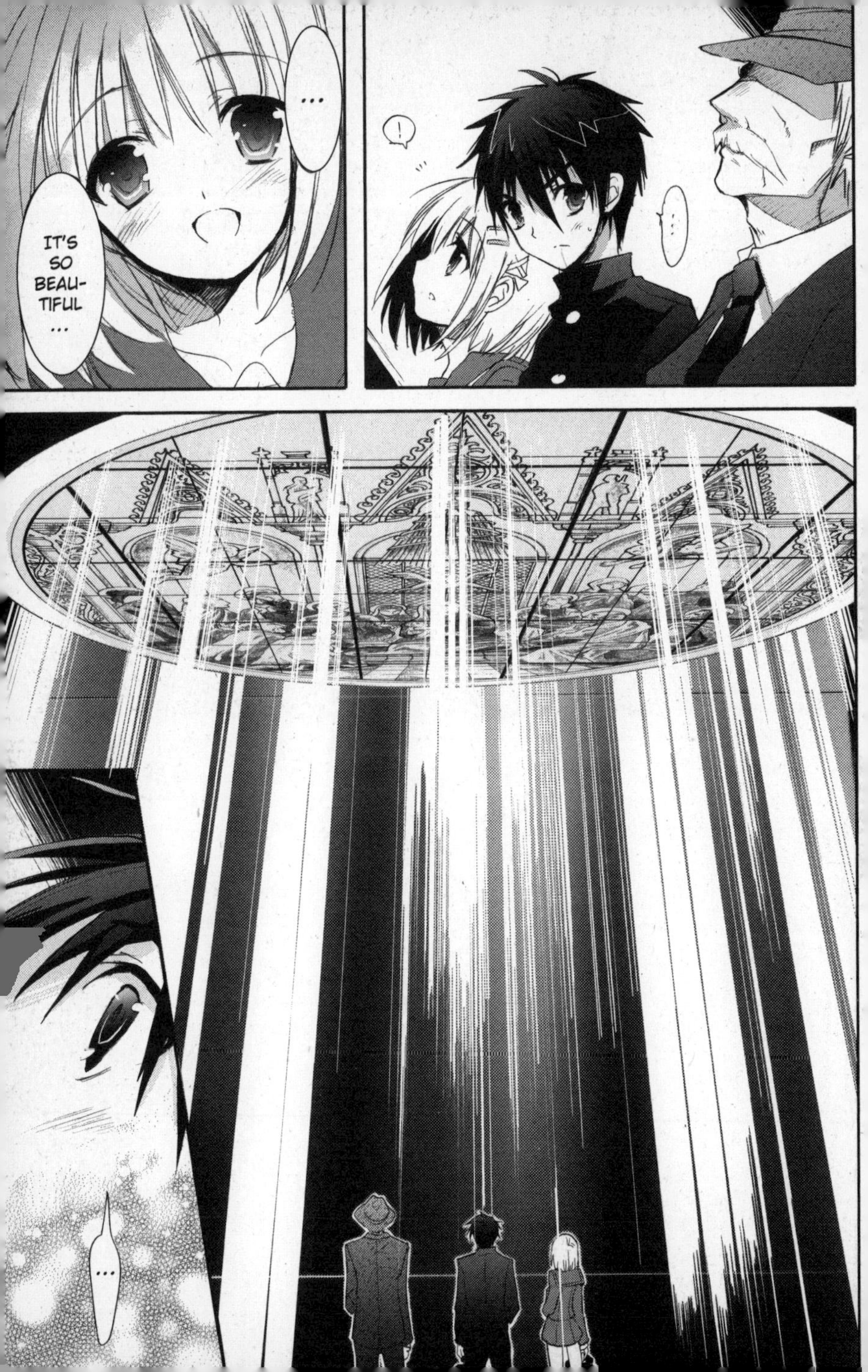
...
!
...
IT'S SO BEAUTIFUL ...
...

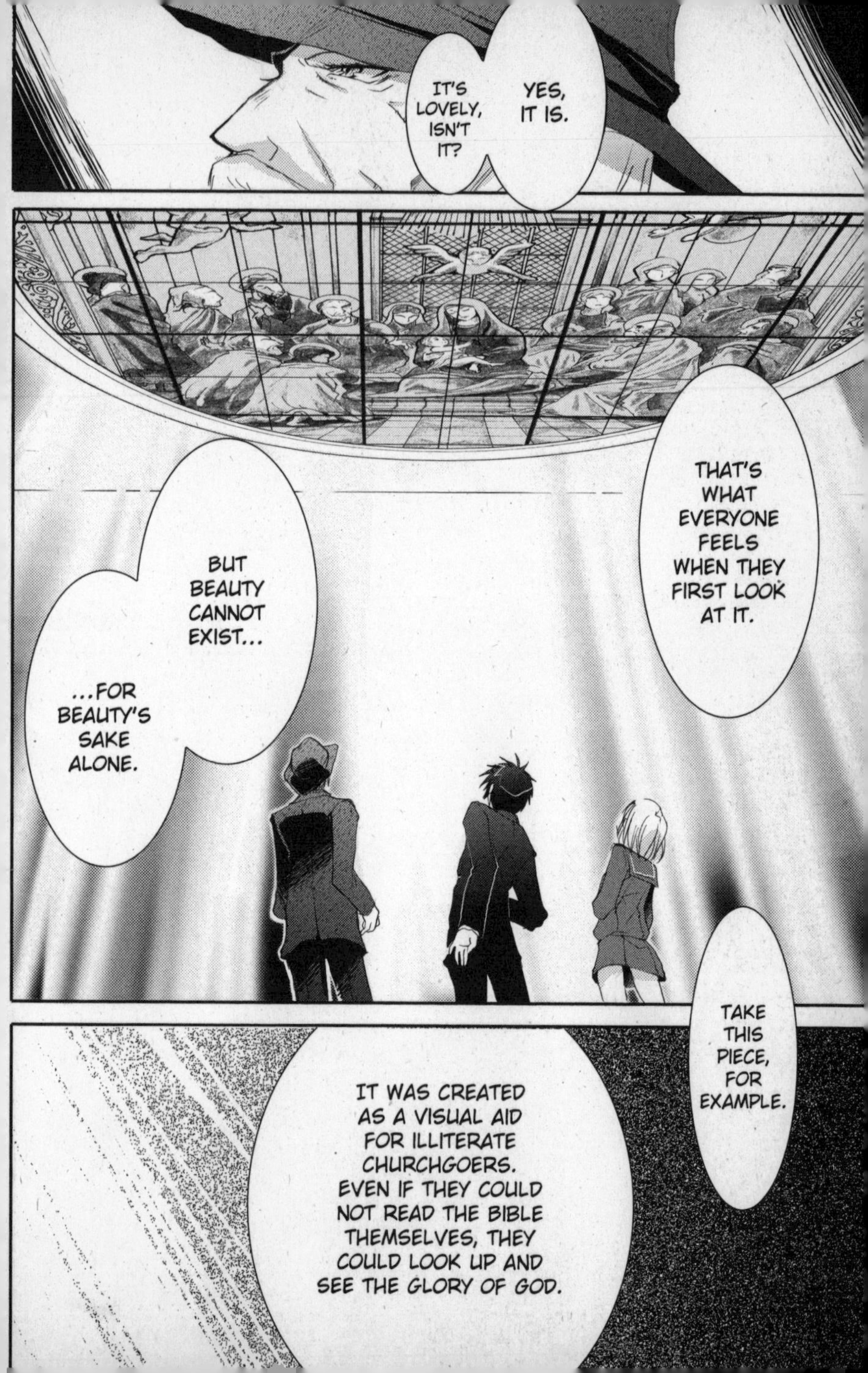
YES, IT IS.
IT'S LOVELY, ISN'T IT?
THAT'S WHAT EVERYONE FEELS WHEN THEY FIRST LOOK AT IT.
BUT BEAUTY CANNOT EXIST...
...FOR BEAUTY'S SAKE ALONE.
TAKE THIS PIECE, FOR EXAMPLE.
IT WAS CREATED AS A VISUAL AID FOR ILLITERATE CHURCHGOERS. EVEN IF THEY COULD NOT READ THE BIBLE THEMSELVES, THEY COULD LOOK UP AND SEE THE GLORY OF GOD.

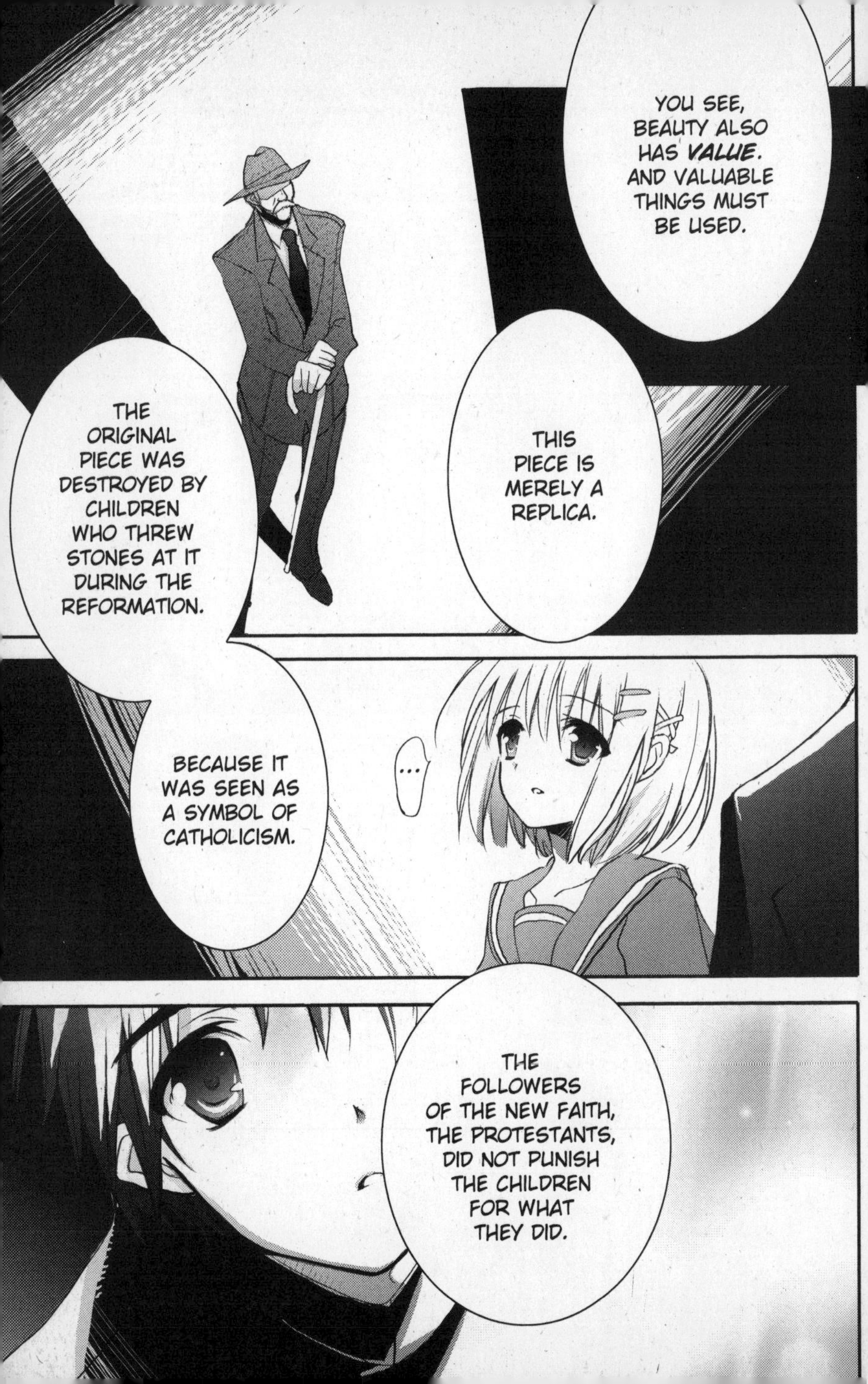
YOU SEE, BEAUTY ALSO HAS *VALUE*. AND VALUABLE THINGS MUST BE USED.
THIS PIECE IS MERELY A REPLICA.
THE ORIGINAL PIECE WAS DESTROYED BY CHILDREN WHO THREW STONES AT IT DURING THE REFORMATION.
BECAUSE IT WAS SEEN AS A SYMBOL OF CATHOLICISM.
...
THE FOLLOWERS OF THE NEW FAITH, THE PROTESTANTS, DID NOT PUNISH THE CHILDREN FOR WHAT THEY DID.

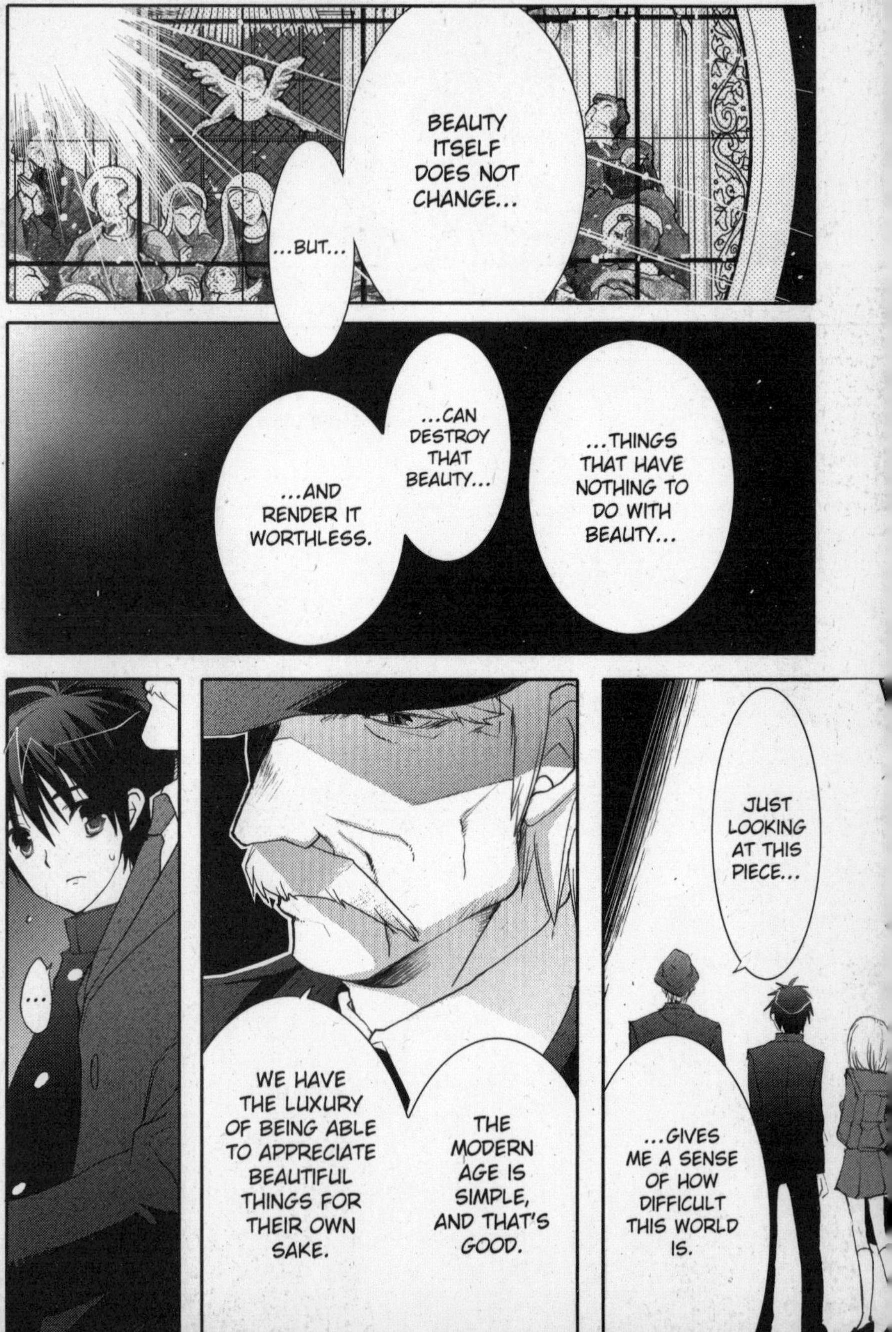
BEAUTY ITSELF DOES NOT CHANGE...
...BUT...
...THINGS THAT HAVE NOTHING TO DO WITH BEAUTY...
...CAN DESTROY THAT BEAUTY...
...AND RENDER IT WORTHLESS.
JUST LOOKING AT THIS PIECE...
...GIVES ME A SENSE OF HOW DIFFICULT THIS WORLD IS.
THE MODERN AGE IS SIMPLE, AND THAT'S GOOD.
WE HAVE THE LUXURY OF BEING ABLE TO APPRECIATE BEAUTIFUL THINGS FOR THEIR OWN SAKE.
...

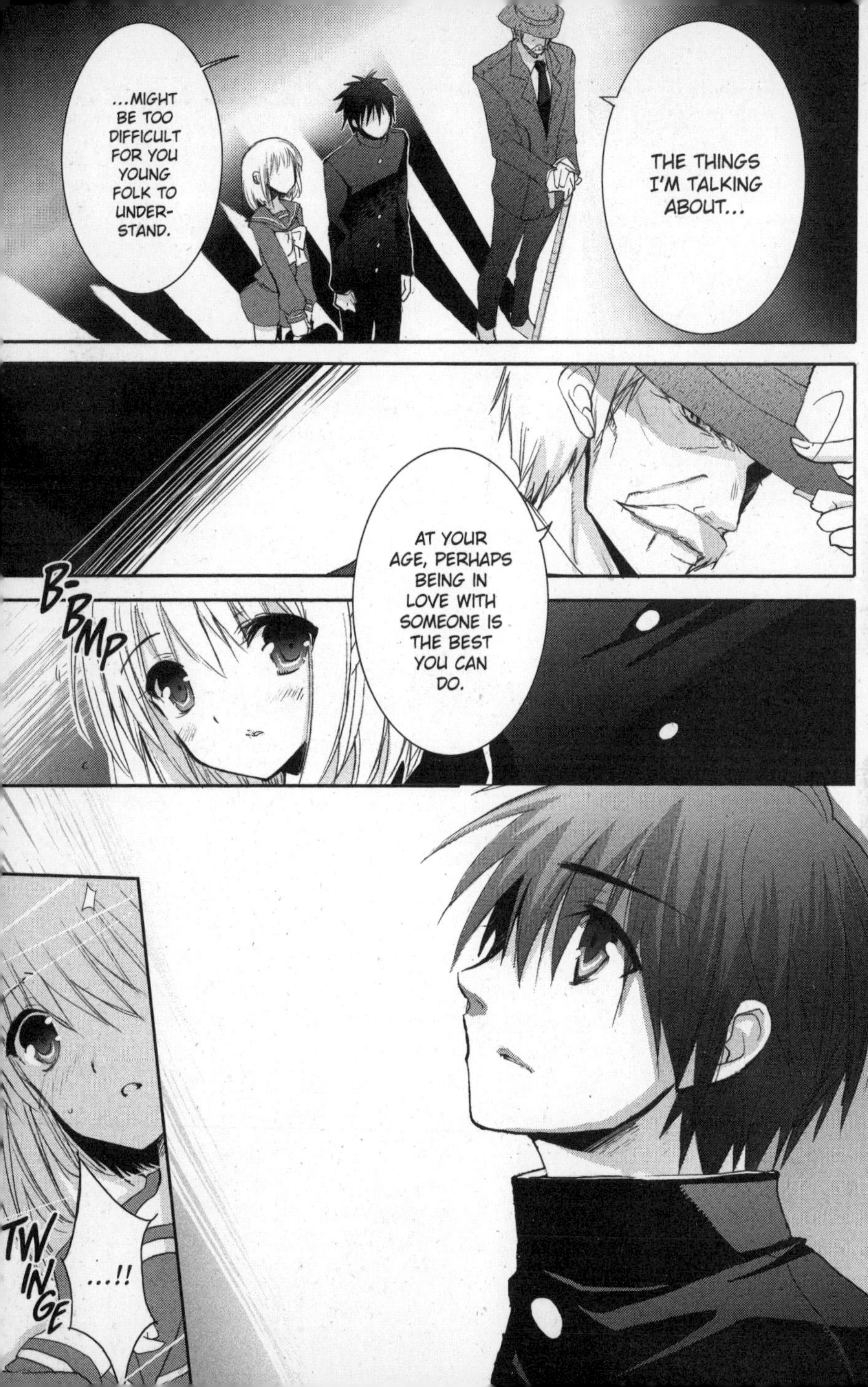
THE THINGS I'M TALKING ABOUT...
...MIGHT BE TOO DIFFICULT FOR YOU YOUNG FOLK TO UNDER-STAND.
AT YOUR AGE, PERHAPS BEING IN LOVE WITH SOMEONE IS THE BEST YOU CAN DO.
B-BMP
TWINGE
...!!

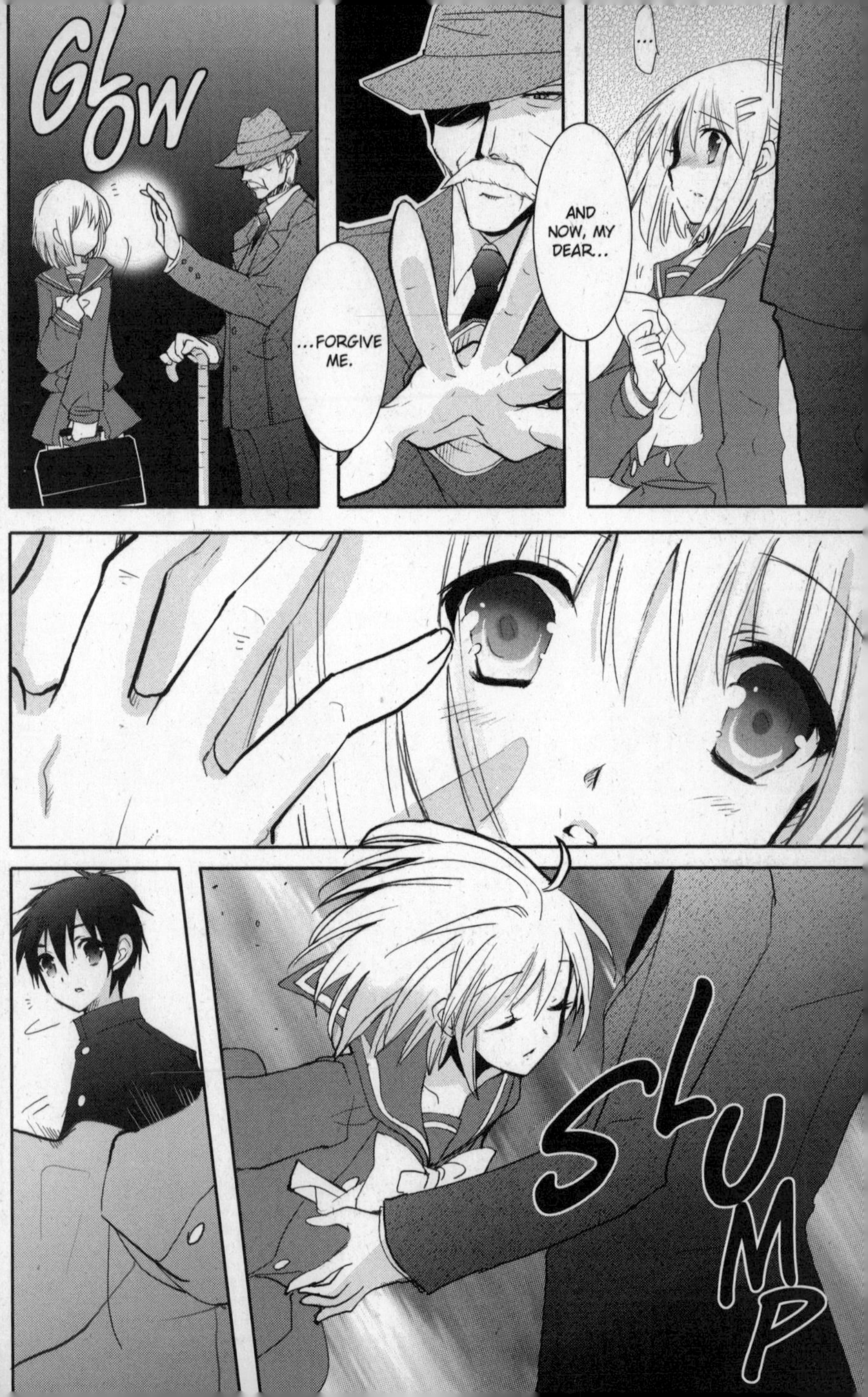
...
AND NOW, MY DEAR...
...FORGIVE ME.
GLOW
SLUMP

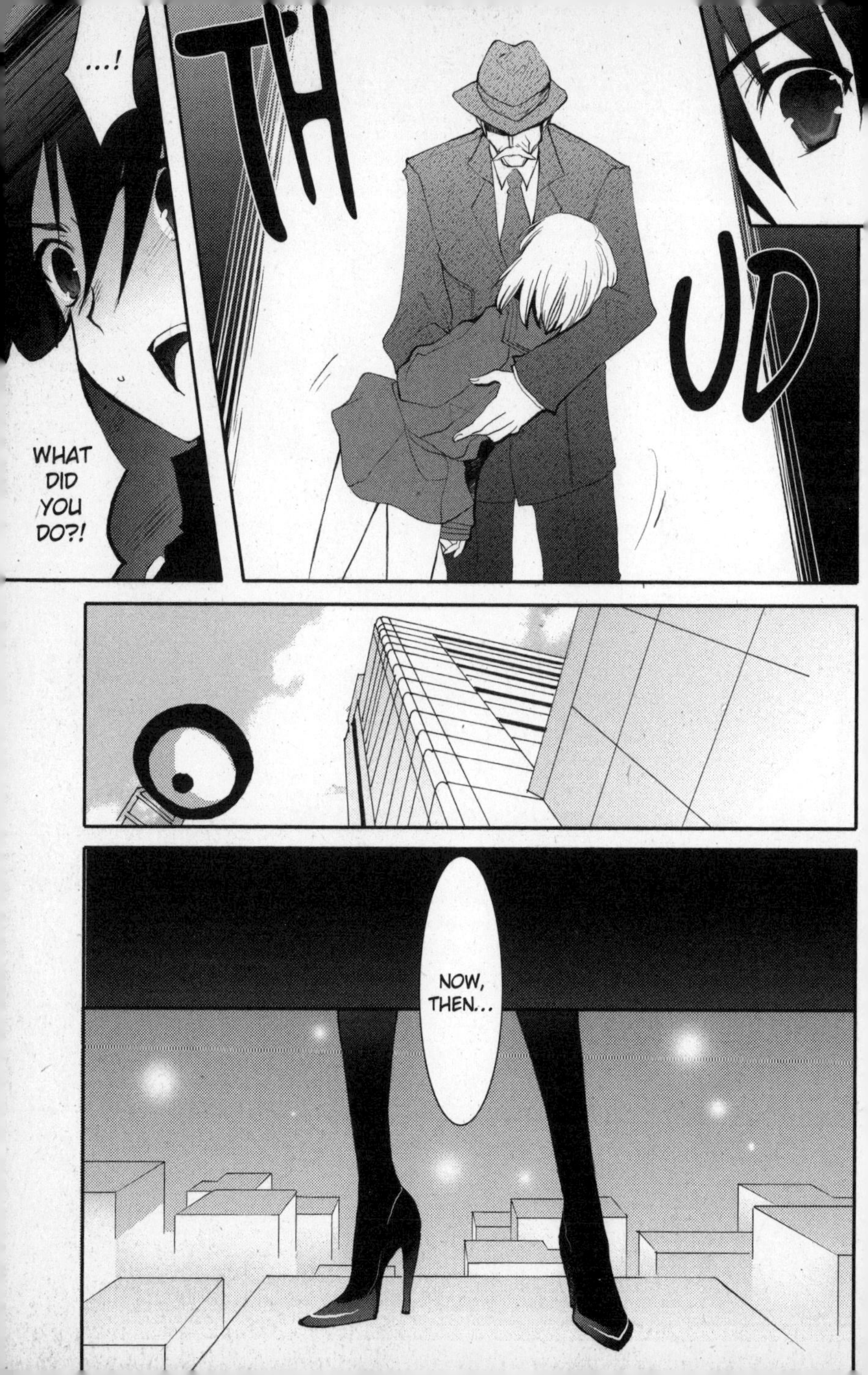
TH
UD
...!
WHAT DID YOU DO?!
NOW, THEN...

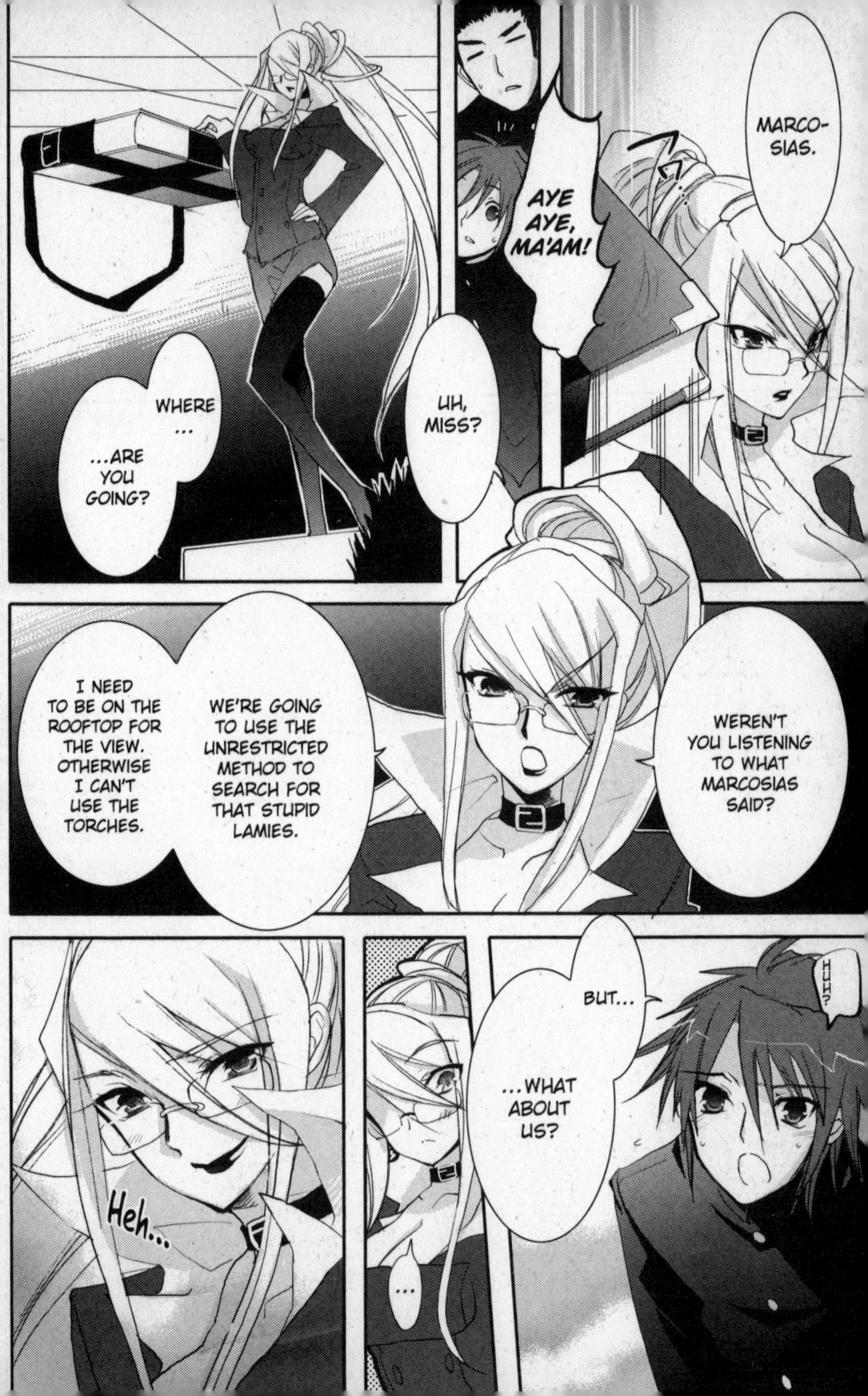
MARCO-SIAS.
AYE AYE, MA'AM!
UH, MISS?
WHERE ...
...ARE YOU GOING?
WEREN'T YOU LISTENING TO WHAT MARCOSIAS SAID?
WE'RE GOING TO USE THE UNRESTRICTED METHOD TO SEARCH FOR THAT STUPID LAMIES.
I NEED TO BE ON THE ROOFTOP FOR THE VIEW. OTHERWISE I CAN'T USE THE TORCHES.
HUH?
BUT...
...WHAT ABOUT US?
...
Heh...

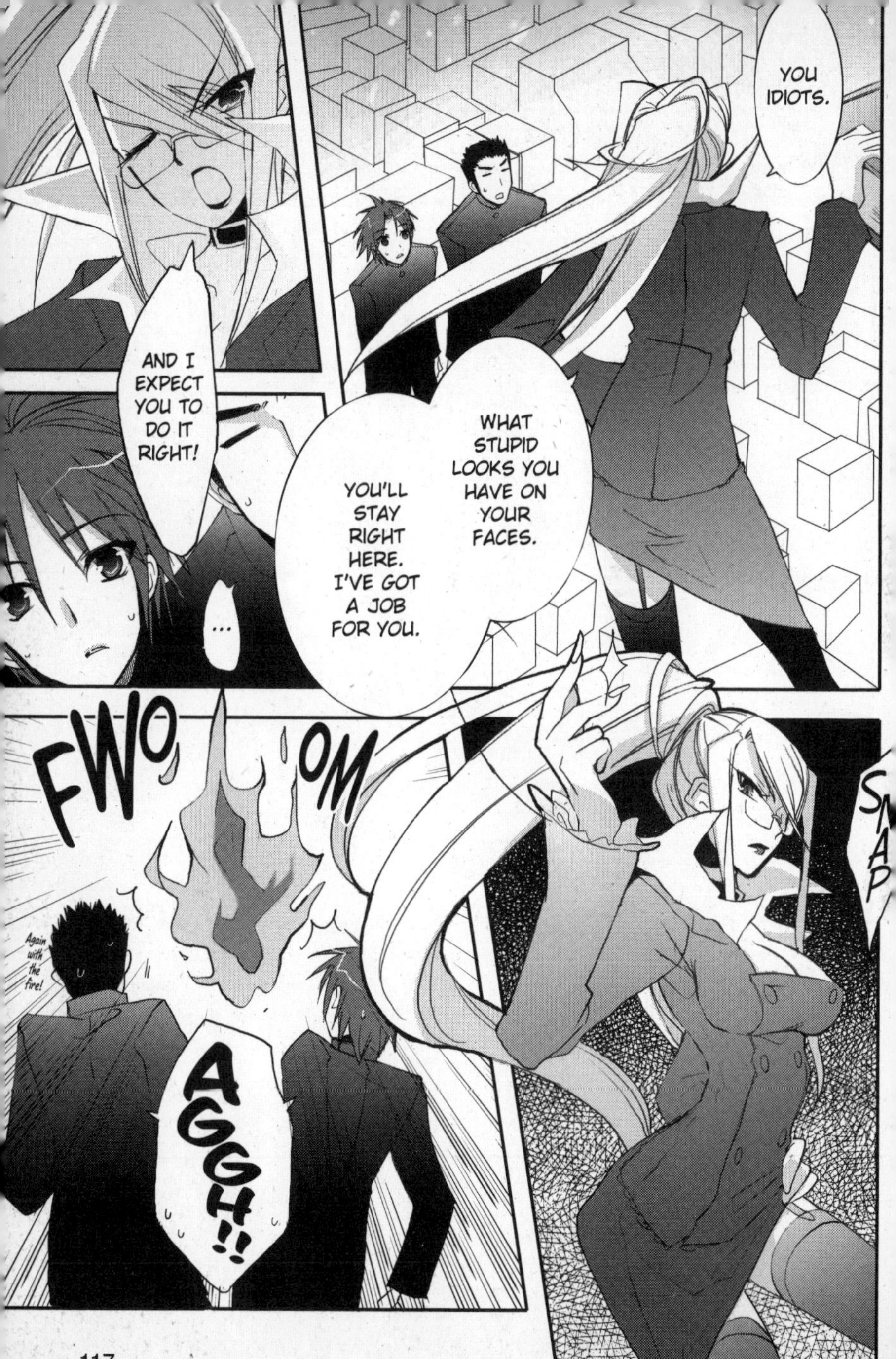
YOU IDIOTS.
WHAT STUPID LOOKS YOU HAVE ON YOUR FACES.
YOU'LL STAY RIGHT HERE. I'VE GOT A JOB FOR YOU.
AND I EXPECT YOU TO DO IT RIGHT!
...
SNAP
FWOOM
Again with the fire!
AGGH!!

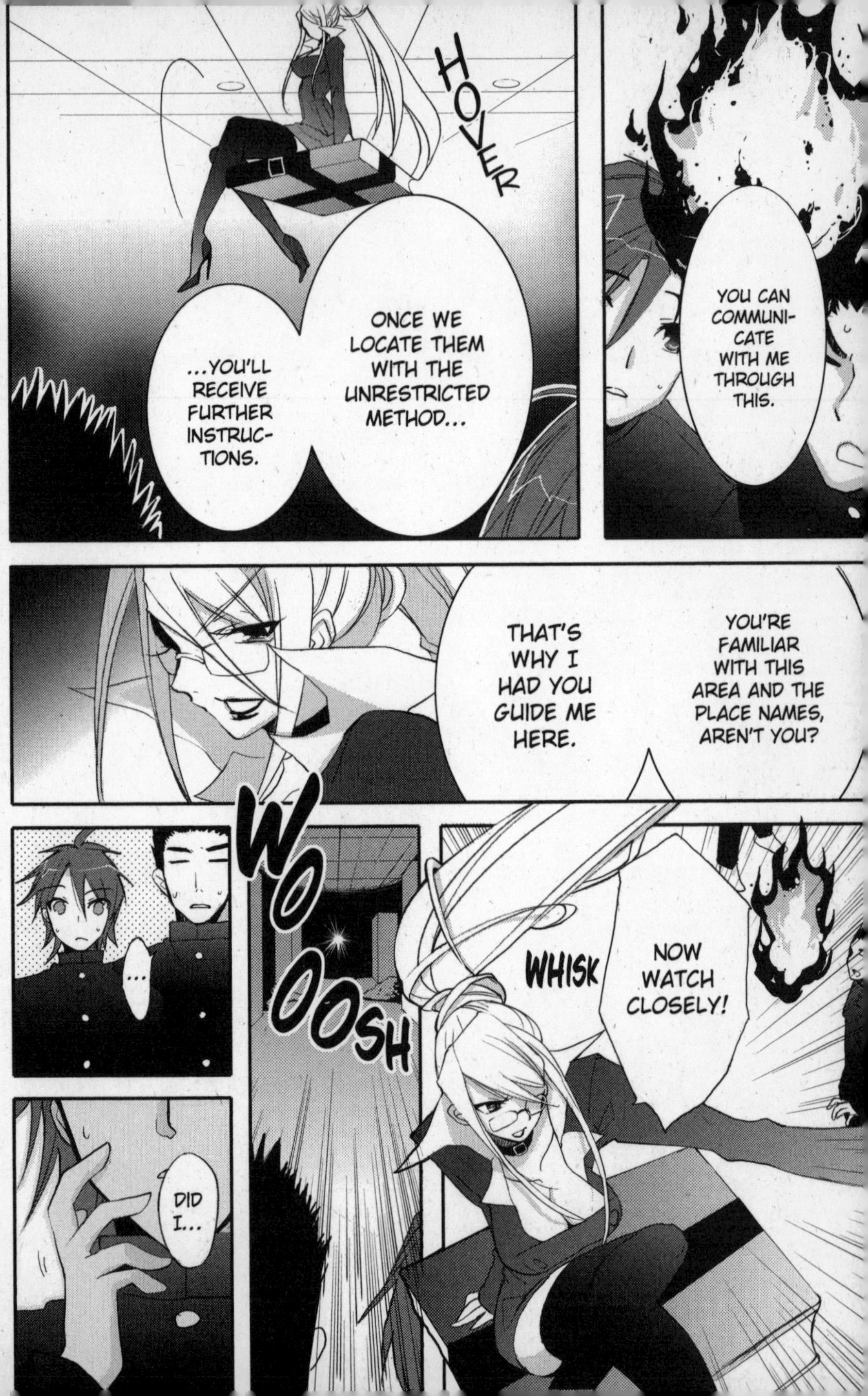
YOU CAN COMMUNI-CATE WITH ME THROUGH THIS.
HOVER
ONCE WE LOCATE THEM WITH THE UNRESTRICTED METHOD...
...YOU'LL RECEIVE FURTHER INSTRUC-TIONS.
YOU'RE FAMILIAR WITH THIS AREA AND THE PLACE NAMES, AREN'T YOU?
THAT'S WHY I HAD YOU GUIDE ME HERE.
NOW WATCH CLOSELY!
WHISK
WOOOSH
...
DID I...

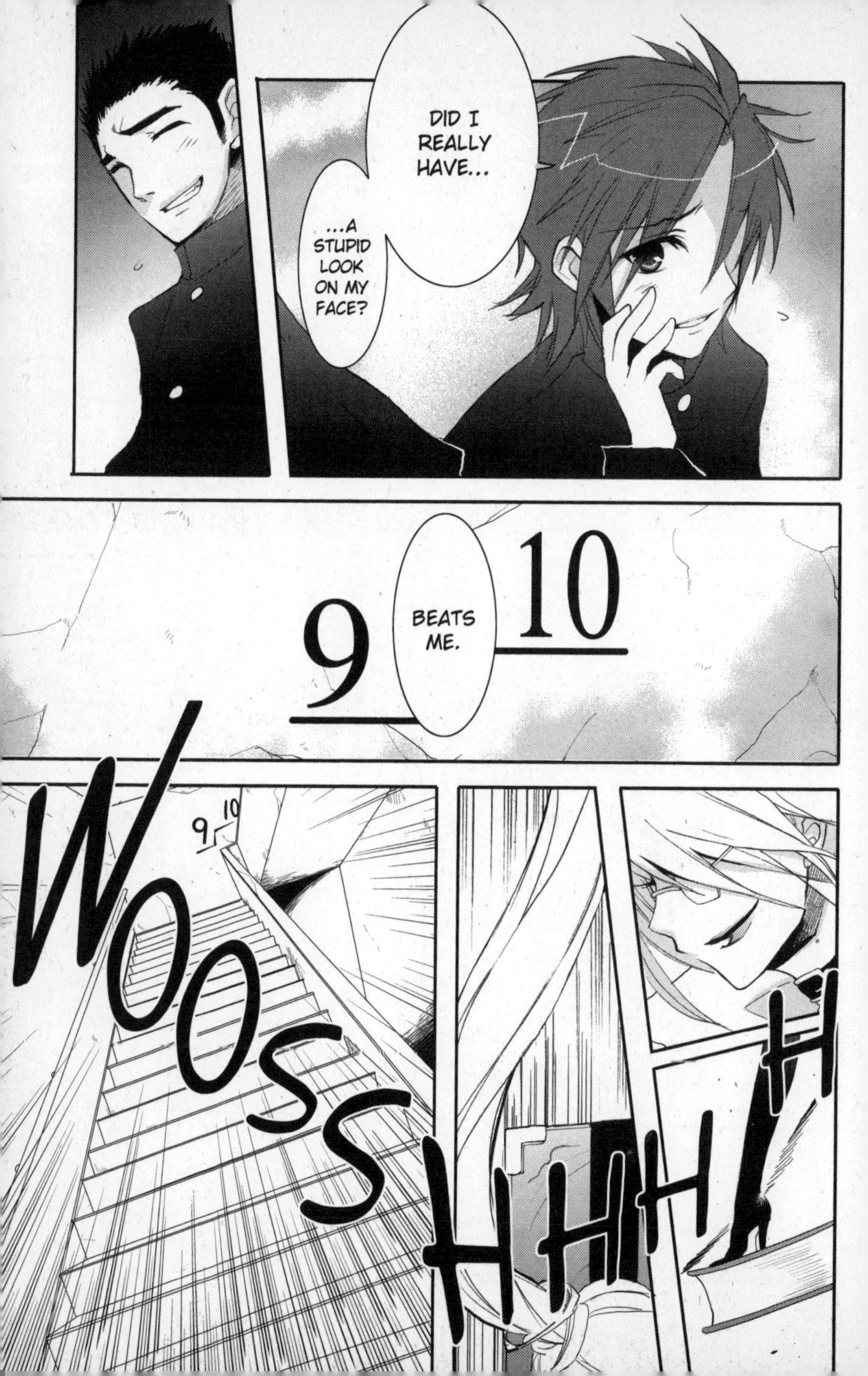
DID I REALLY HAVE...
...A STUPID LOOK ON MY FACE?
BEATS ME.
9 10
WOOSSHHHHH!

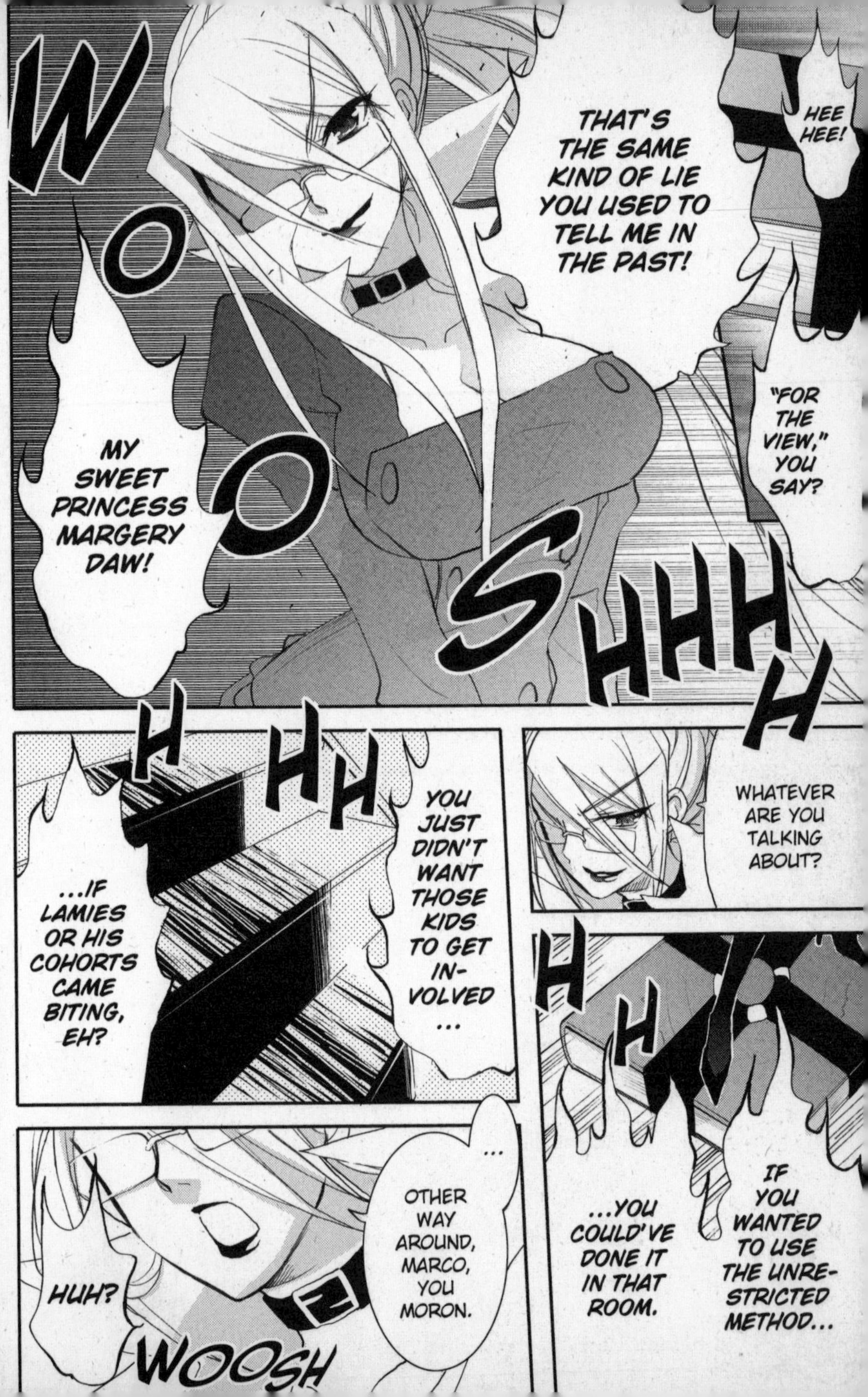
HEE HEE!
THAT'S THE SAME KIND OF LIE YOU USED TO TELL ME IN THE PAST!
"FOR THE VIEW," YOU SAY?
MY SWEET PRINCESS MARGERY DAW!
WOOOSHHHHHHHHHH
WHATEVER ARE YOU TALKING ABOUT?
YOU JUST DIDN'T WANT THOSE KIDS TO GET IN-VOLVED...
...IF LAMIES OR HIS COHORTS CAME BITING, EH?
IF YOU WANTED TO USE THE UNRE-STRICTED METHOD...
...YOU COULD'VE DONE IT IN THAT ROOM.
...
OTHER WAY AROUND, MARCO, YOU MORON.
HUH?
WOOSH

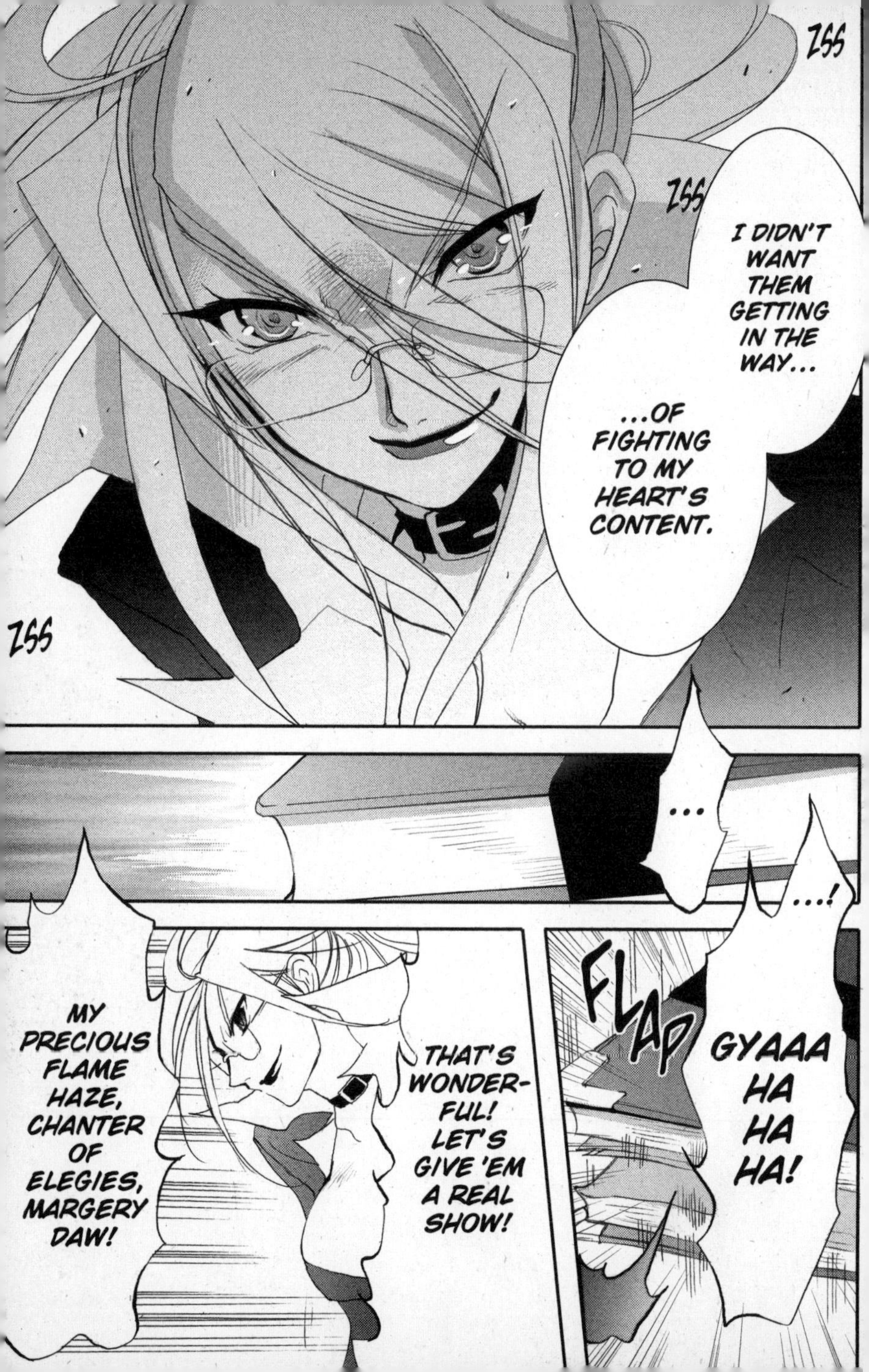
ZSS
ZSS
I DIDN'T WANT THEM GETTING IN THE WAY...
...OF FIGHTING TO MY HEART'S CONTENT.
ZSS
...
...!
FLAP
GYAAA HA HA HA!
THAT'S WONDER-FUL! LET'S GIVE 'EM A REAL SHOW!
MY PRECIOUS FLAME HAZE, CHANTER OF ELEGIES, MARGERY DAW!

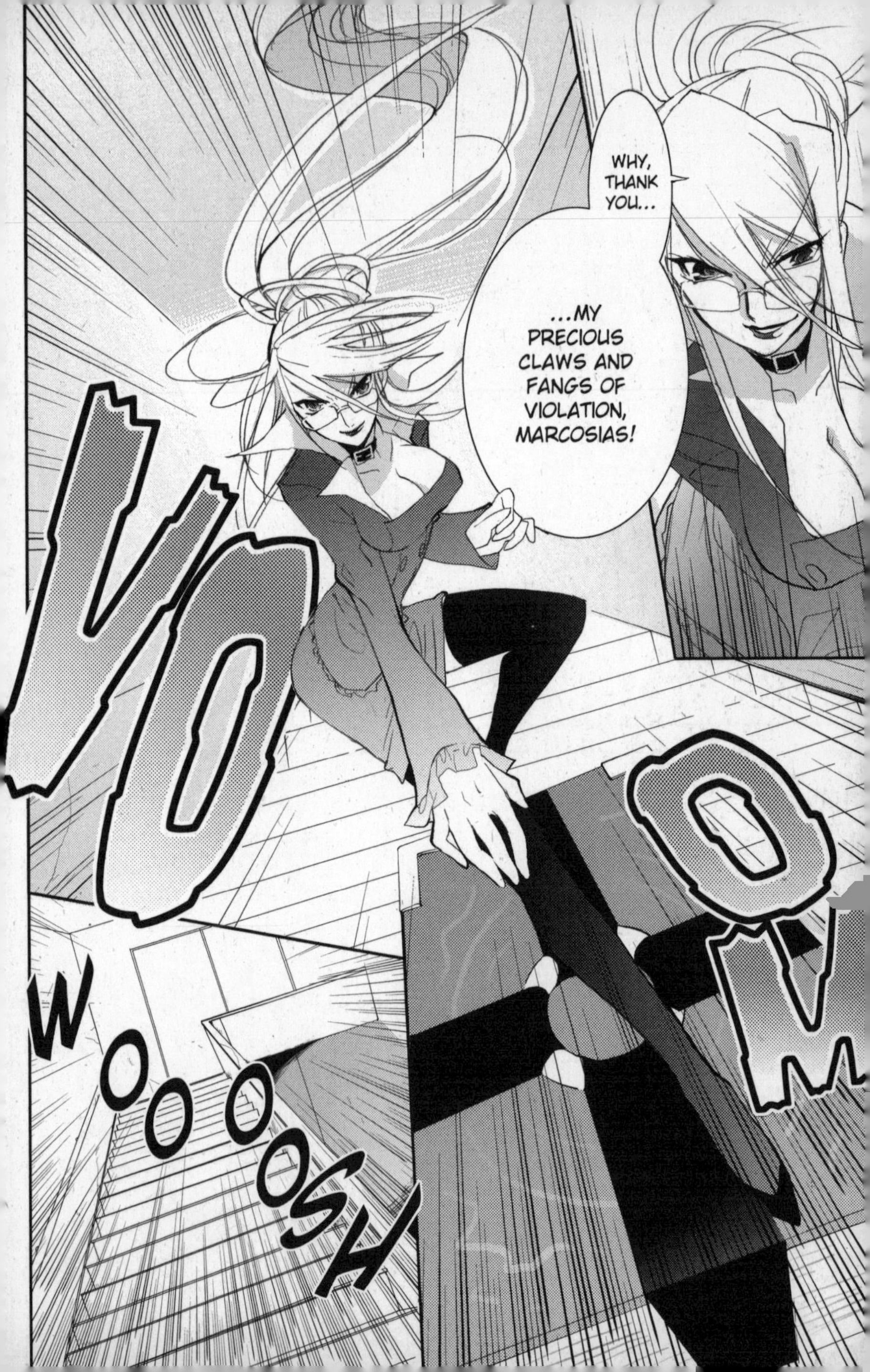
WHY, THANK YOU...
...MY PRECIOUS CLAWS AND FANGS OF VIOLATION, MARCOSIAS!
VOOM
WOOOOSH

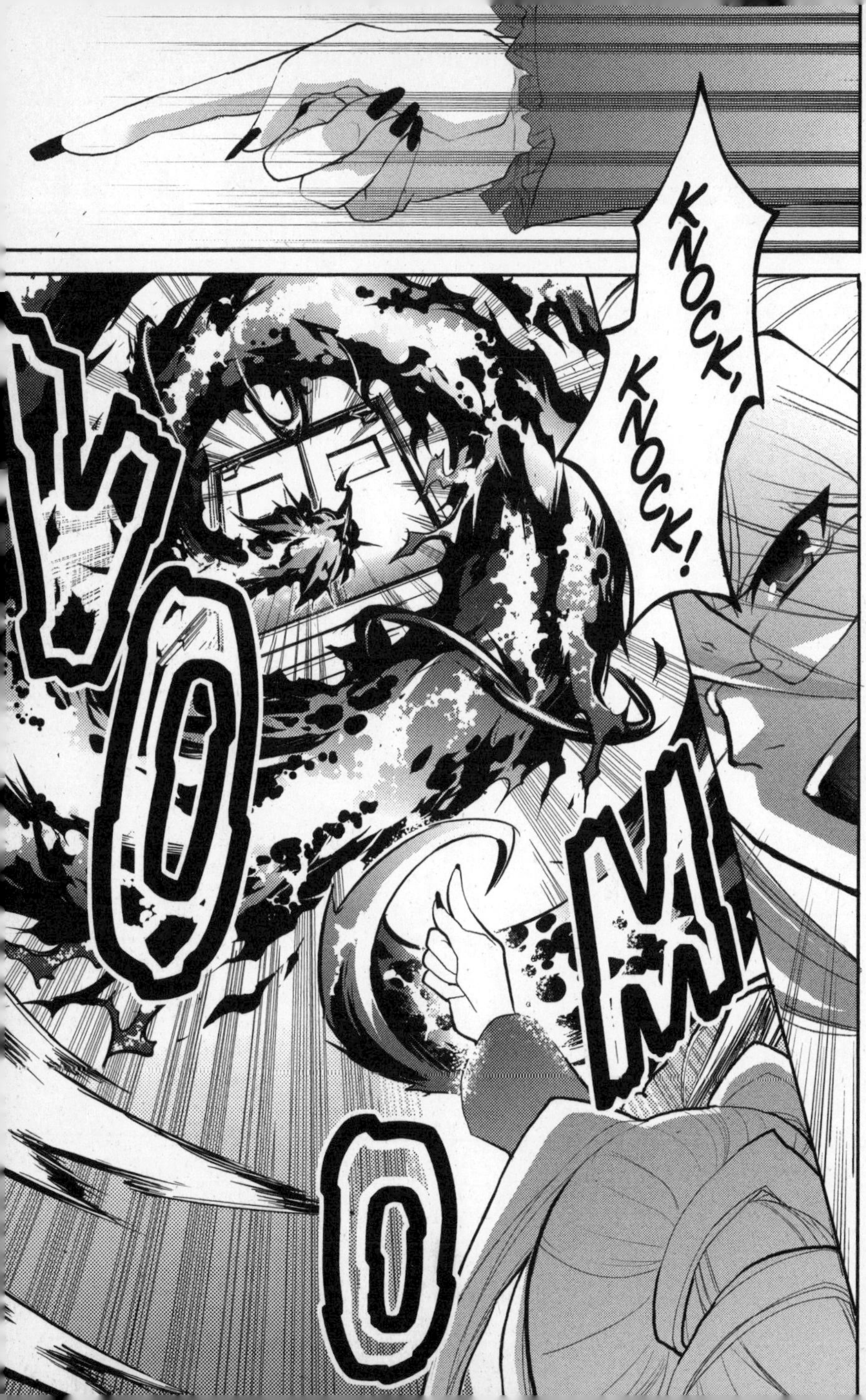
KNOCK, KNOCK!

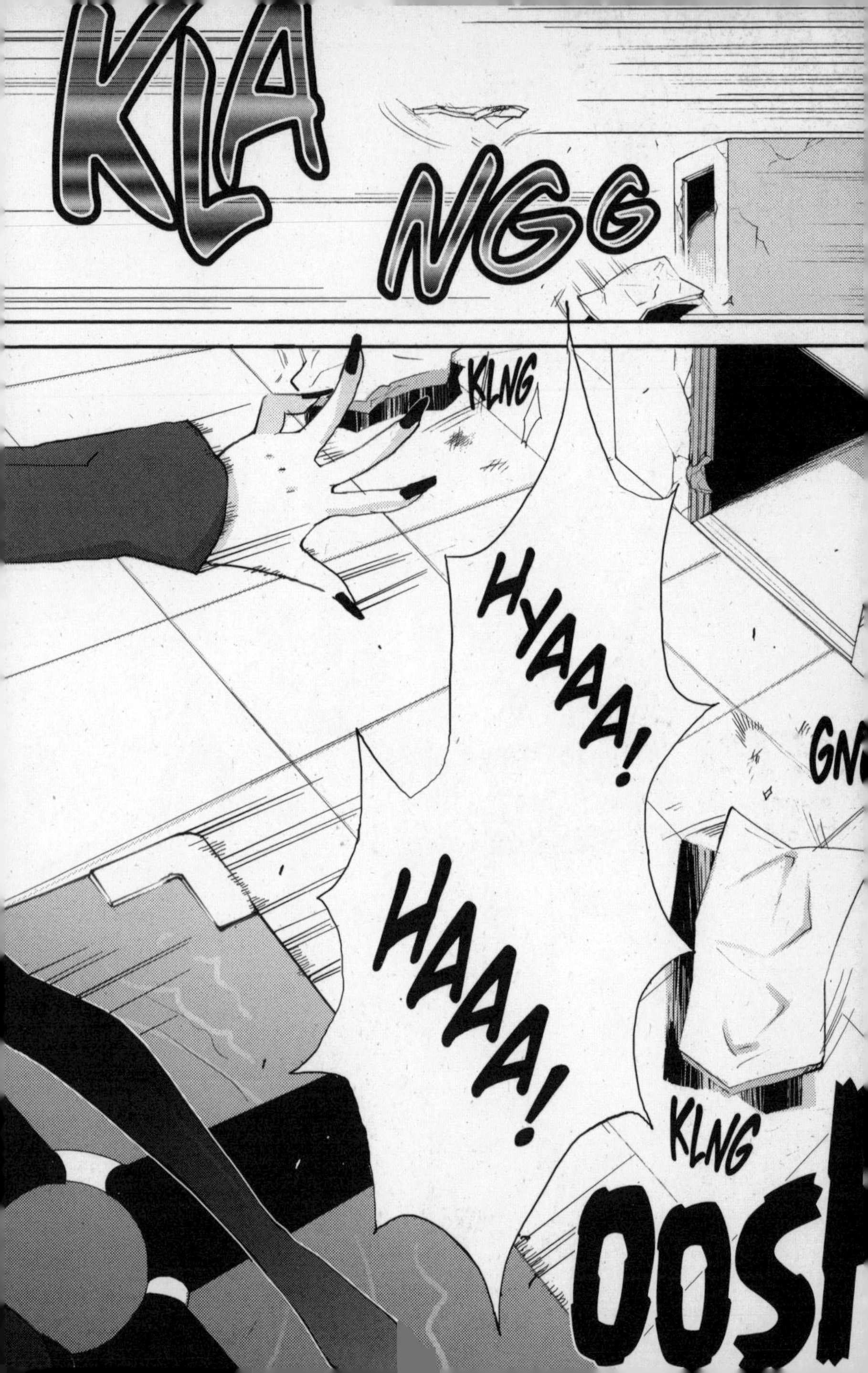
KLANGG
GN
KLNG
HYAAAA! HAAAA!
KLNG
OOSH

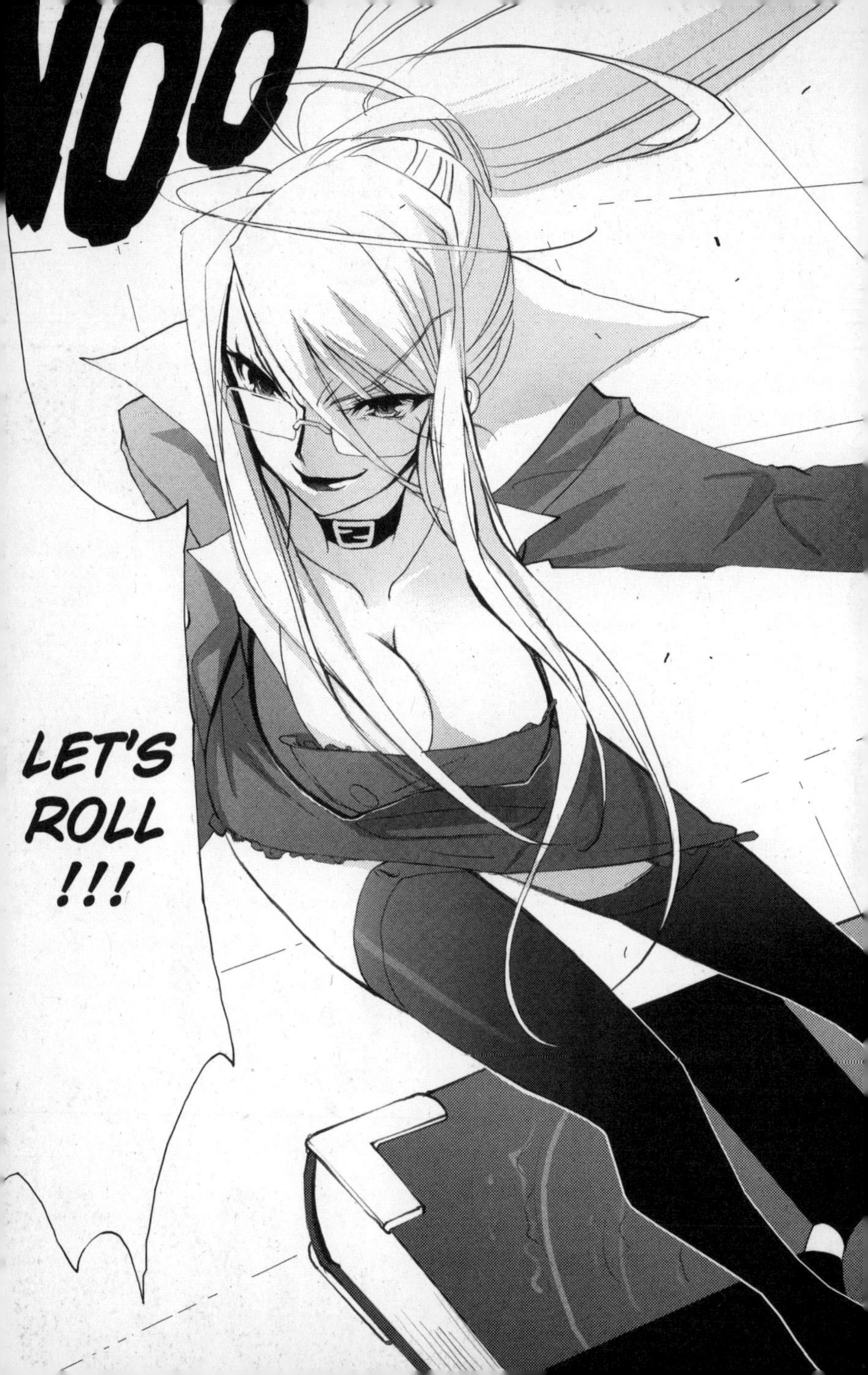
VOO
LET'S ROLL !!!

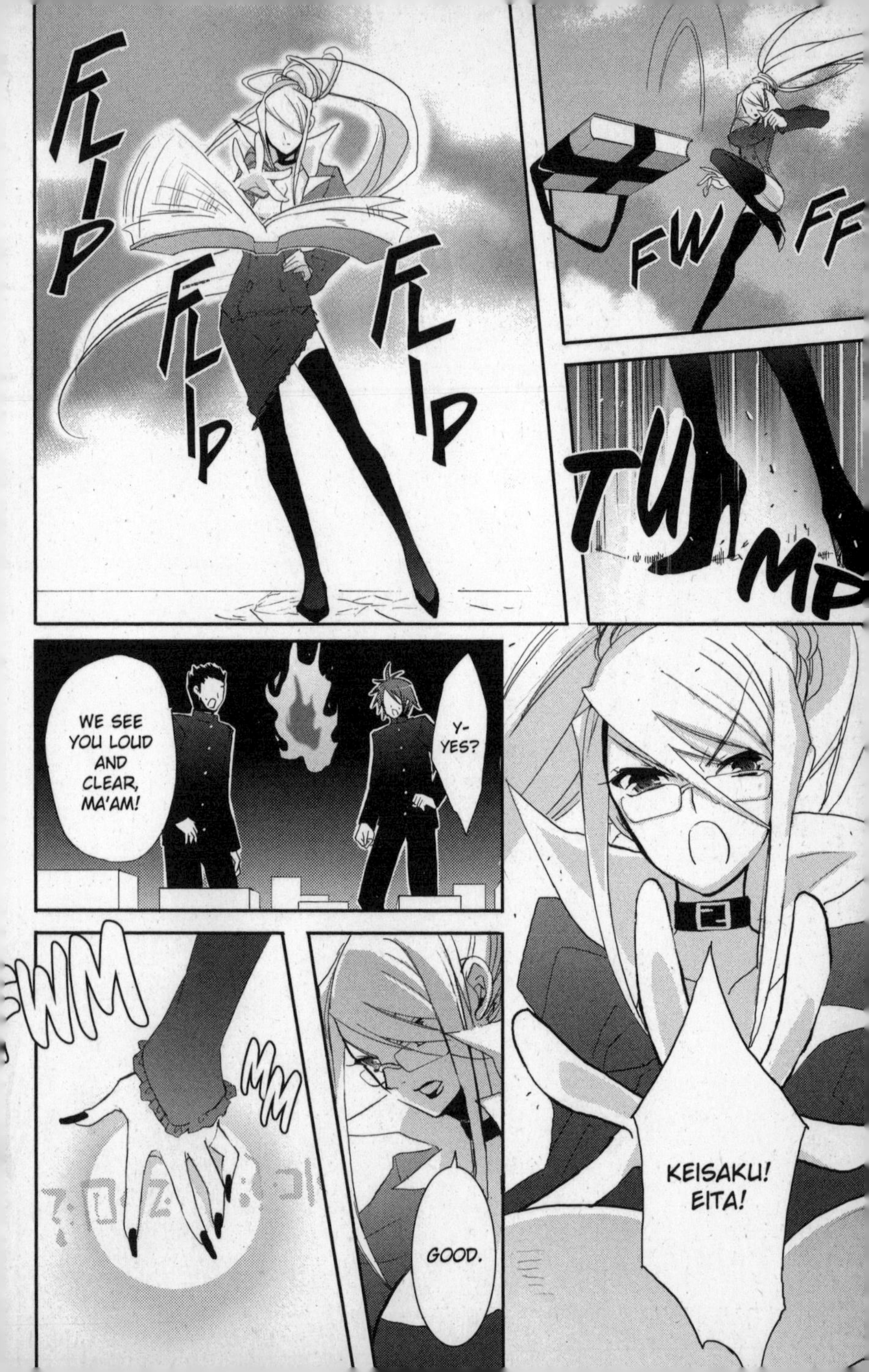
FW
FF
TU
MP
FLIP
FLIP
FLIP
KEISAKU! EITA!
Y-YES?
WE SEE YOU LOUD AND CLEAR, MA'AM!
GOOD.
WM
MM

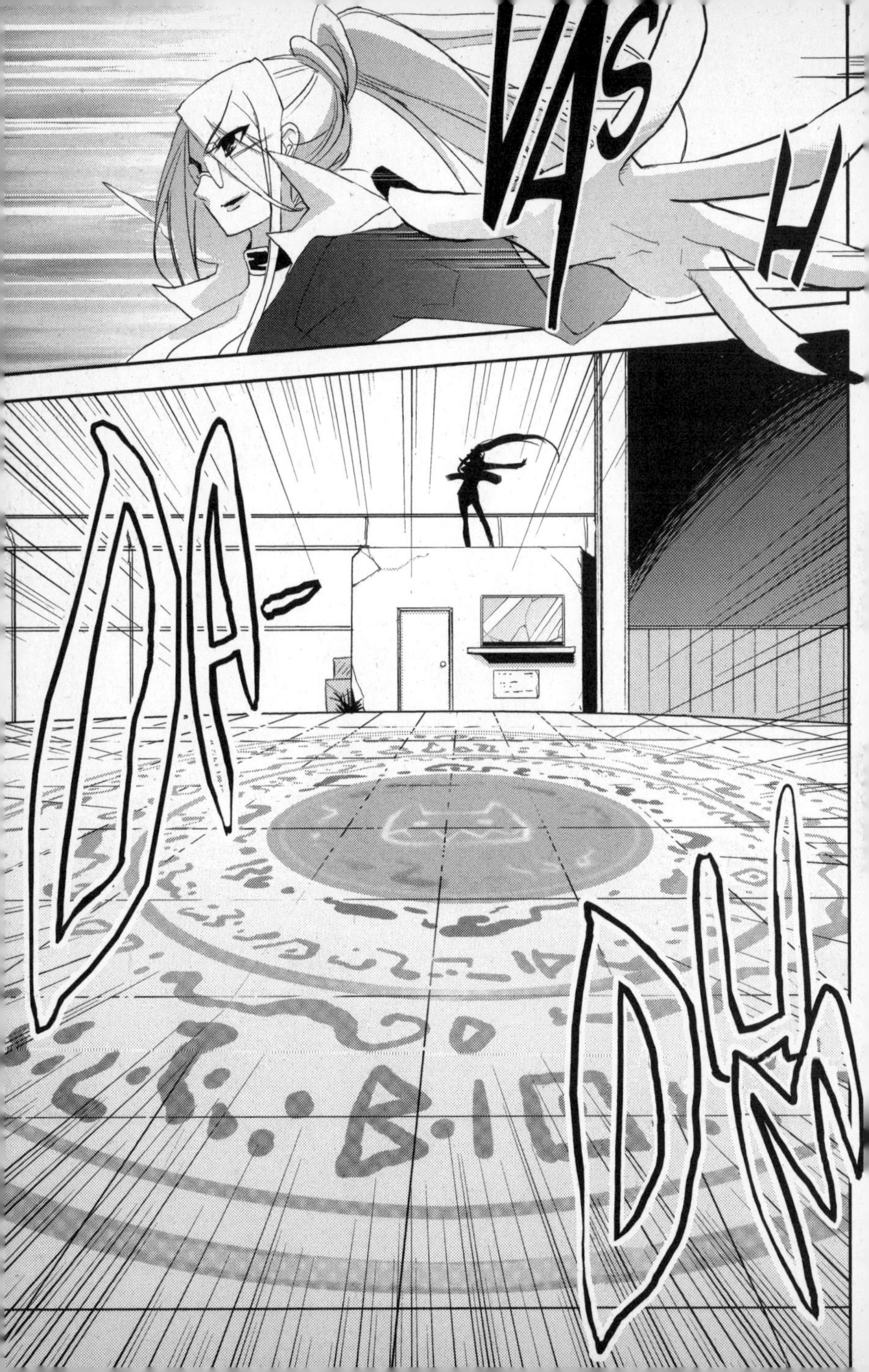
VASH
DA-DUM

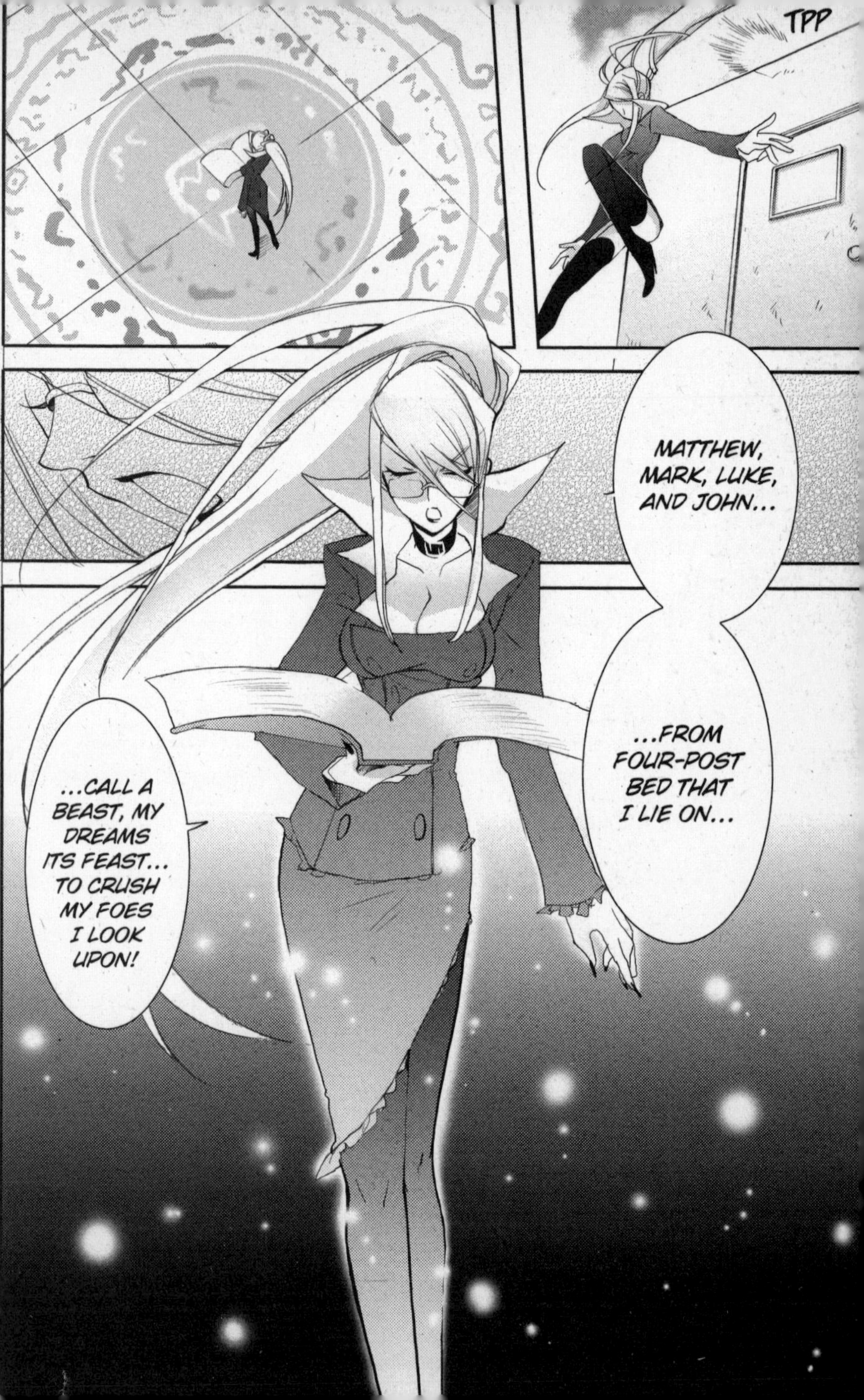
TPP
MATTHEW, MARK, LUKE, AND JOHN...
...FROM FOUR-POST BED THAT I LIE ON...
...CALL A BEAST, MY DREAMS ITS FEAST... TO CRUSH MY FOES I LOOK UPON!

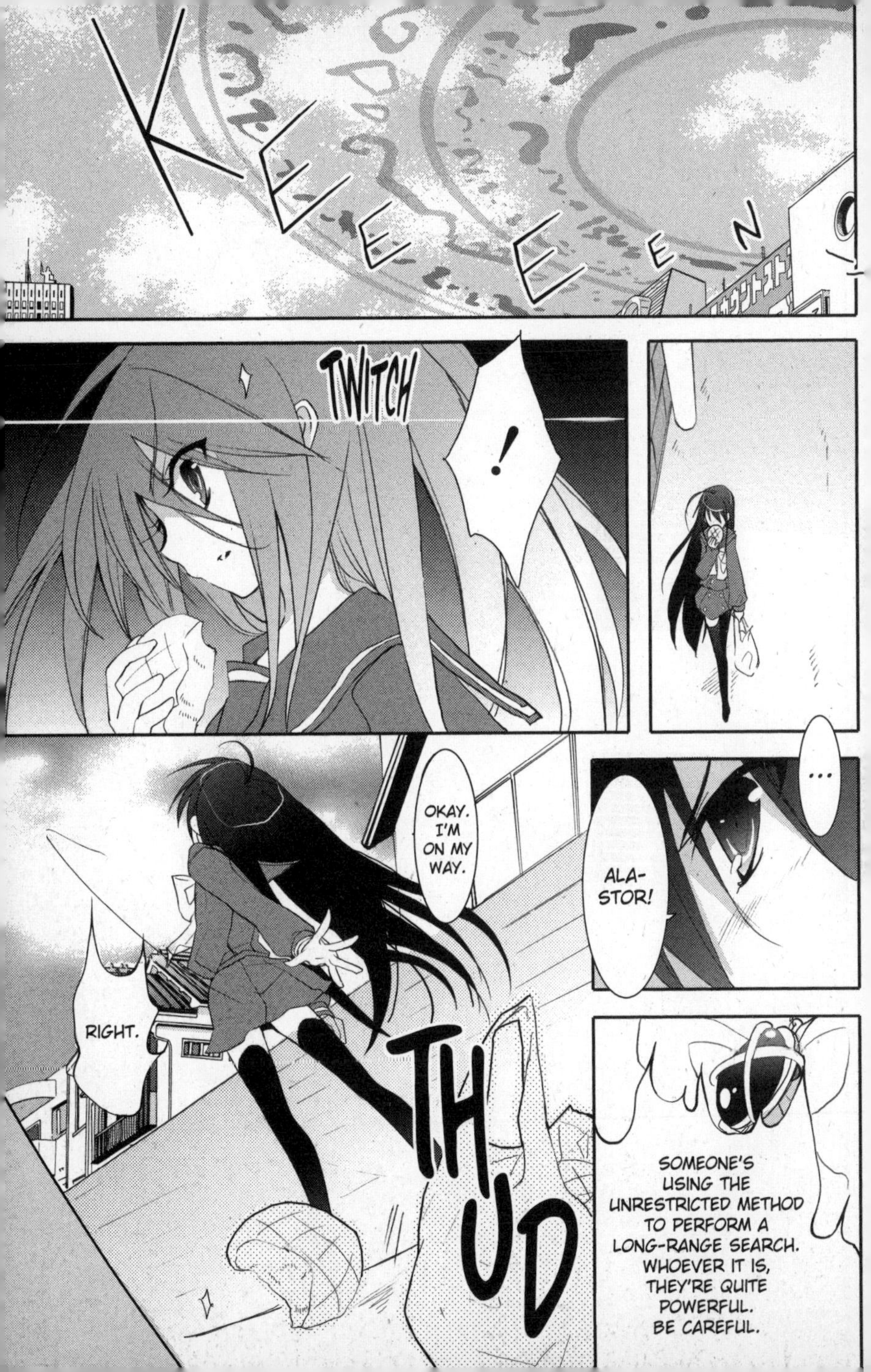
KYEEEEN
!
TWITCH
...
ALA-STOR!
SOMEONE'S USING THE UNRESTRICTED METHOD TO PERFORM A LONG-RANGE SEARCH. WHOEVER IT IS, THEY'RE QUITE POWERFUL. BE CAREFUL.
OKAY. I'M ON MY WAY.
RIGHT.
THUD

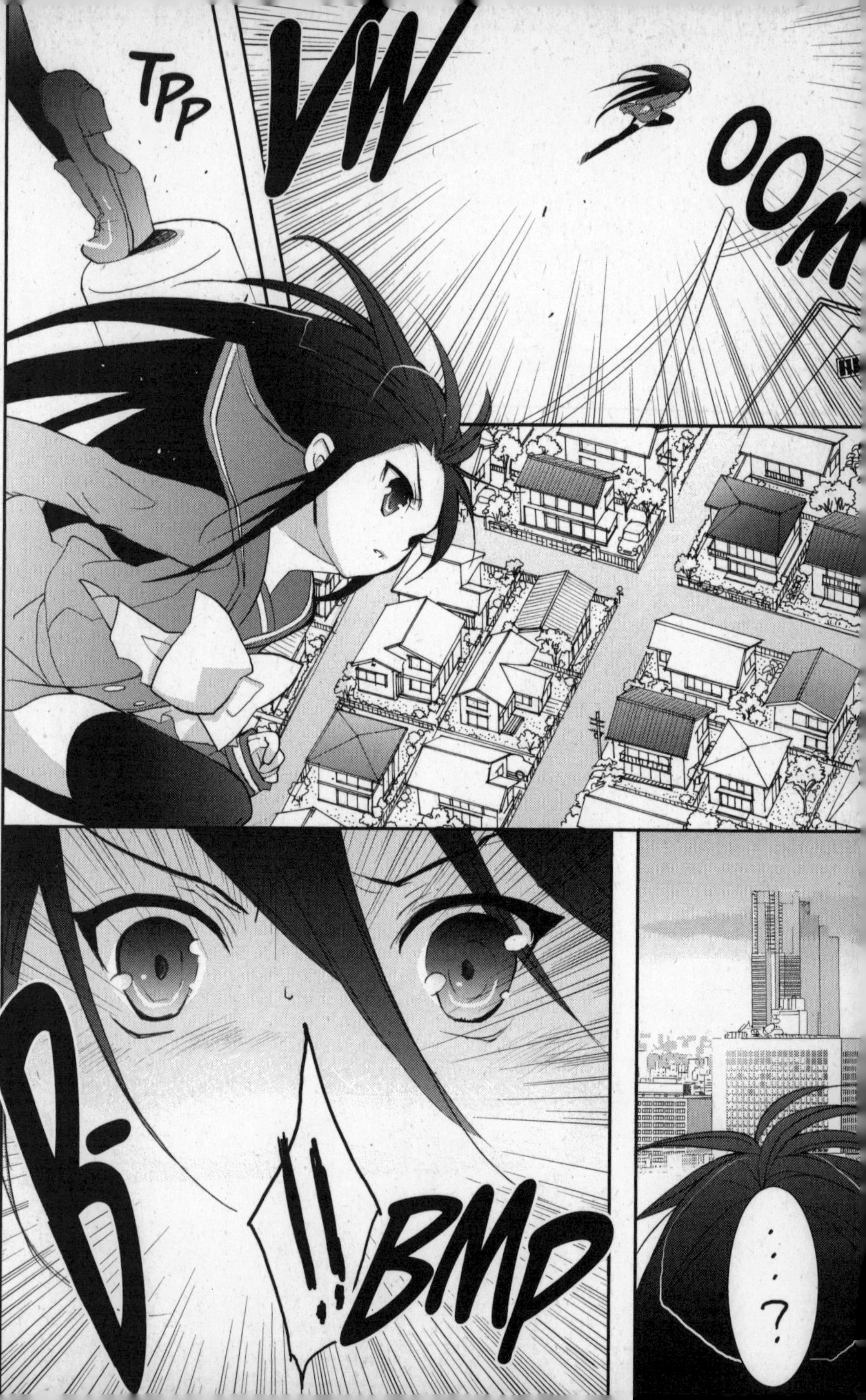
VW
OOM
TPP
...?
B-
BMP
!!

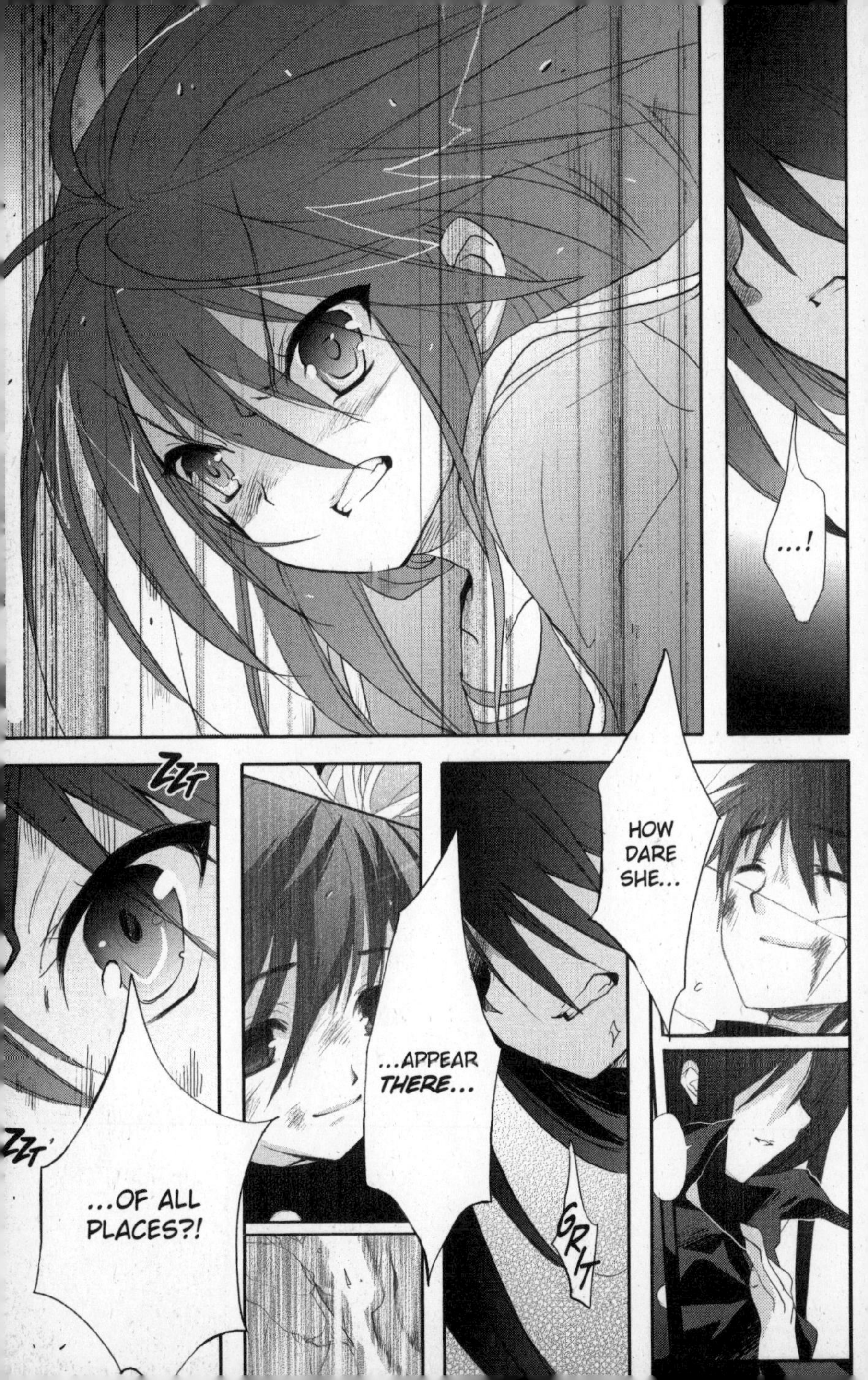
...!
HOW DARE SHE...
GRIT
...APPEAR THERE...
ZZZT
...OF ALL PLACES?!
ZZZT

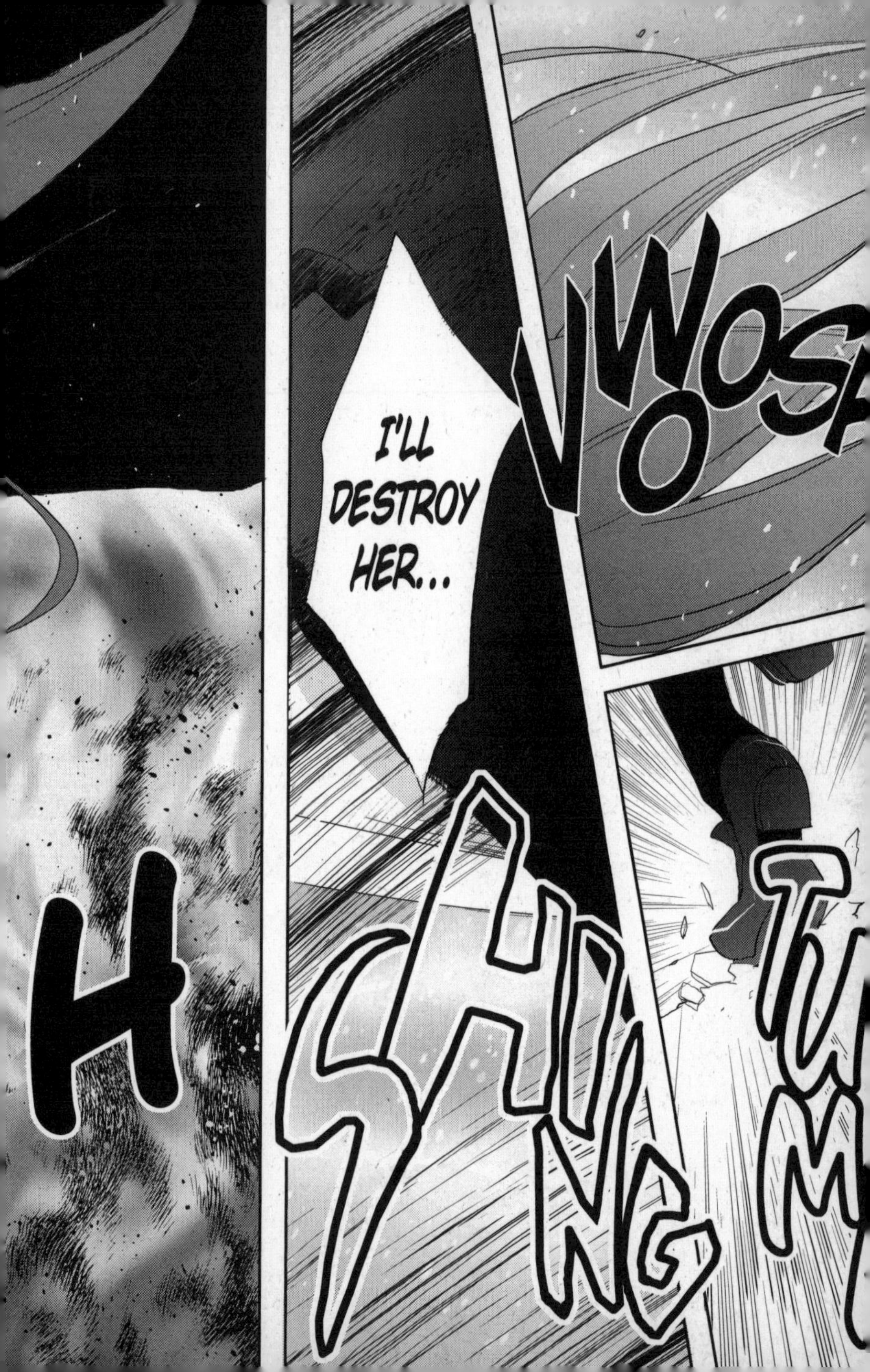
VWOOSH
I'LL DESTROY HER...
SHING
H

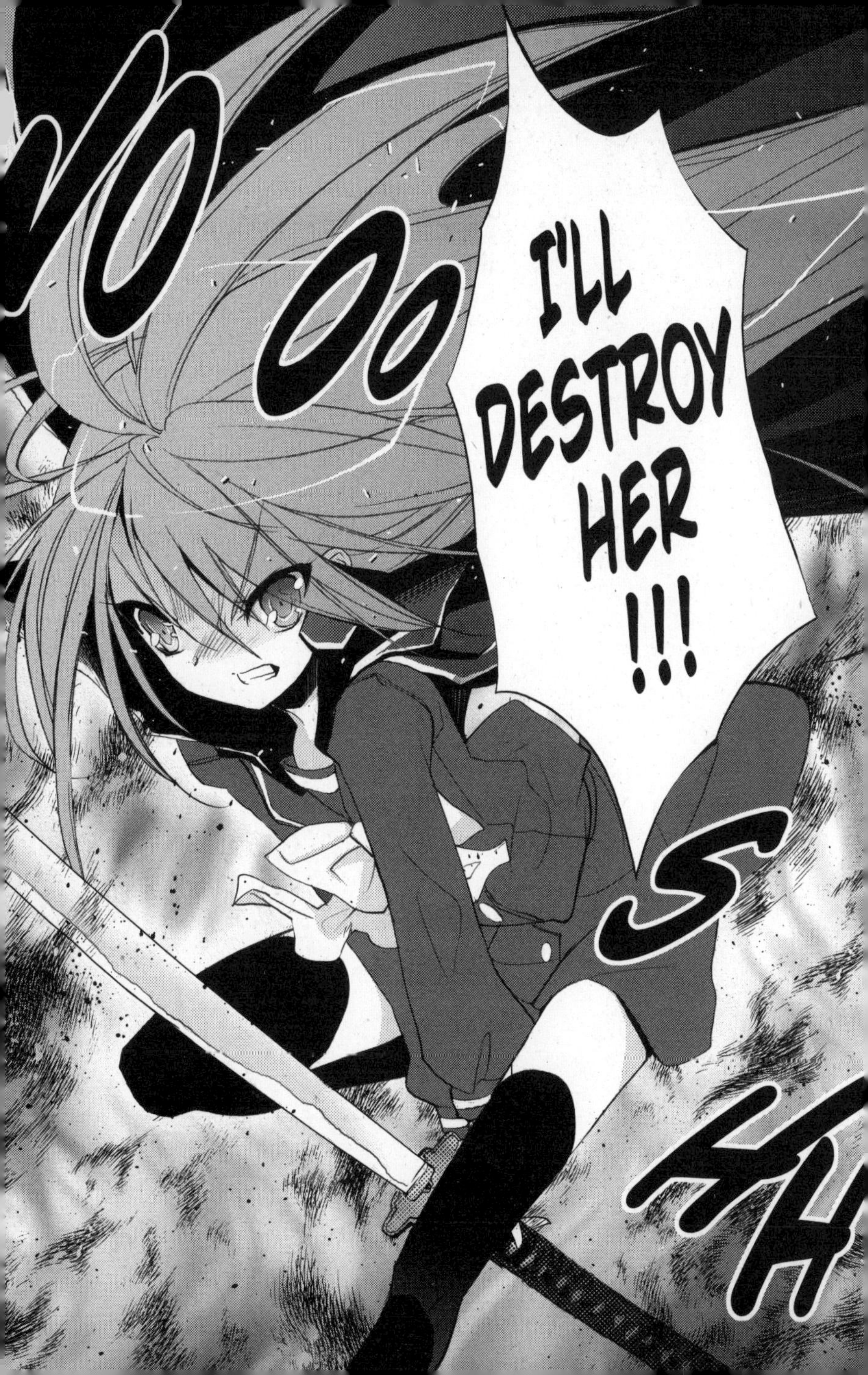
I'LL DESTROY HER !!!

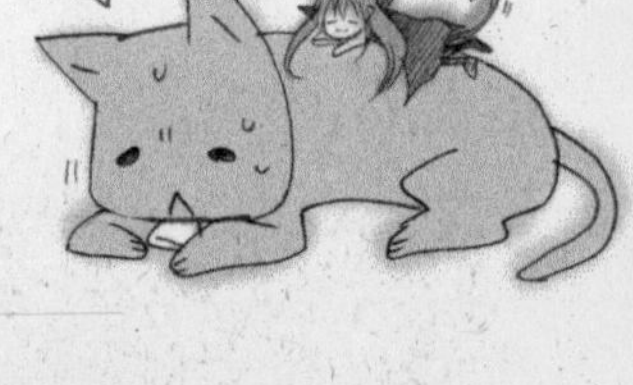
MM
MM

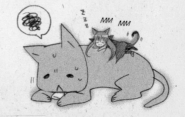

Episode 27: A Chance Meeting of Light and Dark I

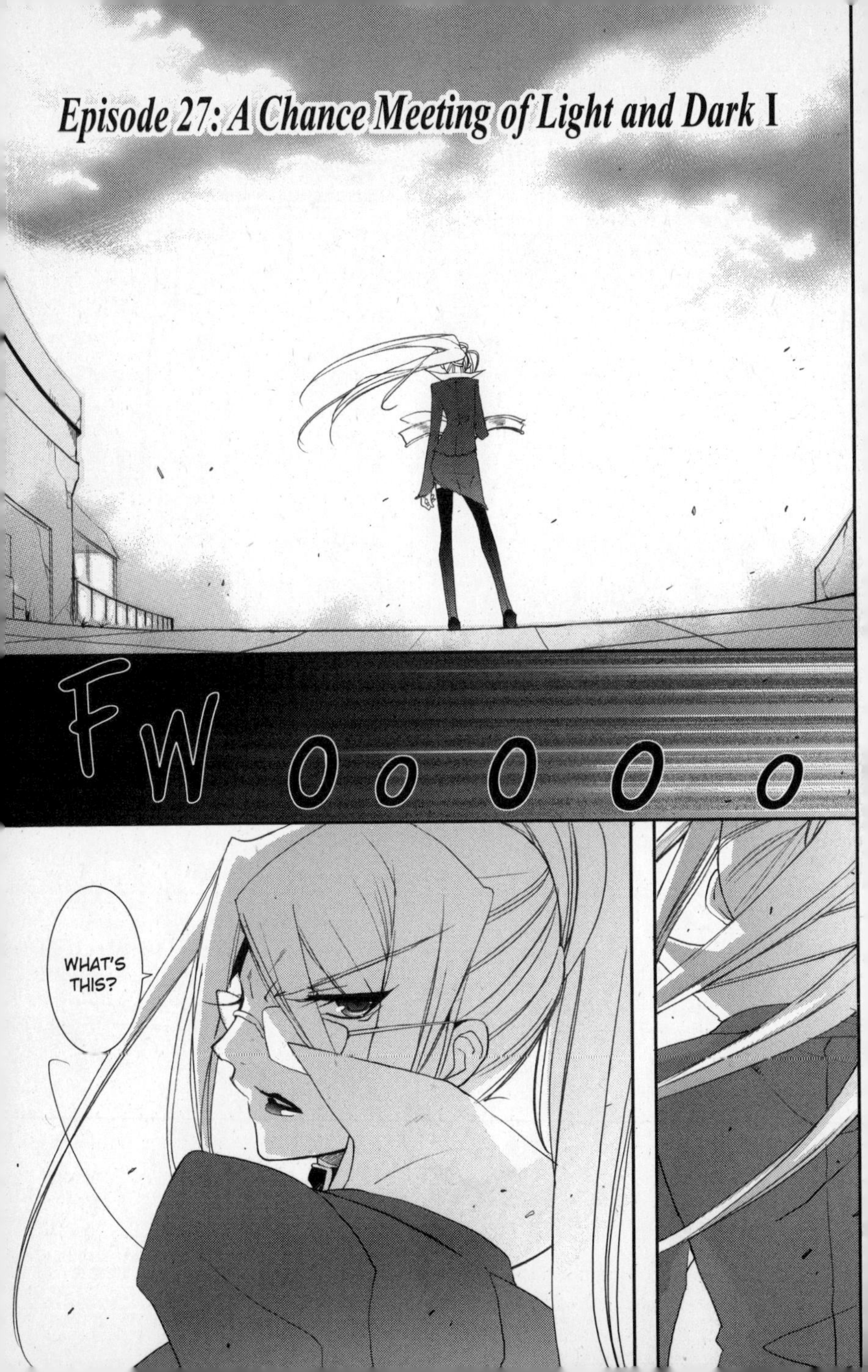
FWOOOOOO
WHAT'S THIS?

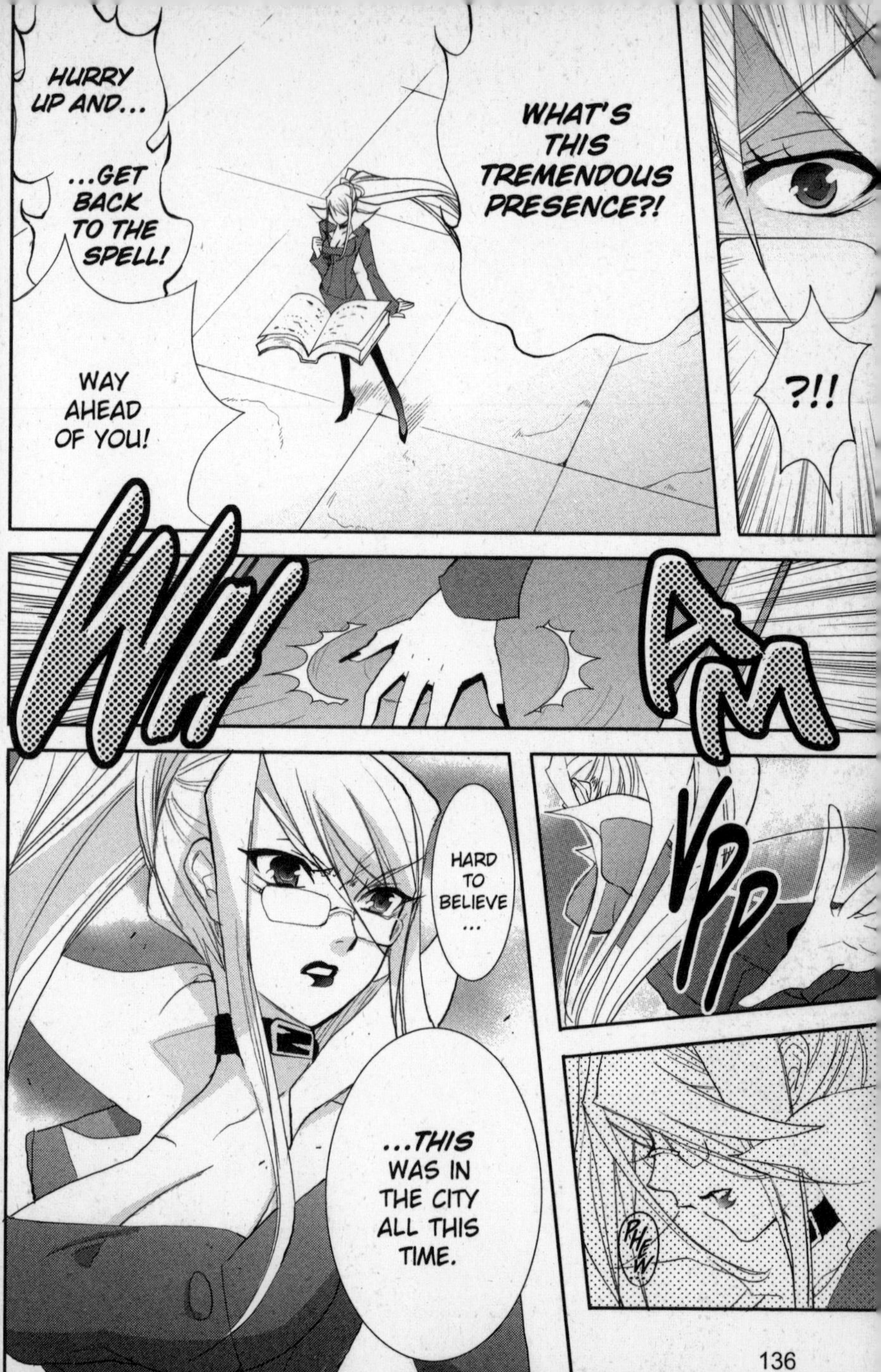
?!!
WHAT'S THIS TREMENDOUS PRESENCE?!
HURRY UP AND...
...GET BACK TO THE SPELL!
WAY AHEAD OF YOU!
WHHAM
VPP
PHEW
HARD TO BELIEVE...
...THIS WAS IN THE CITY ALL THIS TIME.

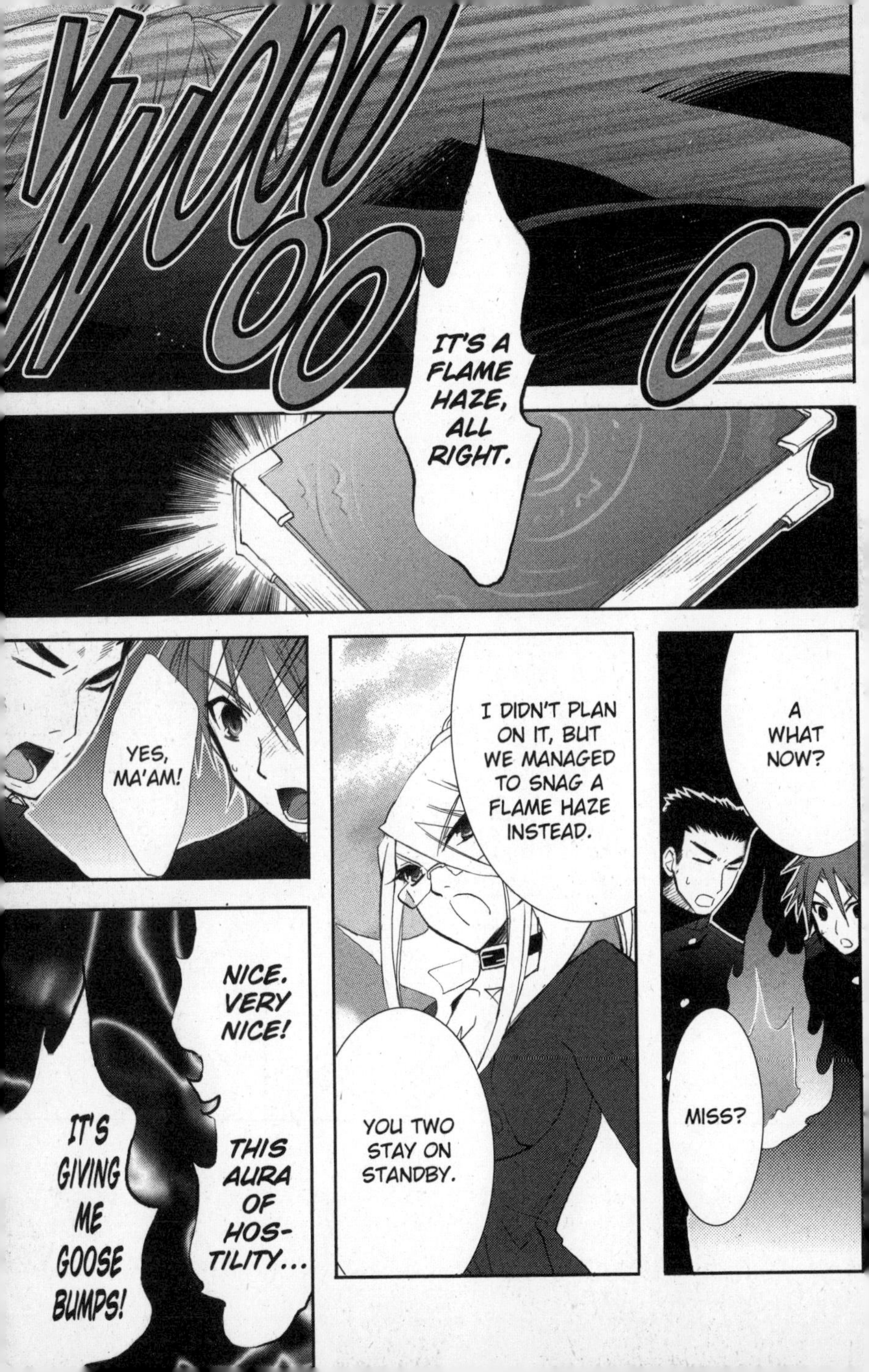
YUGOOOO
OOO
IT'S A FLAME HAZE, ALL RIGHT.
A WHAT NOW?
MISS?
I DIDN'T PLAN ON IT, BUT WE MANAGED TO SNAG A FLAME HAZE INSTEAD.
YOU TWO STAY ON STANDBY.
YES, MA'AM!
NICE. VERY NICE!
THIS AURA OF HOS-TILITY...
IT'S GIVING ME GOOSE BUMPS!

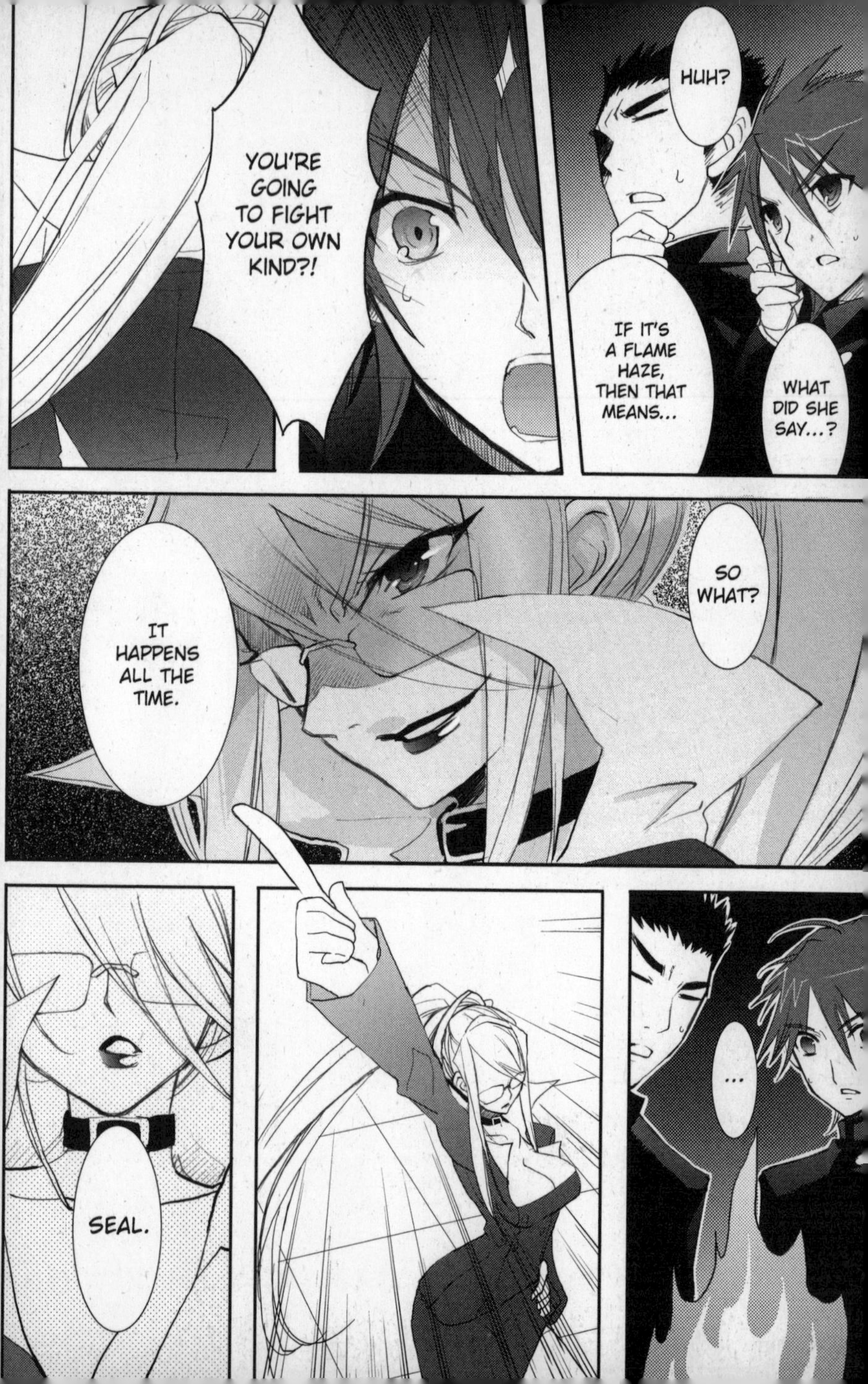
HUH?
WHAT DID SHE SAY...?
IF IT'S A FLAME HAZE, THEN THAT MEANS...
YOU'RE GOING TO FIGHT YOUR OWN KIND?!
SO WHAT?
IT HAPPENS ALL THE TIME.
...
SEAL.

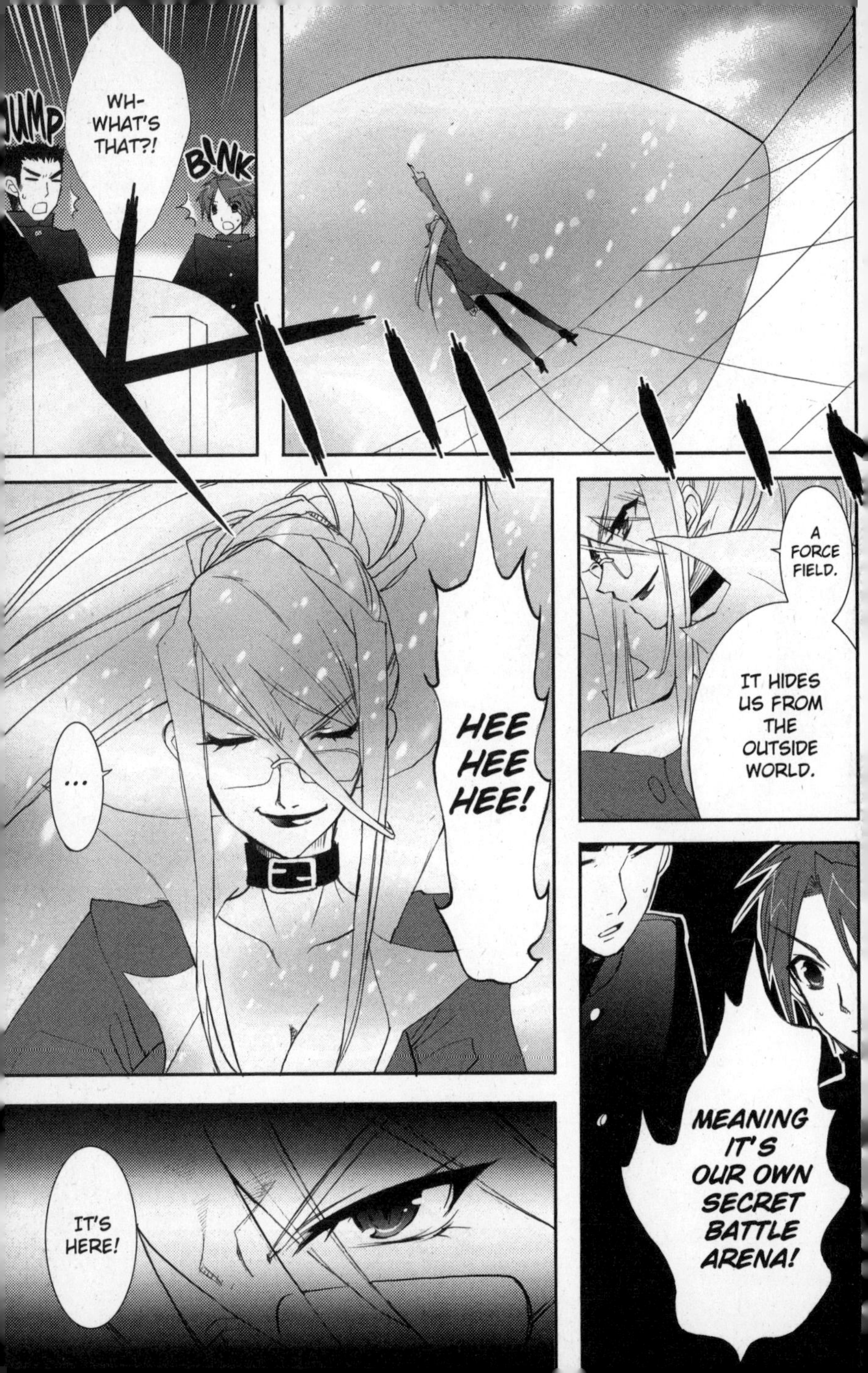
BLINK
WH- WHAT'S THAT?!
JUMP
A FORCE FIELD.
IT HIDES US FROM THE OUTSIDE WORLD.
MEANING IT'S OUR OWN SECRET BATTLE ARENA!
HEE HEE HEE!
...
IT'S HERE!

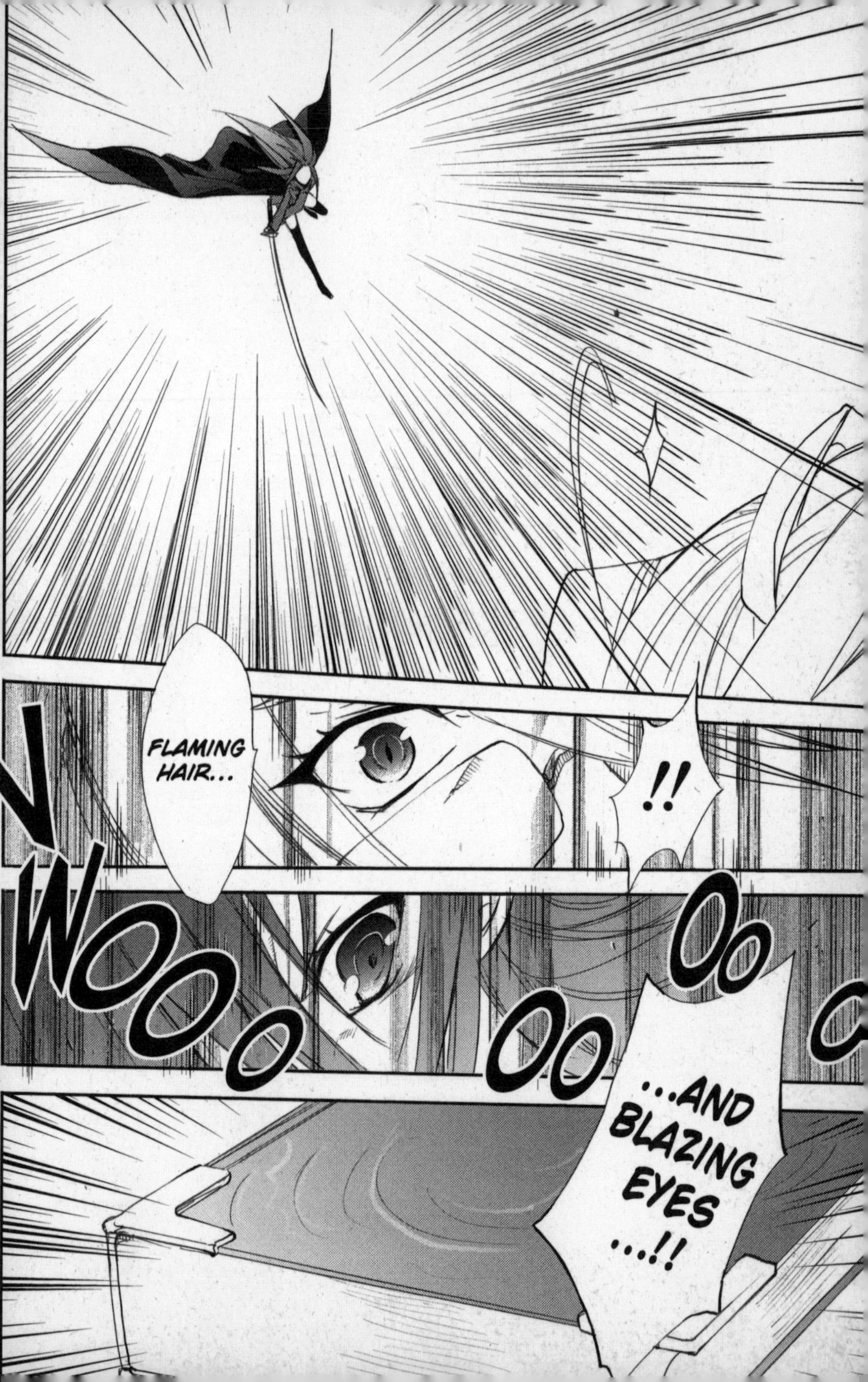
!!
FLAMING HAIR...
WOOOOOOOOO
...AND BLAZING EYES...!!

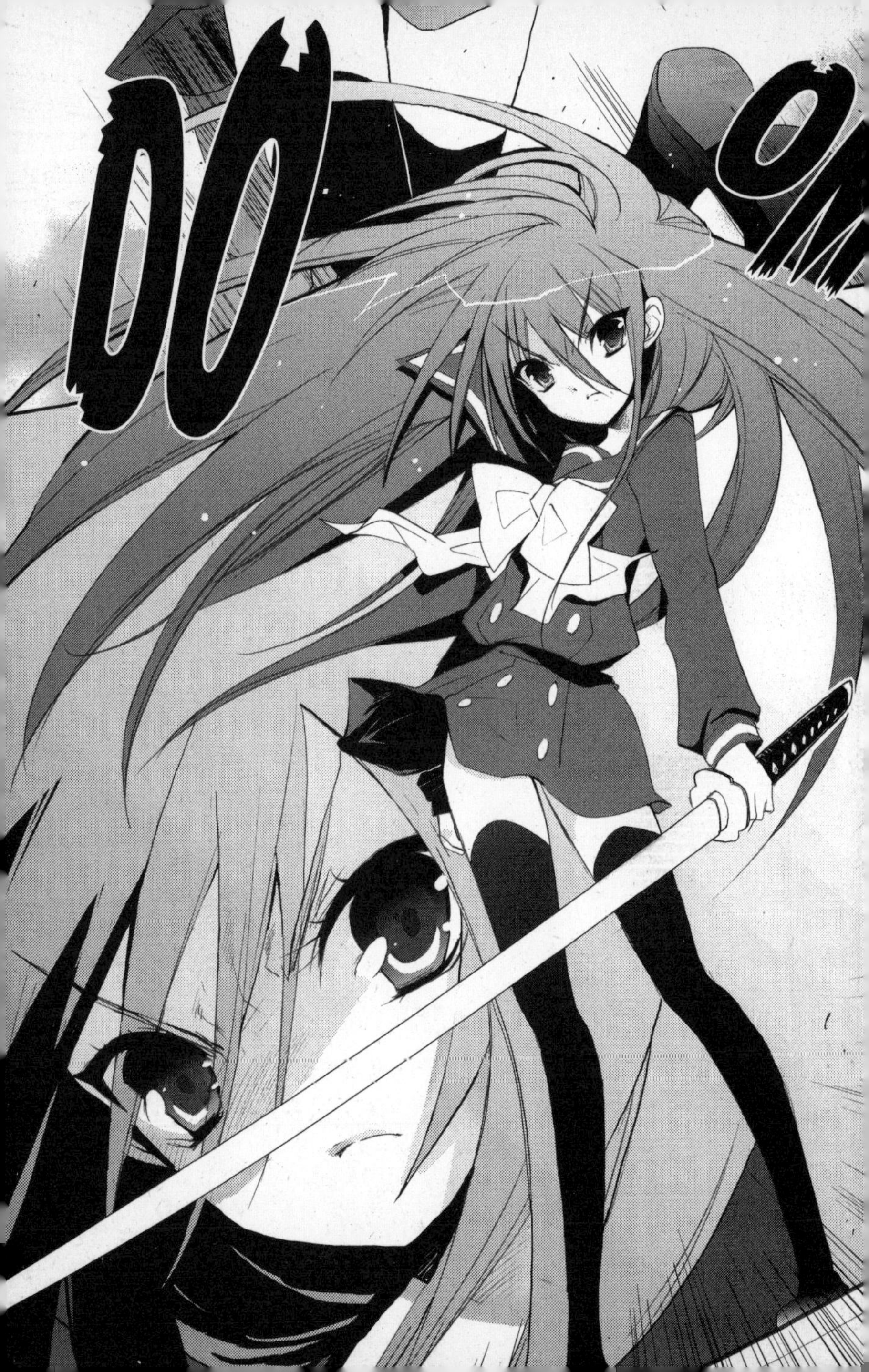
DOOOM

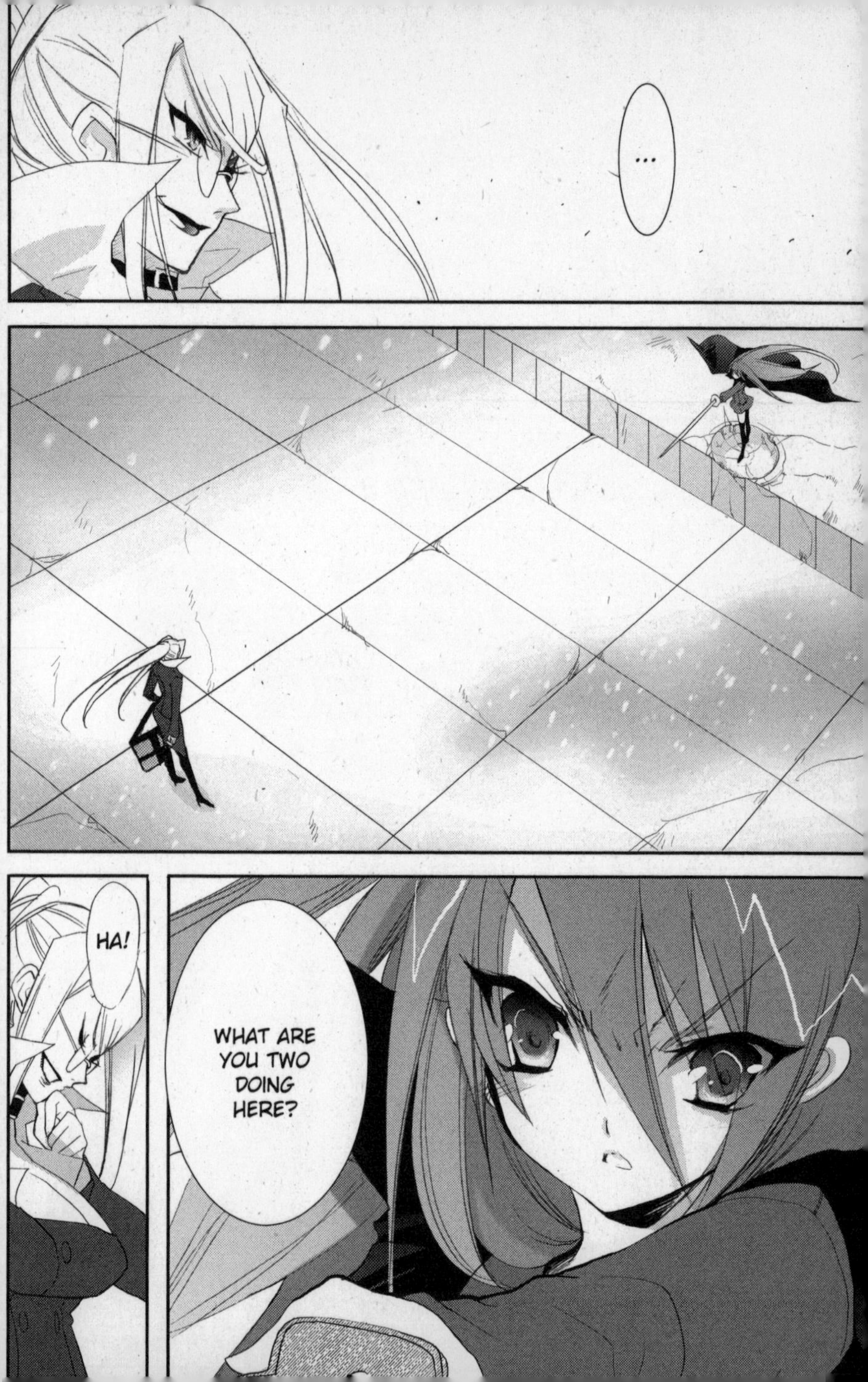
...
WHAT ARE YOU TWO DOING HERE?
HA!

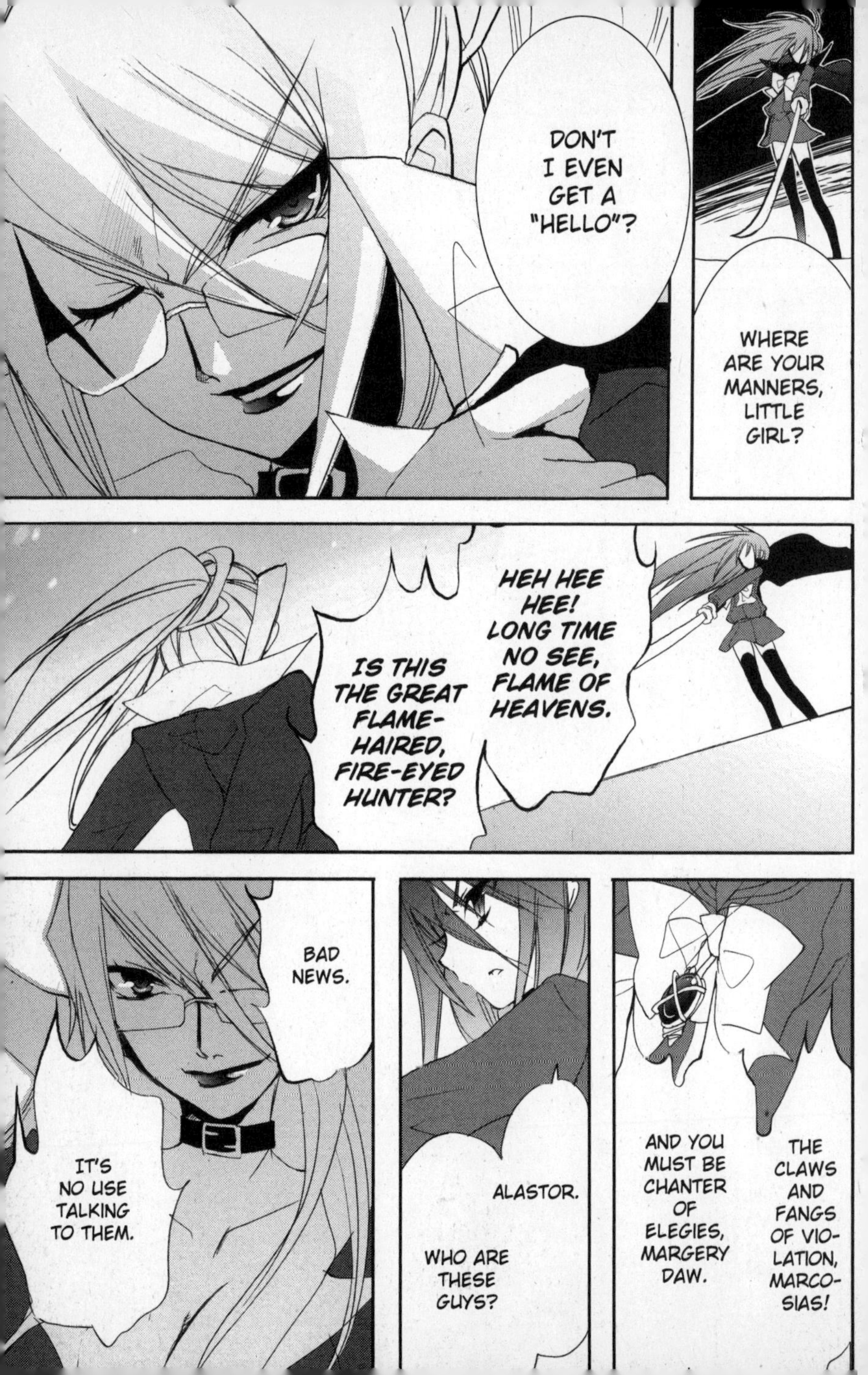
WHERE ARE YOUR MANNERS, LITTLE GIRL?
DON'T I EVEN GET A "HELLO"?
HEH HEE HEE! LONG TIME NO SEE, FLAME OF HEAVENS.
IS THIS THE GREAT FLAME-HAIRED, FIRE-EYED HUNTER?
THE CLAWS AND FANGS OF VIO-LATION, MARCO-SIAS!
AND YOU MUST BE CHANTER OF ELEGIES, MARGERY DAW.
ALASTOR.
WHO ARE THESE GUYS?
BAD NEWS.
IT'S NO USE TALKING TO THEM.

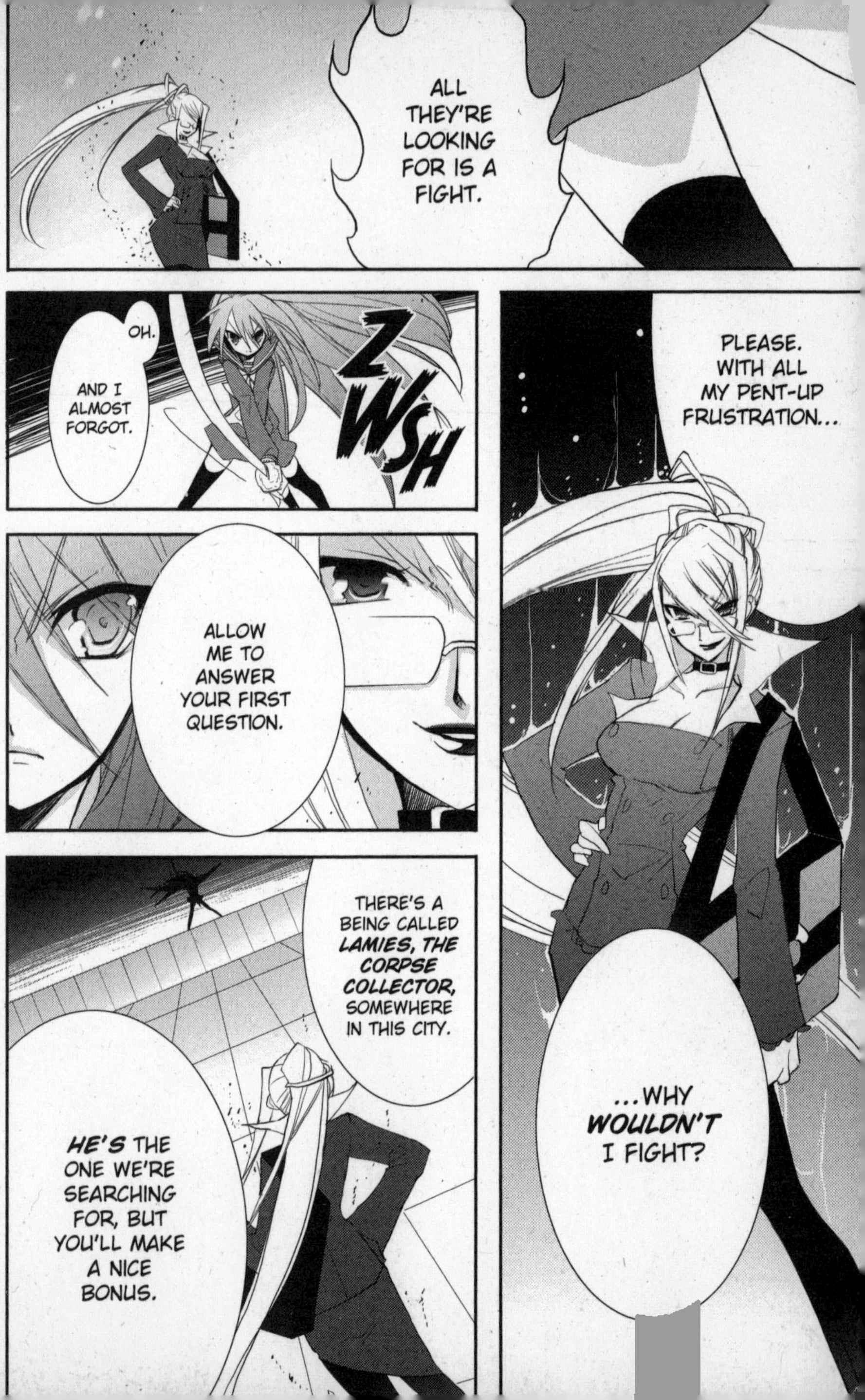
ALL THEY'RE LOOKING FOR IS A FIGHT.
PLEASE. WITH ALL MY PENT-UP FRUSTRATION...
...WHY *WOULDN'T* I FIGHT?
OH.
AND I ALMOST FORGOT.
ZWSH
ALLOW ME TO ANSWER YOUR FIRST QUESTION.
THERE'S A BEING CALLED *LAMIES, THE CORPSE COLLECTOR*, SOMEWHERE IN THIS CITY.
HE'S THE ONE WE'RE SEARCHING FOR, BUT YOU'LL MAKE A NICE BONUS.

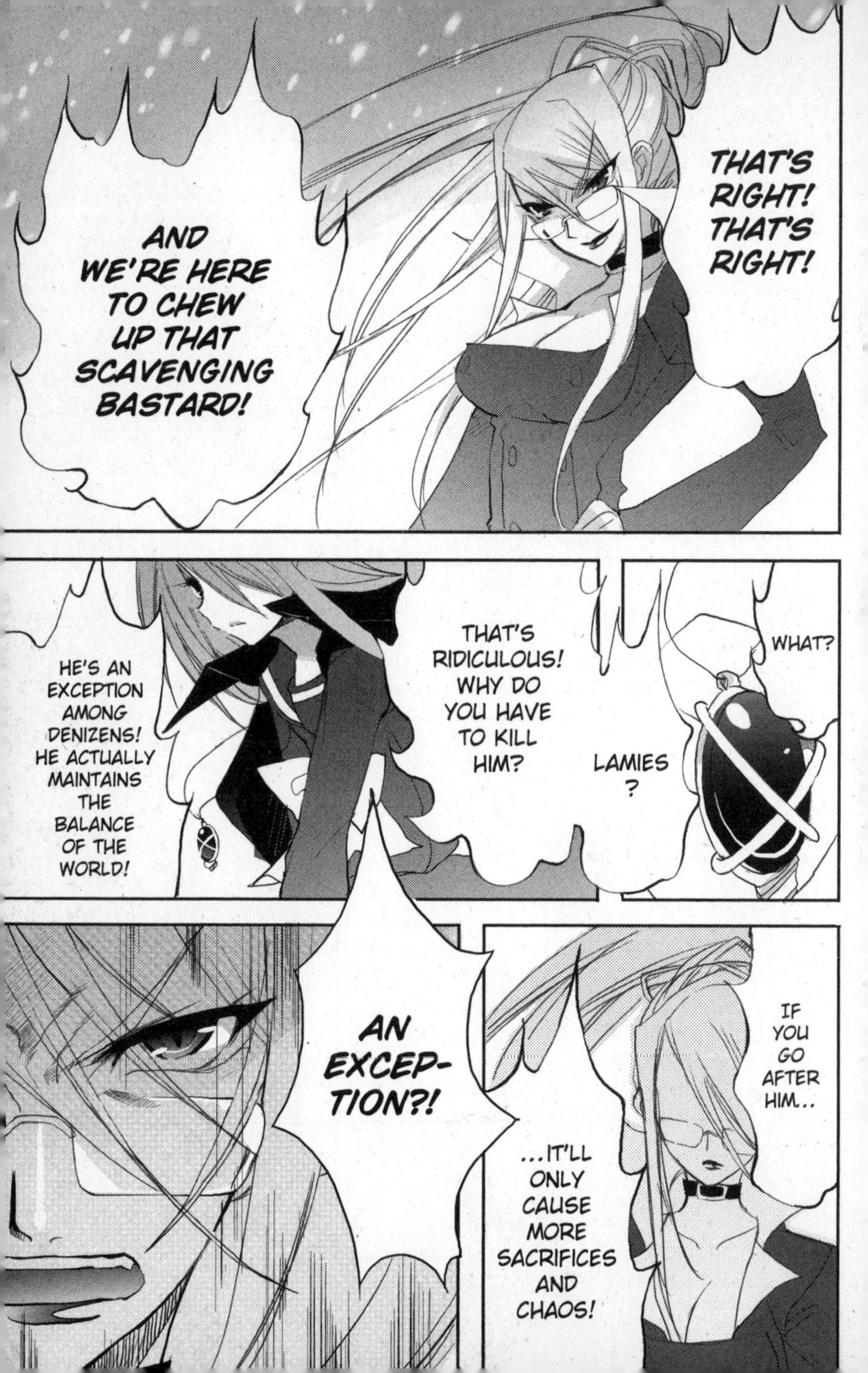
THAT'S RIGHT! THAT'S RIGHT!
AND WE'RE HERE TO CHEW UP THAT SCAVENGING BASTARD!
WHAT?
LAMIES?
THAT'S RIDICULOUS! WHY DO YOU HAVE TO KILL HIM?
HE'S AN EXCEPTION AMONG DENIZENS! HE ACTUALLY MAINTAINS THE BALANCE OF THE WORLD!
IF YOU GO AFTER HIM...
...IT'LL ONLY CAUSE MORE SACRIFICES AND CHAOS!
AN EXCEP-TION?!

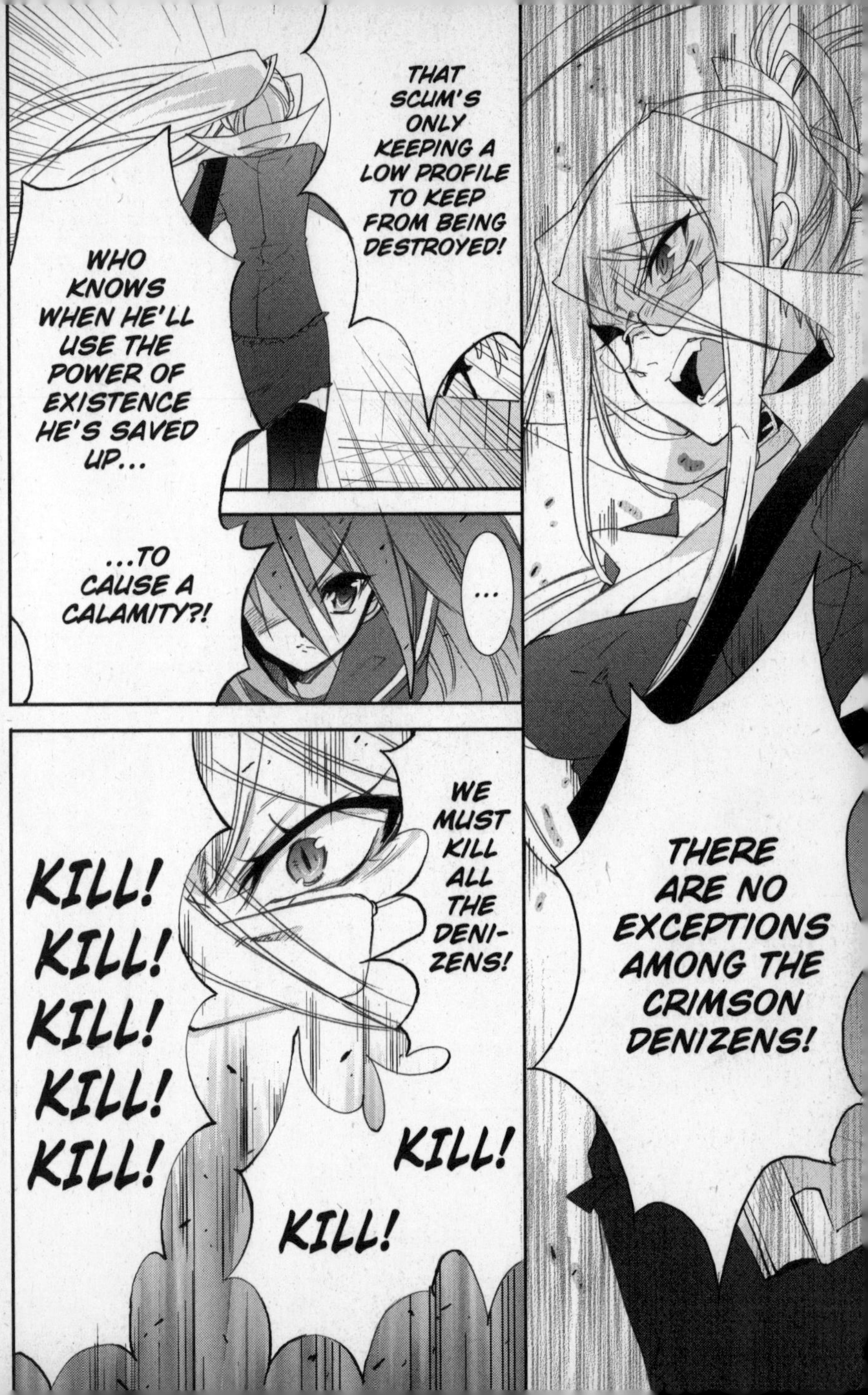

THERE ARE NO EXCEPTIONS AMONG THE CRIMSON DENIZENS!
THAT SCUM'S ONLY KEEPING A LOW PROFILE TO KEEP FROM BEING DESTROYED!
WHO KNOWS WHEN HE'LL USE THE POWER OF EXISTENCE HE'S SAVED UP...
...TO CAUSE A CALAMITY?!
...
WE MUST KILL ALL THE DENI-ZENS!
KILL! KILL! KILL! KILL! KILL!
KILL!
KILL!

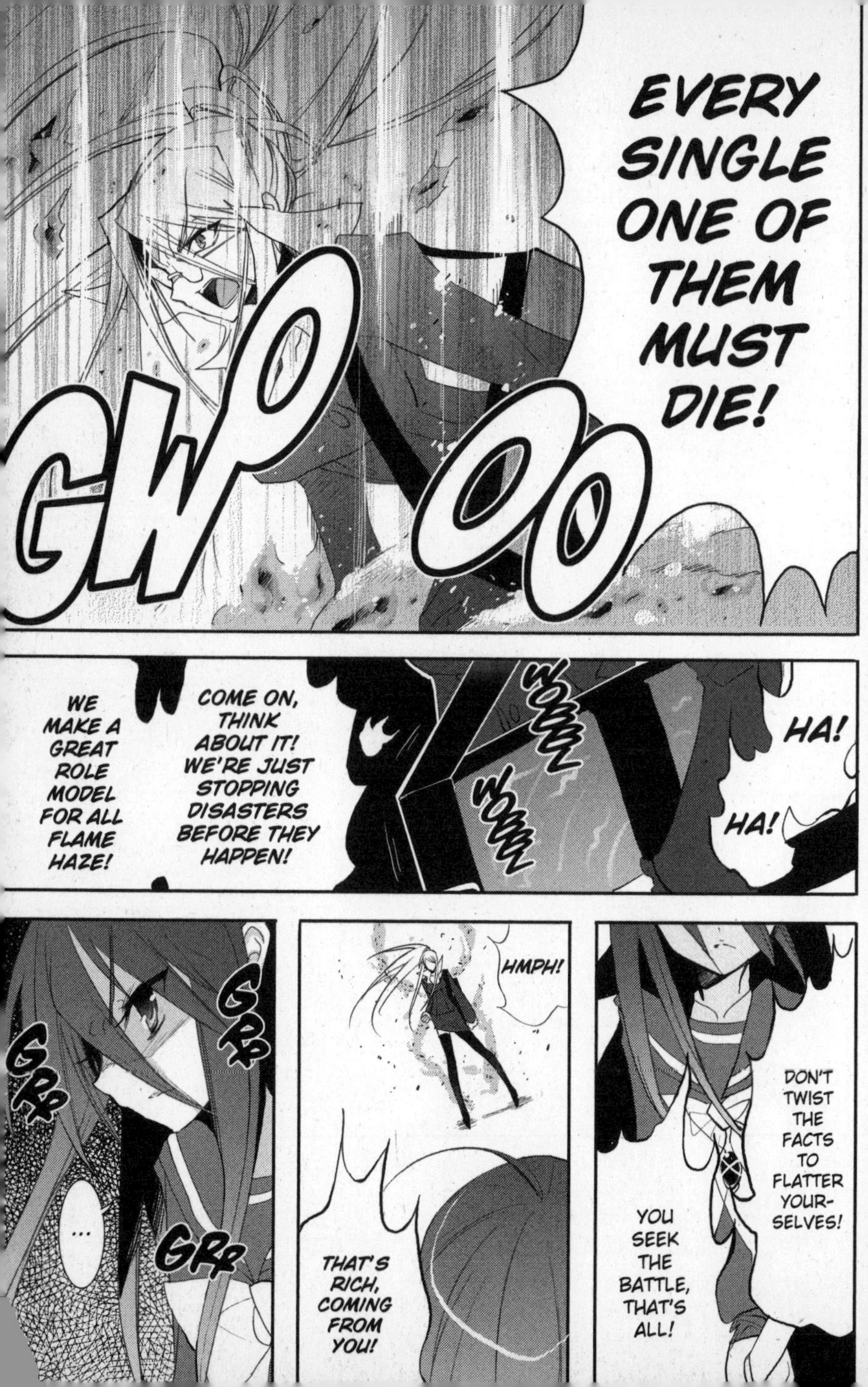
EVERY SINGLE ONE OF THEM MUST DIE!
GWOOO
HA!
HA!
COME ON, THINK ABOUT IT! WE'RE JUST STOPPING DISASTERS BEFORE THEY HAPPEN!
WE MAKE A GREAT ROLE MODEL FOR ALL FLAME HAZE!
DON'T TWIST THE FACTS TO FLATTER YOUR-SELVES!
YOU SEEK THE BATTLE, THAT'S ALL!
HMPH!
THAT'S RICH, COMING FROM YOU!
GRR
GRR
GRR
...

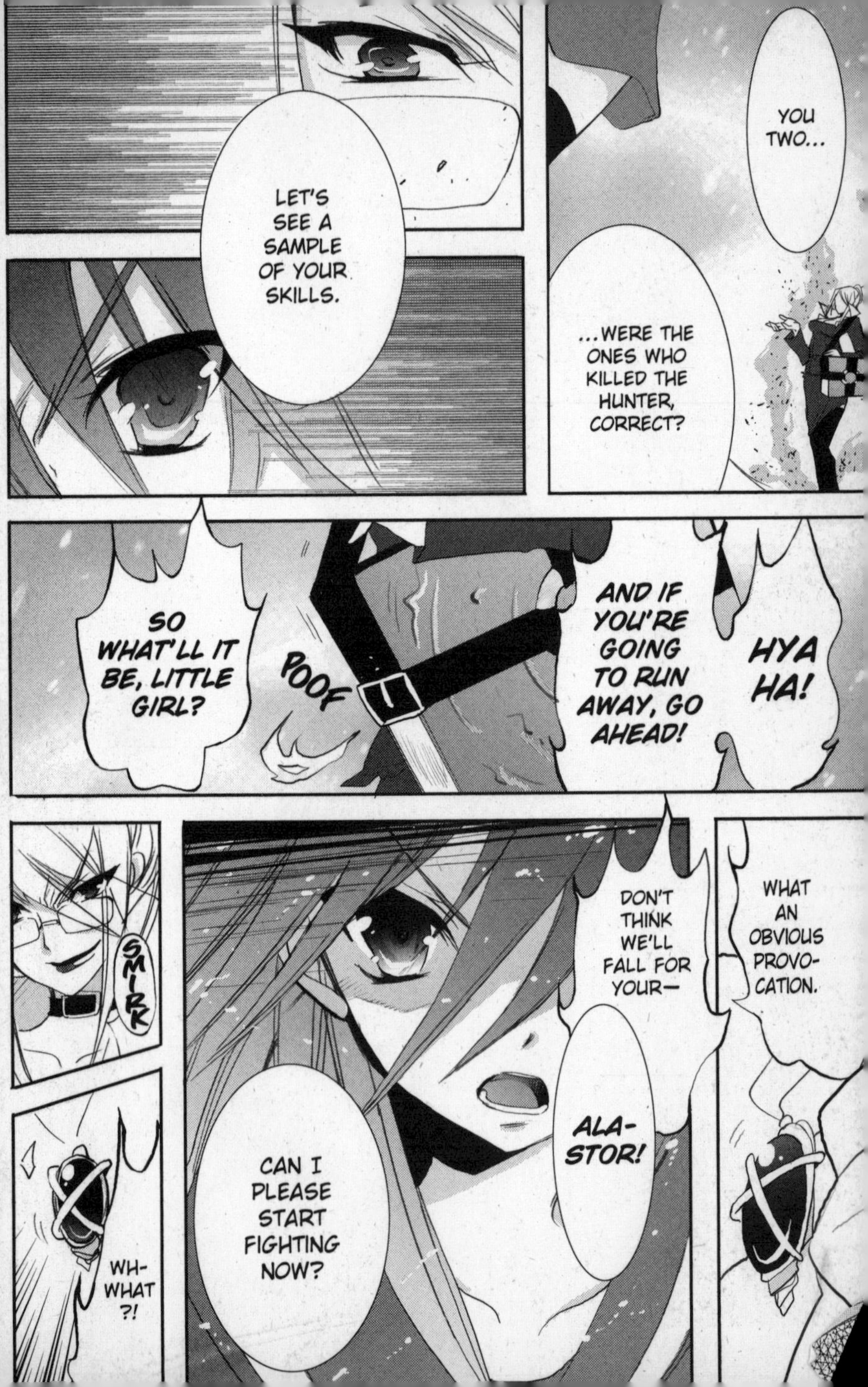
YOU TWO...
...WERE THE ONES WHO KILLED THE HUNTER, CORRECT?
LET'S SEE A SAMPLE OF YOUR SKILLS.
HYA HA!
AND IF YOU'RE GOING TO RUN AWAY, GO AHEAD!
POOF
SO WHAT'LL IT BE, LITTLE GIRL?
WHAT AN OBVIOUS PROVOCATION.
DON'T THINK WE'LL FALL FOR YOUR—
ALA-STOR!
CAN I PLEASE START FIGHTING NOW?
SMIRK
WH-WHAT?!

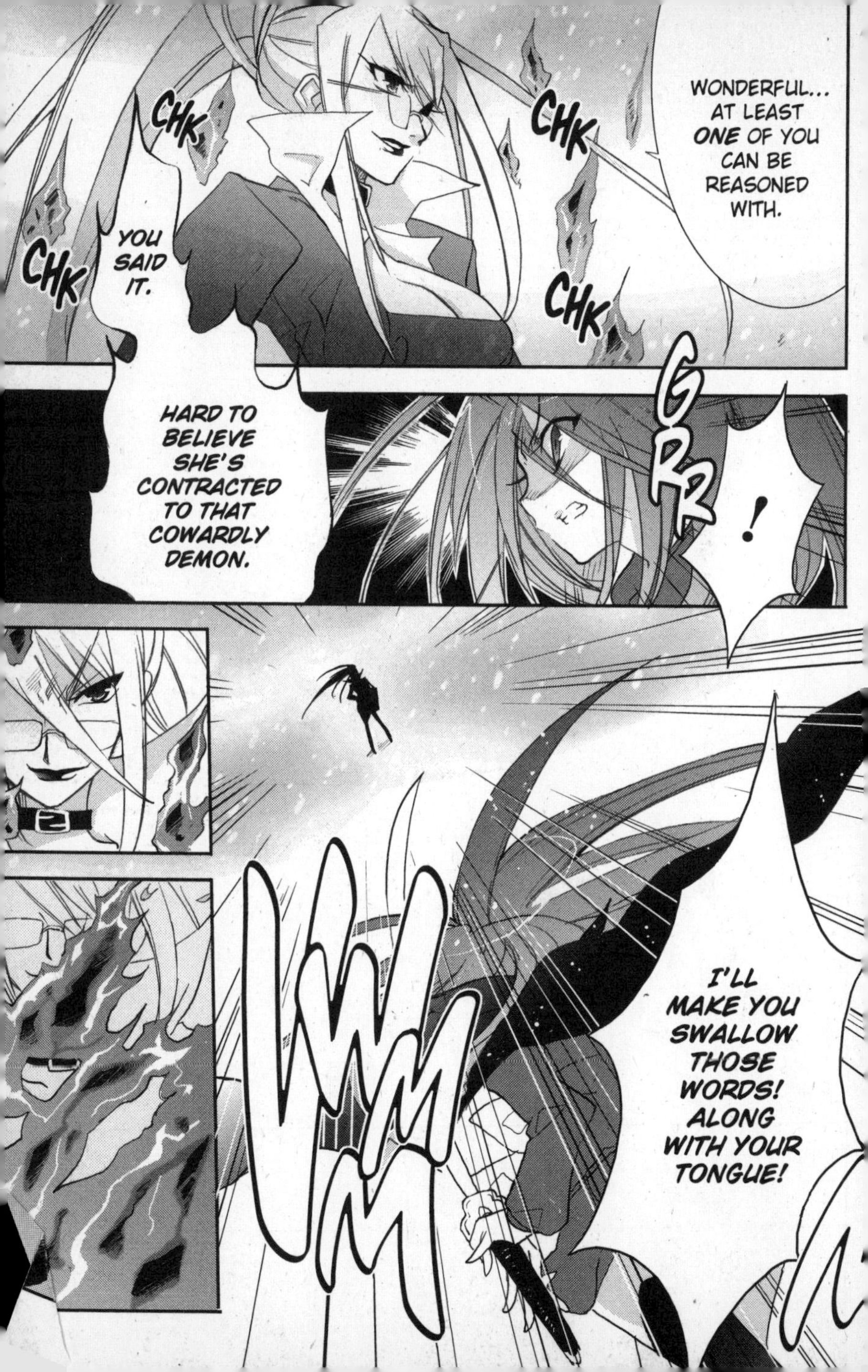
WONDERFUL... AT LEAST ONE OF YOU CAN BE REASONED WITH.
CHK
CHK
CHK
CHK
YOU SAID IT.
HARD TO BELIEVE SHE'S CONTRACTED TO THAT COWARDLY DEMON.
GRR
!
I'LL MAKE YOU SWALLOW THOSE WORDS! ALONG WITH YOUR TONGUE!
VWM

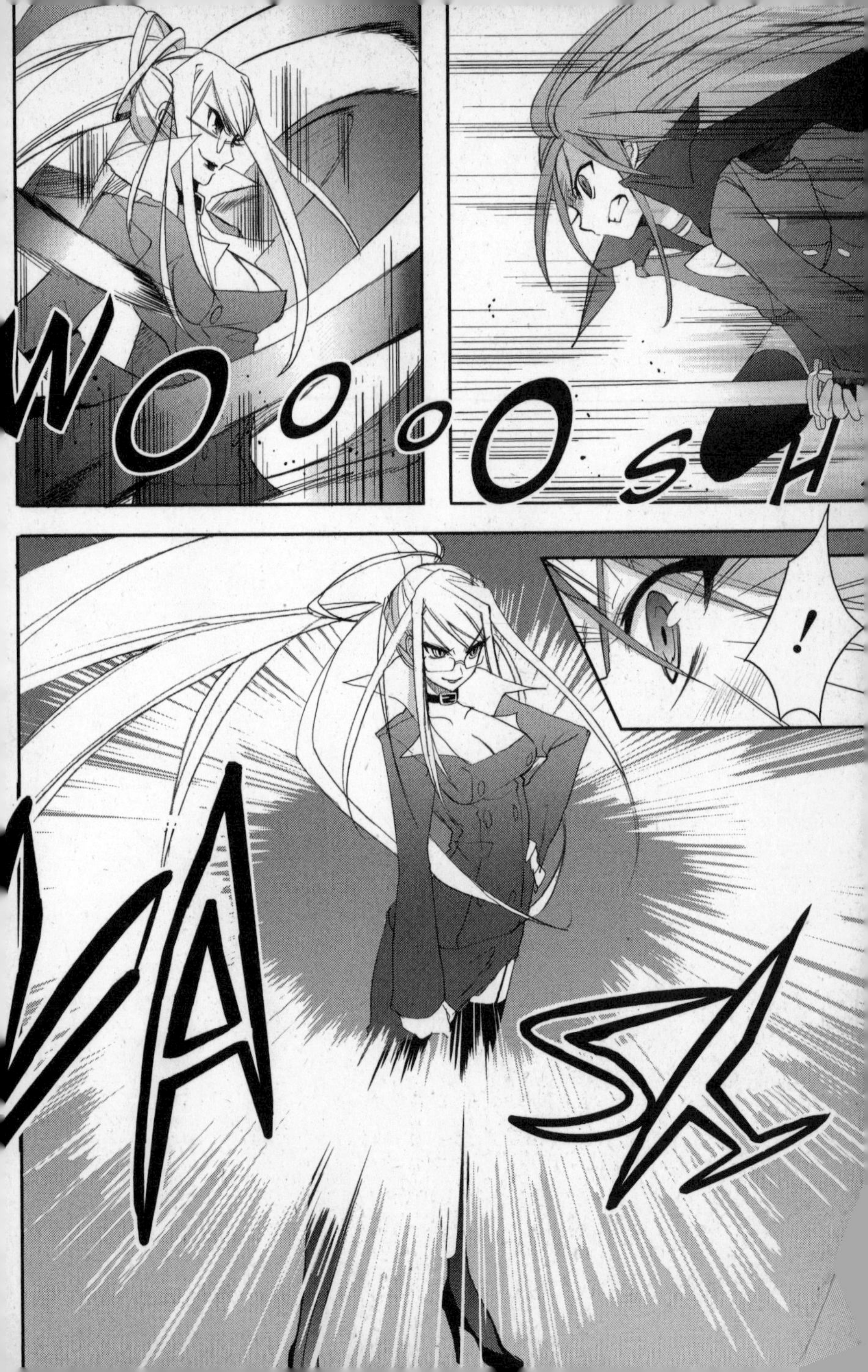
WOOOOSH
!

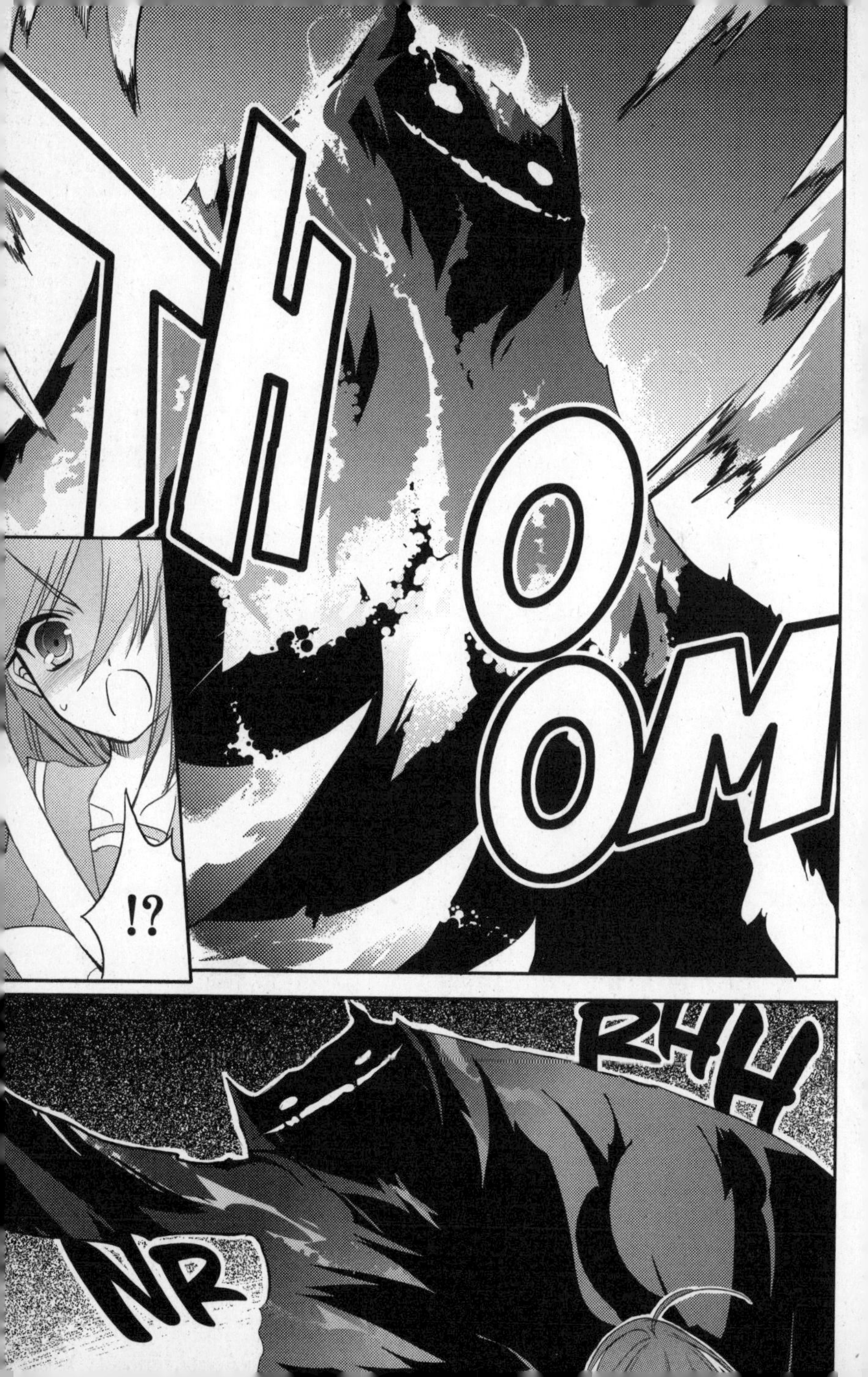
THOOM
!?
NR

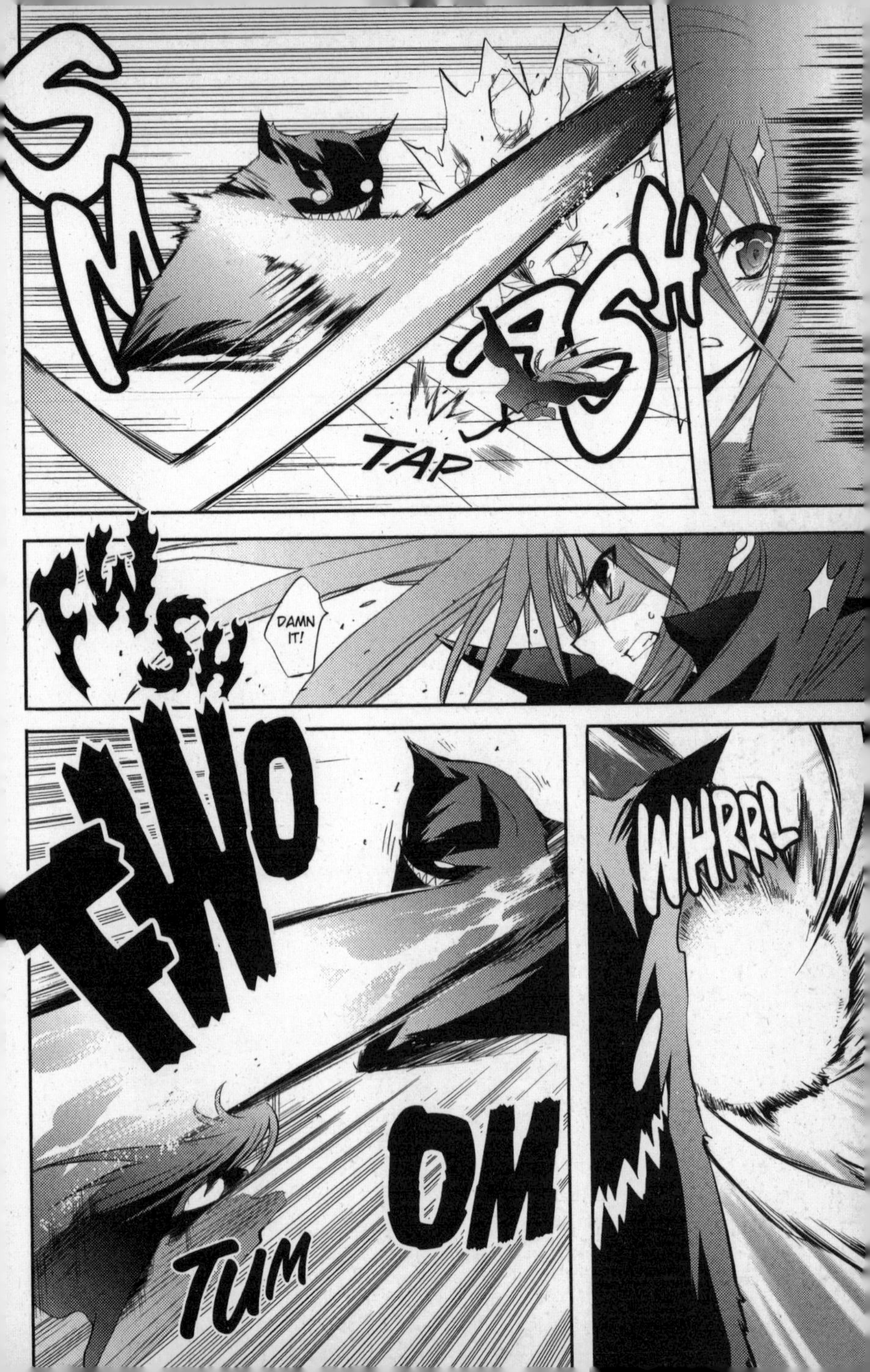
SMASH
TAP
FWSH
DAMN IT!
WHRRL
THOOM
TUM

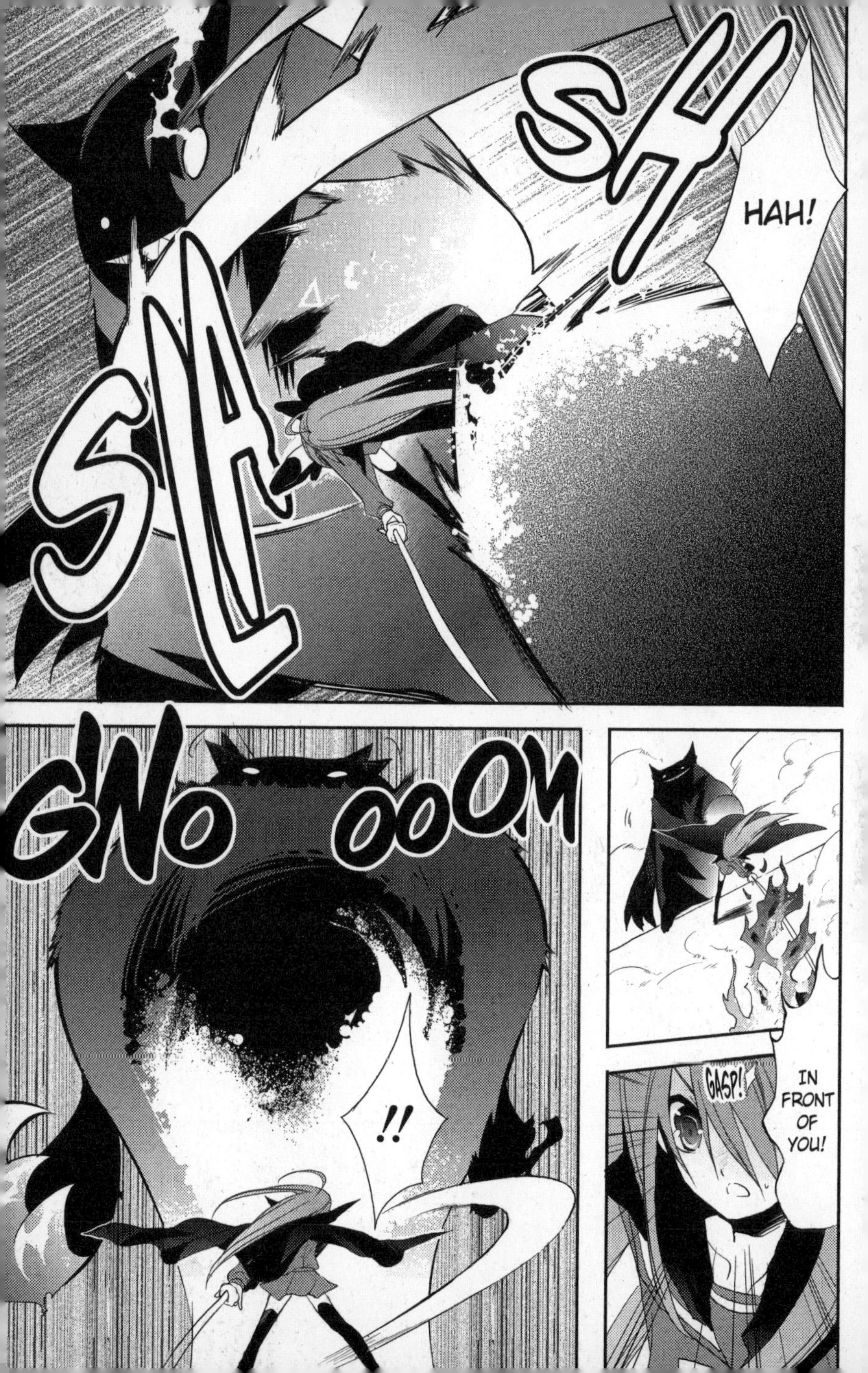
SH
HAH!
SA
IN FRONT OF YOU!
GASP!
G'NO OOOM
!!

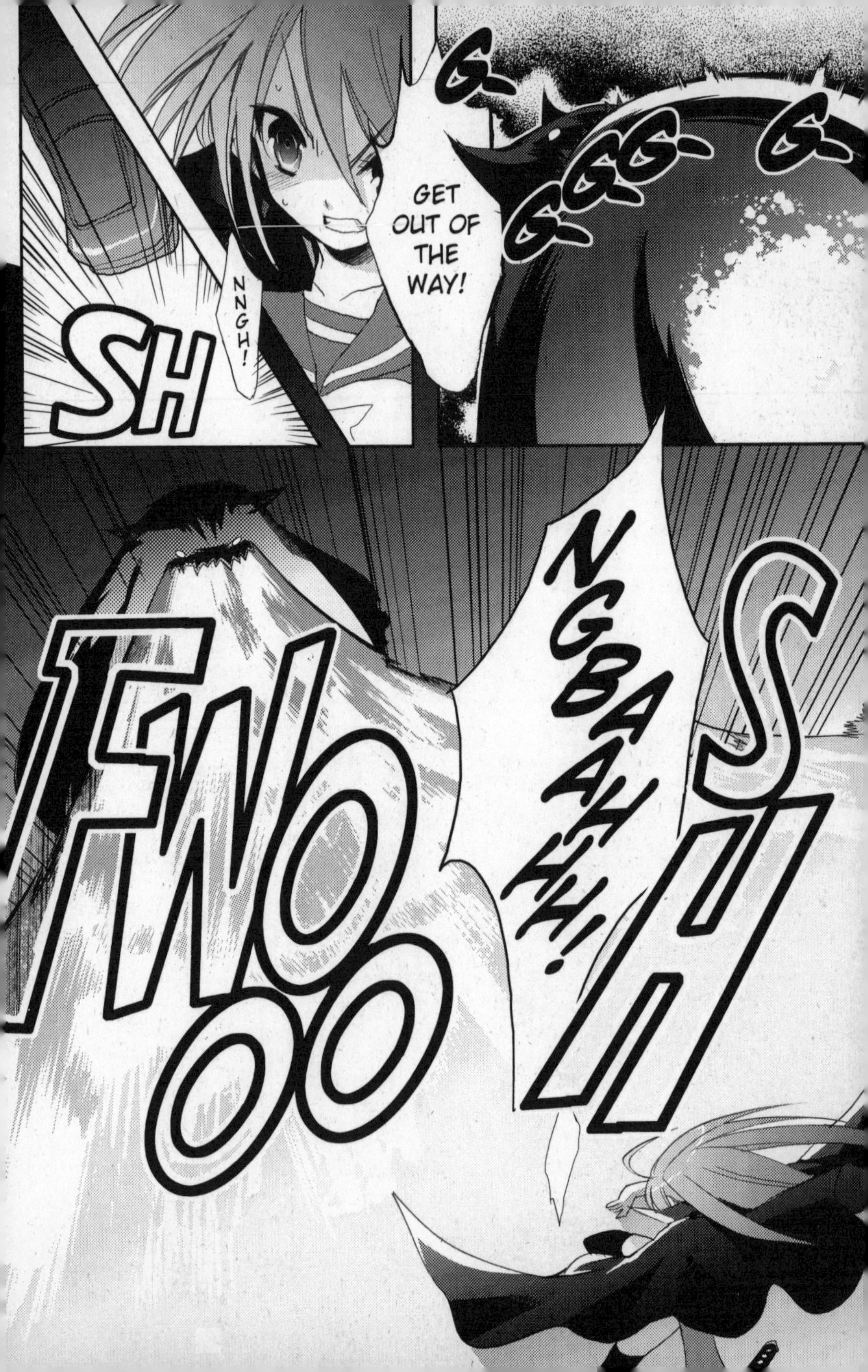
G- GGG- G- G-
GET OUT OF THE WAY!
NNGH!
SH
NGBAAHHH!
FWOOOSH

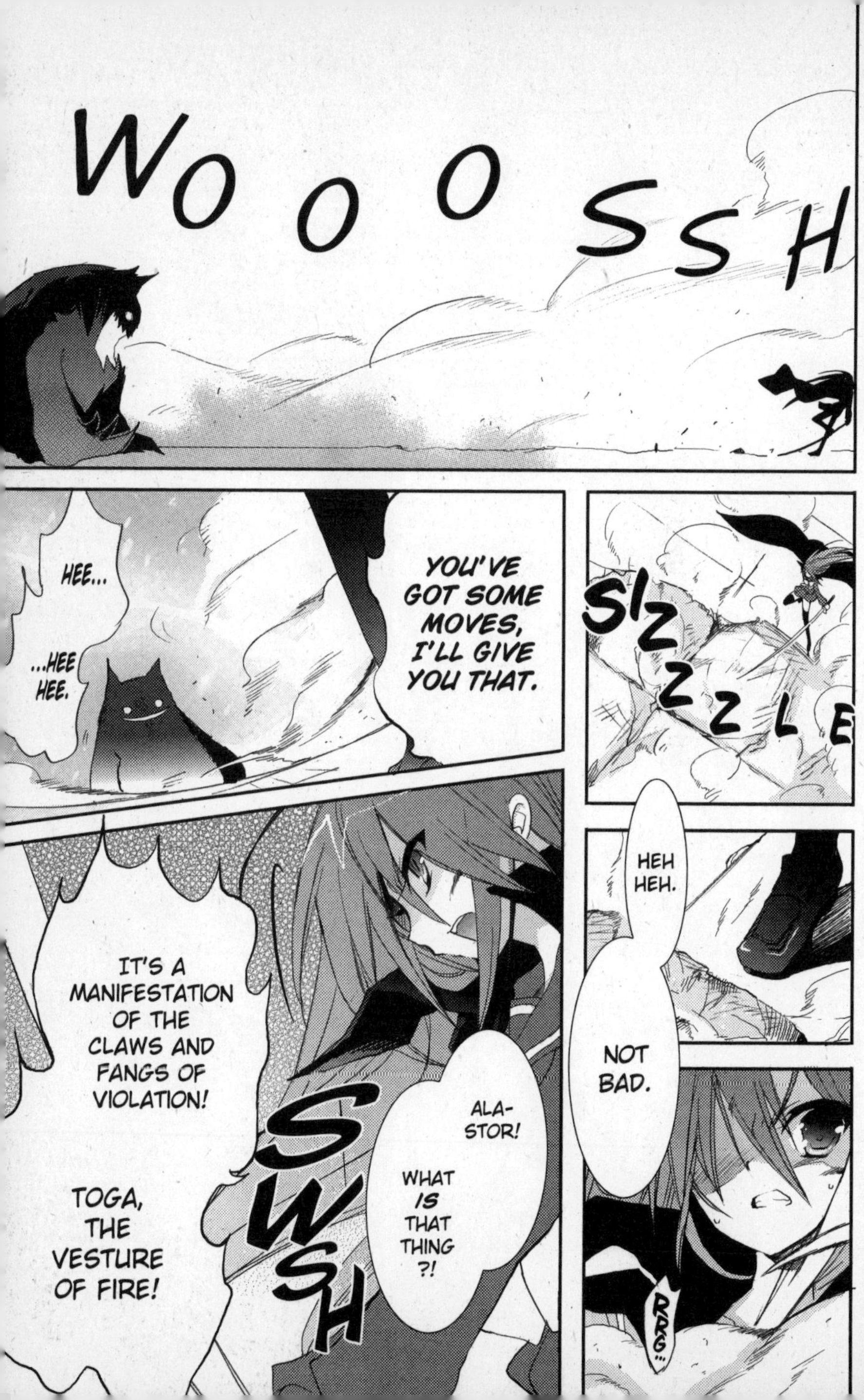
WOOOSSH
SIZZZLE
YOU'VE GOT SOME MOVES, I'LL GIVE YOU THAT.
HEE...
...HEE HEE.
HEH HEH.
NOT BAD.
RRG!!
ALA-STOR!
WHAT *IS* THAT THING?!
SWSH
IT'S A MANIFESTATION OF THE CLAWS AND FANGS OF VIOLATION!
TOGA, THE VESTURE OF FIRE!

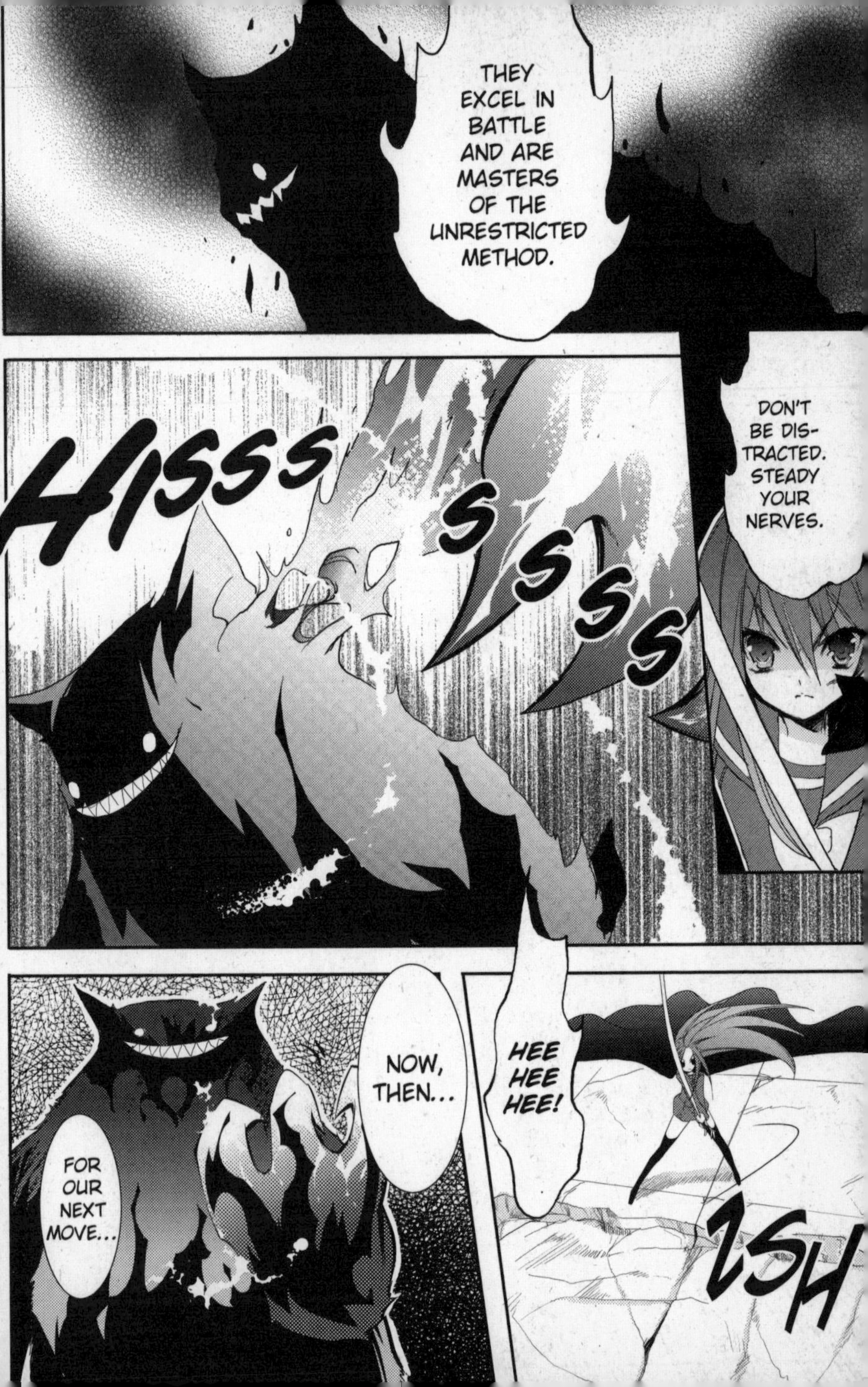
THEY EXCEL IN BATTLE AND ARE MASTERS OF THE UNRESTRICTED METHOD.
DON'T BE DIS-TRACTED. STEADY YOUR NERVES.
HISSSS SSSSS
HEE HEE HEE!
ZSH
NOW, THEN...
FOR OUR NEXT MOVE...

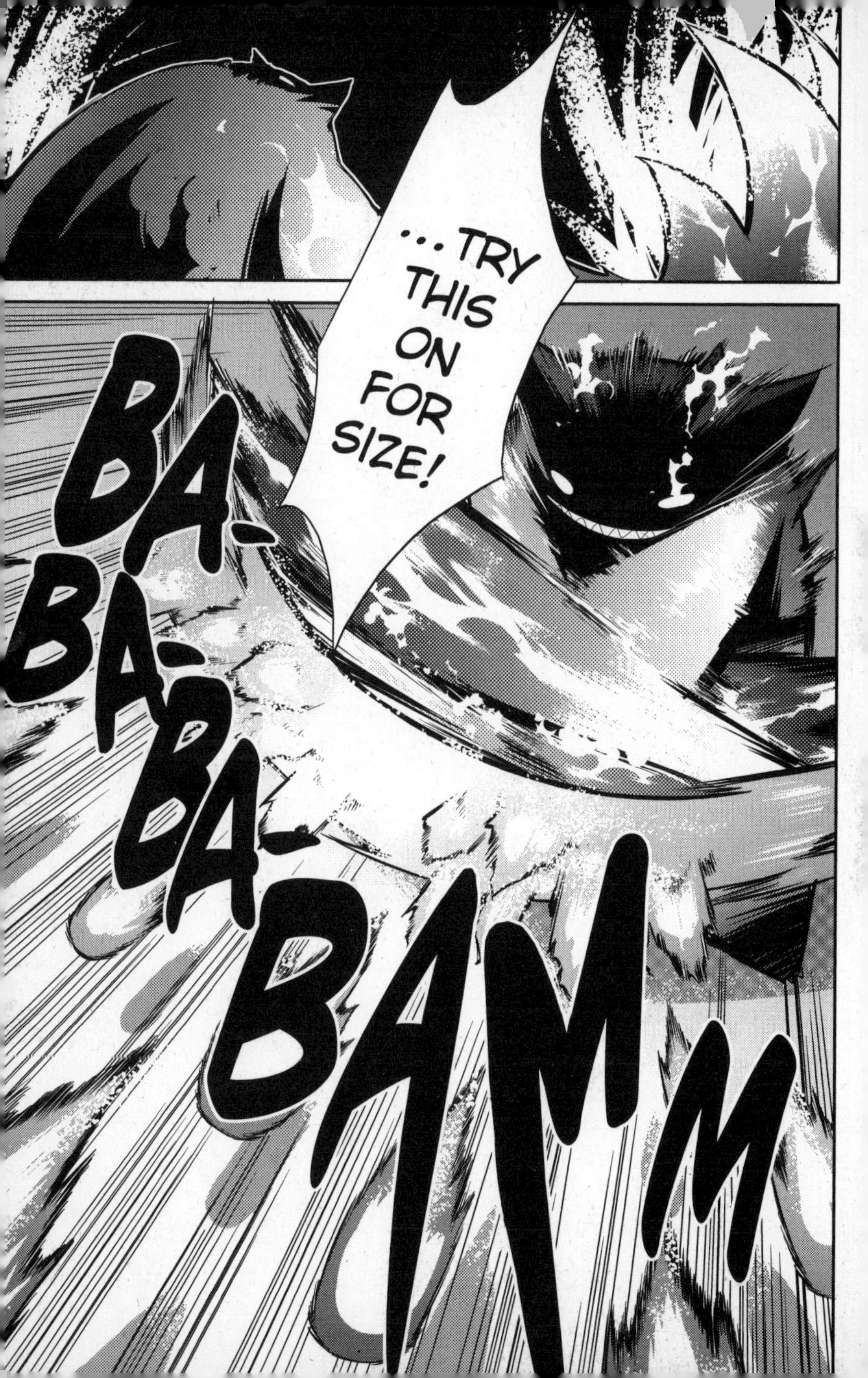
...TRY THIS ON FOR SIZE!
BA-BA-BA-BA-BAMM

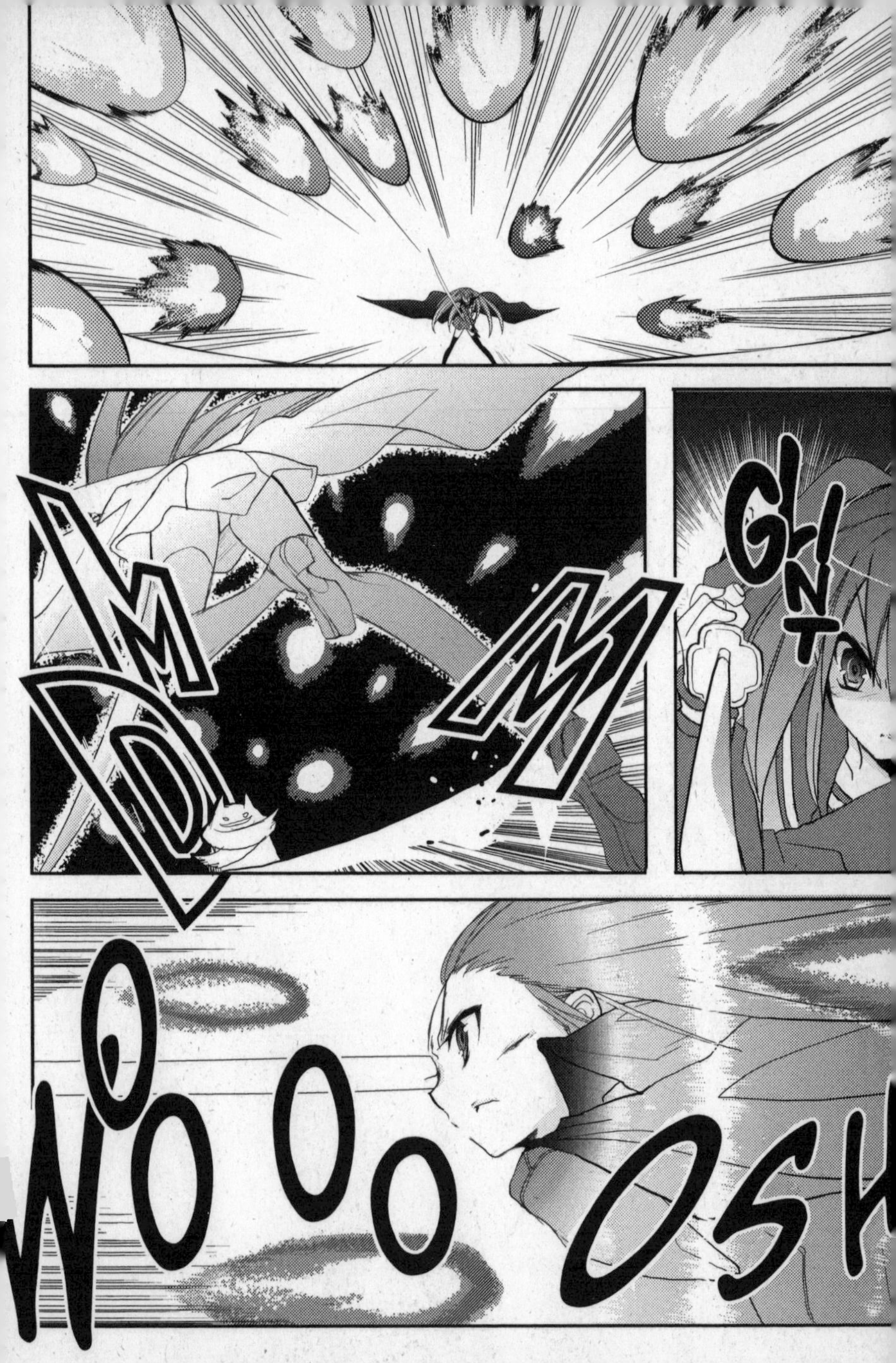
GLINT
DMM
WOOOOOSH

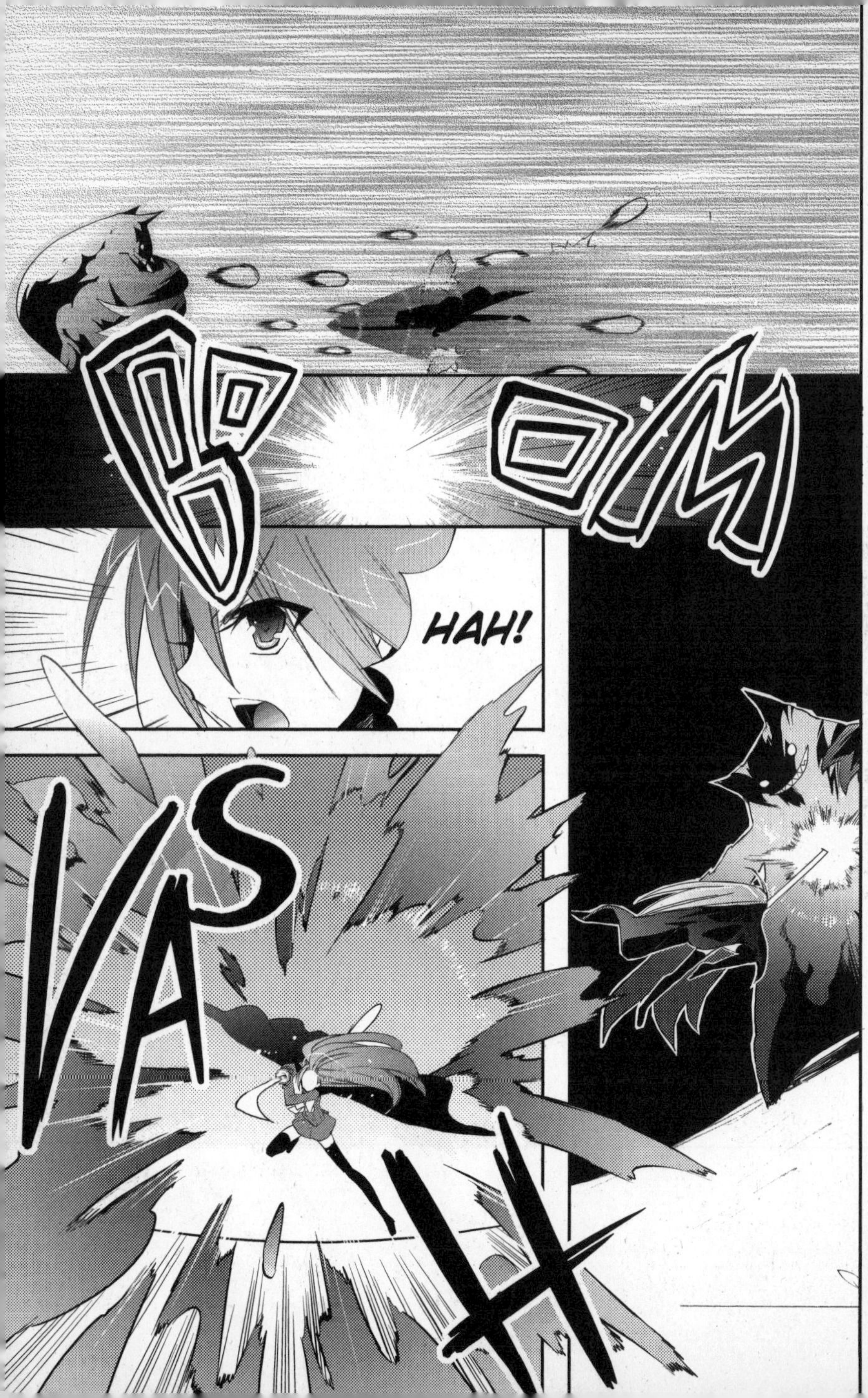
BOOM
HAH!
VASH

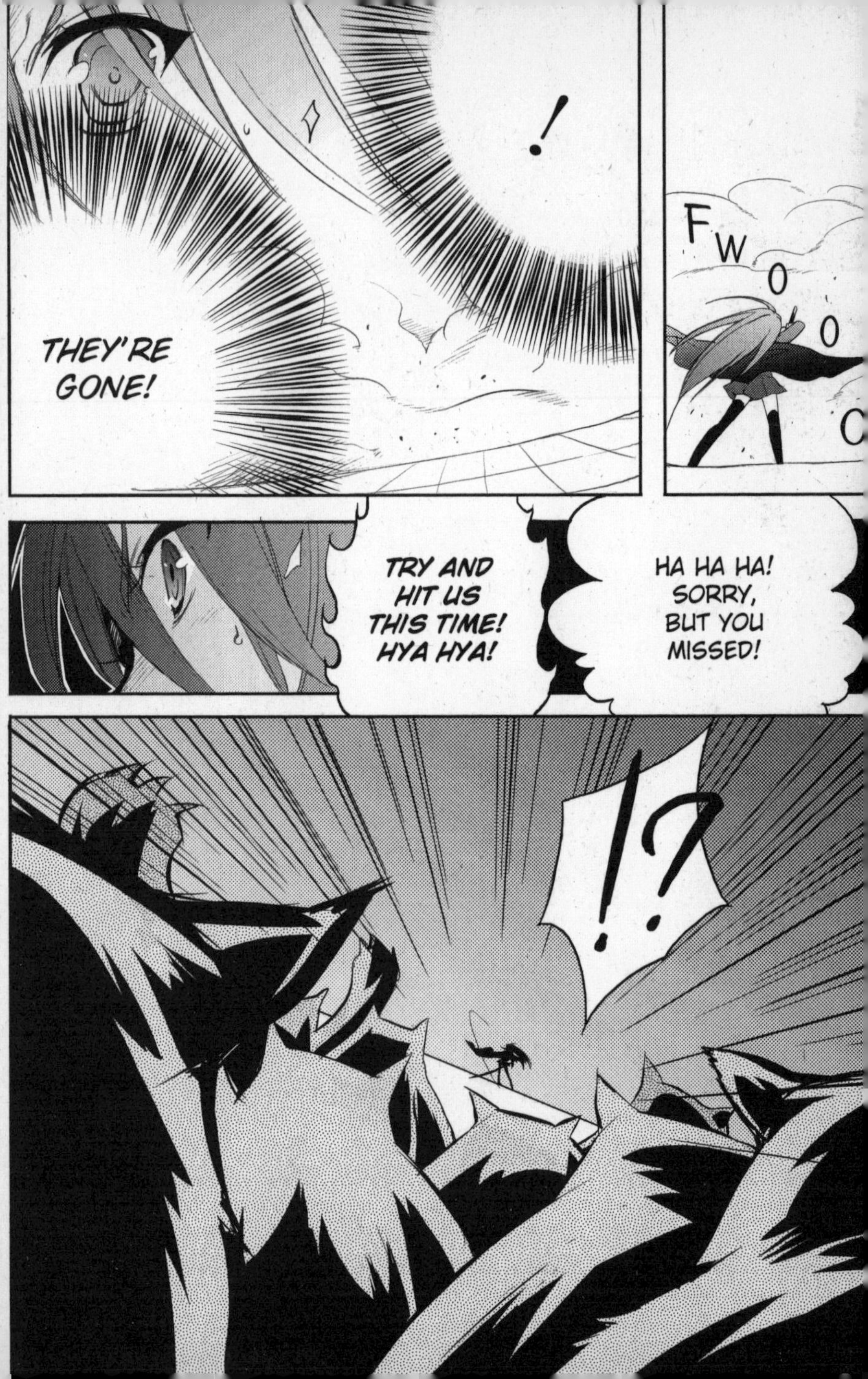
FWOOO
!
THEY'RE GONE!
HA HA HA! SORRY, BUT YOU MISSED!
TRY AND HIT US THIS TIME! HYA HYA!
!?

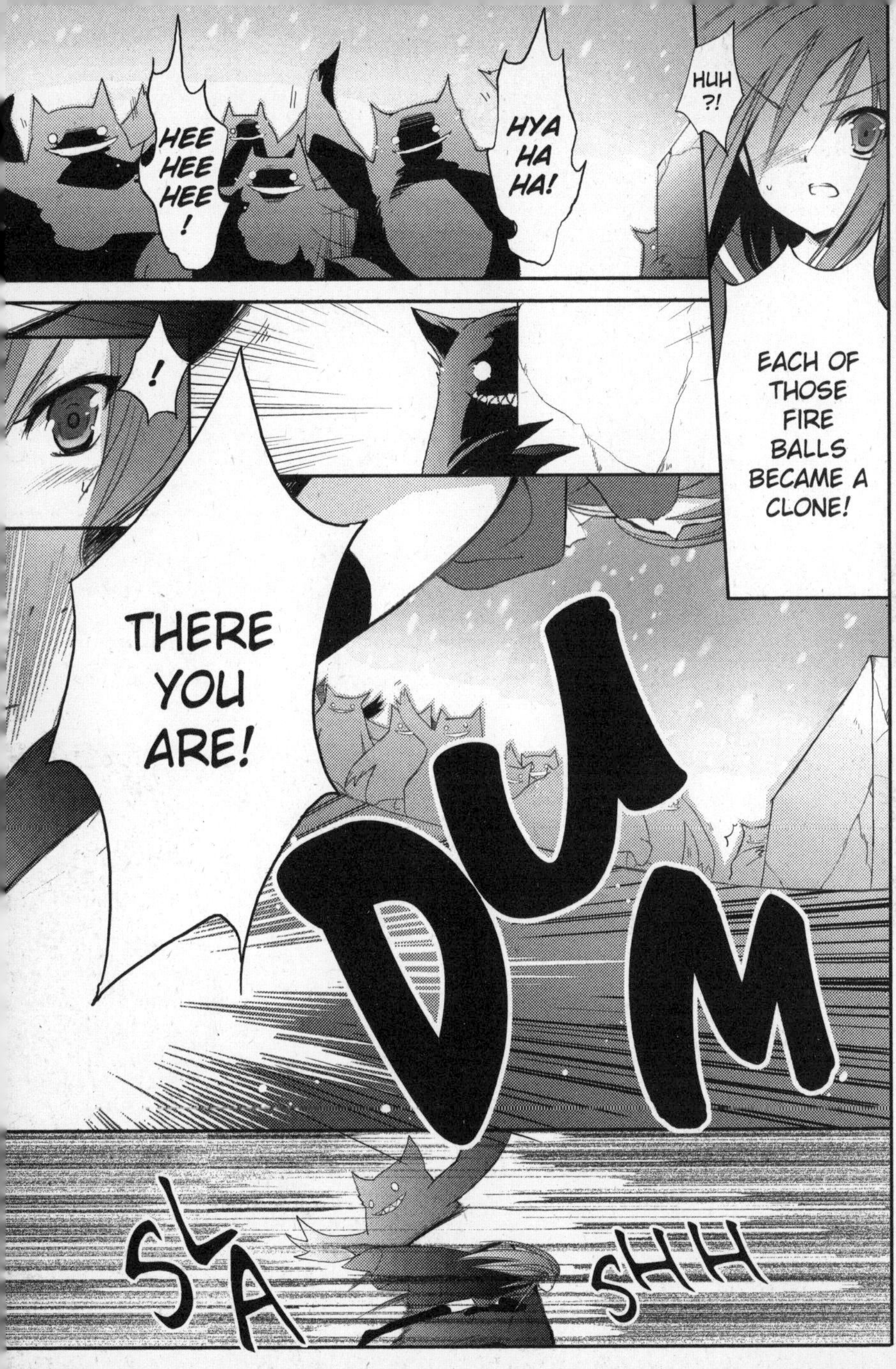
HUH ?!
HYA HA HA!
HEE HEE HEE !
EACH OF THOSE FIRE BALLS BECAME A CLONE!
!
THERE YOU ARE!
DUM
SLASHH

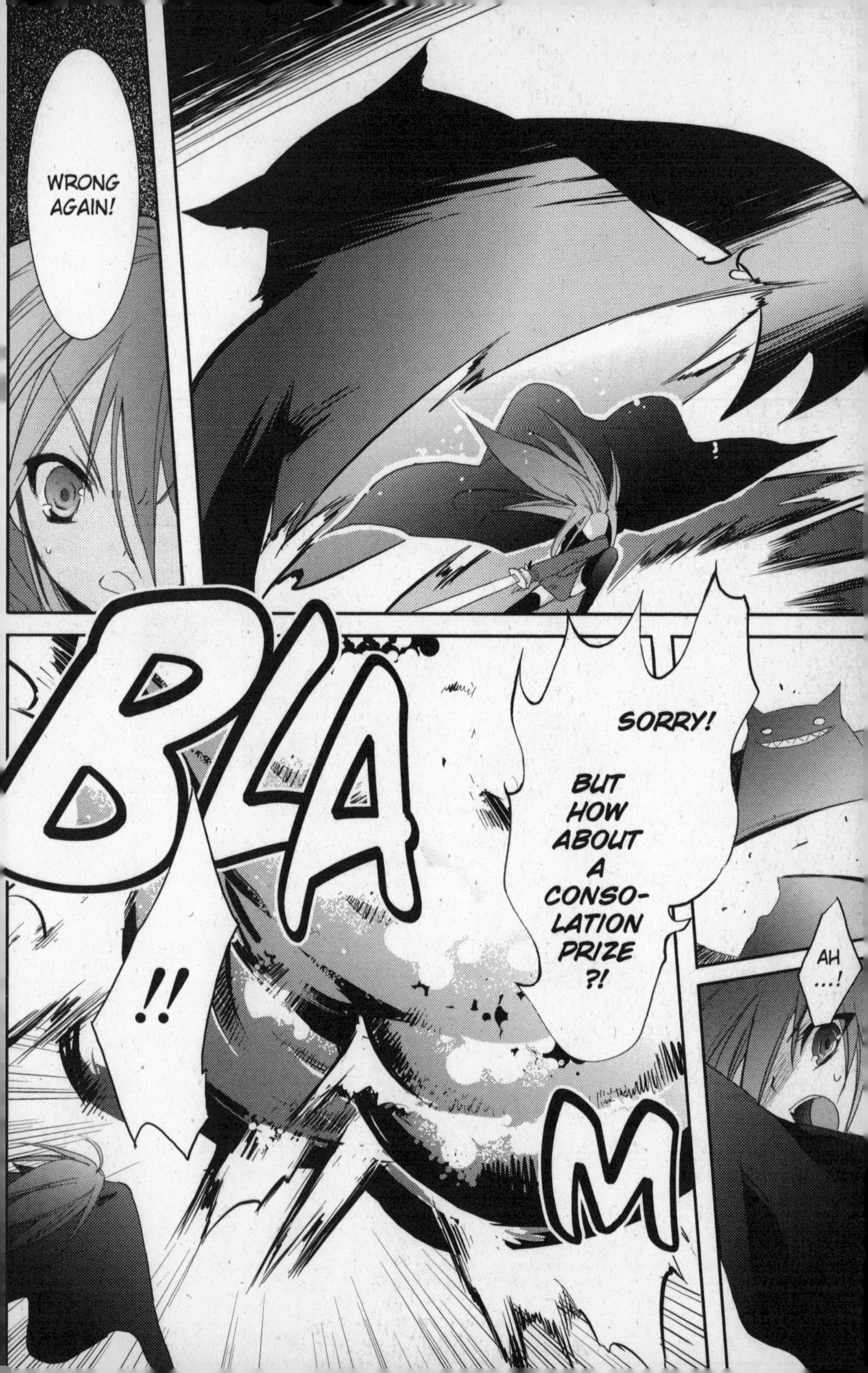
WRONG AGAIN!
AH ...!
SORRY!
BUT HOW ABOUT A CONSO-LATION PRIZE?!
BLAM
!!

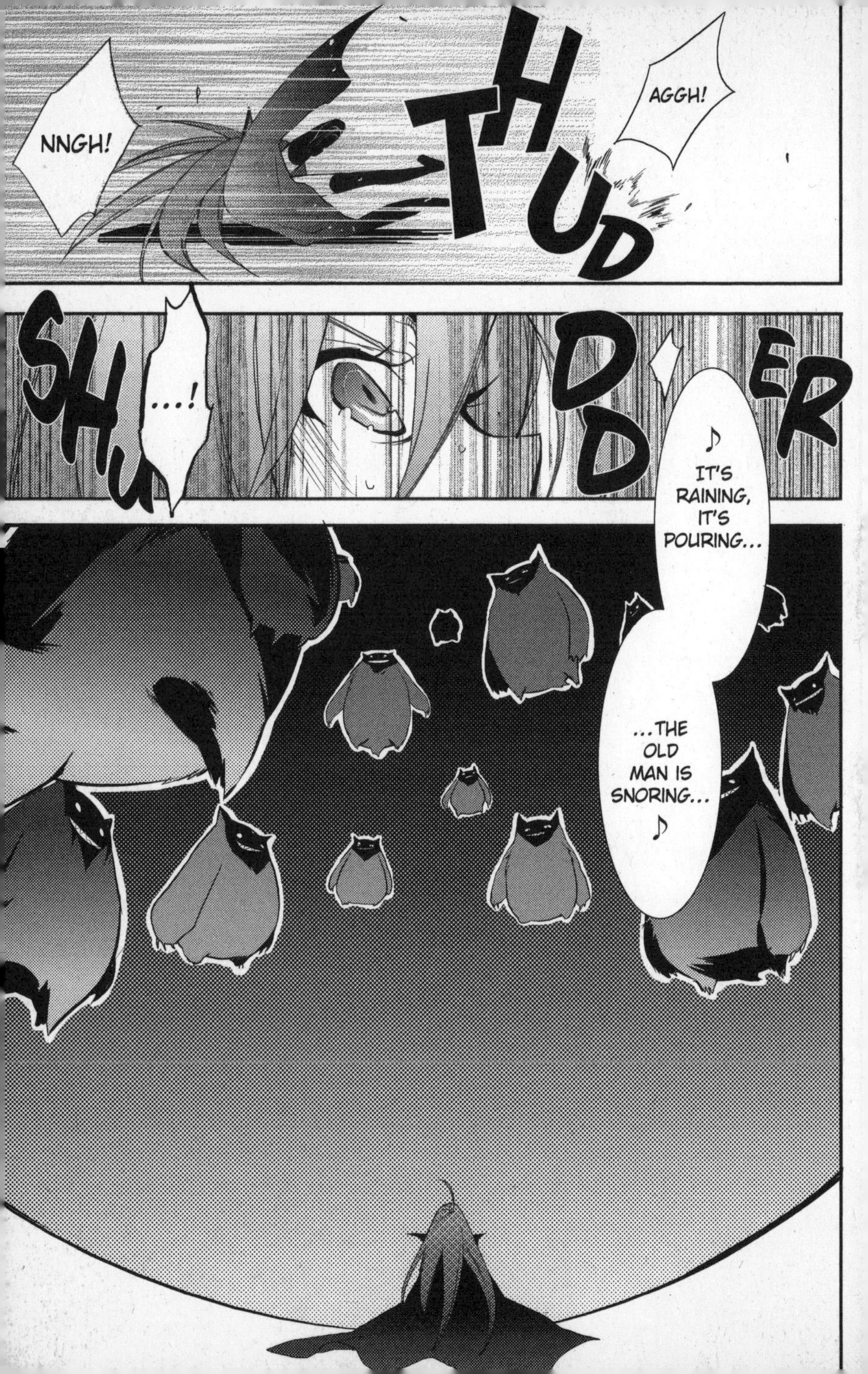
AGGH!
THUD
NNGH!
SHUDDER
...!
♪ IT'S RAINING, IT'S POURING...
...THE OLD MAN IS SNORING... ♪

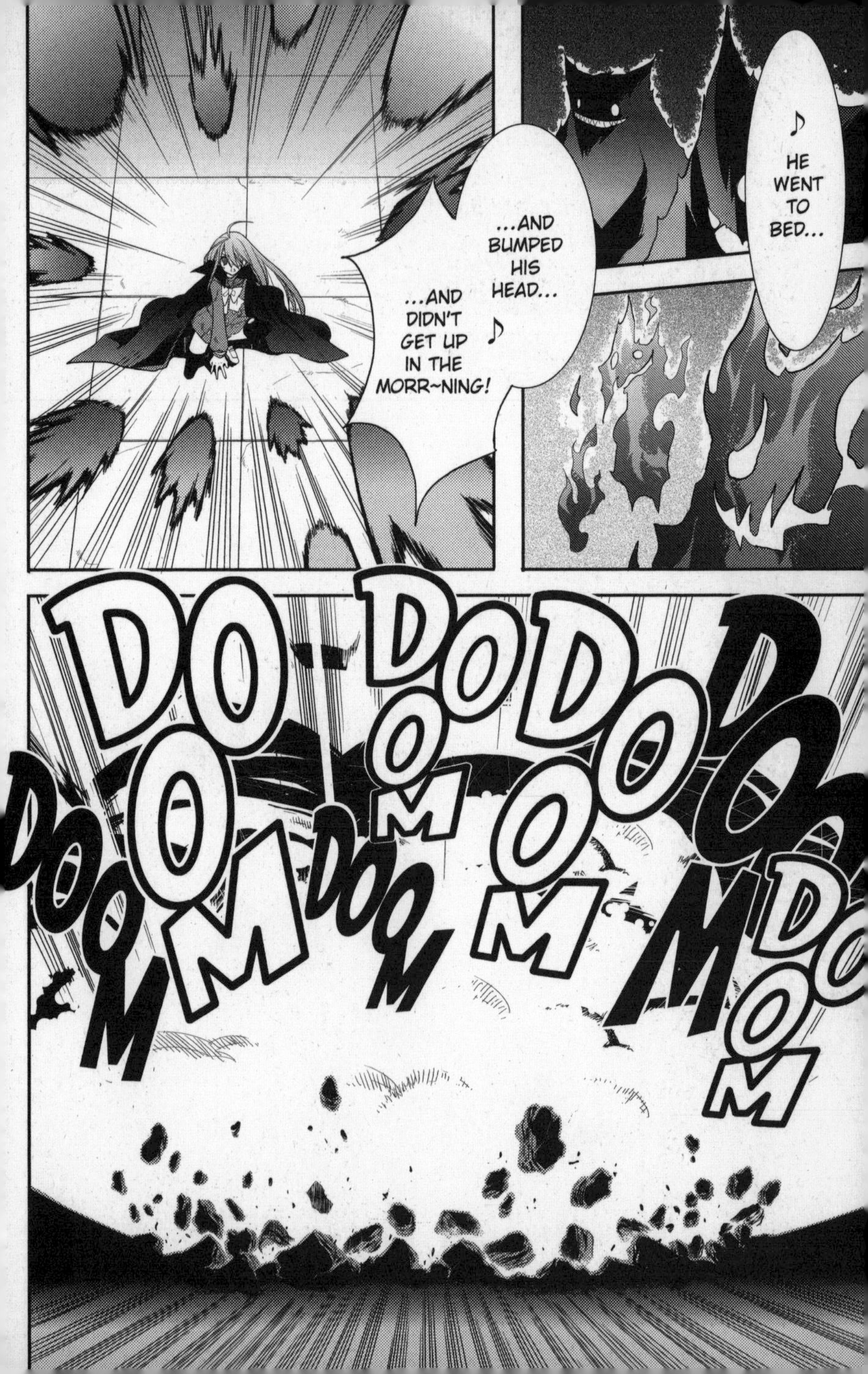
♪ HE WENT TO BED...
...AND BUMPED HIS HEAD... ♪
...AND DIDN'T GET UP IN THE MORR~NING!
DOOM
DOOOM
DOOOM
DOOOM
DOOOM
DOOOM
DOOOM
DOOOM

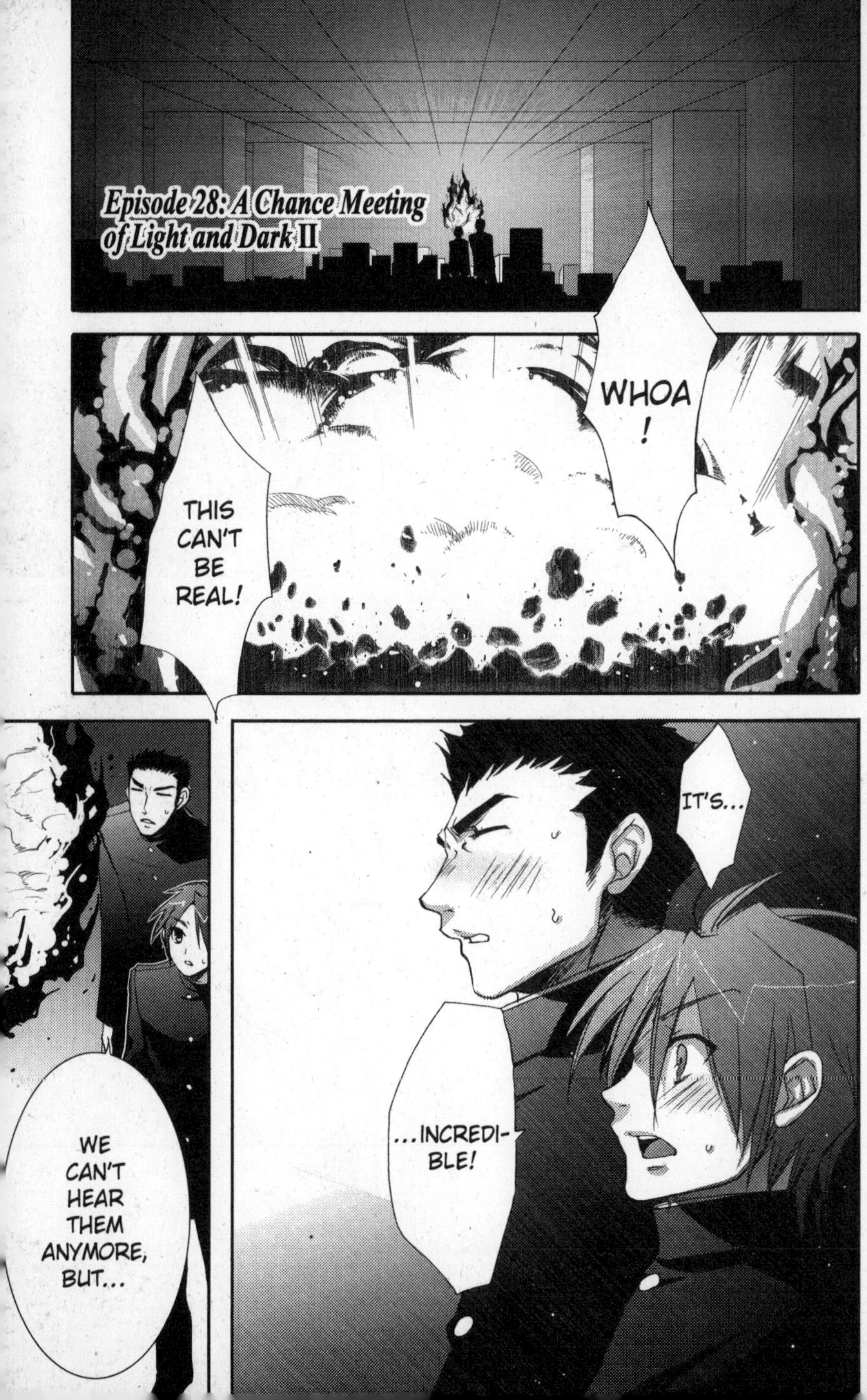
Episode 28: A Chance Meeting of Light and Dark II
WHOA!
THIS CAN'T BE REAL!
IT'S...
...INCREDIBLE!
WE CAN'T HEAR THEM ANYMORE, BUT...

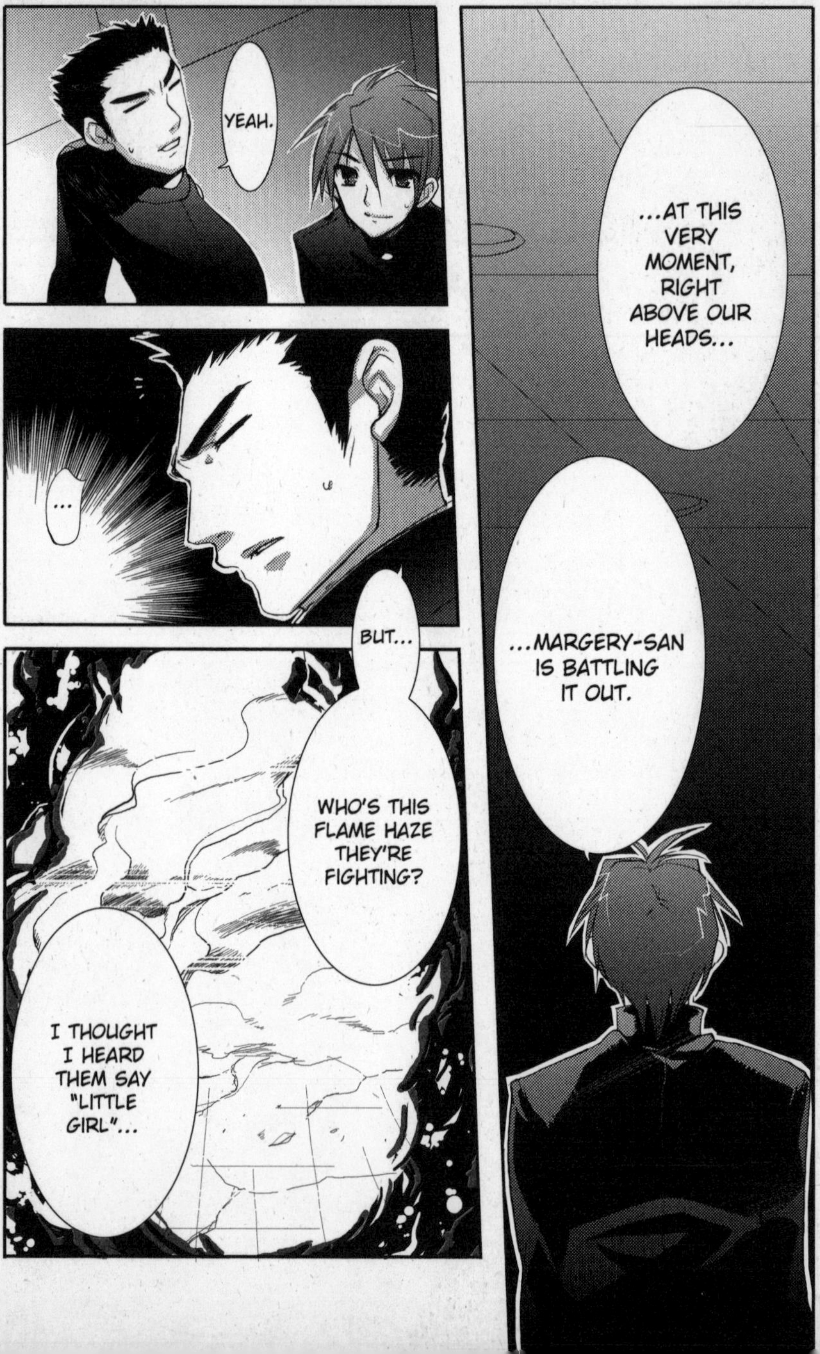
...AT THIS VERY MOMENT, RIGHT ABOVE OUR HEADS...
...MARGERY-SAN IS BATTLING IT OUT.
YEAH.
...
BUT...
WHO'S THIS FLAME HAZE THEY'RE FIGHTING?
I THOUGHT I HEARD THEM SAY "LITTLE GIRL"...

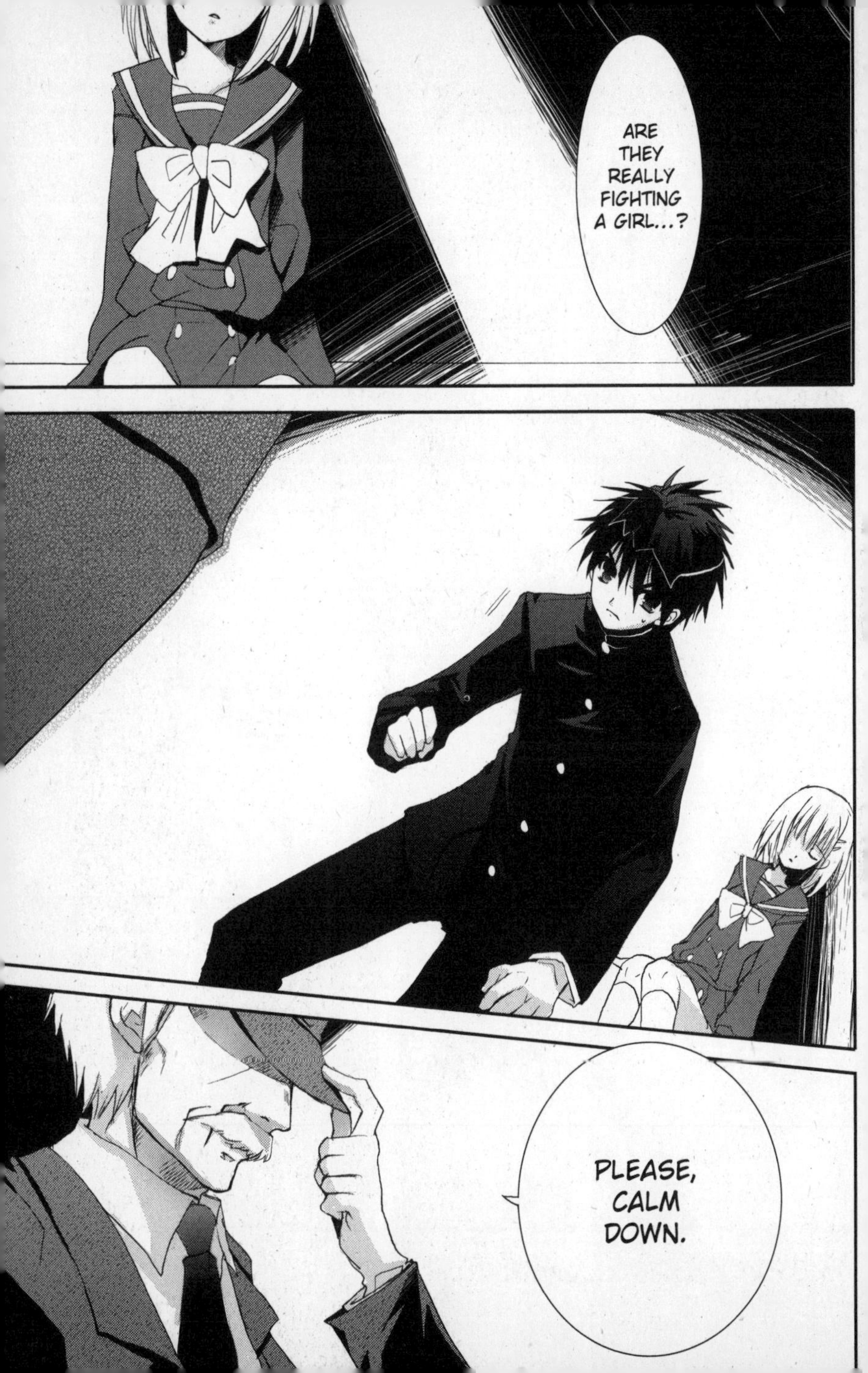
ARE THEY REALLY FIGHTING A GIRL...?
PLEASE, CALM DOWN.

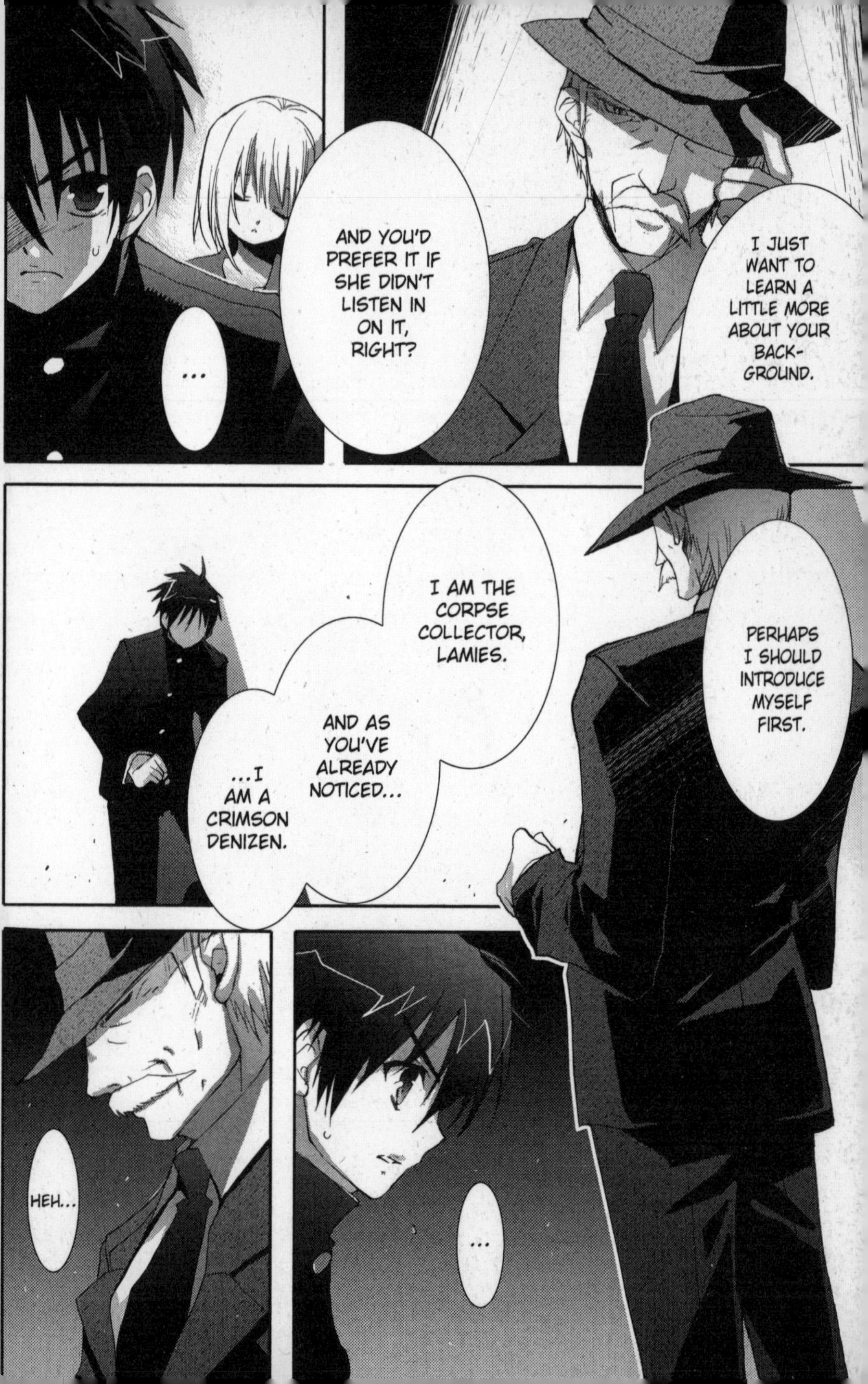
I JUST WANT TO LEARN A LITTLE MORE ABOUT YOUR BACK-GROUND.
AND YOU'D PREFER IT IF SHE DIDN'T LISTEN IN ON IT, RIGHT?
...
PERHAPS I SHOULD INTRODUCE MYSELF FIRST.
I AM THE CORPSE COLLECTOR, LAMIES.
AND AS YOU'VE ALREADY NOTICED...
...I AM A CRIMSON DENIZEN.
...
HEH...

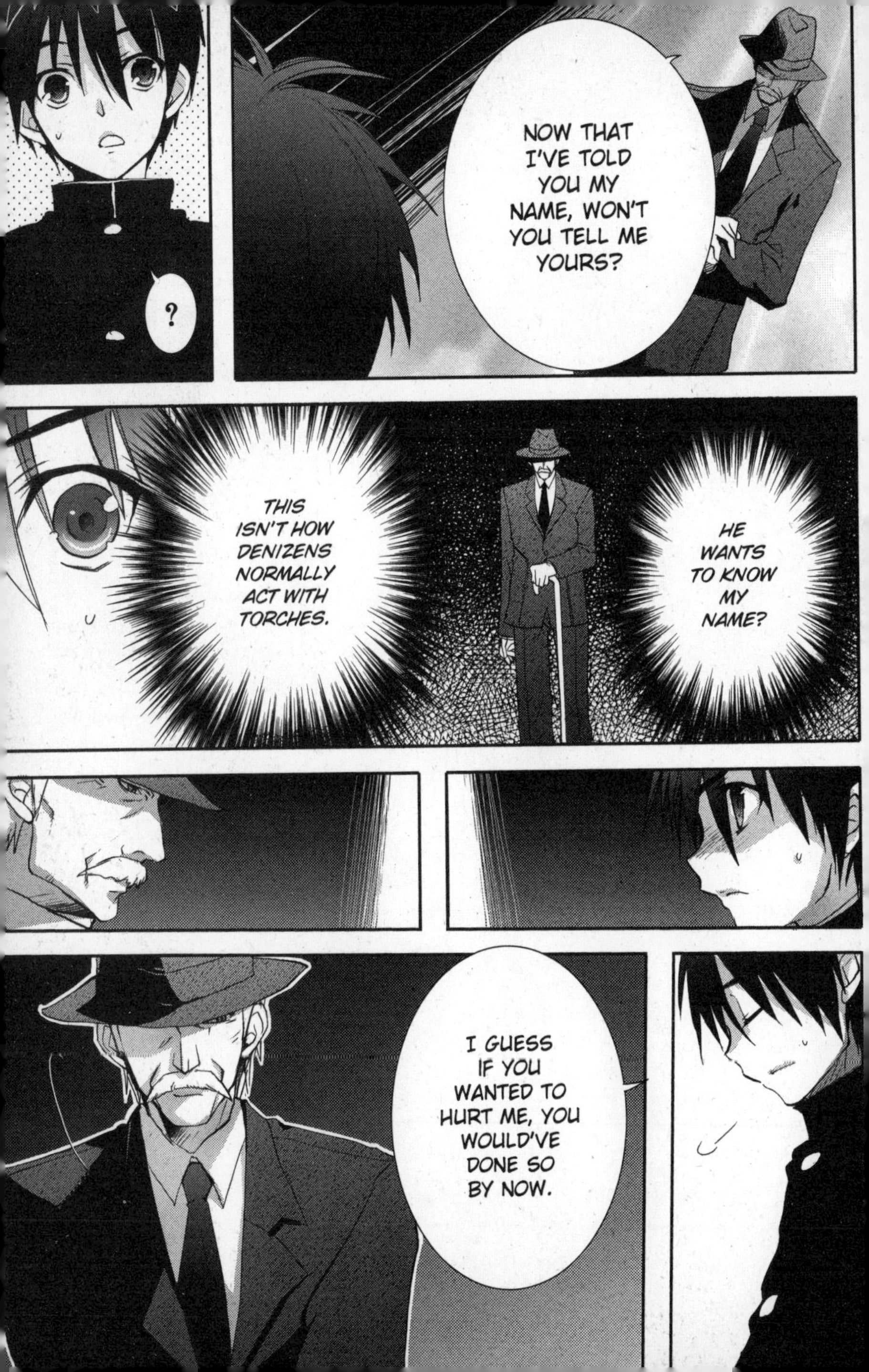
NOW THAT I'VE TOLD YOU MY NAME, WON'T YOU TELL ME YOURS?
?
HE WANTS TO KNOW MY NAME?
THIS ISN'T HOW DENIZENS NORMALLY ACT WITH TORCHES.
I GUESS IF YOU WANTED TO HURT ME, YOU WOULD'VE DONE SO BY NOW.

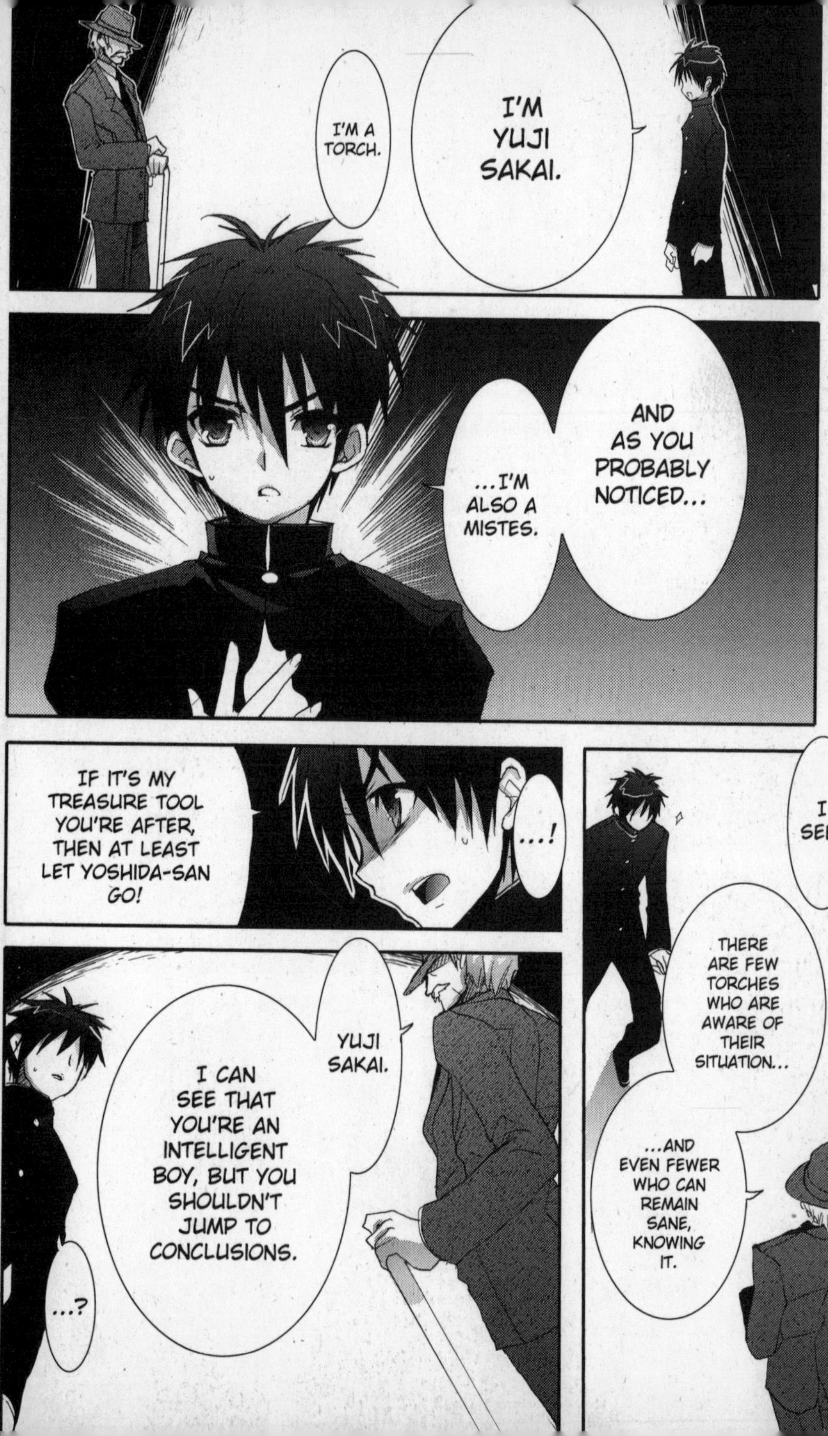
I'M YUJI SAKAI.
I'M A TORCH.
AND AS YOU PROBABLY NOTICED...
...I'M ALSO A MISTES.
I SEE.
THERE ARE FEW TORCHES WHO ARE AWARE OF THEIR SITUATION...
...AND EVEN FEWER WHO CAN REMAIN SANE, KNOWING IT.
...!
IF IT'S MY TREASURE TOOL YOU'RE AFTER, THEN AT LEAST LET YOSHIDA-SAN GO!
YUJI SAKAI.
I CAN SEE THAT YOU'RE AN INTELLIGENT BOY, BUT YOU SHOULDN'T JUMP TO CONCLUSIONS.
...?

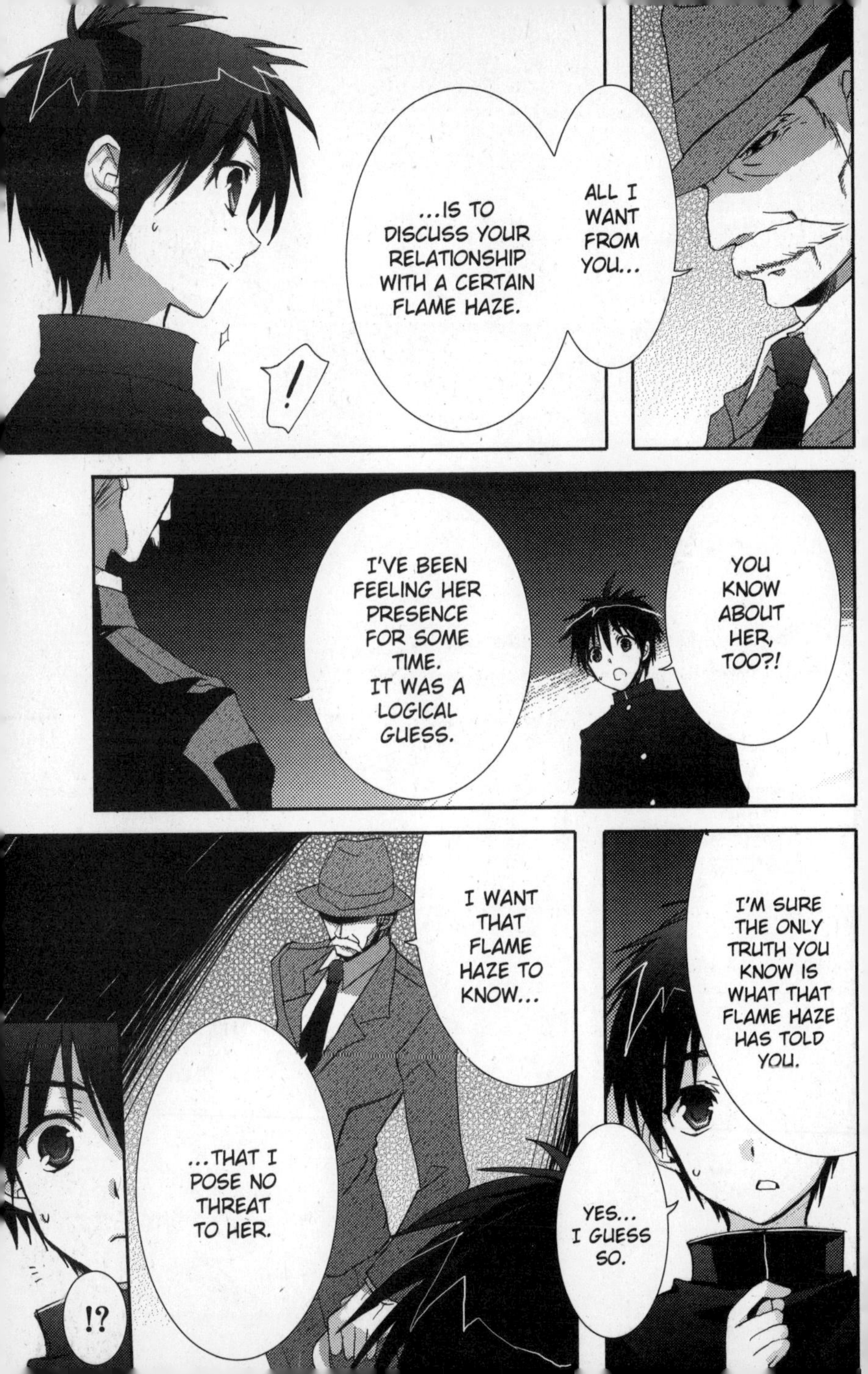
ALL I WANT FROM YOU...
...IS TO DISCUSS YOUR RELATIONSHIP WITH A CERTAIN FLAME HAZE.
!
YOU KNOW ABOUT HER, TOO?!
I'VE BEEN FEELING HER PRESENCE FOR SOME TIME. IT WAS A LOGICAL GUESS.
I'M SURE THE ONLY TRUTH YOU KNOW IS WHAT THAT FLAME HAZE HAS TOLD YOU.
YES... I GUESS SO.
I WANT THAT FLAME HAZE TO KNOW...
...THAT I POSE NO THREAT TO HER.
!?

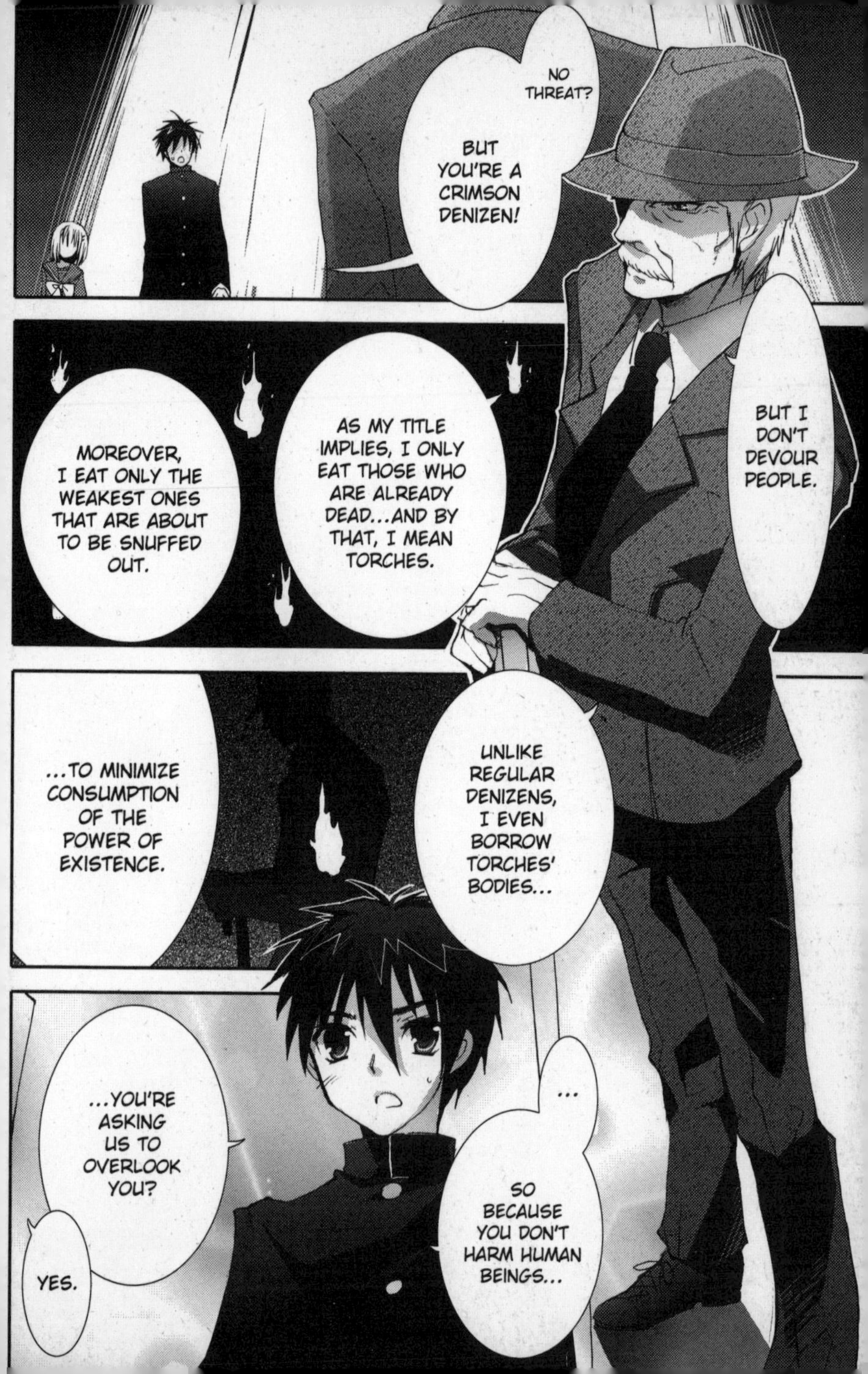
NO THREAT?
BUT YOU'RE A CRIMSON DENIZEN!
BUT I DON'T DEVOUR PEOPLE.
AS MY TITLE IMPLIES, I ONLY EAT THOSE WHO ARE ALREADY DEAD...AND BY THAT, I MEAN TORCHES.
MOREOVER, I EAT ONLY THE WEAKEST ONES THAT ARE ABOUT TO BE SNUFFED OUT.
UNLIKE REGULAR DENIZENS, I EVEN BORROW TORCHES' BODIES...
...TO MINIMIZE CONSUMPTION OF THE POWER OF EXISTENCE.
...
SO BECAUSE YOU DON'T HARM HUMAN BEINGS...
...YOU'RE ASKING US TO OVERLOOK YOU?
YES.

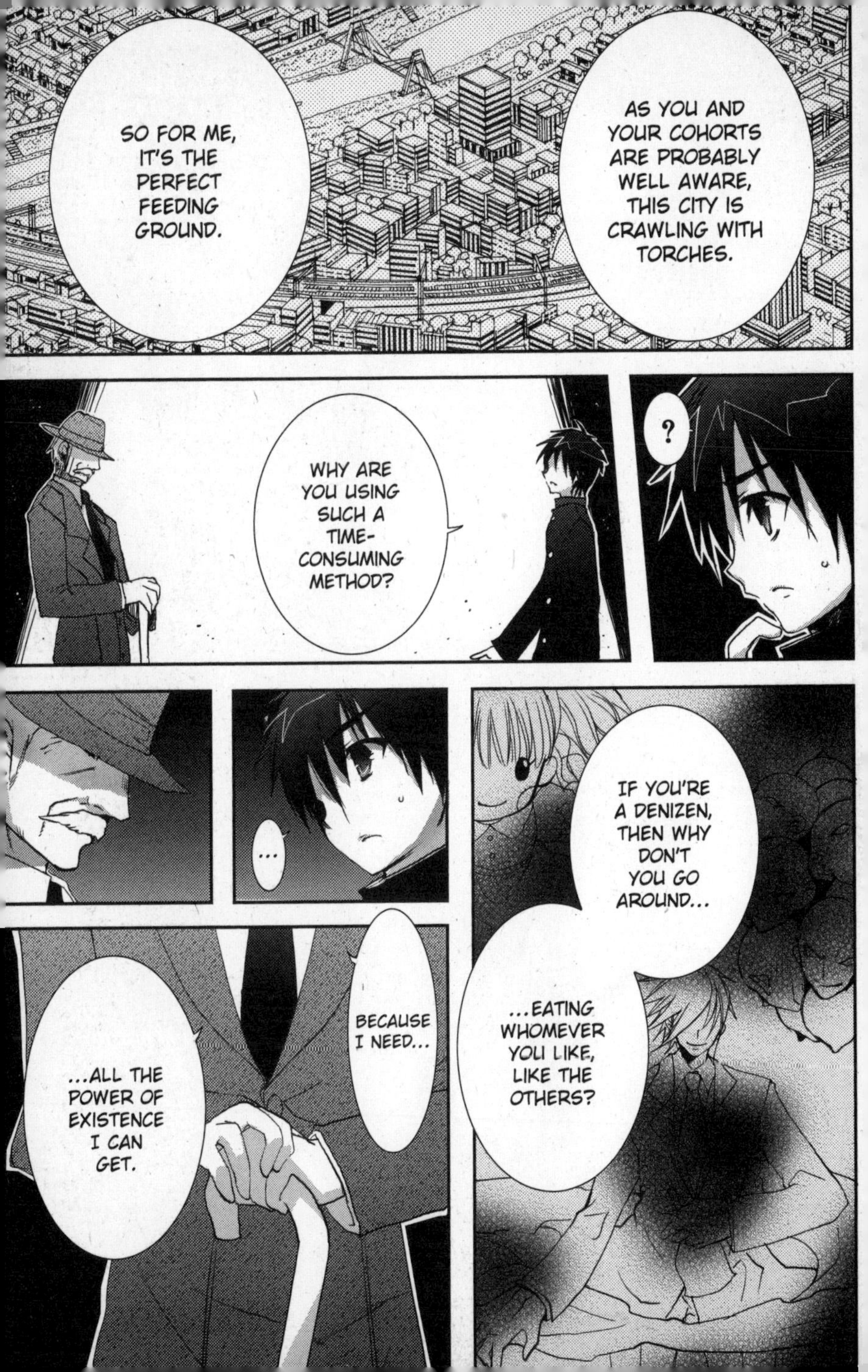
AS YOU AND YOUR COHORTS ARE PROBABLY WELL AWARE, THIS CITY IS CRAWLING WITH TORCHES.
SO FOR ME, IT'S THE PERFECT FEEDING GROUND.
?
WHY ARE YOU USING SUCH A TIME-CONSUMING METHOD?
IF YOU'RE A DENIZEN, THEN WHY DON'T YOU GO AROUND...
...EATING WHOMEVER YOU LIKE, LIKE THE OTHERS?
...
BECAUSE I NEED...
...ALL THE POWER OF EXISTENCE I CAN GET.

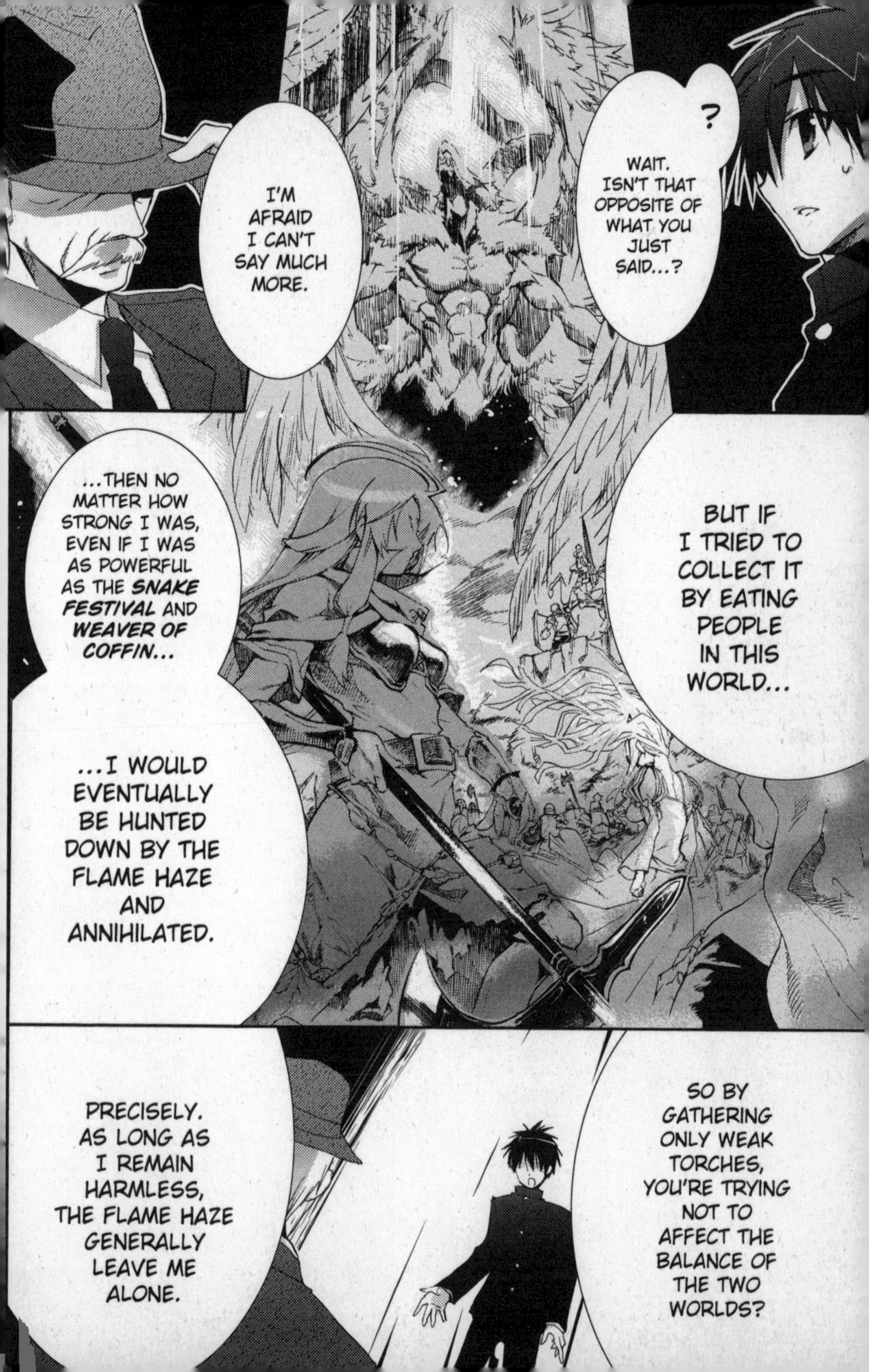
?
WAIT. ISN'T THAT OPPOSITE OF WHAT YOU JUST SAID...?
I'M AFRAID I CAN'T SAY MUCH MORE.
BUT IF I TRIED TO COLLECT IT BY EATING PEOPLE IN THIS WORLD...
...THEN NO MATTER HOW STRONG I WAS, EVEN IF I WAS AS POWERFUL AS THE *SNAKE FESTIVAL* AND *WEAVER OF COFFIN*...
...I WOULD EVENTUALLY BE HUNTED DOWN BY THE FLAME HAZE AND ANNIHILATED.
SO BY GATHERING ONLY WEAK TORCHES, YOU'RE TRYING NOT TO AFFECT THE BALANCE OF THE TWO WORLDS?
PRECISELY. AS LONG AS I REMAIN HARMLESS, THE FLAME HAZE GENERALLY LEAVE ME ALONE.

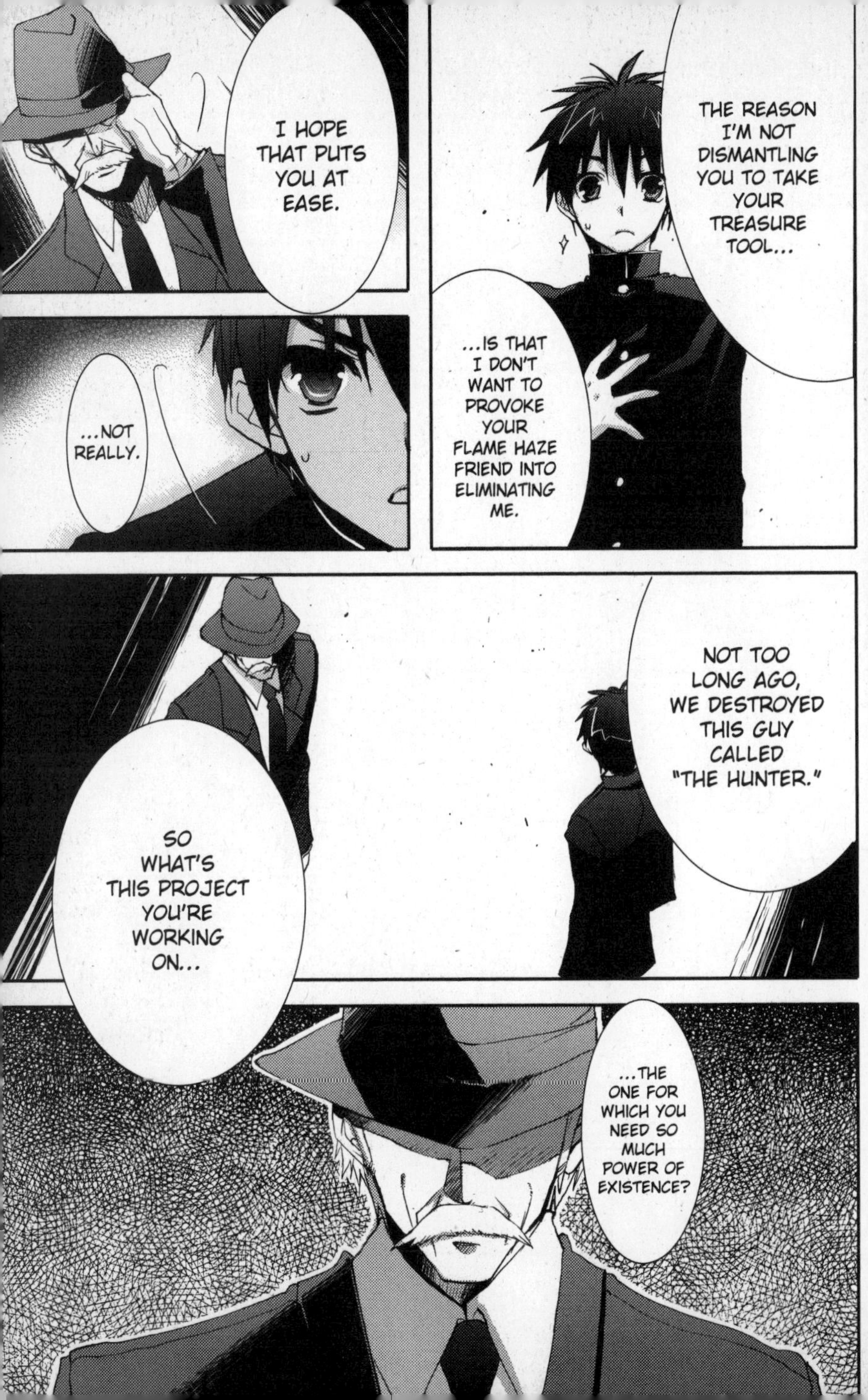
THE REASON I'M NOT DISMANTLING YOU TO TAKE YOUR TREASURE TOOL...
...IS THAT I DON'T WANT TO PROVOKE YOUR FLAME HAZE FRIEND INTO ELIMINATING ME.
I HOPE THAT PUTS YOU AT EASE.
...NOT REALLY.
NOT TOO LONG AGO, WE DESTROYED THIS GUY CALLED "THE HUNTER."
SO WHAT'S THIS PROJECT YOU'RE WORKING ON...
...THE ONE FOR WHICH YOU NEED SO MUCH POWER OF EXISTENCE?

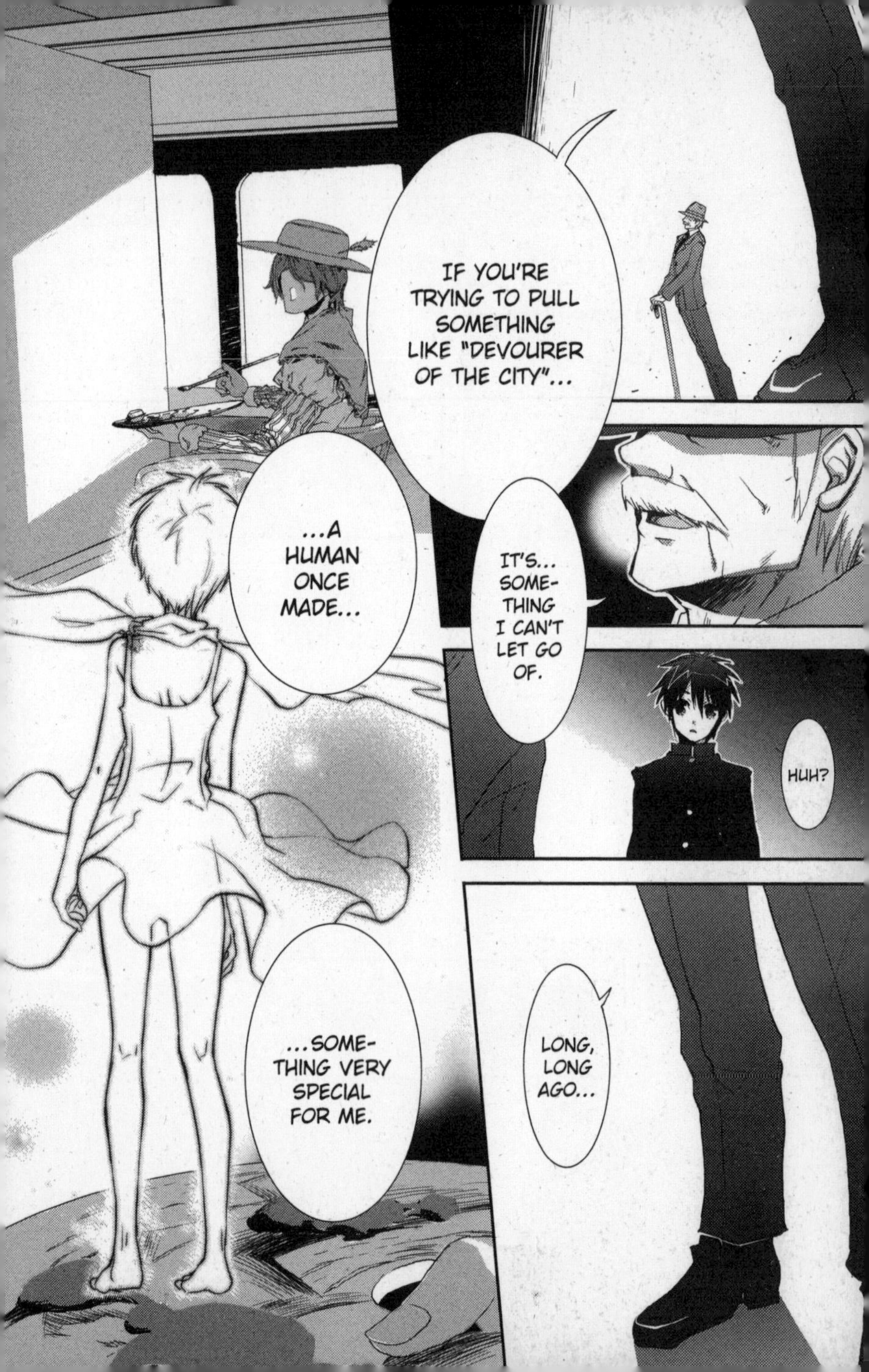
IF YOU'RE TRYING TO PULL SOMETHING LIKE "DEVOURER OF THE CITY"...
IT'S... SOME-THING I CAN'T LET GO OF.
HUH?
LONG, LONG AGO...
...A HUMAN ONCE MADE...
...SOME-THING VERY SPECIAL FOR ME.

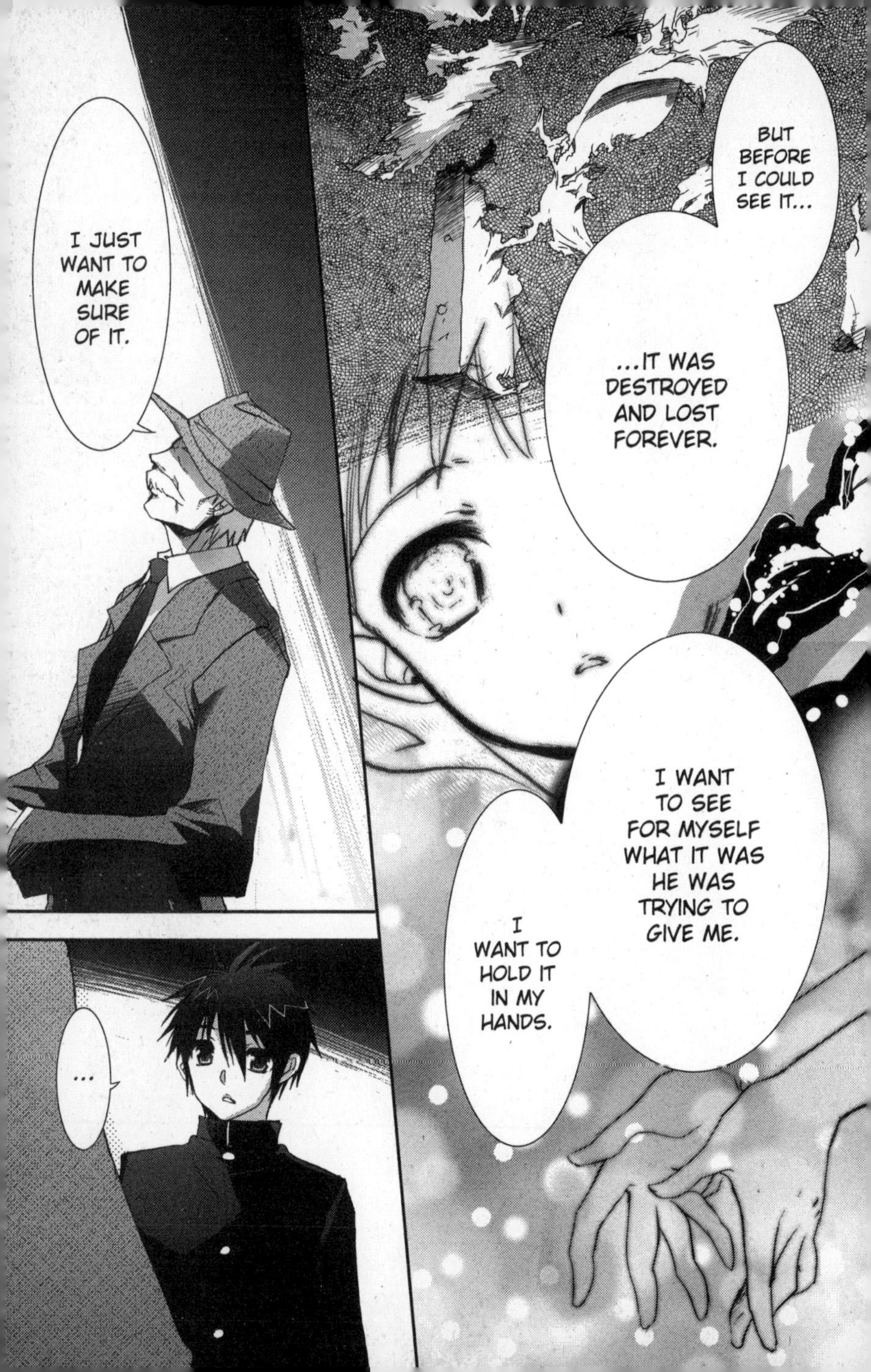
BUT BEFORE I COULD SEE IT...
...IT WAS DESTROYED AND LOST FOREVER.
I WANT TO SEE FOR MYSELF WHAT IT WAS HE WAS TRYING TO GIVE ME.
I WANT TO HOLD IT IN MY HANDS.
I JUST WANT TO MAKE SURE OF IT.
...

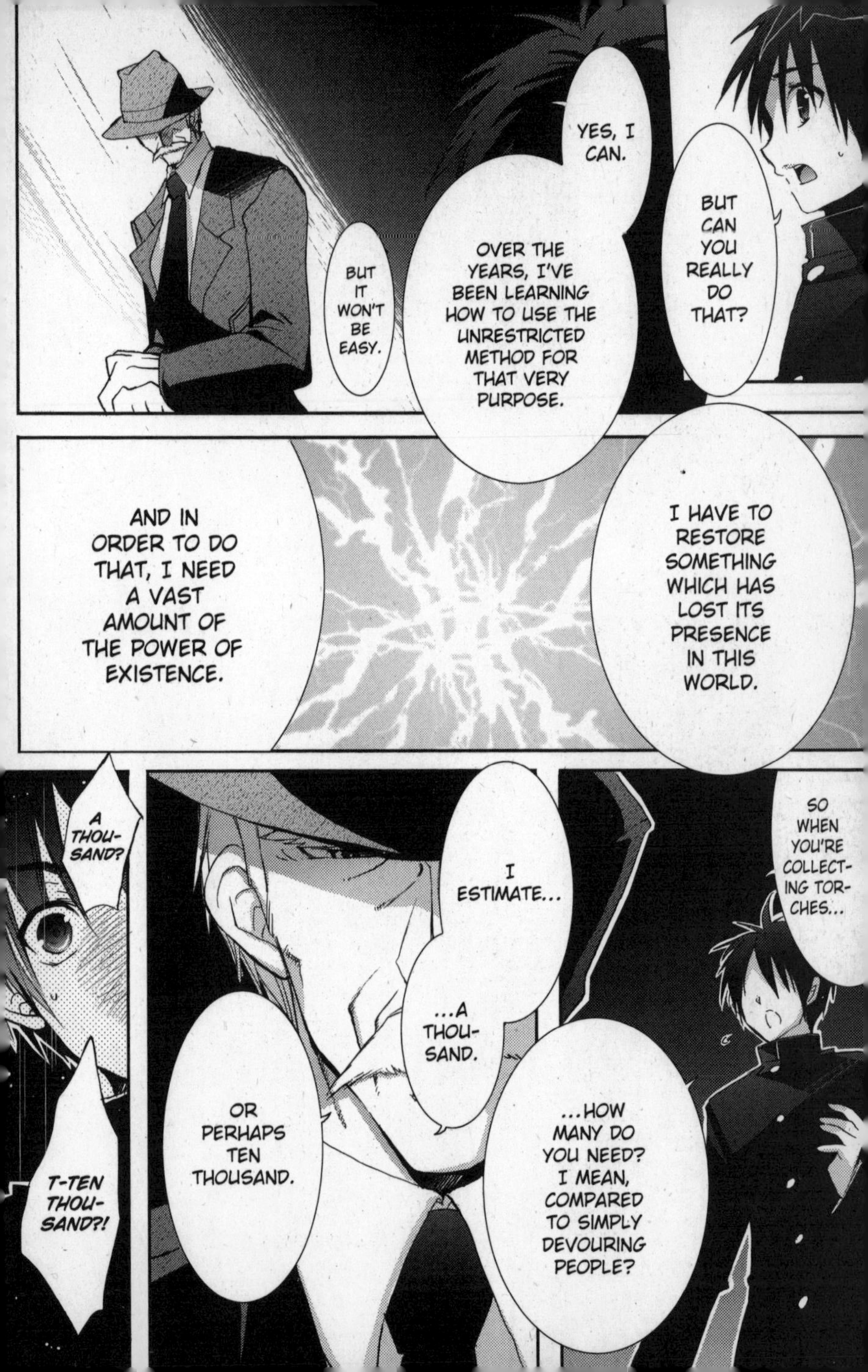
BUT CAN YOU REALLY DO THAT?
YES, I CAN.
OVER THE YEARS, I'VE BEEN LEARNING HOW TO USE THE UNRESTRICTED METHOD FOR THAT VERY PURPOSE.
BUT IT WON'T BE EASY.
I HAVE TO RESTORE SOMETHING WHICH HAS LOST ITS PRESENCE IN THIS WORLD.
AND IN ORDER TO DO THAT, I NEED A VAST AMOUNT OF THE POWER OF EXISTENCE.
SO WHEN YOU'RE COLLECT-ING TOR-CHES...
...HOW MANY DO YOU NEED? I MEAN, COMPARED TO SIMPLY DEVOURING PEOPLE?
I ESTIMATE...
...A THOU-SAND.
OR PERHAPS TEN THOUSAND.
A THOU-SAND?
T-TEN THOU-SAND?!

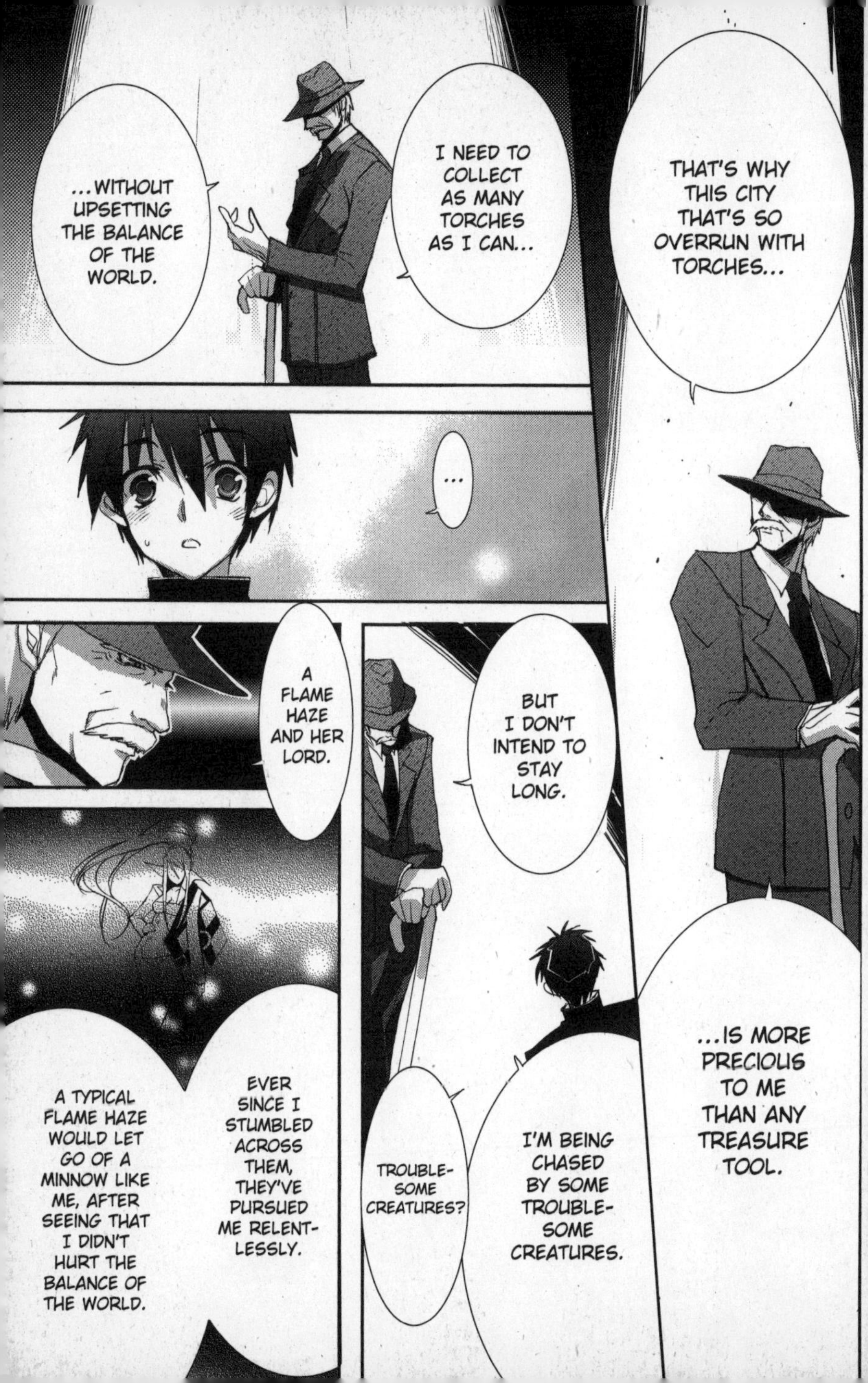
THAT'S WHY THIS CITY THAT'S SO OVERRUN WITH TORCHES...
...IS MORE PRECIOUS TO ME THAN ANY TREASURE TOOL.
I NEED TO COLLECT AS MANY TORCHES AS I CAN...
...WITHOUT UPSETTING THE BALANCE OF THE WORLD.
...
BUT I DON'T INTEND TO STAY LONG.
I'M BEING CHASED BY SOME TROUBLE-SOME CREATURES.
TROUBLE-SOME CREATURES?
A FLAME HAZE AND HER LORD.
EVER SINCE I STUMBLED ACROSS THEM, THEY'VE PURSUED ME RELENT-LESSLY.
A TYPICAL FLAME HAZE WOULD LET GO OF A MINNOW LIKE ME, AFTER SEEING THAT I DIDN'T HURT THE BALANCE OF THE WORLD.

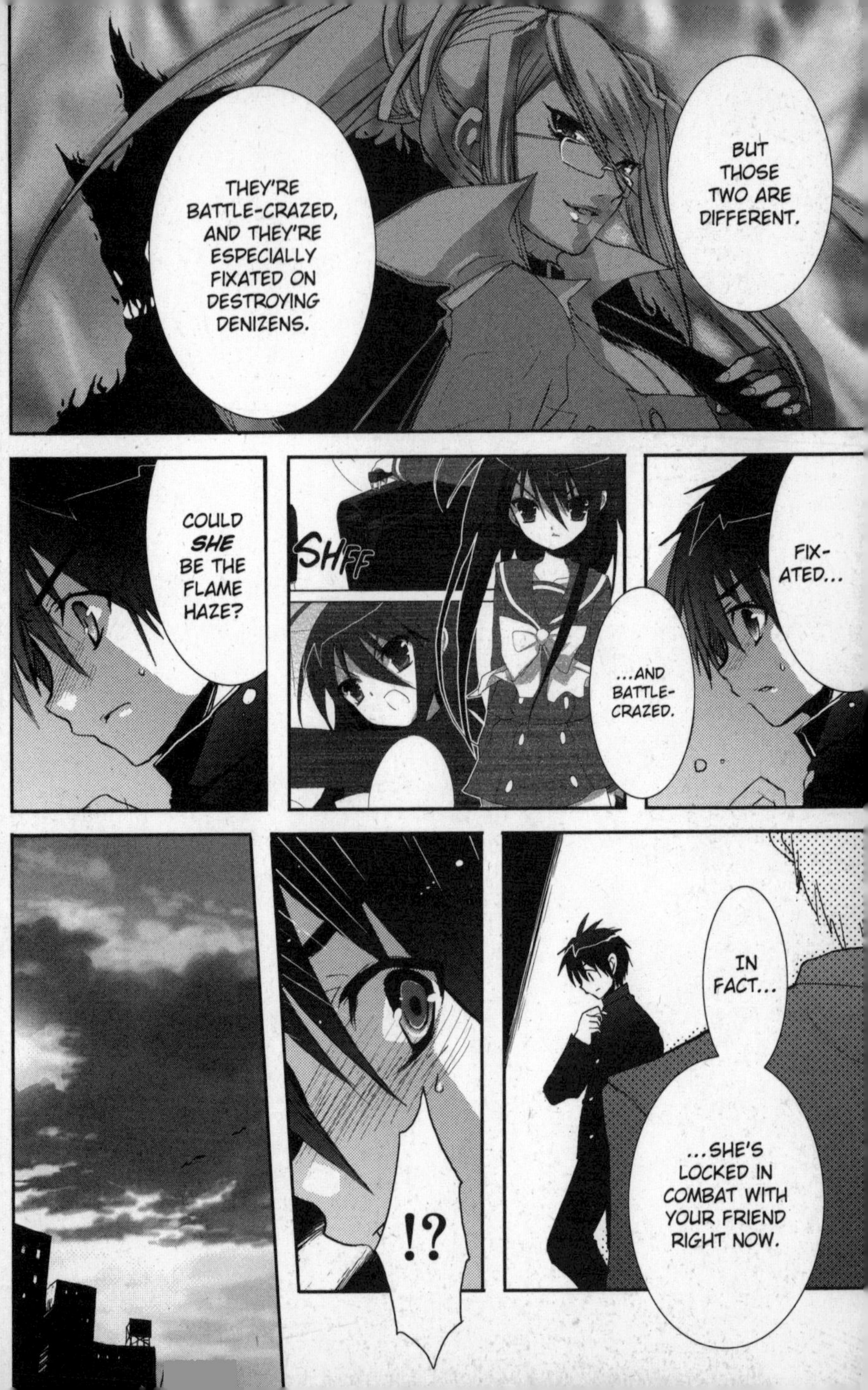
BUT THOSE TWO ARE DIFFERENT.
THEY'RE BATTLE-CRAZED, AND THEY'RE ESPECIALLY FIXATED ON DESTROYING DENIZENS.
FIX-ATED...
...AND BATTLE-CRAZED.
SHFF
COULD SHE BE THE FLAME HAZE?
IN FACT...
...SHE'S LOCKED IN COMBAT WITH YOUR FRIEND RIGHT NOW.
!?

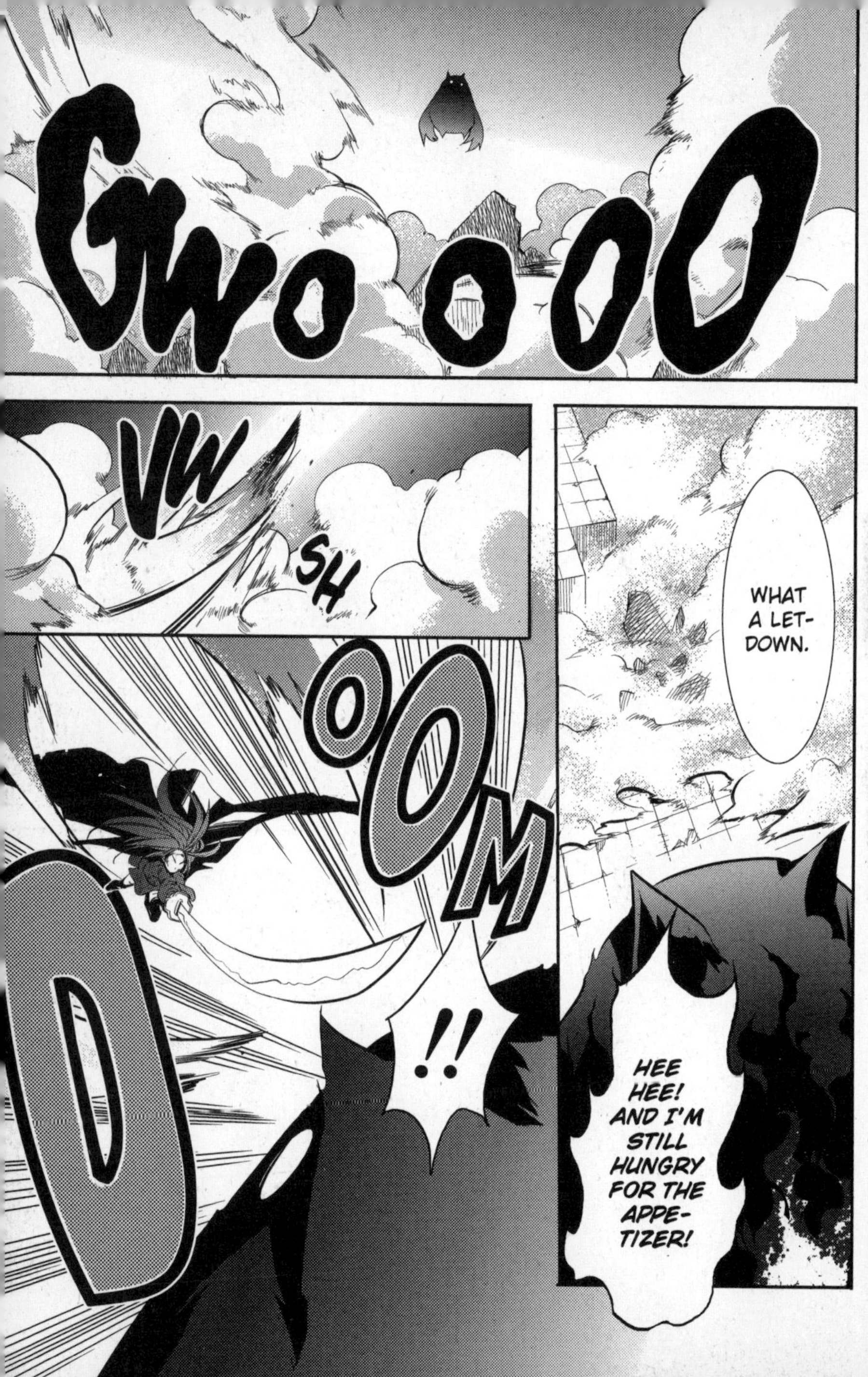
GWOOOOO
WHAT A LET-DOWN.
HEE HEE! AND I'M STILL HUNGRY FOR THE APPE-TIZER!
VWSH
DOOM
!!

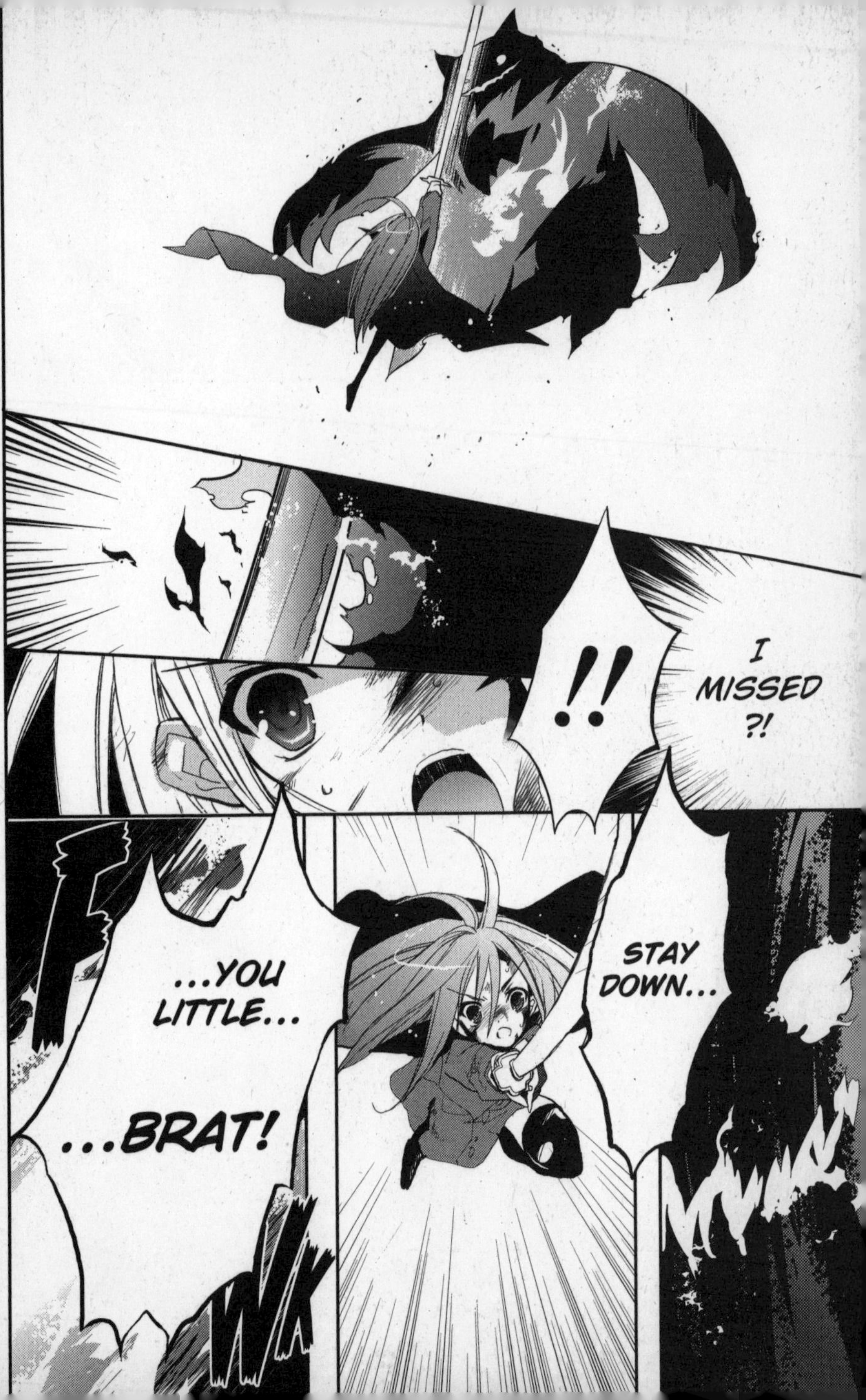
I MISSED ?!
!!
STAY DOWN...
...YOU LITTLE...
...BRAT!

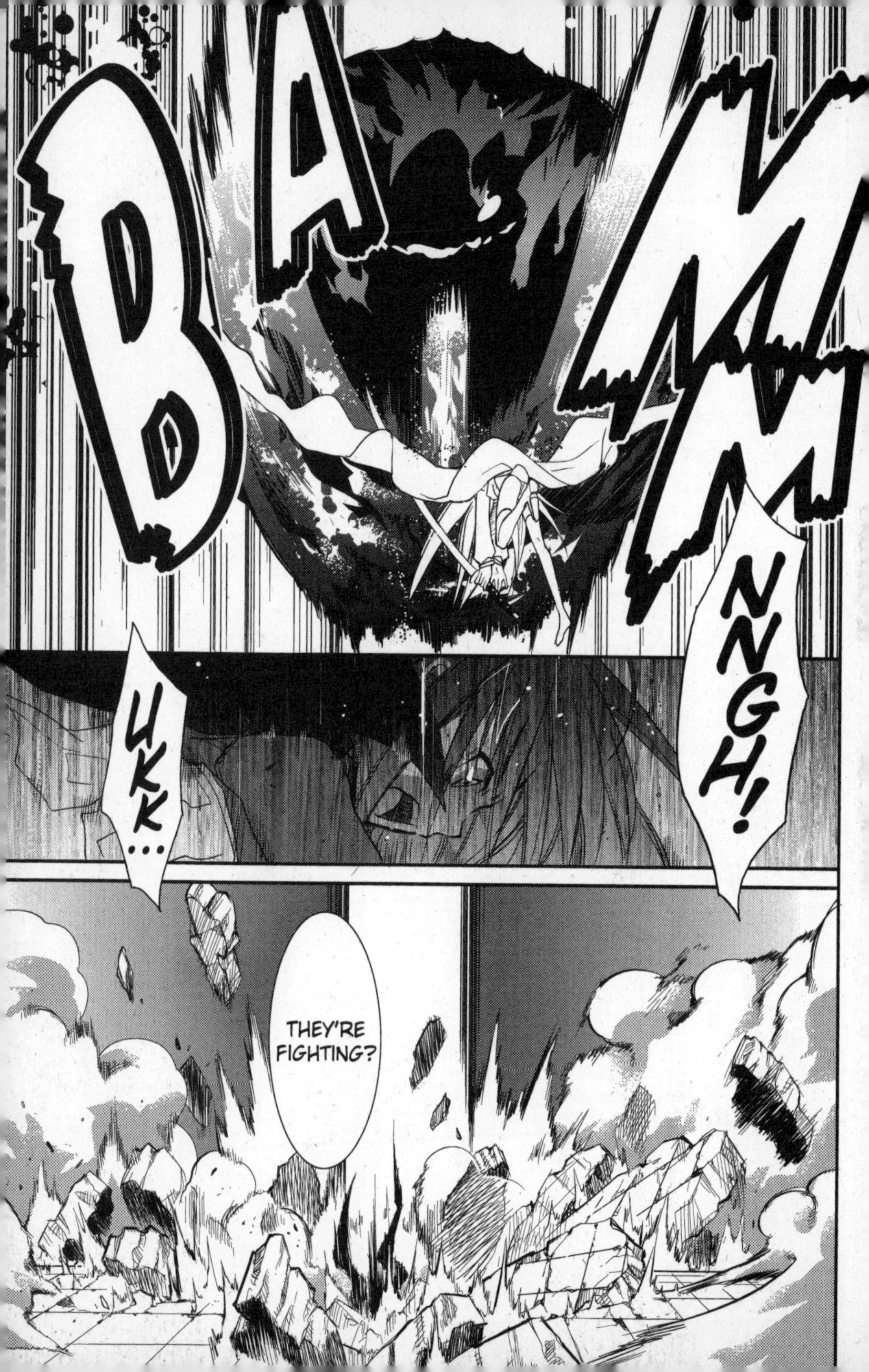
BAMMM
NNGH!
UKK...
THEY'RE FIGHTING?

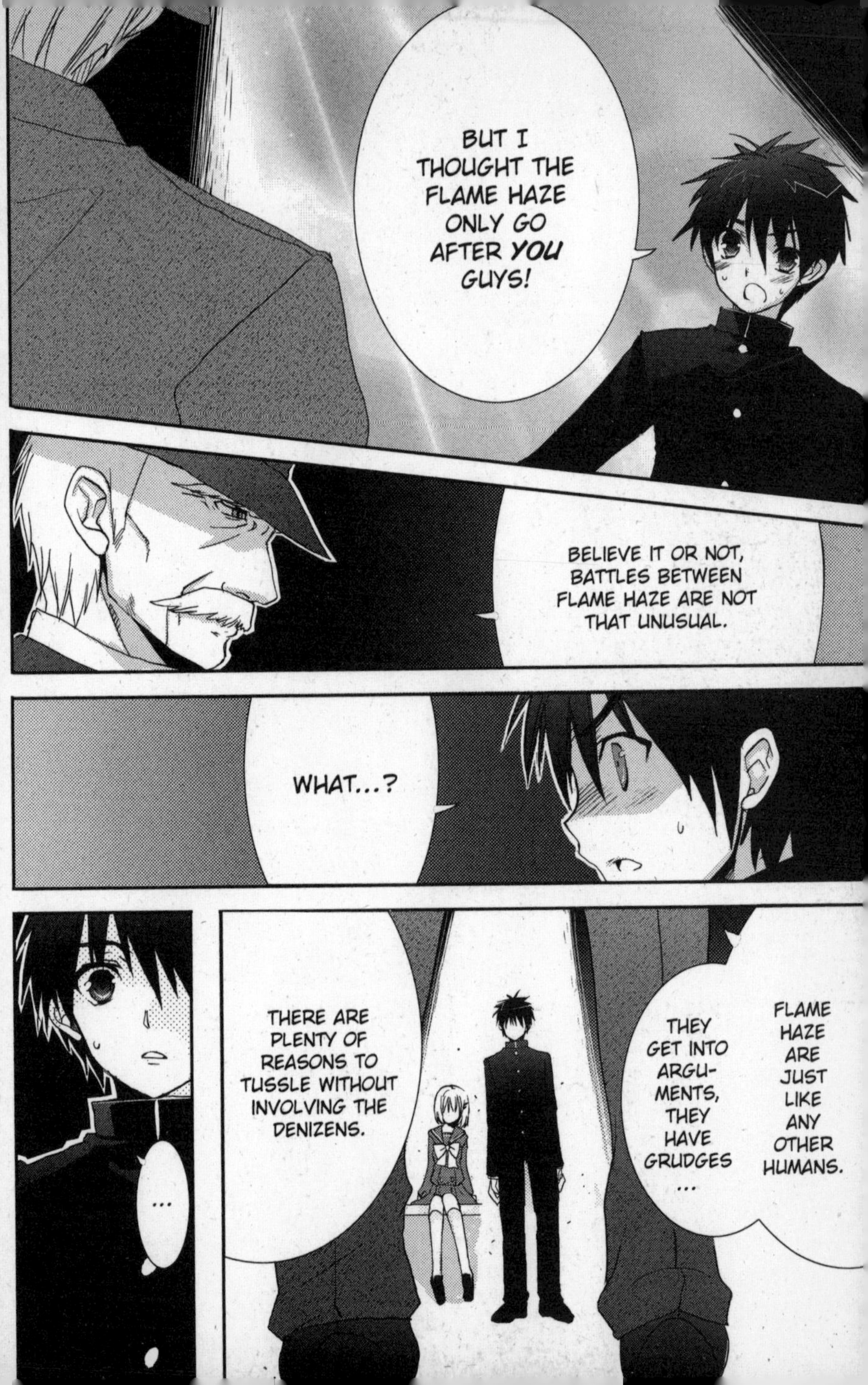
BUT I THOUGHT THE FLAME HAZE ONLY GO AFTER YOU GUYS!
BELIEVE IT OR NOT, BATTLES BETWEEN FLAME HAZE ARE NOT THAT UNUSUAL.
WHAT...?
FLAME HAZE ARE JUST LIKE ANY OTHER HUMANS.
THEY GET INTO ARGU-MENTS, THEY HAVE GRUDGES...
THERE ARE PLENTY OF REASONS TO TUSSLE WITHOUT INVOLVING THE DENIZENS.
...

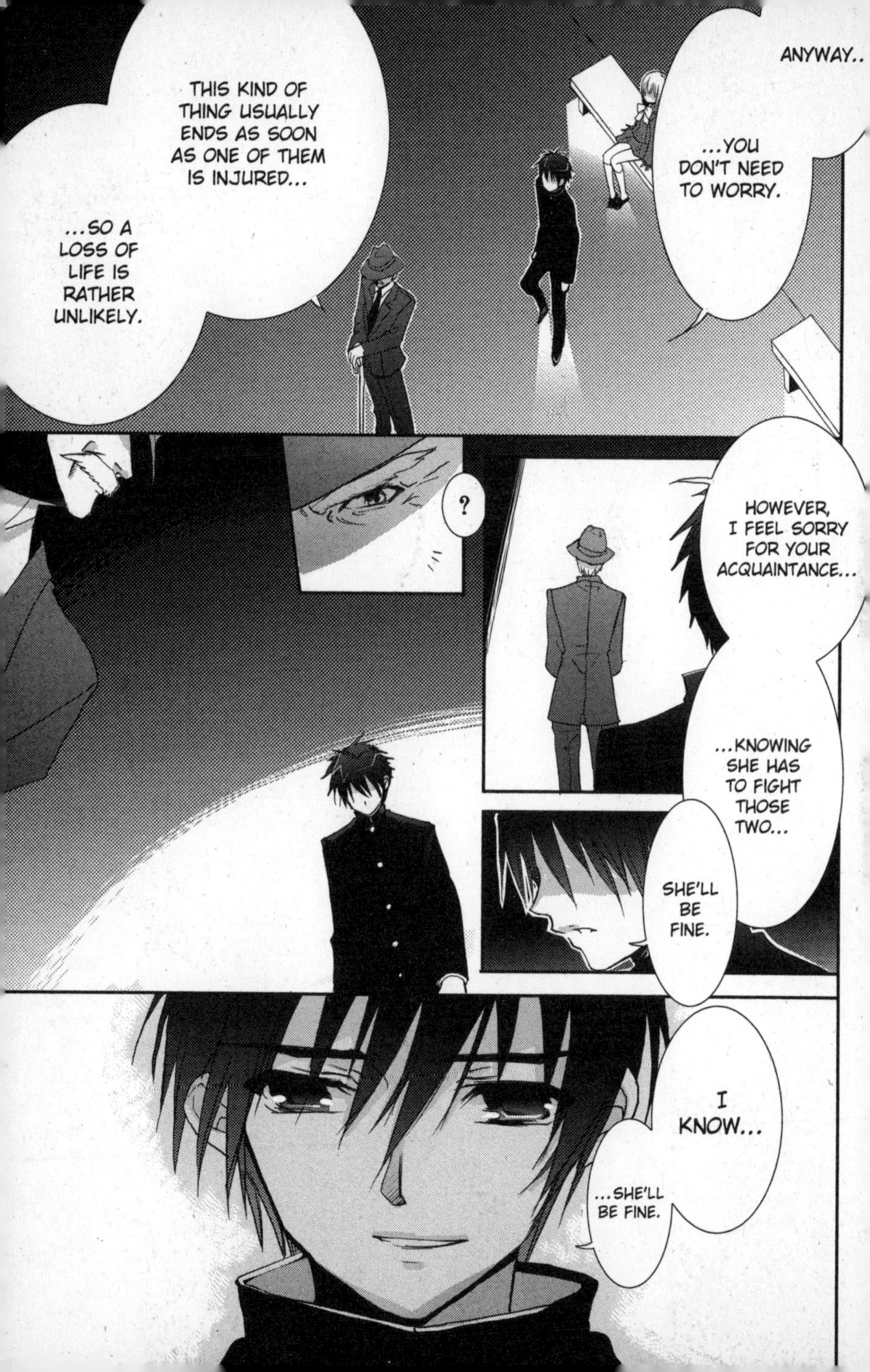
ANYWAY..
...YOU DON'T NEED TO WORRY.
THIS KIND OF THING USUALLY ENDS AS SOON AS ONE OF THEM IS INJURED...
...SO A LOSS OF LIFE IS RATHER UNLIKELY.
HOWEVER, I FEEL SORRY FOR YOUR ACQUAINTANCE...
...KNOWING SHE HAS TO FIGHT THOSE TWO...
SHE'LL BE FINE.
?
I KNOW...
...SHE'LL BE FINE.

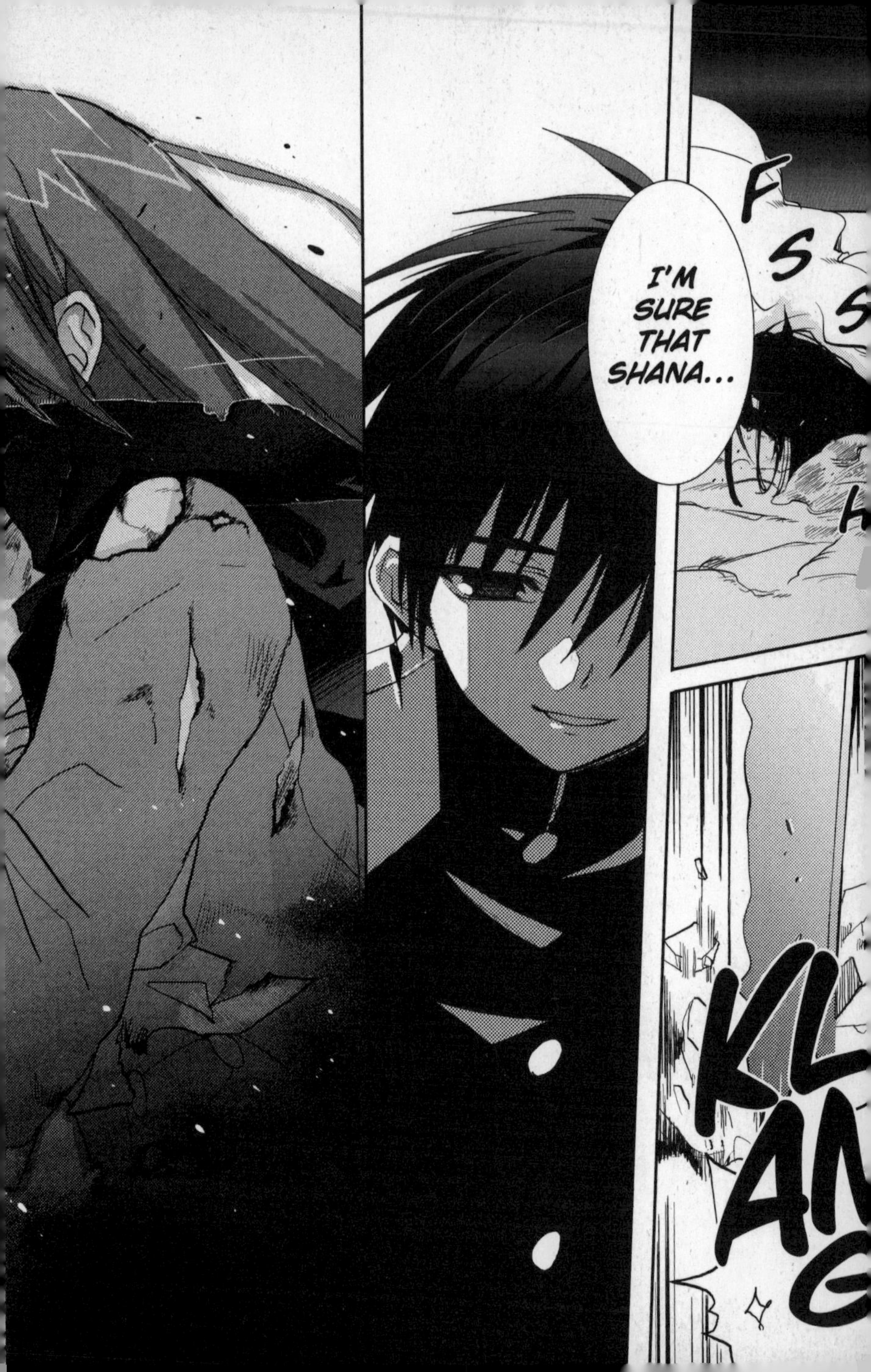
FSSH
KLANG
I'M SURE THAT SHANA...

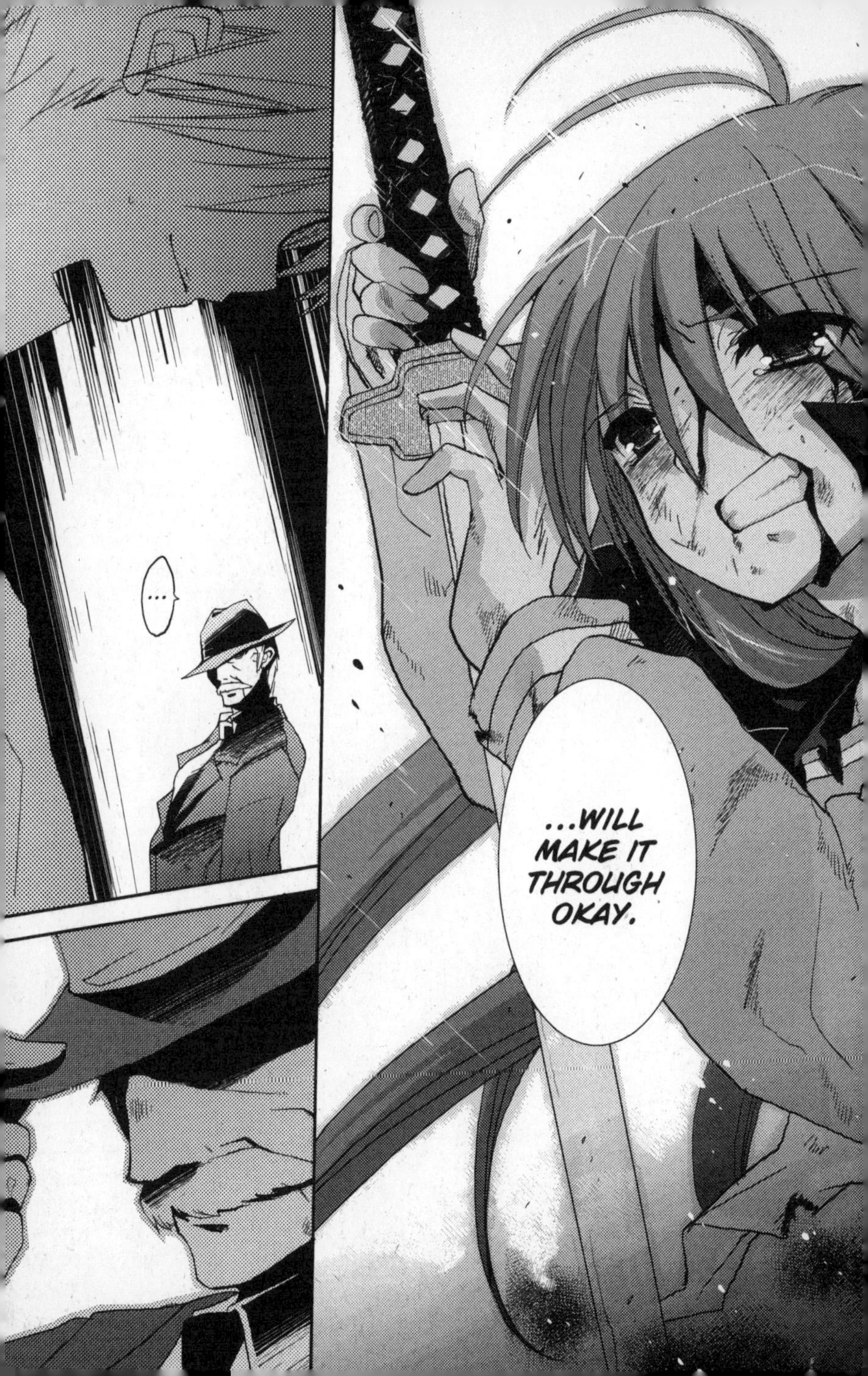
...WILL MAKE IT THROUGH OKAY.
...

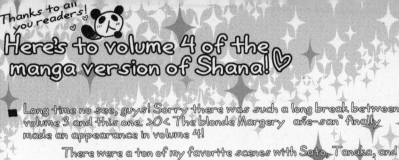

Thanks to all you readers!

Here's to volume 4 of the manga version of Shana!

■ Long time no see, guys! Sorry there was such a long break between volume 3 and this one. >O< The blonde Margery "ane-san" finally made an appearance in volume 4!

There were a ton of my favorite scenes with Sato, Tanaka, and Marcosias!

The fight between Margery ane-san and Shana is far from over, so all you Margery fans, hang tight until next time. >_O

Now, there were a lot of people who helped me get to where I am, so I'd like to send out my heartfelt thanks to them. And I wouldn't have been able to finish the fight scenes if I ever lost this person! Shiro Sensei is truly a master choreographer at sword-fighting for the Shana manga series.

I'd like to thank my assistant Az, the train station attendants, and Suiden Sensei for all his help. I should always apologize to my editor Hagino-san for all the stress I've put him through. Oh, and Takahashi Sensei, Noizi-tan, Mitsugi-san, and, well, everyone! Here's a big "thank you"! And I look forward to working with all of you again!

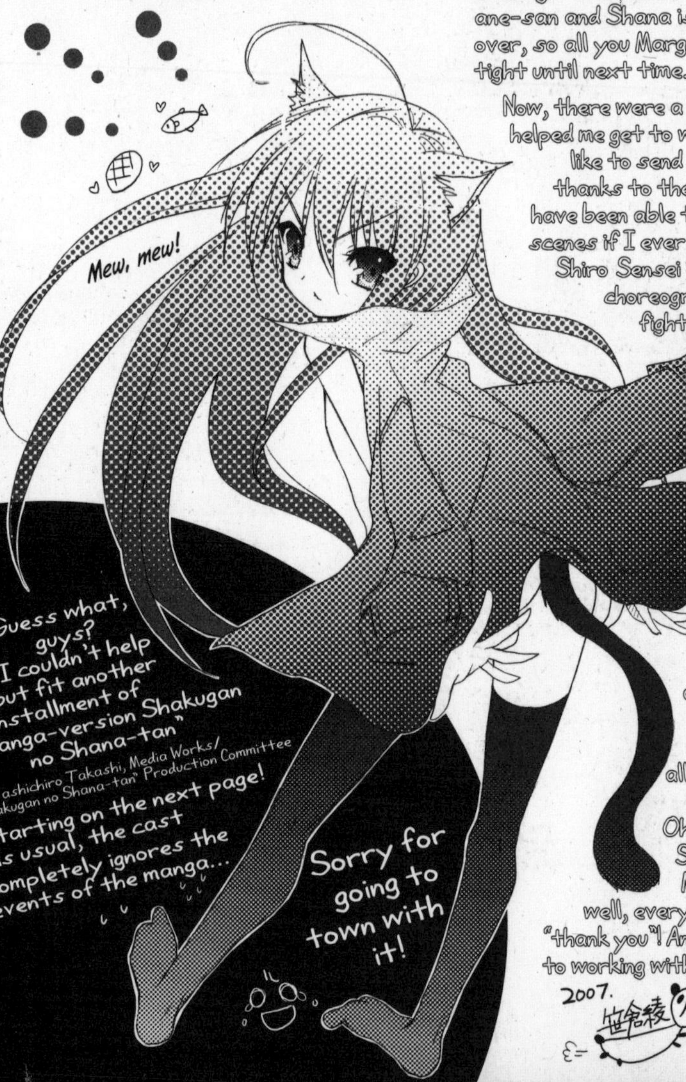
Mew, mew!
Sorry for going to town with it!

Guess what, guys? I couldn't help but fit another installment of "Manga-version Shakugan no Shana-tan"

Yashichiro Takashi, Media Works/ "Shakugan no Shana-tan" Production Committee

starting on the next page! As usual, the cast completely ignores the events of the manga...

2007.

笹倉綾人 Thanks! Ayato Sasakura 2007

① Lock On Target!

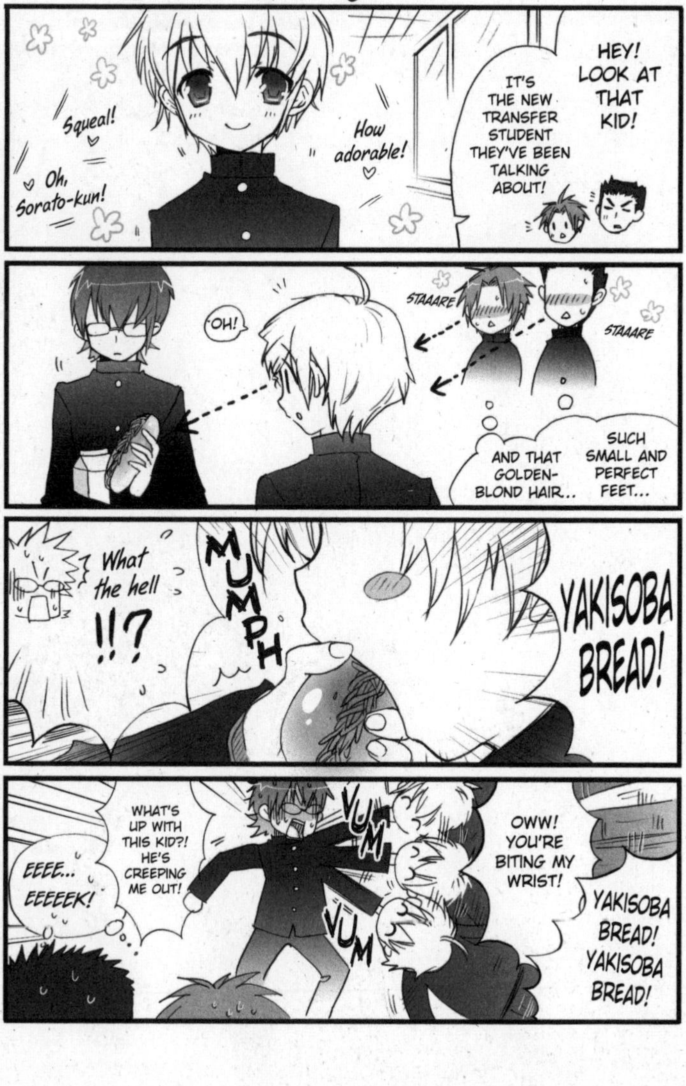
HEY! LOOK AT THAT KID!
IT'S THE NEW TRANSFER STUDENT THEY'VE BEEN TALKING ABOUT!
How adorable!
Squeal!
Oh, Sorato-kun!
STAAARE
STAAARE
SUCH SMALL AND PERFECT FEET...
AND THAT GOLDEN-BLOND HAIR..
OH!
YAKISOBA BREAD!
MUMPH
What the hell !!?
YAKISOBA BREAD! YAKISOBA BREAD!
OWW! YOU'RE BITING MY WRIST!
VUM
VUM
WHAT'S UP WITH THIS KID?! HE'S CREEPING ME OUT!
EEEE... EEEEK!

② Something I've Always Wanted to Try

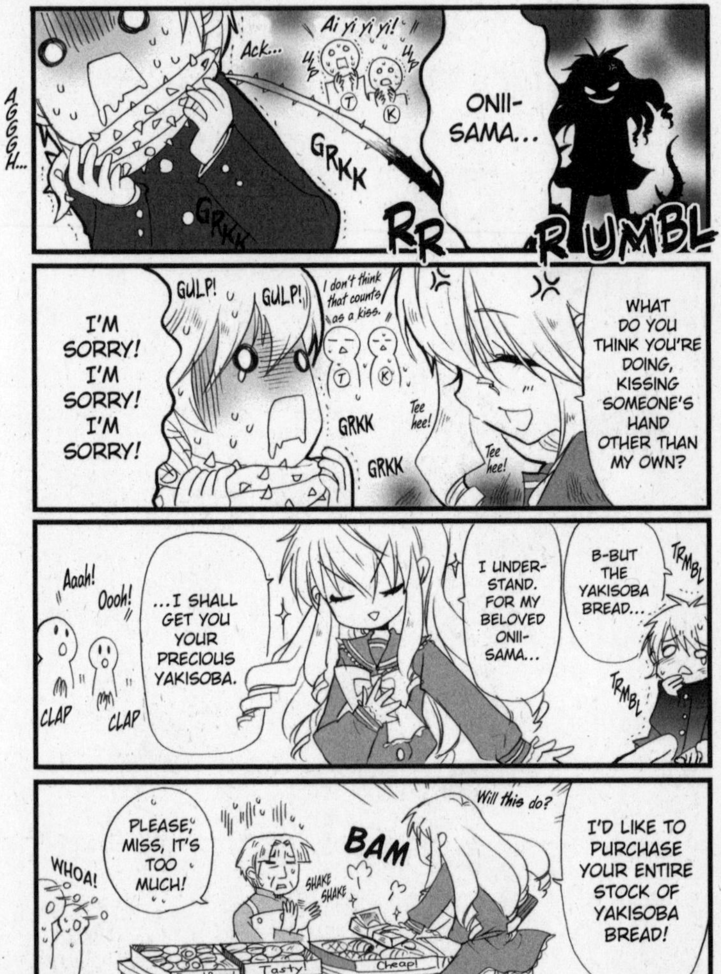
ONII-SAMA...
RR RUMBL
GRKK
Ai yi yi yi!
Ack...
GRKK
AGGGH...
WHAT DO YOU THINK YOU'RE DOING, KISSING SOMEONE'S HAND OTHER THAN MY OWN?
Tee hee!
Tee hee!
I don't think that counts as a kiss.
GULP!
GULP!
GRKK
GRKK
I'M SORRY! I'M SORRY! I'M SORRY!
TRMBL
B-BUT THE YAKISOBA BREAD...
TRMBL
I UNDER-STAND. FOR MY BELOVED ONII-SAMA...
...I SHALL GET YOU YOUR PRECIOUS YAKISOBA.
Oooh!
Aaah!
CLAP
CLAP
I'D LIKE TO PURCHASE YOUR ENTIRE STOCK OF YAKISOBA BREAD!
Will this do?
BAM
SHAKE SHAKE
PLEASE, MISS, IT'S TOO MUCH!
WHOA!
Cheap!
Tasty!
Dorrel Bread

③ It...Spoke?

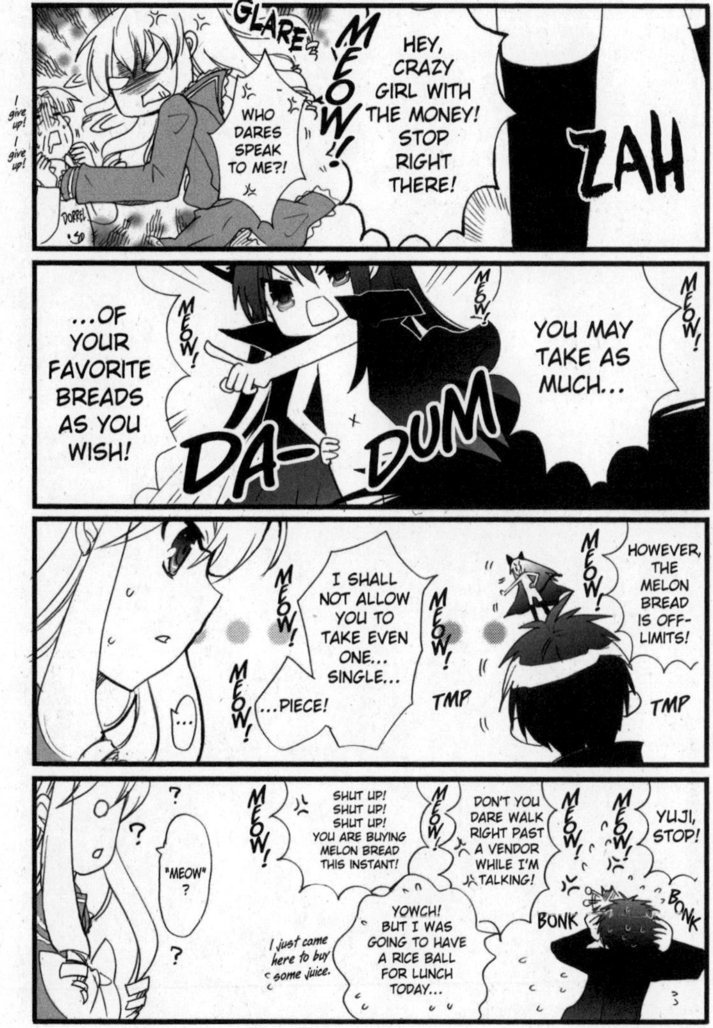
ZAH
HEY, CRAZY GIRL WITH THE MONEY! STOP RIGHT THERE!
MEOW!
GLARE
WHO DARES SPEAK TO ME?!
I give up! I give up!
MEOW!
YOU MAY TAKE AS MUCH...
MEOW!
DA-DUM
MEOW!
...OF YOUR FAVORITE BREADS AS YOU WISH!
MEOW!
HOWEVER, THE MELON BREAD IS OFF-LIMITS!
TMP
MEOW!
TMP
I SHALL NOT ALLOW YOU TO TAKE EVEN ONE... SINGLE...
MEOW!
...PIECE!
MEOW!
...
YUJI, STOP!
MEOW!
MEOW!
BONK
BONK
DON'T YOU DARE WALK RIGHT PAST A VENDOR WHILE I'M TALKING!
MEOW!
SHUT UP! SHUT UP! SHUT UP! YOU ARE BUYING MELON BREAD THIS INSTANT!
MEOW!
YOWCH! BUT I WAS GOING TO HAVE A RICE BALL FOR LUNCH TODAY...
I just came here to buy some juice.
"MEOW"?
?
?
?

④ Ponytails

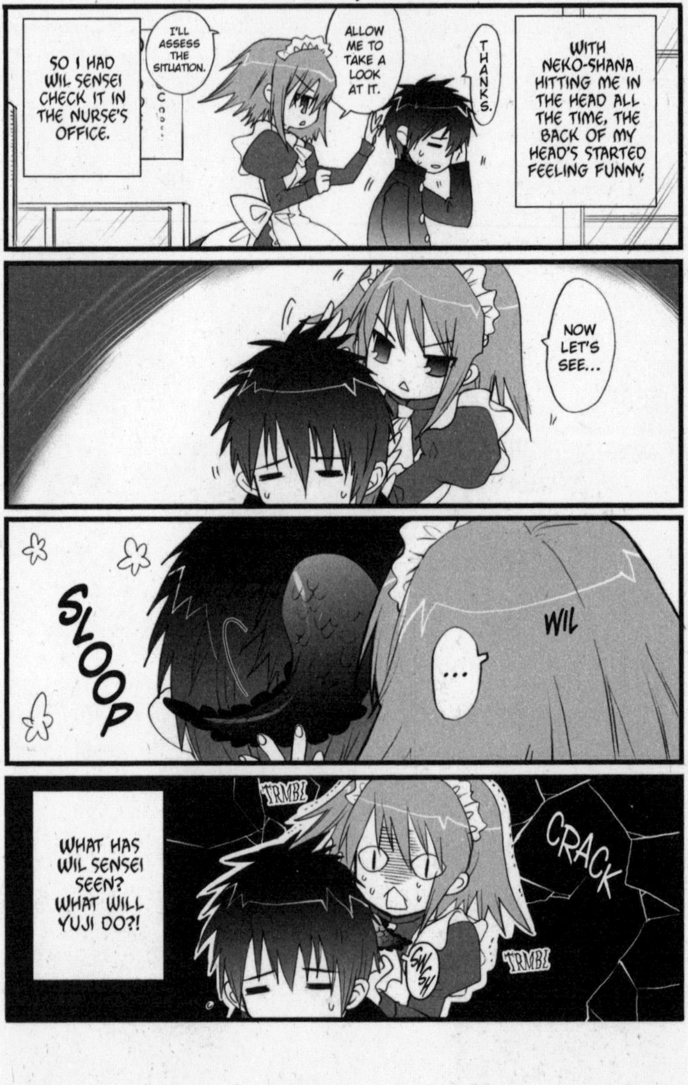
WITH NEKO-SHANA HITTING ME IN THE HEAD ALL THE TIME, THE BACK OF MY HEAD'S STARTED FEELING FUNNY.
THANKS.
ALLOW ME TO TAKE A LOOK AT IT.
I'LL ASSESS THE SITUATION.
SO I HAD WIL SENSEI CHECK IT IN THE NURSE'S OFFICE.
NOW LET'S SEE...
WIL
...
SLOOP
CRACK
TRMBL
WHAT HAS WIL SENSEI SEEN? WHAT WILL YUJI DO?!
SWSH
TRMBL

A Bit About the Story & Character Designs☆

Hello, faithful readers. It's Takahashi, the one behind the original story of *Shakugaun no Shana*. Thank you very much for buying volume 4 of the manga version. I felt we did an excellent job turning the first encounter with Margery Daw into something for manga. It took a high level of skill to reconstruct those scenes, and I think it turned out great!

I think you'll understand just how magnificent it was after you look at the lively features and character actions brought to life by Ayato Sasakura—all based on the original illustrations found in the novels. I only have words of praise and admiration when it comes to the skill it took to make Margery, Lamies, and other characters fit into the manga with faces that readers of the original novels could connect with.

And so I hope all of you readers were able to accept this new and improved Shana as you continue reading.

As usual, I count my blessing as I write this.

December 2007
Shichiro Takahashi

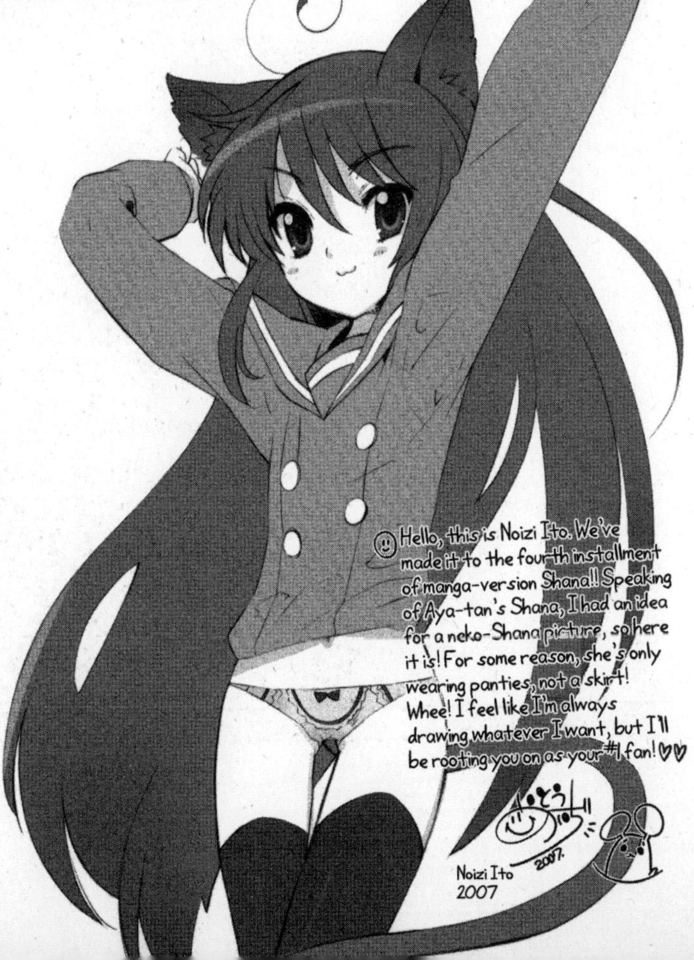
Hello, this is Noizi Ito. We've made it to the fourth installment of manga-version Shana!! Speaking of Aya-tan's Shana, I had an idea for a neko-Shana picture, so here it is! For some reason, she's only wearing panties, not a skirt! Whee! I feel like I'm always drawing whatever I want, but I'll be rooting you on as your #1 fan! ♡♡
2007.
Noizi Ito
2007

SHAKUGAN NO SHANA
Vol. 4
VIZ Media Edition

Story by
YASHICHIRO TAKAHASHI

Art by
AYATO SASAKURA

Character design by
NOIZI ITO

Translation/Katherine Schilling
Touch-Up Art & Lettering/Susan Daigle-Leach
Design/Matt Hinrichs
Editor/Jason Thompson

VP, Production/Alvin Lu
VP, Publishing Licensing/Rika Inouye
VP, Sales & Product Marketing/Gonzalo Ferreyra
VP, Creative/Linda Espinosa
Publisher/Hyoe Narita

Printed in the U.S.A.

Published by VIZ Media, LLC
P.O. Box 77010
San Francisco, CA 94107

10 9 8 7 6 5 4 3 2 1
First printing, July 2009

store.viz.com

www.viz.com

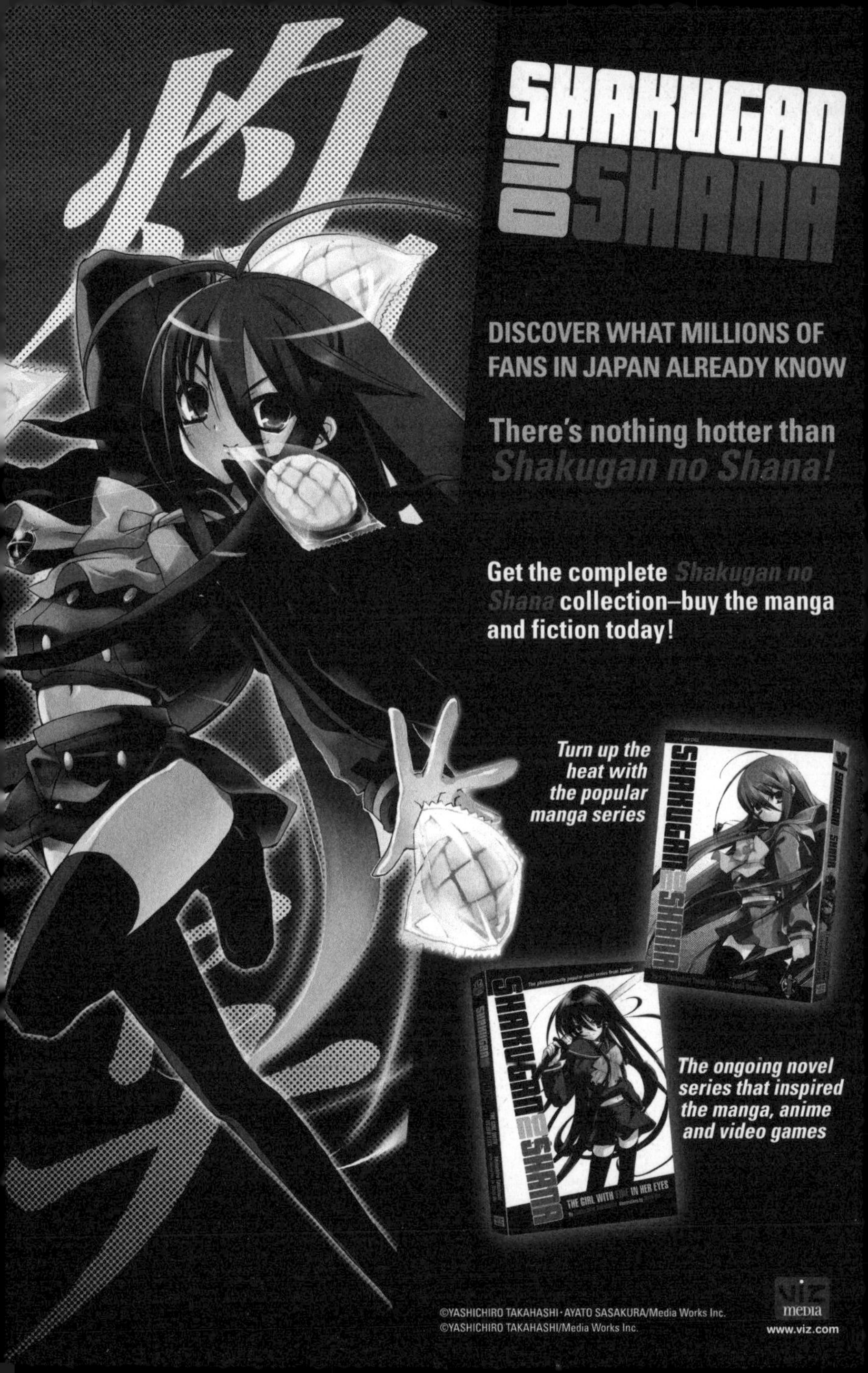

SHAKUGAN no SHANA
DISCOVER WHAT MILLIONS OF FANS IN JAPAN ALREADY KNOW
There's nothing hotter than Shakugan no Shana!
Get the complete Shakugan no Shana collection–buy the manga and fiction today!
Turn up the heat with the popular manga series
The ongoing novel series that inspired the manga, anime and video games
©YASHICHIRO TAKAHASHI · AYATO SASAKURA/Media Works Inc.
©YASHICHIRO TAKAHASHI/Media Works Inc.
viz media
www.viz.com

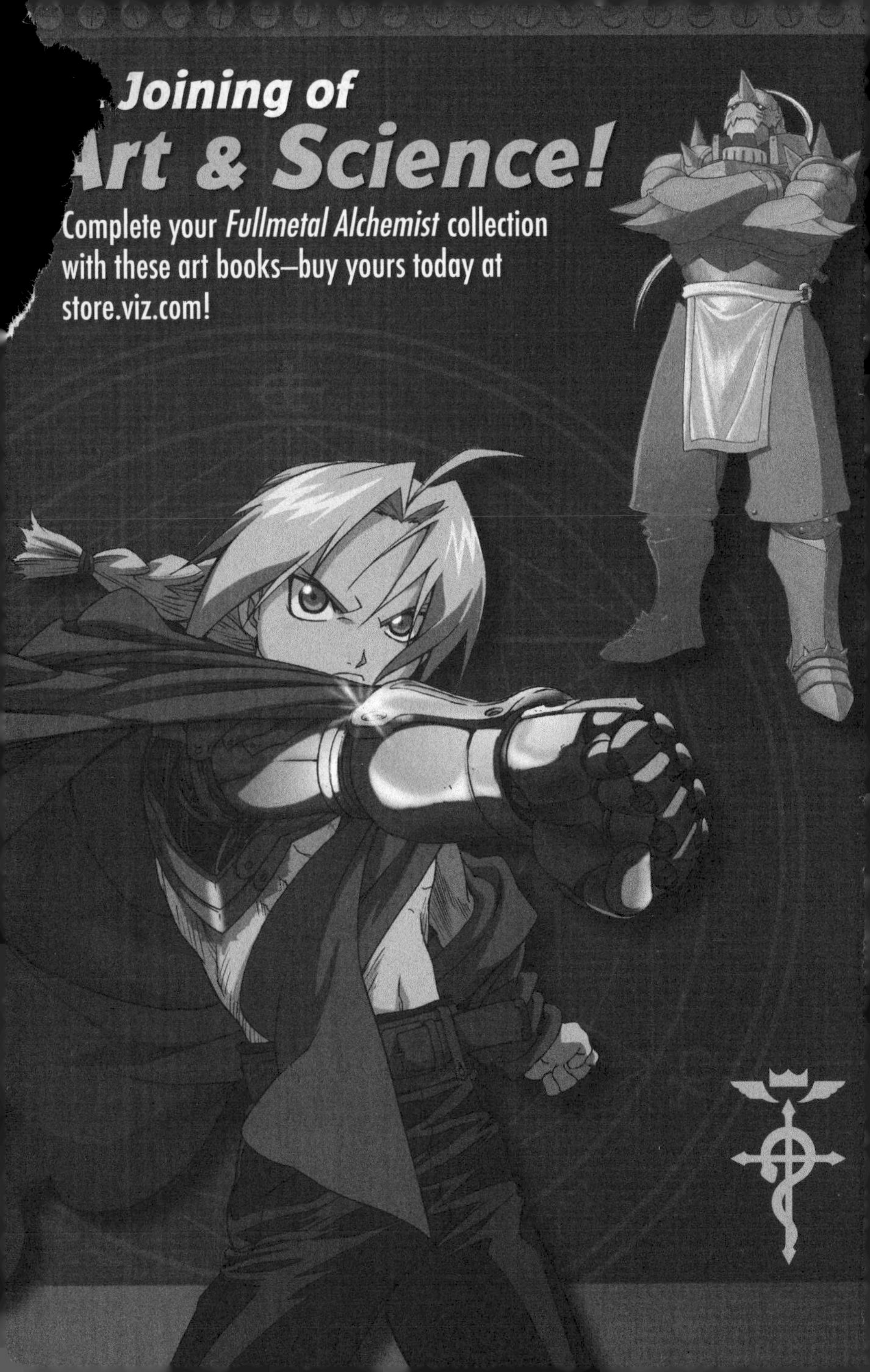
Joining of
Art & Science!
Complete your *Fullmetal Alchemist* collection with these art books—buy yours today at store.viz.com!